THE

MOODY

HANDBOOK

OF

PREACHING

Haimei chen

THE
MOODY
HANDBOOK
OF
PREACHING

THE

MOODY

HANDBOOK

OF

PREACHING

GENERAL EDITOR

JOHN KOESSLER

MOODY PUBLISHERS

CHICAGO

Editor: Jim Vincent
Interior Design: Ragont Design
Cover Design: Smartt Guys design
Cover Image: iStockphoto / Zbigniew Kościelniak

Library of Congress Cataloging-in-Publication Data

Koessler, John, 1953-
The Moody handbook of preaching.
    p. cm.
Includes bibliographical references and index.
ISBN-13: 978-0-8024-7064-5 (alk. paper)
ISBN-10: 0-8024-7064-5 (alk. paper)
1. Preaching. I. Title.
BV4211.3.K63 2008
251--dc22
                                        2007048912

CONTENTS

ACKNOWLEDGMENTS

Clearly a book like this is a collaborative affair. In addition to the fine authors who have contributed chapters to this book, there are others to whom I owe a debt of gratitude. I want to express my appreciation to Dr. Michael Easley, who initially encouraged me to take on this project. I must also thank Greg Thornton, Dave DeWit, and Tracey Shannon at Moody Publishers for their enthusiasm and support.

As a writer, I learned long ago that the unsung heroes of every book are the editors who labor behind the scenes and wrestle with the language and egos of the writers they serve. I am not speaking here of the general editor but of the real editors, the women and men who dwell in that murky world of grammar, syntax, and footnotes. Billie Sue Thompson and Jamie Janosz served in this capacity for this project. It has been a privilege to have them as my colleagues at the Moody Bible Institute and it is a particular pleasure to labor with them on this book. Jim Vincent served as the developmental editor for this project. If there is any elegance or style in it the credit must go not only to the fine authors who contributed the chapters but to them. Their names deserve to be on the cover.

Most of all, I must express my deep gratitude to the Lord Jesus

Christ, whose calling in my life brought me to the pulpit. I began preaching more than thirty years ago. After all these years, the excitement and mystery of this task continue to captivate my heart. It is my prayer that this book will kindle a similar fire in the hearts of those who read it.

INTRODUCTION

I once heard master homiletician Haddon Robinson say that he had devoted his life to answer one question: Why is it that some can preach for an hour and it seems like five minutes while others preach for only five minutes and it seems like an hour? This book attempts to provide an answer to that question. Its aim is to do more than merely help the reader understand the basics of a good sermon—the contributors fill in some of the gaps left by other books on homiletics.

In our effort to accomplish this goal, we have added to the basic question posed by Dr. Robinson. Is expository preaching still necessary? What role does the sermon play in today's worship? How do we make sure our use of story does not take over the sermon? Does technology help or hurt the sermon? Why do many of today's sermons seem so dull? How do men and women hear the sermon differently?

The contributors to this book also deal with some of the fundamental questions of sermon formulation. How should a sermon based on a biblical narrative differ from a sermon based on a didactic passage? When and how should the preacher refer to the original language? How has the use of Bible software changed sermon preparation?

A key distinctive of this handbook is its multidisciplinary approach to preaching. The contributors come from a wide range of disciplines and ministry experiences. They teach in the undergraduate and graduate schools of the Moody Bible Institute with backgrounds in Bible, theology, pastoral ministry, communications, education, and even sacred music. It includes the insights of three presidents of Moody Bible Institute. Michael Easley, current president, explains why he favors expository method in preaching, while his predecessor, Joseph Stowell, tells us why he loves to preach. George Sweeting, who preceded Dr. Stowell, brings his experience as an evangelist and his knowledge of evangelistic history to bear on the subject of evangelism and the sermon.

Reading about preaching is a little like reading about kissing. The subject is worthy of interest and the techniques helpful, but nothing compares with the actual experience. It is our hope that this book will arouse your interest in preaching and enhance the experience of the sermon for you and your listeners.

Part One

FORMING A

PHILOSOPHY OF

PREACHING

L O S I N G

T H E

C E N T E R

by
John Koessler

Every sermon has a center of gravity. Whether the goal of the sermon is to explain, prove, or apply, the expositor must stand on something to make his or her point. In expository preaching, the weight is placed upon God's Word. It is this emphasis that makes a sermon truly biblical. Thomas Long, professor of preaching at Candler School of Theology, observes, "Faithful engagement with Scripture is a standard by which preaching should be measured, and the normal week-in, week-out practice of preaching should consist of sermons drawn from specific biblical texts." According to Long, this type of preaching should be normative in churches. "Biblical preaching in this strict sense should be the rule and not the exception."[1]

But in this postmodern age a seismic change is taking place, and the reverberations are shaking the pulpits of the West. In postmodern preaching the center of gravity has shifted away from the text to the preacher's own experience and that of the audience. In this kind of preaching the traditional relationship between text and anecdote is reversed. Instead of using anecdotes to illustrate the central truth of the text, personal story is the central truth of the message and is corroborated by Scripture. The weight of proof in the sermon does not rest on proposition but on identifiable experience.

THE SEISMIC SHIFT:
FROM METANARRATIVE TO MICRONARRATIVE

The term that is often used to refer to this approach is *micronarrative*. It is rooted in the thinking of twentieth-century philosopher Jean-François Lyotard who asserted that the legitimation of knowledge in postmodern society occurs differently than in the modern era. Lyotard claimed that "the grand narrative" has lost its credibility for people in the postmodern age.[2] The weakness of these "metanarratives," according to Lyotard, is that they do not fit everyone.

D. A. Carson, research professor of New Testament at Trinity Evangelical Divinity School, alludes to this when he writes that the fundamental change in postmodernism has been in the area of epistemology—the way in which we know things.[3] In the premodern era truth began with God.[4] It was a matter of revelation and tradition. This kind of knowledge was certain because it came from an all-knowing or trusted source. The modern era did not put an end to tradition but made it subordinate to experience and empiricism. The perspective of the modernist is characterized by Anthony Giddens this way: "To sanction a practice because it is traditional will not do; tradition can be justified, but only in the light of knowledge which is not itself authenticated by tradition."[5] Therefore, in the modern age, truth was considered reliable when it could be validated by experientially based knowledge—the observable, measurable, repeatable data of science. Postmodernism shifts the locus of knowledge away from the external sources of tradition and scientific method (premodernism) and from empirical—measurable—experience (modernism) to the internal realm of subjective experience.

In preaching, this change of perspective is reflected in a shift from metanarrative to micronarrative. If a metanarrative is the big story that explains everything, its alter ego is the micronarrative, the little story that tells others what the world looks like from one's personal angle of vision. The key distinctive of a micronarrative is that it is "local" rather than universal. This local perspective is the source of the micronarrative's appeal—and its greatest weakness. When the micronarrative becomes the center of the sermon, personal experience becomes the final arbiter of truth instead of the text. The Bible does not disappear and may even play a prominent role in the message. However, a sermon grounded in micronarrative tends to treat the Bible in an ornamental fashion. Biblical texts are strung throughout the sermon like the glittering bulbs on a Christmas tree, giving the impression that Scripture is prominently featured in the message. But in the micronarrative-based sermon the text serves the story and not the other way around.

THE ROLE OF STORY IN PREACHING

Story has always played a part in evangelical preaching. The use of story in preaching is validated by the fact that narrative is often God's chosen method of communicating about Himself. Much of the truth of God's Word is conveyed in narrative form. J. Kent Edwards, who directs the doctor of ministry program at Talbot School of Theology in La Mirada, California, warns that genre influences meaning, with dangerous theological implications: "The correct genre can enhance and support a message; the wrong genre can distort and even destroy a message."[6] Author Walter Wangerin describes the power of story when he tells how he used stories to catechize the children of his congregation. "Storytelling conveys the realities and the relationships of our faith better than any other form of communication we have," Wangerin explains, "for in story the child does more than think and analyze and solve and remember: the child actually experiences God through Jesus and through Jesus' ministry."[7] Some truths may be best communicated by way of narrative.

Story, however, can be a double-edged sword. "People have many ways of narrating the story of their lives," Thomas Long observes. "They can tell the 'Christian story' of their lives, but they can also relate their family story, their national story, their racial story, their vocational story, the story of their psychological growth, and so on."[8] The hope, Long points out, is that the Christian story will function as the "narrative center" of all the other stories. But this is not always the case. Sometimes the order is reversed so that "the lesser story erodes or replaces the gospel story."[9] This is the danger of the sermon that is rooted in micronarrative.

Despite this danger, micronarrative does have a legitimate place in the message. Jesus sometimes appealed to personal experience to validate His point to His audience. In Matthew 7:9–11 he asks, "Which of you, if his son asks for bread, will give him a stone? Or if he asks for a fish, will give him a snake? If you, then, though you are evil, know how to give good gifts to your children, how much more will your Father in heaven give good gifts to those who ask him!" In these verses Jesus appeals to human experience in a line of reasoning that moves from the lesser to the greater. He uses the "local" experience of his listeners as a signpost to point them to the larger metanarrative of God's goodness.

Personal experience was the evidence offered by the man in John 9:25, when he was questioned by the leaders of the synagogue. The religious leaders claimed that Jesus was a sinner, but the man replied, "Whether he is a sinner or not, I don't know. One thing I do know. I was blind but now I see!"

This is the essence of micronarrative: "I do not know everything, but I do know my own experience and this is what it tells me."

THE PLACE OF PERSONAL TESTIMONY

Micronarratives in the form of personal testimony were an integral part of the Christian witness in the New Testament era and in the early church.[10] The apostle Paul used a micronarrative of personal experience to support his contention that Jesus was the Christ (Galatians 1:11–24). The contrast between his "previous way of life" and his present behavior offered strong evidence of the truth of his gospel. He pointed to the Galatians' personal experience to help them see the flaw in their slip back into legalism. "I would like to learn just one thing from you" he challenged in Galatians 3:2–3. "Did you receive the Spirit by observing the law, or by believing what you heard? Are you so foolish? After beginning with the Spirit, are you now trying to attain your goal by human effort?"

The use of anecdotes as sermon illustrations first appeared in Christian preaching in the sixth century, when Gregory the Great introduced the use of non-scriptural stories into the sermon as illustrations of biblical truth.[11] Gregory compiled an encyclopedia of anecdotes, known as *exempla*. This medieval precursor to the modern sermon illustration database, consisting mostly of miracle stories involving Italian saints, was widely used by the mendicant friars of the thirteenth and fourteenth centuries to flesh out the doctrine of the sermon for the audience.[12]

During the Reformation the dimension of personal experience was evident in the sermons of Martin Luther, who often relied on personal testimony and utilized the first person.[13] Luther appealed to audience experience through "the copious heaping up of linked examples, and the establishment of antithesis through imagined dialogue."[14]

Narrated experiences also show up frequently in the preaching of the great evangelical preachers of the nineteenth century, exemplified by evangelist D. L. Moody. Moody often incorporated testimony stories into his messages that described his own experience and the experiences of others. Testimony as proof of the gospel runs through all of Moody's sermons.[15]

Testimony also figured importantly in the theology of the burgeoning fundamentalist movement. The use of personal testimony loomed so large in the fundamentalist tradition, in fact, that it appeared in the five-volume theological work that gave the movement its name. George Marsden explains, "Each of the first five volumes, which were otherwise heavy on higher criticism and doctrine, concluded with personal testimony."[16] Fundamentalist theologian J. Gresham Machen contended that Christian experience was "one of the primary evidences for the truth of the gospel record."[17]

However, Machen was no postmodernist. He believed that the micronarrative of the believer's experience was subordinate to the metanarrative of the gospel events. "Christian experience is rightly used when it confirms the documentary evidence," he wrote, "but it can never possibly provide a substitute for the documentary evidence."[18] Machen was convinced that dichotomizing biblical truth and scientific truth was dangerous. He argued that truth is harmonious in nature and that what is true in religion cannot also be false in science and philosophy: "All methods of arriving at truth, if they be valid methods, will arrive at a harmonious result."[19]

THE DANGER OF PERSONAL EXPERIENCE

Stories of personal experience are interesting and can be a powerful tool for today's preacher. But the sermon's foundation must be laid with better material. Personal experience provides an uncertain footing for the expository message. Experience can be a strong testimony when it is used in a corroborative way but experience is not self-validating. One person's personal experience can be used to contradict that of another.

Many years ago I heard a pastor whom I deeply respected challenge a world-renowned atheist's assumptions about the Christian faith with these words: "There isn't anything I can tell you about Jesus Christ that you don't already know, but there is one thing I can tell you that you haven't heard, that is my personal testimony." He went on to describe his conversion experience and the subsequent change that the work of Christ produced in his life.

I was so impressed by this approach that a few months later I attempted to use the same line of reasoning on a bald-headed devotee of eastern mysticism in Ann Arbor, Michigan. I bumped into him on my way out of a bookstore and he asked me to buy a colorful magazine filled with stories about the gods he worshiped. I attempted to engage him with the gospel. When I told him I knew the gospel was true because of the change Jesus Christ had brought about in my life, he flashed a beatific smile. "I know exactly what you are talking about," he declared. "Lord Krishna did the same for me."

Machen is correct: "Christian experience is rightly used when it helps to convince us that the events narrated in the New Testament actually did occur; but it can never enable us to be Christians whether the events occurred or not."[20] All experiences may be true experiences, but the conclusions we draw from them are not always true.

The believer's experience confirms the testimony of the biblical record. But it is the biblical record and the events it recounts that interpret the believer's experience. If Christ's resurrection did not actually take place, it does not change our experiences, but it does change their significance. If Christ did not rise, "we are to be pitied more than all men," no matter what our experience has been (1 Cor. 15:19).

Preaching that makes the micronarrative its center of gravity is interested primarily in the audience. As laudable as this is, it is not a sufficient focus for biblical exposition. The goal of the expositor is to convey God's message. The prophet Jeremiah captures this idea when he speaks of the "burden of the Lord" in Jeremiah 23:33–38. The burden is the heart of the prophetic message, the essential content that the prophet must convey to God's people. In this respect, every preacher feels the weight of the prophetic mantle when standing before the congregation.

THE PREACHER AND THE PROPHET

The preacher, however, differs from the prophet in an important respect. Although both aim to communicate the Word of God, the preacher's words are not God's words. When the prophets spoke, they were "carried along" by the Holy Spirit (2 Peter 1:21). Such language, while not necessarily implying dictation, speaks clearly of divine control. The prophets spoke from God. This unique ministry of the Holy Spirit guaranteed that the true prophet would say only what God intended. The expositor, on the other hand, speaks about God's Word.

This does not mean that the Holy Spirit is absent from the process of sermon formulation and preaching. Paul's request that the Ephesians pray for him, so that whenever he opened his mouth words might be "given" to him, is a clear indication of the preacher's dependence upon God (Eph. 6:19). But unction, in this sense, is not the same thing as inspiration. The distinction between God's Word and the preacher's words is an important one and must be maintained. God's Word is inerrant and infallible. It is authoritative and must be obeyed. Those who reject God's Word reject God Himself.

The preacher cannot make such a claim. While the expositor speaks with authority, it is derived authority. The preacher's words do not have the same inherent authority that the prophet's words possessed. When speaking in the capacity of his office, the prophet's words were God's words. The expositor's words remain his own, no matter how good the sermon may be. The authority of the expositor is contingent in nature and extends only as far as the text itself. Those who reject the preacher's words reject God only when the preacher conveys the truth of the biblical text.

Consequently, the burden placed upon the preacher is both the same and different from the obligation laid upon the prophet. The prophet was charged with the task of accurately conveying the words of God to his audience. The expositor shares this responsibility. Kent Edwards warns, "Good preaching is not based on original idea. It strives to say to a contemporary audience what the original author of the biblical text said to the original audience."[21]

A MEDIATOR OF THE TEXT

But the biblical expositor bears an added burden—the responsibility of being a mediator of the text. In a sense, the preacher stands between the text and the congregation and acts on behalf of both. The preacher studies what God has said in order to know what He intended to communicate. The preacher also listens to the text on behalf of the congregation, in an effort to discern its implications for them. The expositor tries to anticipate how the audience will hear the text and frames the message in a way that is best suited to their needs. In short, the preacher's challenge is to convey the "unoriginal" idea of the text in an original and practical way. The difficult task assigned to God's messenger is that of being interesting and relevant without altering the message.

How, then, do we make certain that the center of gravity in the message is rooted in the metanarrative of God's Word? It is not necessarily a question of whether the sermon begins with a reading of the text or a personal story. Micronarrative may be a very effective starting point for the sermon. Preachers often use personal experience to establish common ground and raise concerns that the text will eventually address. Personal experience can even be used as a running narrative in the sermon, functioning as a kind of antiphonal reply or thematic "call and response" that answers the main assertions of the biblical text. The story serves as a bridge to the text and a living metaphor that reflects the sermon's central idea and exemplifies the points being made from the Scripture text.

Three tests can help us determine whether the sermon's center of gravity is rooted in the metanarrative of Scripture or the micronarrative of personal experience. First, ask yourself where the critical mass of the sermon is found. In nature, gravity is related to mass. The same is true of the sermon. Is the sermon grounded in the idea of the biblical text or in the concepts that are conveyed by story? This is not a mathematical matter, as if you could determine the answer simply by calculating the number of verses read during the message. Rather, it is conceptual. Where do the ideas in your sermon come from? Do they originate with the text? Or are they grounded in the stories you use? Sermons where the biblical content has a low center of gravity relegate the ideas of Scripture to the periphery of the message. The use of Scripture is incidental and superficial.

Second, when it comes to gravity, the presence of mass causes objects to accelerate toward each other. The same should be true of the relationship between story and text in the sermon. When you use personal experience in the message, it should move the audience closer to an understanding of the text and its implications for them. Does your use of story point listeners to the text? Does it clarify the text for them and help them to see what implementation looks like in real life? Does it motivate them to follow through on the admonition of the text? Or does the story seem to function as an end in itself?

Third, gravity gives weight to objects. Where is the weight in this sermon? Is it a function of the truth of the text or the stories you tell? Suppose you eliminated all the Scripture from your message. Could you still preach the sermon? If the answer is yes, the biblical center of gravity is too low and needs to be adjusted.

Personal experience is a useful touch point in the sermon but it should never be the final reference point. In nature the center of gravity is the location where the weight of an object is concentrated. A proper center of gravity is essential for keeping one's balance. In the realm of preaching the delicate balance between biblical truth and personal experience can be maintained only when the sermon's center of gravity is oriented around the biblical text.

JOHN KOESSLER is chairman and professor of pastoral studies at Moody Bible Institute. He has earned the D.Min. degree from Trinity Evangelical Divinity School in Deerfield, Illinois, and holds degrees from Biblical Theological Seminary, Hatfield, Pennsylvania, and Wayne State University, Detroit.

NOTES

1. Thomas G. Long, *The Witness of Preaching* (Louisville: Westminster John Knox, 2005), 45.

2. Jean-François Lyotard, *The Postmodern Condition: A Report on Knowledge*, trans. Geoff Bennington and Brian Massumi, in *Theory and History of Literature,* vol. 10 (Minneapolis: Univ. of Minnesota Press, 1984), 37.

3. D. A. Carson, *Becoming Conversant With the Emerging Church* (Grand Rapids: Zondervan, 2005), 27.

4. Ibid., 88.

5. Anthony Giddens, *The Consequences of Modernity* (Palo Alto, Calif.: Stanford Univ. Press, 1990), 38.

6. J. Kent Edwards, *Effective First-Person Biblical Preaching* (Grand Rapids: Zondervan, 2005), 19–20.

7. Walter Wangerin Jr., "Making Disciples by Sacred Story," *Christianity Today* February 2004, 66–69.

8. Long, *The Witness of Preaching,* 45.

9. Ibid.

10. Michael Green, *Evangelism and the Early Church* (Grand Rapids: Eerdmans, 1970), 316.

11. Frederick Homes Dudden, cited by O. C. Edwards Jr., *A History of Preaching* (Nashville: Abingdon, 2004), 140.

12. Claire M. Waters, *Angels and Earthly Creatures: Preaching, Performance and Gender in the Later Middle Ages* (Philadelphia: Univ. of Pennsylvania Press, 2004), 40.

13. Fred W. Meuser, "Luther as a Preacher of the Word of God" in *The Cambridge Companion to Martin Luther,* ed. Donald K. McKim (Cambridge: Cambridge Univ. Press, 2003), 143.

14. Andrew Pettegree, *Reformation and the Culture of Persuasion* (Cambridge: Cambridge Univ. Press, 2005), 20.

15. Stanley N. Gundry, *Love Them In: The Life and Theology of D. L. Moody* (Chicago: Moody, 1976), 215.

16. George Marsden, *Fundamentalism and American Culture* (Oxford: Oxford Univ. Press, 1980), 120.

17. J. Gresham Machen, *Christianity and Liberalism* (Grand Rapids: Eerdmans, 1923), 70.

18. Ibid., 72.

19. Ibid., 58.

20. Ibid., 72.

21. Edwards, *Effective First-Person Preaching*, 20.

WHY

EXPOSITORY

PREACHING?

by
Michael J. Easley

In the spring of 2005, my wife, Cindy, and I began searching for a church to attend. This was a new experience for us since I had been a pastor for twenty years. A ministry change from the pastorate to college president took me out of the pulpit and into the pew, and this relocation meant we had to "find a church." As soon as we settled in our new home, we started visiting congregations in the Chicago area. We did not expect it to be difficult to find a church where the Scripture is clearly and accurately explained.

During this period, I was approached by search committees, friends, and key leaders who were looking for a Bible expositor for their churches. Many of these inquiries represented strategic congregations with large numbers in attendance and a long history of significant ministry. Again and again, I heard the same lament: "We cannot find a man who teaches the Bible."

I no longer wonder if this is simply a trend. I believe it is an epidemic. It is not as if exposition has been carefully analyzed, appreciated for its strengths, and criticized for its weakness. It has been abandoned. What was once a process of disciplined exegesis honed into exposition has become something else. Once preaching was a craft; now it is merely creative. At one time sermon development demanded careful Bible study, a rigorous hermeneutic, the use of languages, an awareness of the historical context with a close eye on biblical theology. This kind of "old-school" exposition seems to be disappearing. How did this happen?

"Every generation blames the one before," a popular song from the eighties declared. We might also turn this around and say that the aging generation blames the one that comes after it. Both hold true when it comes to the decline of expository preaching. Fifty years ago Merrill Unger decried the diminishing role of expository preaching in the twentieth century church: "The Word of God has been denied the throne and given a subordinate place. Human eloquence, men's philosophies, Christian ethics, social betterment, cultural progress and many other subjects good and proper in their place have captured the center of interest and have been enthroned in the average pulpit in the place of the Word of God."[1]

His observation still rings true. Western culture is forever developing "isms" and "ologies." In my lifetime, a new Christianese has developed. We now loathe terms like "saved," "sin," or "repent," preferring less offensive and innocuous terms like "seeker," "emerging," "orality," "narrative," "storytelling," "parabolic," and more. Some blame our shift away from exposition on "postmodernity," "emerging" trends, or on this culture's entertainment-oriented, MTV-conditioned attention span.

A survey of articles, journals, abstracts, and recent books on preaching is telling. This literature points to a seismic shift that is reflected in a new vocabulary. Academicians call for a greater emphasis on narrative, orality, or the like. This is not merely a matter of semantics. This change in emphasis has resulted in a frenetic jumble that is less grounded in Scripture and more focused on "tickling ears" (cf. 2 Tim. 4:3). Bible colleges and seminaries still produce many who will fill a pulpit or stand at a podium (or who will sit on a stool or wander a stage holding a cup of coffee). Search google.com for several schools of your choice and read the course descriptions, and it may surprise you to see what those who are teaching homiletics are writing, preaching, and doing themselves. The fruit does not fall far from the tree.

Some of these changes are needful. Some expositors can be tedious and thoroughly boring. Some are chained to the pulpit or out of touch with the world. They may need to critically evaluate what they are doing. But no preacher can afford to forsake the text of Scripture.

SUPERSIZE ME

Another factor that has contributed to the decline of biblical exposition has been the growth of the "supersized" church. We used to call churches with more than two thousand people "megachurches." Some have suggested a new label for churches in the ten-thousand-plus range: "superchurches." Mega and superchurches have—in the main—moved to a vastly different model of the sermon. While you may find in rare cases expository messages, more pastors seem to favor "how-to" messages and short series. They base sermons on themes from television: reality, survival, makeover, or even cooking shows. Perhaps this is what is required to capture the interest of a culture afflicted with attention deficit. Perhaps it has a place in our Christian world. But what if the loss of exposition is dangerous? What if it is creating a doctrinal vacuum?

The American church equates success with blessing and too often evaluates in terms of numbers. Certainly, if we were in sales, this might be valid. But if spiritual health, vitality, discipleship, and Christlike character are the church's goals, can veiled or scarce references to the Bible be a sufficient strategy for clearly explaining the living Word of God?

The growth in pastors' conferences is another telling indicator. The first question many of us ask before attending a conference is, "Who are the speakers?" If the roster includes the latest church-growth guru, the celebrity *du jour*, or the pastor of "The First Big Church of the World," we will be inclined to attend. But which one of us would attend a conference with unknown and unpublished presenters? In many cases it is not biblical exposition that draws us, but the speaker's track record of success.

Conferences can be helpful. The Bible college I serve hosts several. But what draws a crowd and what we want to see and hear often has nothing to do with the quality of biblical exposition. It is all about the trappings of success—and success in these terms must be carefully examined. The comparison of ourselves with these superstar Christians and the ambition to transform our congregation into a "supersized" church may cause us to doubt whether biblical exposition works.

WHY EXPOSITORY PREACHING?

For more than twenty-five years I have been a student and practitioner of expository preaching. I have been privileged to study under and learn from some of the finest biblical expositors. I have listened to and delivered many sermons. I remain convinced that expository preaching is the most effective way to communicate God's Word.

Expository preaching relies on the authority of the Word of God. Eloquence, craft, and creative methodologies can help package a message. But without the authority of God's Word, a sermon will at best be a persuasive or entertaining speech. I believe in expository preaching because it is a method that can accommodate all the genres of biblical literature and be adapted to a variety of learning styles. I believe in expository preaching because it is a dependable vehicle for communicating to others about the person and work of Jesus Christ. In short, I remain committed to expository preaching because I remain committed to the authority of God's Word.

Years ago, I traveled abroad with a brilliant professor of religion who held degrees from Ivy League schools. He was far more liberal than I, so rather than trying to enter into a debate with him, I asked a lot of questions. On one leisurely stroll down a German alley, I asked him about "truth." He dazzled me with his knowledge of German philosophers and then explained that truth is like a giant sphere. Holding his hands apart as if he was holding an invisible ball, he pointed to one side.

"Your truth is over here," he said.

Then, he pointed to the opposite side of his invisible sphere.

"My truth is over here. We both have 'truth' but we cannot see how they agree because it is too big."

OK, I thought. I'll bite. So, I asked a follow up question :"What if they are directly opposite? How can they be the same truth?"

My question made him angry. He dismissed me as a simpleton. I may be simple, but I'm not stupid. Relativism has perverted the idea of truth and distorted modern notions of right and wrong. It used to be that we could call something morally wrong or morally right. We could say that stealing is wrong or murder is wrong. Today the distinction between right and wrong has been blurred by relativistic thinking. Stealing is not wrong, many would assert, if a person is dying of hunger. Murder is not wrong, they might conclude, if a person lives in an environment that has programmed them to see murder as common and acceptable.

CREEPING RELATIVISM

This broader atmosphere of cultural relativism has infected the church. The church used to hold the position, now not much more than an old-fashioned notion in some circles, that the Bible is God's Word, authoritative and without error. The idea was that if this is indeed true, we ought to believe and obey it. While plenty of churches still pay lip service to this assumption, too many Christians are practicing relativists.

Recently a young woman approached me with a question. She had been raised in a good Christian home and worshiped in a solid church. She was a very mature college graduate. Despite this heritage, she was confused about what the Scriptures have to say about homosexuality.

"Does it really matter if a person has a different sexual orientation?" she asked. "After all, they were born that way. How can we say it's wrong?"

She had been taught one thing in the church but had learned a different set of values from the culture. Friends, university instructors, the media, and even some who identify themselves as Christians systematically and persistently contradicted the scriptures she had learned in the church of her childhood. "It's about tolerance," they say. "It's about love. It's about welcoming everyone to the table."

But what about those troublesome verses in Scripture that say something else? Jesus was clear when He said, "Sanctify them in the truth; Your word is truth" (John 17:17).[2] Paul wrote in the same vein, elaborating on how we are "sanctified" by the truth of God's Word: "All Scripture is inspired by God and profitable for teaching, for reproof, for correction, for training in righteousness" (2 Tim. 3:16). The Bible we hold in our hands and read from is God's Word. It does not merely *contain* God's Word; it *is* His Word. All of Scripture is true. That is why Paul told Timothy, "Prescribe and teach these things" (1 Tim. 4:11).

But how can we be sure that the things Timothy was to prescribe and teach were not simply a reflection of the social prejudices of Paul's day or a result of his ignorance? How do we know they were not simply a reflection of his culture?

One of my professors described what he called the big "A" Author and the little "a" author in God's Word. He said that God superintended the writing of Scripture, but we see undeniable little "a" style. Though they wrote in little "a" style, God "moved" men by His Spirit to write these things. The most crucial factor in expository preaching is the commitment to accurately teach, explain, and apply the authoritative and inerrant Word of God.

STILL EFFECTIVE

Expository preaching is well suited for communicating to a postmodern culture. One way to think about culture is simply as context. We all live, work, and play in a context. Maybe we live in a suburb, neighborhood, inner city, or out in the country. Our context may be homogeneous or diverse. Maybe it's upper, middle, or lower class. It might be religious or agnostic. These and many other factors combine to define our "culture."

The gospel accounts show Jesus Christ moving in several different cultures. Yet, in all His dealings, He was—in His very nature—the same Word. He was speaking for His Father. He was speaking as the one and only Son of God. He was inseparably the very Word of God. In other words, if we are to communicate the person and work of Jesus Christ to a changing culture, our moorings must be clearly tied to the biblical text. We serve our context best by showing a clear light toward the Bible.

This is why one of the expositor's primary goals is to show that the sermon has its origin in the biblical text. The listener should be able to say, "There is no mistake. I can clearly see this in the passage." According to the apostle Paul, the aim of every preacher should be: "Holding fast the faithful word which is in accordance with the teaching, so that he will be able both to exhort in sound doctrine and to refute those who contradict" (Titus 1:9). A preacher's comments, opinions, anecdotes, and applications are then to support the clear meaning of the text.

THEOLOGY AND EXPOSITION

Biblical exposition is also a good way to teach theology in context. In general terms, we approach theology in one of two ways. One is systematic theology. Systematic theology is deductive in nature. It organizes the theological truth of Scripture thematically. Biblical theology is theology in context. It examines the themes of systematic theology by studying the entire corpus of an individual writer or looking at a particular period in biblical history. Biblical theology is exegetical theology. Both approaches are necessary, and expository preaching draws from both disciplines.

Because it is grounded in grammatical, historical, and literary exegesis, expository preaching is a particularly effective method of exploring the theology of a biblical author or a particular book of the Bible. But good exposition must also be informed by the discipline of systematic theology. When exposition is presented, the hearer can be exposed to theology. Whenever a passage addresses key doctrines such as salvation, sanctification, forgiveness, God's sovereignty or mercy—or a hundred other crucial subjects—the expositor can readily explain these ideas along with the text.

However, there are also times when important theological truths are not directly mentioned in the text but have a bearing on the ideas contained in the passage. The content of the text may indirectly trigger questions about theological doctrines that can be explained only from systematic theology. When I served as a pastor, I frequently employed what I called a "sidebar" in the sermon to address these questions. I literally took a few steps away from the pulpit and said, "This verse brings up a little sidebar. While this is not the main point of this passage, it does clearly speak to a core theological doctrine." Then I gave a brief explanation of the concept. Good preaching is always theological in nature.

MAKE IT INTERESTING

The difficulty postmodern audiences have in listening to propositional truth has been grossly overstated; still it is fair to say that much expository preaching is unnecessarily dull. Part of good exposition involves the use of illustrative material. We might support a point by citing sources. We could quote some expert, a well-known spokesperson, or someone famous. We might read a recent article from the news or a popular book. When we illustrate a point, we explain it with something the audience can identify with and understand. We may tell a story that elaborates and illustrates the point. If I expound on the term "faith," I would do well to explain how we have faith in someone or something.

If I say, "Have faith in Christ," that can fall flat. I might explain: "Having faith in Christ is not the same thing as having faith in faith. Most of us remember the children's story, *The Little Engine That Could.* The idea of 'I think I can, I think I can, I think I can,' is faith in faith. Nor is faith in Christ the same as Zen faith. When one of my daughters played soccer, all the parents inadvertently had Zen faith. We'd all cheer on the team, throw our energies toward them, and 'will' them to make the goal. That's nonsense. That's Zen faith. To have faith in Christ is to believe in a person, to know that He is trustworthy and to know that He will do what He says. I can 100 percent count on, believe, and know that He will make good on His promise. That is what it means to believe in Christ, to have faith in Him."

Illustrations, like this one, help to flesh out the point. But, be careful not to let the illustration overpower the point or become the point. In other words, let the Bible guide your use of illustrations, rather than finding a great story and building the message around it.

The use of DVD clips provides a good example of this danger. These clips can be powerful. I have several in my arsenal that are very compelling. But if the clip becomes the centerpiece or the main idea or takes a large chunk of time to develop, it is probably taking away from the passage. A friend recalled attending one conference that was essentially one DVD clip after another with very little explanation in between. The speaker simply assembled several of his favorite clips and felt they made the point sufficiently. If the illustration becomes the foundation of the message with a few principles tacked on to make it a sermon, then our audience is left with a nice preview of a cool clip. But can they easily find their way to the biblical passage or point?

When the DVD illustration overshadows the scriptural passage, we've moved from exposition to entertainment. To toss up a DVD clip is easy. The video image supplants the need to do the tough work of exegesis and exposition.

Another way to make the expository message interesting is to draw on a variety of biblical genres. Not all the Bible is didactic in nature. Nor should we give the impression that all exposition must be pedantic and highly detailed. Sound exposition takes into account different kinds of literature, like narrative, prose, discourse, song, lyric, structure, parable, metaphor, and prophecy. It carefully accommodates the nature of the literature and considers how it is best taught, explained, and applied. A character study can still be grounded in exposition. Teaching through a narrative can make issues of faith, obedience, commitment, patience, endurance, suffering, and joy come alive for the audience.

Those who are committed to exposition must also be committed to a lifelong analysis of their teaching style. Are you willing to carefully and painfully examine your method of teaching? Exposition does not negate creativity or freshness in preaching. The danger in today's context is that we will overemphasize delivery systems, media, arts, drama, technologies, and production quality. Somewhere, we can lose the Bible as our base, our foundation, the centerpiece of all we hold true.

The Joy of Discovery

One of the most compelling motivations for exposition is the interest, hunger, and longing it can engender in the life of the believer. When executed well, exposition draws a listener in to use his or her mind to grow, learn, and mature in their walk with Jesus Christ. Pastor Ray Stedman wrote,

> Exposition is preaching that derives its content from the Scripture directly, seeking to discover its divinely intended meaning, to observe its effect upon those who first received it, and to apply it to those who seek

its guidance in the present. It consists of deep insight into and under-standing of the thoughts of God, powerfully presented in direct personal application to contemporary needs and problems. It is definitely not a dreary, rambling, shallow verse-by verse commentary, as many imagine. Nor is it a dry-as-dust presentation of academic biblical truth, but a vigorous, captivating analysis of reality, flowing from the mind of Christ by means of the Spirit and the preacher into the daily lives and circumstances of twentieth century people.[3]

Exposition. You know it when you hear it. Expository preaching reveals clear lines, moored to the biblical text. Exposition begins with the Scripture. Applying exegetical skills, Bible study methods, and systematic theology, the student determines to let the text govern the message. The Scripture, not the speaker, determines the message. We are students in search of the meaning of the text, not students in search of a proof text.

As such, if you are an expository preacher, recognize yours is a special calling, one requiring specific gifts of the Spirit. Bruce Theilman put it this way:

> Preaching is the most public of ministries, and therefore the most conspicuous in its failure and the most subjective to the temptation of hypocrisy. It is imperative that only those undertake it who are appropriately gifted by the Holy Spirit. Such "gifting" includes prophecy, evangelism, the consciousness of an unavoidable call, providential endowments, and outward confirmation as evidenced by the Holy Spirit's making the preaching effort into a new Bethlehem.[4]

THE BOTTOM LINE

So, why expository preaching? Because when you stand before a group of children, students, adults, men and women, you will be able to tell them, "This is what God says." Being clever and entertaining and even using some video clips and/or drama might have its place. But if we supplant Scripture for the sake of expedience, we are in danger.

Jesus declared, "For I did not speak on My own initiative, but the Father Himself who sent Me has given Me a commandment as to what to say and what to speak. I know that His commandment is eternal life; therefore the things I speak, I speak just as the Father has told Me" (John 12:49–50).

At the end of the day—at least at the end of the sermon—will you be able to say the same? I want to be able to say, "This is my very best explanation of the very Word of God." He deserves no less.

MICHAEL J. EASLEY is president of the Moody Bible Institute and Bible teacher on the national radio program *inContext*. He has served as a pastor more than twenty years.

NOTES

1. Merrill F. Unger, "The Need of Expository Preaching in the Twentieth Century," *Bibliotheca Sacra,* 111, no. 433 (1954): 231.

2. All Scriptures are from the New American Standard Bible (NASB).

3. Ray C. Stedman, "On Expository Preaching," The Ray C. Stedman Library. Archives of Elaine Stedman. July 30, 1996, http://www.raystedman.org.

4. Bruce W. Theilmann, *The Wittenburg Door*, no. 36, April–May 1977.

Three

THE

SERMON IN

PUBLIC WORSHIP

by

H. E. Singley III

Why would the general editor of a book on preaching ask a *church musician* to write about the sermon? I am not a preacher, but I am no stranger to preaching. I have listened to sermons from the time I was a young boy. Because my wife, our children, and I were privileged to serve in music ministry and evangelism in Latin America, I even learned to understand sermons in the beautifully expressive Spanish language as well as my native English. In the more than forty years since I began to participate in the music ministry of public worship, as well as evangelistic crusades and Bible conferences, I have listened to a wide spectrum of preachers from a number of different nationalities, some well-known and some not so well-known.

Additionally, I serve in an academic community and a local church where biblical exposition is consistently emphasized and exemplified. I have a profound appreciation for the art of preaching and am deeply committed to the indispensability of biblical exposition. I am also committed to the vital interplay among preaching, music, and all other elements of corporate worship to complete the church's total worship experience.

THE SERMON PLACED IN CONTEXT

As a church musician who thinks about the sermon in public worship, it seems to me that many congregations fail at being intentional about Word-centeredness in the other aspects of corporate worship. They put too much responsibility on the sermon as the principal bearer of the Word or do not provide enough of a biblically focused context to surround and undergird the church's preaching. Regarding the role of music in gathered worship, Dietrich Bonhoeffer wrote: "Why do Christians sing when they are together? The reason is, quite simply, because in singing together it is possible for them to speak and pray the same Word at the same time; in other words, because here they can unite in the Word. . . . Thus the music is completely the servant of the Word. It elucidates the Word in its mystery."[1]

Much has been written about church music in the last few years. Some critics cast church music—or a particular musical style—as the culprit for irrelevancy in a given local church or denomination. Others see music as the crucial element that can catapult a church into a new period of vitality. Composer, author, and music professor Samuel Adler put it this way, "The music of worship has been cast in the role of convenient scapegoat for all maladies afflicting the attendance at, participation in, and comprehension of worship services."[2]

Yet Harold Best suggests, " . . . a congregation is just as responsible to sing the gospel as the preachers are to preach it."[3] Put simply, God's Word should be not only preached but also *sung, read,* and even *prayed* in the gathered worship of His people. In other words, every element of corporate worship functions in tandem with everything else to proclaim the Word.

Thus, any consideration of the sermon's role in public worship must begin with the broader subject of *worship.*

THE NATURE OF WORSHIP

Formed by the combination of two Old English words, *weorth* and *scipe*, antecedents of the modern words *worth* (or *worthy*) and *-ship* (as in state, condition, or quality), *worship* is a term that could be defined most basically as "worthiness." Put another way, something that is worshiped possesses the quality of worth. As a noun, worship is defined as "a person of importance," "reverence offered a divine being or supernatural power," "a form of religious practice with its creed and ritual," or "extravagant respect or admiration for or devotion to an object of esteem."[4]

Though for many the word *worship* is primarily associated with divine worthiness, the word is, in reality, used more broadly. The use of the word for a person of importance is less known to English speakers in the United States than those in Great Britain. "Your worship" is the means of addressing a judge in court, or a city official could be referred to as "his worship, the mayor." Merriam-Webster's Eleventh Collegiate Dictionary tells us that the verb *worship* means "to honor or reverence as a divine being or supernatural power" or "to regard with extravagant respect, honor or devotion." In this broader sense, one could worship—or extend worship to—an idol or false god (cf. Isa. 2:20, Acts 17:23).

Worship as it is associated with the triune God, is what concerns us here, and, as such, it is an especially descriptive word. Not all languages have an equivalent. By way of example, the typical term for "worship service" in Spanish is "culto de adoración," which could be understood as "service (literally, *cultus*) of adoration." Though adoration is part of what Christian worship includes, the English word in its religious connotations extends beyond, encompassing things such as respect, devotion, and giving reverence.

Yet today, the vividness and utility of the word is truncated, even eviscerated, in common parlance. In his excellent book, *Return to Worship*, Ron Owens describes this tendency: "Often when people think of worship, their minds immediately turn to music. They think of music styles and talk of the type of 'worship' or music they 'like.' To them, worship is seen only in the context of music. . . . Music can be and often is a part of worship, but it is not fundamentally necessary. . . . To many, worship is music, and music is worship, and many worship music."[5]

Pastors, music leaders, and others who participate in leading public worship perpetuate this misuse by saying phrases like, "We're going to have a time of worship," when what they really mean is, "We're going to have a time of singing" (or praise or music) or, more precisely, "Let us continue in worship as we lift our hearts and voices in song." Similarly, the term "worship leader" confounds the issue. Pastor Kent Hughes writes, "Neither must we be allowed to think that 'worship' is only a part of the service—as if singing and praise were worship in contrast to the preaching. And 'worship leader?' What an odd term! Does the worship end when his or her part is done?"[6]

A more accurate title would be "music leader," "minister (or pastor) of music," or some other word combination that avoids making "worship" nothing more than an unfortunate euphemism for the perfectly viable word "music."

Still, despite the significance of our English word, the original Hebrew and Greek words that are translated "worship" are even more descriptive. A case in point is the Old Testament term *shâchâ*, which means, "to prostrate oneself (especially in homage to royalty or God), bow down, crouch, fall down [flat], humbly beseech, do [make] obeisance, do reverence, make to stoop, [or] worship."[7] This is the word rendered "worship" in passages like Genesis 22:5, "Then Abraham said to his young men, 'Stay here with the donkey while I and the boy go over there. We will worship [*shâchâ*] and then come back to you.'" As the apostle John describes the throne of heaven, he employs a Greek word quite similar in meaning to *shâchâ*, the word *proskyneō*. Revelation 4:9–10 reads, "Whenever the living creatures give glory, honor and thanks to him who sits on the throne and who lives for ever and ever, the twenty-four elders fall down before him who sits on the throne, and worship [*proskyneō*] him who lives for ever and ever."

This word *proskyneō* means "to prostrate oneself in homage (do reverence to, adore) [or] worship."[8] Among the other New Testament words translated as "worship" is *latreuō*, meaning "to minister (to God), i.e., render religious homage, serve, do the service, worship(-er)." Paul uses *latreuō* in Philippians 3, "For we are the circumcision, who worship [*latreuō*] by the Spirit of God and glory in Christ Jesus and put no confidence in the flesh" (v. 3 ESV). Of *proskyneō* and *latreuō*, church musician and theologian Marva Dawn writes, "These words convey a profound sense of humble and loving adoration along with appropriate gestures."[9]

Despite the richly descriptive virtues of *worship*, *shâchâ*, *proskyneō*, and *latreuō*, there is still more to the whole concept of worship. In his provocative book, *Unceasing Worship*, Harold Best contends, "Worship, along with every iota of Christian living, is a seamlessness, a continuity, a unity that in no way can be broken down into chronological or spatiotemporal segments."[10] He continues, "We begin with one fundamental fact about worship: at this very moment, and for as long as this world endures, everybody inhabiting it is bowing down and serving something or someone—an artifact, a person, an institution, an idea, a spirit, or God through Christ. . . . We are, every one of us, unceasing worshipers and will remain so forever. . . ."[11]

Thus the question is not whether one worships but rather *what*—or *who*—it is that is worshiped. Is worship directed to the Triune God or is its focus on one or more of the countless idols the human heart can devise? God desires worship from His people that is, as Hughes describes, "Day-in-day-out living for Christ, the knees and heart perpetually bent in devotion and service."[12]

This is consistent with Paul's words to the Colossians, "And whatever you do, whether in word or deed, do it all in the name of the Lord Jesus, giving thanks to God the Father through him" (Colossians 3:17 ESV).

CORPORATE WORSHIP

If worship is an ongoing, all-encompassing reality for the believer, why should corporate worship be of concern to pastors, elders, or other church leaders, and for that matter, the average person in the pew? Christian worship—the perpetual Christocentric, upward focus of the believer's life—is subtly counterfeited, particularly in our day, by an indeterminate, amorphous spirituality, often expressed as an inward-directed, highly subjective self-absorption.

Various news media and the entertainment industry have profiled and helped to proliferate this type of spirituality. For those accustomed to God-directed worship and a spirituality rooted in the Scriptures, many contemporary cultural manifestations of spirituality lack an objective or fixed foundation and offer a greatly exaggerated focus on the *self*, either as the basis for one's spirituality or the chief reason for pursuing spirituality. In the United States, it seems that the self-focus in much of contemporary spirituality is only exacerbated by the rugged individualism that is endemic to the American psyche, often expressing itself in a kind of cultural Pelagianism[13]—"If *I* just do enough good things, I'll be OK with God."

This egocentric mindset can even affect believers. In one of his landmark books *God in the Wasteland*, David Wells cautions, "The sovereignty of the self destroys the character of the church as the one people of God who are united by a common redemption in Christ, a common identity as children by adoption of the Father, and a common understanding in his written Word. It destroys as well worship of the God who stands outside all sinners and whose greatness and glory are the objects of their adoration."[14]

When carefully planned with intentionality and attention to detail, corporate worship expresses—week in and week out—to the Triune God, to other believers, and to the watching world the common redemption, identity, and Word-based understanding that Wells has written about and believers worldwide share.

Corporate worship is a palpable expression of the body of Christ, a clear representation that being a Christian extends beyond the individual believer. Hebrews 10 offers this obvious emphasis on the community of believers, "Let us hold fast the confession of our hope without wavering, for he who promised is faithful. And let us consider how to stir up one another to love and good works, not neglecting to meet together, as is the habit of some, but encouraging one another, and all the more as you see the Day drawing near" (vv. 23–25 ESV).

Through the music, the prayers, the affirmation of the historic creeds, the reading of the Scriptures, and the faithful exposition of the Word, God's people—gathered together in His presence—are compelled to "forget not all his benefits" (Psalm 103:2), "make known his deeds among the peoples" (Psalm 105:1 ESV), "seek the Lord and his strength; seek his presence continually" (Psalm 105:4 ESV), and "remember the wonders he has done, his miracles, and the judgments he pronounced" (Psalm 105:5).

Corporate worship serves as an essential antidote to the seemingly inexorable compulsion toward our culture of self-preoccupation. Corporate worship allows God and His people to engage in a weekly dialogue where:

- God convenes His people for worship (articulated through the "call to worship").
- The gathered congregation responds with praise and adoration.
- The people confess their sins and hear the assurance of God's forgiveness.
- God speaks through the reading and preaching of His Word as well as through the sacraments (or ordinances, viz., the Lord's Table and baptism).
- The people respond with the giving of offerings and recommitment of life.
- God sends the people from gathered worship to return once again into the world to love and serve Him (articulated through the benediction).

The subjectivity and ambiguity of *spirituality* is countered with the objectivity of Word-permeated, Christ-focused *worship*.

THE PLACE OF THE SERMON

As already intimated, the reading and exposition of God's Word are indispensable components in the dialogue of public worship. God speaks to His people through His written Word. If God is not allowed to speak through His Word as it is faithfully read and preached, the more important of the two parties in the dialogue of worship is muted.

Referring to the sermon in the context of corporate worship, Dawn writes, "The essential goal of preaching is that the listener be transformed."[15] The concept of *transformation* is one of the characteristics distinguishing *preaching* from *teaching*. Granted, the Bible—even when read, studied, or taught for intellectual reasons in private or academic settings—can bring about transformation in the reader, the student, or the teacher and, in fact, often does so in surprising ways that can only be understood as God's Spirit working through His Word.

The difference between teaching and preaching is perhaps more of *intent*. Among Webster's several definitions, to *teach* is "to cause to know a subject" or "to impart the knowledge of" a given subject. Conversely, to *preach* is "to urge acceptance or abandonment of an idea or course of action," "to exhort in an officious or tiresome [hopefully not!] manner," "to set forth in a sermon," or "to advocate earnestly."[16] Stated another way, preaching the Word in corporate worship is not primarily for the purpose of conveying cognitive knowledge but, instead, achieving conformity of the human will to God's will.

Because worship is more about God than human beings, the tendency toward moralistic preaching must be deliberately avoided, especially given the intrinsic pragmatism and results orientation of our surrounding culture. William Willimon cautions:

> Moralizing usually occurs when the preacher attempts to draw simple moral inferences from a biblical text. The gospel is presented in the form of suggestions for better living, principles for correct behavior, or obligations to be met. Careful exegesis reminds us that the scriptures, again and again, are focused primarily upon God and only secondarily or derivatively upon us.
>
> The primary function [of the sermon as a liturgical act] is proclamation—again and again naming the Name, telling the Story, keeping time, rehearsing the truth, stating the way things are now that God has come among us, announcing the fact of our adoption as children and heirs. Any ethical payoff from the sermon must derive from this essentially theocentric function.[17]

The sermon in corporate worship should be theocentric, which is to say that it should faithfully *proclaim* God's truth to the listener and, in turn, should direct the people to God. The sermon should stand in contrast to a lecture, for instance, or a motivational speech.

THE USE OF PROJECTION TECHNOLOGIES IN A SERMON

In this regard, it is needful to reflect on visual technologies (such as PowerPoint) and the place such media have in the corporate worship of many congregations. Taking into consideration what she calls the "dark side" of these technologies, *Chicago Tribune* cultural critic Julia Keller posits,

> [PowerPoint] squeezes ideas into a preconceived format, organizing and condensing not only your material but—inevitably, it seems—your way of thinking about and looking at that material. A complicated, nuanced issue invariably is reduced to headings and bullets. And if that doesn't stultify your thinking about the subject, it may have that effect on your audience—which is at the mercy of your presentation.[18]

Keller expresses pessimism about the widespread use of Power-Point—greater than three hundred million users worldwide—and what she calls the "PowerPoint way," characterized by "chopping up complex ideas and information into bite-sized nuggets of a few words and then further pureeing those nuggets into bullet items of even fewer words."[19] She cites a 1970 essay which, even then, lamented the "technological compulsiveness" of Western culture and the "technological imperative [to not only] foster invention and constantly to create technological novelties, but equally the duty to surrender to these novelties unconditionally just because they are offered, without respect to their human consequences."[20] Think of no more than *some* of the transcendent themes of our faith, e.g., the "unsearchables"— "Great is the Lord, and greatly to be praised, and his greatness is unsearchable" (Psalm 145:3 ESV), "This grace was given [me], to preach to the Gentiles the unsearchable riches of Christ" (Ephesians 3:8 ESV). Or, consider the "mysteries"—of His will (Ephesians 1:9), that the Gentiles are fellow heirs (Ephesians 3:6), of godliness (1 Timothy 3:16). We risk oversimplifying, indeed, handicapping the Scriptures as preaching is distilled into Power-Point presentations. A better approach would draw on the rich potential of *language* for the proclamation of the God who has chosen to reveal himself via the spoken (and then the written) Word.

I must add that musical literacy has suffered in our churches due to projection technologies. For instance, the rapturous sound of a congregation singing an unaccompanied hymn in four-part harmony is a relic of the past in some churches. In addition, the lack of written music due to the projection of words only cripples the learning of new songs. The answer? *Hymnals* along with *printed copies*—with both words *and* music—of songs old or new that may not be in the hymnal.

We often hear that a picture is worth a thousand words, yet the spoken word has not lost its potency even in a culture saturated with television, movies, and all manner of video technologies. The cleverest of radio commercials, for example, stimulate the imagination in ways that video images cannot. One of the great legacies my wife has given to our children is reading to them when they were young, allowing *words* to stimulate their minds and activate their imaginations. I am thoroughly convinced that the benefits of reading far outdistanced what they would have gained from watching a video, even if the subject matter was similar.

Commenting on the compulsive, perhaps undiscriminating use of technology, communications professor Quentin Schultze observes, "Churches install video projectors in order to get the 'full benefit' of computer-presentation technology, sometimes resulting in entertainment-style worship services laced with slick slide shows, video clips, multimedia bulletin announcements, and dynamic sermon outlines." Then he warns, "These kinds of technological practices often distract a congregation from the spoken message, fragment the liturgical flow, and destroy the solemnity of worship—all in the name of progress."[21] Preachers should become specialists in *language*, not only the biblical languages for purposes of exegesis, but the language of oratory and great literature for purposes of more effective verbal communication.

ELEVATING THE MESSAGE ABOVE THE MESSENGER

We must also distinguish between the *message* and the *messenger*. This does not mean that we overlook the biblical qualifications for elders, for example, or that we ignore other details such as grammar, vocabulary, and rhetoric. Nevertheless, where the proclamation of God's Word is concerned, we must recognize that the preacher is not as important as what is being preached and, more specifically, *the One* the preacher seeks to make known.

Some years ago, I had the privilege of traveling as the conductor of the Moody Men's Collegiate Choir for a musical ministry in Ireland and

Scotland. I had heard about churches in that part of the world with large, elevated pulpits but had never personally seen one. When I entered one particular church, I saw a cross at the center and immediately below it an elevated pulpit. As we were preparing for our concert, I stood behind the pulpit. I remember thinking that the preachers for whom that kind of pulpit was designed must have been taller than my five-foot eight-inch frame or they would have been dwarfed by the pulpit's enormity! That, however, was exactly the point: The pulpit was designed to lift up *God's Word* and not the preacher! These pulpits convey visually that any authority that the preacher has is not his own but that of the *Word*.

What a contrast the older type of pulpit is to the transparent, comparatively small, Plexiglas pulpits many churches use today. Perhaps unwittingly, those pulpits enable the one standing behind them (or moving about around them in the manner of a television personality) to receive inappropriate attention. Hughes suggests, "It is not too much to say that some preachers have debased the sermon to a form of mass entertainment."[22]

This alluring tendency to emulate entertainment in our preaching, church music, and the other elements of corporate worship must be confronted. In commenting on churches "with plenty of excitement, entertainment and emotion where there is little good teaching but everyone has a great time," Richard Winter concludes that people "want instant pain relief and entertainment," probably even more in our day of increasingly complex and frenetic lifestyles. "When God does not come through like that, we manufacture techniques and teaching to give us the excitement and experience we crave," compelling the corporate worship experience in many settings "to be ever more entertaining and thrilling." The result? Winter proffers, "An ever-increasing desire for something more—another gift of the Spirit, another healing miracle, more dramatic experiences in worship." He concludes, "God does indeed offer something deeper and more fulfilling now and in the future, but these are not often associated with the instant thrills and excitement promised by the culture of advertising and entertainment."[23]

ENTERTAINMENT-ORIENTED VERSUS
CHRIST-CENTERED WORSHIP

The most viable and enduring alternative to consumer-driven, entertainment-oriented corporate worship is *Christocentric* worship—palpable Christ-centeredness from the beginning to the end of a worship service in order that God's *Word* will permeate all that takes place. This will ultimately satisfy because, therein, God is most glorified and God's people most drawn to eternal verities. J.C. Ryle, the godly Anglican bishop of Liverpool in the nineteenth century, specified a framework for public worship that, in summary, includes the following:

- God's people in a given congregation gathering on the Lord's Day
- Leaders of worship who are theologically sensitive, set apart, and truly prepared for service
- God's Word publicly read and faithfully preached
- Public prayer, which is purposeful and biblical (e.g., following the "ACTS" outline—adoration, confession, thanksgiving, supplication)
- Praise and adoration, which are all-encompassing
- The consistent inclusion of the Lord's Table and Baptism as part of the worship experience.[2]

From the vantage point of our "free church" traditions, many evangelicals seem averse to the kind of structure that Ryle described as the norm for public worship. Yet, as another writer maintains, "Every service, whether a Pentecostal revival meeting . . . or a Roman Catholic high mass . . . has a structure, a pattern for praise" so that those who plan public worship really are not deciding "between structured or unstructured worship, but between thoughtful or unthoughtful structure."[25] Emphasizing the importance of how worship services are planned and carried out, this author cautions, "Rituals of public worship deeply influence us, imprinting themselves on our subconscious minds and thus shaping the pattern of our personal spirituality." Thus, he surmises, "Considerable attention should be given to the forms of praise we regularly employ, for they will significantly affect the dynamics of our relationship with God."[26]

Hughes states it even more explicitly: "Thus, I have come to see that while all of life is worship, gathered worship with the body of Christ is at the heart of a life of worship. Corporate worship is intended by God to inform and elevate a life of worship. In this respect, I personally view how we conduct gathered worship as a matter of life and death."[27]

Corporate worship must not imitate entertainment's emphasis on personality and performance carried out before an onlooking, often passive audience. Anne Ortlund (paraphrasing Kierkegaard) writes that worship leaders (i.e., preachers, music leaders, et al) are nothing more than *prompters* and that the entire congregation are the *actors* with God as the *audience* in the drama of worship.[28]

In his book *The Supremacy of God in Preaching*, John Piper asserts: "I am persuaded that the vision of a great God is the linchpin in the life of the church, both in pastoral care and missionary outreach. Our people need to hear God-centered preaching. They need someone, at least once a week, to lift up his voice and magnify the supremacy of God. They need to behold the whole panorama of his excellencies."[29]

The Shorter Catechism of the Westminster Confession begins with a question of foundational essence, one of those issues of "first things." It asks, "What is the chief end of man?" The answer: "Man's chief end is to glorify God, and to enjoy him for ever."

May it be so! Worship, in the "all of life" sense and in the corporate sense, is ultimately about the glory of God. May that be the theme of those who lead His church, and may all our efforts in corporate worship—singing, praying, reading, giving, and, yes, preaching—be untiring and persistent in that pursuit.

H.E. SINGLEY III is professor of sacred music at Moody Bible Institute. He earned the D.M.A. degree in church music from Southwestern Baptist Theological Seminary, Fort Worth, Texas. He is a graduate of Moody Bible Institute and also holds degrees from the University of Nebraska-Lincoln and the American Conservatory of Music.

NOTES

1. Dietrich Bonhoeffer, *Life Together*, Trans. by John W. Doberstein (San Francisco: HarperSanFrancisco, 1993), 59.

2. As quoted in Paul Westermeyer, "Professional Concerns Forum: Chant, Bach, and Popular Culture," *The American Organist* 27, no. 11 (November 1993), 35.

3. Harold Best, *Music Through the Eyes of Faith* (San Francisco: Harper, 1993), 192.

4. *Webster's Eleventh New Collegiate Dictionary*, s.v. "worship."

5. Ron Owens, *Return to Worship: A God-Centered Approach* (Nashville: Broadman and Holman, 1999), 3, 6.

6. R. Kent Hughes, *Worship by the Book*, ed. D. A. Carson (Grand Rapids: Zondervan, 2002), 141.

7. James Strong, ed., *A Concise Dictionary of the Words in the Hebrew Bible* (Madison, N. J.: publisher unknown, 1890; repr., Nashville: Abingdon, 1980), 114.

8. James Strong, ed., *A Concise Dictionary of the Words in the Greek Testament* (Madison, NJ: publisher unknown, 1890; repr., Nashville: Abingdon, 1980), 61.

9. Marva Dawn, *Reaching Out without Dumbing Down: A Theology of Worship for the Turn-of-the-Century Culture* (Grand Rapids: Eerdmans, 1995), 81.

10. Harold Best, *Unceasing Worship* (Downers Grove, Ill.: InterVarsity, 2003), 12.

11. Ibid., 17.

12. Hughes, *Worship by the Book*, 140.

13. According to Louis Berkhof, the Pelagian view of humankind includes the following: "Whether a man will do good or evil simply depends on his free and independent will," "There is no such thing as original sin," and " . . . in turning from evil to good, man is not dependent on the grace of God. . . ." Louis Berkhof, *Systematic Theology* (Grand Rapids: Eerdmans, 1939), 234, and *The History of Christian Doctrines* (Carlisle, Pa.: The Banner of Truth Trust, 1969), 133.

14. David F. Wells, *God in the Wasteland* (Grand Rapids: Eerdmans, 1994), 113.

15. Dawn, *Reaching Out without Dumbing Down*, 210.

16. *Webster's Seventh New Collegiate Dictionary*, s.v. "teach" and "preach."

17. William H. Willimon, *The Service of God* (Nashville: Abingdon, 1983), 141–151.

18. Julia Keller, "Killing Me Microsoftly," *Chicago Tribune Magazine*, 5 January 2003, 10.

19. Ibid., 11.

20. Ibid.

21. Quentin J. Schultze, *Habits of the High-Tech Heart* (Grand Rapids: Baker, 2004), 97.

22. Hughes, *Worship by the Book*, 149.

23. Richard Winter, *Still Bored in a Culture of Entertainment: Rediscovering Passion and Wonder* (Downers Grove, Ill.: InterVarsity, 2002), 133–134.

24. J.C. Ryle, *Knots Untied* (1874), 226–230, cited in Warren W. Wiersbe, *Real Worship*, 2d ed. (Grand Rapids: Baker, 2000), 108.

25. Donald W. McCullough, *The Trivialization of God* (Colorado Springs: Nav-Press, 1995), 114–115.

26. Ibid.

27. Hughes, *Worship by the Book*, 142.

28. Anne Ortlund, *Up with Worship: How to Quit Playing Church*, rev. and updated (Nashville: Broadman and Holman, 2001), 18.

29. John Piper, *The Supremacy of God in Preaching* (Grand Rapids: Baker, 1990), 11.

Four

APPLYING

SCRIPTURE TO

CONTEMPORARY LIFE

by
Winfred Omar Neely

Real expository preaching exists only when application takes place. Without application we do not have an expository message. We may have a running commentary on a passage of Scripture, or a word study, but without the vital ingredient of application we do not have an expository sermon.

The absence of application in a message does not even do justice to the nature of Scripture. Thus A. W. Tozer notes, "The Scriptures not only teach truth, they show its *uses* for mankind. The inspired writers were men of like passion with us, dwelling in the midst of life. What they learned about God became to them a sword, a shield, a hammer; it became their life motivation, their good hope, and their confident expectation. From the objective facts of theology their hearts made . . . many thousands of joyous deductions and personal *applications*!"[1]

Recognizing the key role of application in an expository message, noted preacher and professor Haddon Robinson includes application in his definition of expository preaching. He describes expository preaching as the communication of a biblical concept "which the Holy Spirit first *applies* to the personality and experience of the preacher, then through the preacher, *applies* to the hearers [emphasis added].[2] Not only does application have a vital role in the expository message, applying the theme of the passage to contemporary life is "the main thing to be done."[3] This is not to say that such components as the exposition and illustration of the text are not important. They are, but they and every other element of the expository message should be employed in the interest of relating God's eternal Word to contemporary life.

THE APPLICATIONAL PATH

Application is the intersection of the eternal truth of God with contemporary life. Application takes place when the expositor finds the road where the theme of a passage of Scripture intersects with human life and experience. When the expositor finds the place where God's truth and human experience meet, then people will see the relevance of Scripture to their own experience. How does the expositor go about finding the place where the truth of God touches the life and experience of the listener?

The path toward competent application begins with rigorous exegetical work and in-depth study of the cultural, social, and historical circumstances of the first readers of the passage of Scripture under consideration. In the letters of the New Testament, the expositor determines what is the Holy Spirit's big idea in the passage. He will also consider matters such as verb tense and may be involved in word study in order to get at the meaning of the passage. In narrative literature, expositors must consider matters such as plot, exposition, tension, rising tension, resolution, and conclusion. They also determine the "big idea" of the story.

However, no matter what the literary genre, expositors must also deal with key questions about the original audience. What issues were the readers facing? What sins were they dealing with? Are there cultural and social factors that contribute to the meaning and application of the passage to their experience? The expositor's understanding of the text and the social and cultural factors in the background of the text lay the foundation for competent application of the passage to identical or comparable issues and struggles today.

The path toward competent application is also the result of an in-depth understanding of the mind-set, issues, problems, and struggles of contemporary society. It is imperative that the biblical communicator understands the people whom he is trying to reach and help.

While knowing the Bible is paramount, the biblical expositor must also understand his own audience and the issues that they face every day. Some politicians have lost elections because they made statements that indicated they were out of touch with the lives and experiences of their constituents. Of course, the preacher must have an uncompromising commitment to let the Scriptures speak for themselves, yet, as the great Scot preacher James Stewart suggests, "It is a damaging criticism of any preacher, that he is out of touch with the actualities of other men's lives, ignorant of the conditions which they have to grapple, and therefore incompetent to speak to their needs or to give them counsel and guidance for their struggle."[4]

To get in touch,[5] expositors should read the newspaper, weekly magazines, novels, and plays, and watch the news. From time to time a pastor should watch a popular TV sitcom or go to the movies. I am amazed at some of the profound issues being raised in films and sitcoms today, issues such as: guilt, fear, abortion, adultery, temptation, homosexuality, prejudice, racism, drug addiction, abuse, ambition, truth, justice! These burning issues are the stuff of popular entertainment. In fact, some people watch plays and films in order to get help for their personal lives! They develop their worldviews and theology through these venues. Through critically studying these various media and art forms, an expositor is able to put his homiletical finger on the cultural pulse of life, feeling the beating of postmodern pains, fears, aspirations, and worries. Hearing and feeling the heartbeat of contemporary society, he will be better able to speak God's word with clarity, precision, and compassion.

In addition to understanding contemporary culture well, an expositor needs to know the specific issues and needs of the people he will address. In this case, the local pastor is in a strategic position, and, the longer he remains in a place, the more strategic this position becomes. When life throws people a curveball, often the local pastor is the first person they seek for counsel, prayer, and help. Passing through the prism of pastoral care and involvement, a minister may find himself involved in the broad spectrum of a family's life: the birth of a baby, graduation from high school or college, the marriage of a son or daughter, academic failure, pregnancy out of wedlock, drug addiction, the diagnosis of a terminal illness, or the death of a family member. During such times, the pastor may gain insight into the lives of people he serves, sharing their joys and sorrows, having a better idea of how to apply God's Word to their lives and experience.

Deepening one's relationships and gaining insight into the needs of a local body requires years of involvement. This is one reason why longevity in ministry is important. Through years of ministry to a church and getting to know the people entrusted to his charge, a pastor will be able to deftly connect the truth of God to the lives of his local church, making application more meaningful and thoughtful.

The pastor, however, is not the only one in a local church who exercises a strategic caring role. For example, a director of women's ministries may regularly address the women in her sphere of ministry. Working with these women, getting to know them, she is in a better position to apply the texts of Scripture to their lives. Deacons are often in touch with the needs of the congregation and may bring that knowledge to bear on the sermon when they serve as lay preachers.

APPLICATION AND THE TEXT

Application begins with text selection. In most cases, the selection of the text for the message is the first step in the expository message preparation process. When prayerfully selecting texts that will be the foundation of expository messages, it is wise to take into consideration the needs of the people. Understanding the unique needs of his audience, the expositor—under the direction of the Holy Spirit—is able to choose texts that will help listeners in their walk with God and encourage them to deal with life biblically. Text selection and the needs of the congregation ought to walk together. Ringing through the cavern of the preacher's heart and mind should be the question: "What portion of Scripture will address the current needs of those entrusted to my care?"

Effective application is an outgrowth of the purpose of the text. Every passage or literary unit of Scripture has an intention, an objective, and a purpose. Every passage of Scripture is aiming at the target of some desired change in the thinking, attitude, and behavior of the readers. Our job, as expositors, is to determine through the exegetical study of the text what that purpose is. During our study we must ask ourselves, Why is this portion of Scripture here? What did the Holy Spirit want to see happen in the lives of the first recipients of this portion of Scripture? We must intentionally look for purpose statements in the text such as John 20:30–31. If the biblical writer's purpose is not explicit, we look for clues in the text, such as: imperatives and exhortations in the letters; and, plot, characters, and dialogue in the narratives. When you discover the Holy Spirit's intention in the text, write it out.

This exegetical purpose ought to be the sermonic purpose of an expository message. Remember, the expository message agrees with the text in content, structure, mood, and purpose. The Holy Spirit's intention with the original recipients is still His intention today. Therefore, the exegetical purpose and the sermonic purpose should be the same. We need to be concerned with what the Holy Spirit desires to do in the lives of our audience through their interaction with the text under consideration.

Understanding the purpose of the text is critical to application. How can we correctly apply a text to our contemporaries, if we do not know what the purpose of the text is in the first place? At best we may hit the Holy Spirit's target, but more often than not we miss the mark, misapplying and misusing the biblical text. And, in some instances, we may lead the Lord's people to make unwise decisions. Too much is at stake for us to be haphazard and inept in doing the principle thing in the message: the application! For these reasons, the purpose of the text must drive application.

As an expositor, write out the sermonic purpose in a way that matches the purpose of the text and relates to the listeners. You should have a clear and measurable goal in mind, knowing where the Holy Spirit wants to go in the message. Aiming at a desired target focuses application. So get ready, aim, and preach!

APPLICATION AND THE PREACHER'S LIFE EXPERIENCE

Application begins with the life and experience of the expositor. The

Spirit of God first applies the truth to the preacher, then, through the preacher, applies the truth to the audience. Haddon Robinson says that "God's dealing with the preacher is at the center of the process" of message preparation and delivery.[6] As the expositor is wrestling with the text in his personal study, he must ask himself some questions. "So what? What difference does this truth or principle make in my life?" "Lord, what would you have me to think, say, or do?"

Expositors of Scripture need to be sensitive to the prompting of God the Holy Spirit. Sometimes, without even asking these questions, the Spirit of God will begin to speak to us about the purpose of the passage working itself out in our lives.

Years ago, I was preparing a message on why we should love one another. In my study I worked with Ephesians 5:25: "Husbands, love your wives, just as Christ loved the church." I knew from my study that the love here was not mere sentiment, but agape love, love that serves, gives, and sacrifices for the highest good of the object loved. At this time in my life, my wife and I had three children. My first child, Eden, for the first few months of her life, woke often during the night and would not go back to sleep. My wife was up often for several hours during the night, and, during this period, I did not get up once to help her with the baby. Then Rachel came along, and, almost from the very beginning of life, she slept all night. Not much of a challenge there. Then, while my wife and I were missionaries in Senegal, West Africa, our son was born. He woke up at night, but my wife would feed him and he would go right back to sleep. However, I did not get up to help Stephne.

Now, while I was studying what it meant to love my wife, the Holy Spirit said to me, "Winfred, I want you to love your wife as Christ loved the church."

I thought to myself, "Okay, Lord, what do You want me to do? Shall I go and buy her some flowers, or shall I take her out to dinner?"

"No, Winfred."

"Okay, Lord, what do I do?"

"Winfred, go change your son's diaper and prepare him a bottle!"

"Lord, You can't be serious! What if my son has made a mess?"

I knew that it was God calling me to do this as an expression of love to my wife, but I struggled. I realized how deeply selfish and self-centered I was. Still, I did what the Holy Spirit told me to, and I rejoiced as I changed my son's diaper and gave him a bottle. The light kind of went off in my head as well. I realized that I was the baby's father and needed to be involved in the process. Helping Stephne was a practical expression of my love for her.

This went on two weeks before I even delivered the message. One of my parishioners came to me after the sermon and said, "Pastor, don't preach that! If you do, my wife may ask me to get out of the bed at night and help her with our little boy!" Another man said to me, "Winfred, my wife and I don't have children at home, but I helped her with the dishes this afternoon as an expression of love!" The message had a valuable application—one rejected (in jest perhaps) by one listener and accepted in a creative way by another. As the Spirit of God deals with us and we yield to Him, there may be some examples from our own lives that can be used in application for the audience.

APPLICATION AND THE AUDIENCE

Application begins with the life and the experience of the expositor, but it does not stop there. The Holy Spirit also applies the truth through the preacher to those who listen. The expositor wants the audience to make joyous deductions of their own and draw corporate and personal applications from the truth of the passage. Graham Johnston writes that sometimes a "preacher may spend hours poring over the text, but little or no time considering the people who will receive the message."[7] The expositor then needs to ask himself some questions relative to his audience. What differences does this truth make in the lives of my audience? What does this truth look like in the lives of people in the church? What use does the objective truth of this passage have for the lives of my people who are "dwelling in the midst of life"? How can this passage become a shield, a hammer, life motivation, confident expectation, and good hope for my listeners?

Working through these questions, the preacher needs to visualize the audience and think about individuals and representative groups in the audience: single mothers, married couples, single men and women, teenagers, children, etc. Thinking about the audience, the expositor asks himself, "What does this truth look like in a teenager's life? What does it look like in a single mother's life?" Imagine having a conversation with each person and telling what the truth looks like in his or her life. Since the sermon is oral communication, write these applications down the way that you would say them.

WEAVING APPLICATION THROUGHOUT THE MESSAGE

Understanding what the truth looks like in the life of the audience, the expositor of Scripture must determine how the application will be woven into the message as a whole. If the message has a theme that will be developed in several points, the expositor should apply the main point of each move (concerning moves, see chapter 22) to the audience. Ideally, the closing sentences of the move should be the application of the main point in question to contemporary life and experience. If the message has a theme with only one point, such as we may find in some narrative portions of Scripture, the message will have two moves: the telling and reliving of the story and the application of the point of the story to contemporary life.

Not only should application of the points of the message to contemporary life characterize the body of the message, application needs to begin in the introduction and reach its climax and final focus in the conclusion.

Application begins in the introduction of the message. One of the goals of an effective introduction is to address the needs and concerns of the audience. This is why understanding the reason a particular passage was written in the first place is so important. Those needs, concerns, and sins of the first recipients are likely to be the same needs, concerns, and sins of your contemporary audience. Keep in mind that events and conversations recorded in the Bible reflect real life, and the distance between the biblical world and the twenty-first century is not as great as we sometimes imagine. Of course, there are technological, social, and cultural differences. But remember that people have not changed. The human heart today still has the same struggles, doubts, emptiness, evil desires, and frustrations that plagued the hearts of the men and women of biblical antiquity.

The expositor aligns the introduction with the Holy Spirit's purpose in the text by focusing on the needs of the people, the very needs and concerns that the Spirit of God Himself is focusing on in the passage. For example, Ephesians 1:3–14 is the eulogy section of the epistle to the Ephesians. Here Paul gives us various reasons for which we are to praise God. One could focus on the need raised in this passage in an introduction by saying something like:

"Sometimes praising God does not come easy, especially when we are not content with our lot in life. Occupied with our own problems, frustrations, and dashed dreams, some of us may find it difficult or may consider it foolish to express words of praise to our heavenly Father. You wonder, 'Why praise God?' Why should you praise Him when you are going to have surgery in the morning? Why should you praise Him when the ravages of old age slowly eat away at your godly and once vibrant mother, leaving her with debilitating arthritis and memory loss? Why should you praise Him when you have been single for so long, caught in the grip of loneliness with the prospect of intimacy and marital companionship light years away from the galaxy of your personal experience? Why should we praise God today? Why? Why? We find some help with this burning question in our text for today. Open your Bible to Ephesians 1:3–4."

At this point, the audience is ready to get into the Word and hear what God says to their situations. Surfacing needs in the introduction whets the appetite of the audience for God's Word.

The sermon application should reach its climax and final focus in the conclusion. This may be done in several ways. The expositor may give a list of suggestions of how a truth or principle can be put into practice. The expositor may make a final appeal—an appeal that challenges the audience to respond to the truth in some way. This is a final call to put the principle of the passage into practice. The expositor may tell a story that shows what the truth looks like in contemporary life, helping the audience see how the truth may express itself in their own lives.

An illustration can be a powerful and emotional means of applying truth in the conclusion. This is especially helpful if the preacher has told a story in the opening sentences of the introduction, and returns to that story in the closing words of the message, bringing out the illustrative implications of the story. The expositor may decide to use prayer as the final appeal in the message. Here, the prayer is centered around the thrust of the message. As the expositor, write this prayer out and give it thought before the Lord! Sometimes, in your reading, you may come across a written prayer that could be useful in the conclusion. For instance, one of A. W. Tozer's prayers would be a fitting conclusion to a message on 1 Peter 2:1–3:

> O God, I have tasted Thy goodness, and it has both satisfied me and made me thirsty for more. I am painfully conscious of my need of further grace. I am ashamed of my lack of desire. O God, the Triune God, I want to want Thee; I long to be filled with longing; I thirst to be made more thirsty still. Show me Thy glory, I pray Thee, so that I may know Thee indeed. Begin in mercy a new work of love within me. Say to my soul, "Rise up, my love, my fair one, and come away." Then give me grace to rise and follow Thee up from this misty lowland where I have wandered so long. In Jesus' name. Amen.[8]

I have invited audiences to close their eyes and pray this prayer with me as I read it to them. What better way to end a message than with the audience doing business with God! In these contemplative moments, the Holy Spirit applies these wonderful words with power and meaning to people!

The language we use is an important aspect of application. One of the attractions of Tozer's prayer is its simplicity of language. Simple language, concrete language, the everyday language of the streets used in creative ways is genius! By using language that the audience understands, your listeners feel included. When you and I do not use language that they understand, we fail to get the message across. This is disastrous in a sermon where immediacy of understanding is critical. Application should drive the very words that we use. One of the reasons why I demand that all of my preaching students write out manuscripts of their sermon is so that they acquire the discipline of laboring with word choice in their study, selecting words that are driven by application so that they are able to relate meaningfully the eternal Word of God to today's world.

LEAVE ROOM FOR MYSTERY

Yet there is another word that needs to be said about application. There is *mystery* involved here. I have been involved in the preaching ministry for nearly thirty-one years. What I find interesting is that sometimes in preaching I have said something that I did not think was all that important, but the Holy Spirit took that seemingly unimportant sentence and influenced someone's life. Describing the impact of the Spirit, Jesus said, "The wind blows where it wishes, and you hear sound, but you do not know where it comes from or where it goes" (John 3:8 ESV). There is mystery involved. The Holy Spirit Himself is at work in the preaching process. We give Him all of the glory for everything that is done.

The fact that as expositors we are called to apply God's Word to contemporary life should sober us as well. We must do our work and make sure that our use of Scripture in application is skillful and correct. The misapplication of Scripture has done a lot of harm in the lives of people. Let us then be careful in handling and applying the Word of God.

Without application, we do not have expository preaching. Effective application of the Word of God to life is the hallmark of biblical exposition. We must always keep in mind the question "So what?" Or, as the Puritans used to ask, so we need to still ask, "What is the use of this portion of Scripture for life?"

WINFRED OMAR NEELY is an associate professor of pastoral studies at the Moody Bible Institute. He holds the doctor of ministry degree from Trinity Evangelical Divinity School, Deerfield, Illinois, and degrees from Wheaton College Graduate School and Trinity International University.

NOTES

1. A. W. Tozer, *The Knowledge of the Holy* (San Francisco: HarperSanFrancisco, 1961), 80 (emphasis added).

2. Haddon W. Robinson, *The Development and Delivery of Expository Messages*, 2nd ed. (Grand Rapids: Baker, 2001), 21.

3. John A. Broadus, *On The Preparation and Delivery of Sermons*, 4th ed. (San Francisco: HarperSanFrancisco, 1944), 165.

4. James S. Stewart, *Heralds of God* (1946; repr. Vancouver, British Columbia: Regent, 2001), 105. *Preaching* magazine identified Stewart as the greatest preacher of the twentieth century. His two books on preaching, *The Heralds of God* and *A Faith to Proclaim*, are classics.

5. For a more in-depth discussion of how the preacher goes about studying contemporary culture, see John R. W. Stott, *The Art of Preaching in the Twentieth Century* (Grand Rapids: Eerdmans, 1982), 190–200. For help with developing a life of study, see Fred B. Craddock, *Preaching* (Nashville: Abingdon, 1985), 69–83.

6. Haddon W. Robinson, *The Development and Delivery of Expository Messages* (Grand Rapids: Baker, 2001), 25.

7. Graham Johnston, *Preaching to a Postmodern World* (Grand Rapids: Baker, 2001), 149.

8. A.W. Tozer, *The Pursuit of God* (Camp Hill, Pa.: Christian Publications, 1982), 20.

WHY I

LOVE TO

PREACH

by
Joseph M. Stowell

How do I feel about preaching? To say, "I love to preach," seems too simplistic. I love to eat pasta, hang out with my wife, Martie, play golf, or drive a fast car. But do I love preaching? Well, maybe . . . ? It depends!

Preaching is not like anything else I love to do. I do not agonize over eating a great dinner, spending time with my wife, hitting a perfect drive, or nailing the accelerator. But I do agonize over preaching. I don't have to dig deep to do most of the things I love, but I have to dig deep to preach.

Most of the things I love don't bring my worst insecurities to the surface. They don't tighten my gut on a Friday night or ruin an otherwise good Saturday. Although I love preaching, I usually have the nagging thought that the sermon I am about to preach could still be improved. Even after preaching, my anxiety level elevated because I forgot a key transition or muffed the introduction.

I'm never plagued about how to grip a putter when I golf, but I am often haunted by the thought that there may be something pivotal in the biblical text that I have not yet seen. As I preach, I agonize about how to articulate the message in the most compelling way.

THE AGONY OF PREACHING

I am haunted by the words of my professor and mentor Howard Hendricks, who warned me that one of the worst sins is boring people with the Bible. It is certainly challenging to convince "what-have-you-done-for-me-lately" church members that what I am about to say is more important than what they would like to think about for the next forty minutes.

Preachers are human, and humans wrestle with ego. When you give birth to one sentence at a time, articulating something so intrinsically a part of your soul, there is always a certain risk. It is a blow to a pastor's ego when he walks by the most spiritual people in the church, huddled in the foyer after the morning message, only to overhear them talking about the great insights of their favorite radio preacher. Of course, preaching is not supposed to be about egos, but there is nothing like preaching to remind you that you have one.

As someone who lives in the suburbs, I love to cut my lawn and edge my driveway with precision. There is something satisfying about standing back and thinking, "There, that's done. I'm great with how it looks!" I never feel that kind of satisfaction with preaching. When someone asks me if I'm ready to preach, my response is always "Not really!" I never feel completely ready. There always seems to be a more interesting illustration, a clearer transition, a better thought about the historical and cultural context, on and on, forever and ever—with no amen! Preaching is the ultimate in open-ended art form; it can always be improved.

Preaching never feels like it is over and done. I can walk away from a lousy golf game and get on with my life, but I can't walk away after a poorly preached sermon and forget it. I can't tell you how many times I have preached and afterward promised God I would never embarrass Him like that again.

Why is it that when I feel I have preached a really good sermon, it sometimes seems to go nowhere? And, when I feel I have not done so

well, God often sees fit to use it in someone's life? In moments like these, *Amen!*
I comfort myself with the reminder that God's power is made perfect in
weakness (2 Cor. 12:9). God often uses my inadequacy to keep me appropriately humble. A public display of weakness in the thing that
people expect me to do well isn't very comfortable. I don't enjoy being
humbled. But preaching has a way of doing that to me.

MY GOAL IN PREACHING

I must remind myself that the goal in preaching is not to be a *great*
preacher but to be an *effective* preacher. Hitting this goal consistently is a
complicated, multifaceted enterprise that plays with my head and my
heart. I am humbled when I remember that God even spoke through a
donkey in the Old Testament.

Saying I love preaching seems too simplistic and too flippant a way
to speak of such a profound responsibility. I am awed by the magnitude
of the responsibility. I am the middleman in a divine encounter between
the Almighty God and sinful humanity. When I think of preaching as a
matter of crafting my own words into what God wants me to say, it is a
terrifying and weighty pursuit.

I am always aware that preaching is serious business. It entangles us *good*
in a myriad of conflicting emotions and self-deprecating thoughts.
Preaching demands our best, even while it reminds us that we are not up
to the task. I feel a kinship with Bruce Theilman, who writes, "The
pulpit calls those anointed to it as the sea calls its sailors; and like the
sea, it batters and bruises, and does not rest. . . . To preach, to really
preach, is to die naked a little at a time and to know each time you do it
that you must do it again."[1]

Yet the reality, as strange as it may seem, is that I do return to it again
and again. Not because I have to, but because I want to. No, actually, I
preach because I love to. I'm not sure I can even explain my ambivalence.
But I know this. After thirty-six years of "dying naked a little at a time,"
I still love to preach. To me, in spite of all the challenges and nagging insecurities, preaching is the sweetest agony in the world.

A KEY REASON TO LOVE PREACHING

Whether you are an aspiring preacher or a seasoned veteran, let me try to describe what drives us to publicly fall on the sword of our inadequacies Sunday after Sunday and somehow love it all the same.

First, we should love to preach because you and I are wired for preaching. In the classic movie *Chariots of Fire,* the Olympic runner Eric Liddell says, "I believe God made me for a purpose, but He also made me fast. And when I run I feel His pleasure."[2] My spiritual gifts are bent toward preaching and when I preach I feel His pleasure. This should be true for you if you love Jesus and are gifted to preach.

It is wonderfully rewarding to hear people tell you how God has used the message to impact their lives in a strategic way. If you and I have this spiritual gift, we should use it to honor Him.

Preaching is a way to bring glory to God. Preaching offers the opportunity to proclaim the nature, ways, and will of God on a regular basis so that all of the radiance of His surpassing glory can be comprehended and adored.

MY TOP THREE REASONS

If you were to ask me to give my "short list" of reasons I love to preach, three others would be at the top of my list—and perhaps yours too.

1. Being a voice for God in a world of distracting and destructive voices

Preaching, as it is meant to be, is not an exercise in sharing our thoughts with interested people. Thankfully! After many years of talking, I find that what I think is important and interesting is not always as compelling to those who have to listen to me. I hate to tell you how many times I have launched into a discourse on some topic I thought would be gripping to my listeners, only to watch their eyes glaze over. More than once, I have dogmatically shared my opinions, only to realize later how wrong I have been. To be honest, I sometimes tire of hearing myself talk.

However, I never tire of telling people God's thoughts. His words are always compelling, relevant, and more importantly, always correct. Preaching is the one verbal exercise I can do with confidence. Only when I preach God's Word can I be sure that my words are indisputably true, and, if acted upon, are as transforming as they are profound.

The tricky part is making sure that I am preaching God's thoughts and words, and not simply something I would like to say. The hard work of exegesis—understanding the true meaning of the text in its historical, grammatical, and cultural context—is essential to preaching with confidence. It is not always easy. I have studied many texts that at first blush seemed to contain a great sermon idea, for which I have both a passion and a bunch of killer illustrations, only to have the dream of that great sermon die on the battlefield of exegesis.

No matter how tempting it was to try to revive the original sermon idea, integrity demands that I preach God's intention in the text. There is no power in preaching what I *wish* the text would say. The power comes only when the sermon is aligned with what God is saying in the text. His Word, not mine, is the sword that plunges deep into the heart of the listener, piercing all the way to its hidden intentions and motives (Hebrews 4:12).

Preaching that is effective and powerful is the intentional commitment of the preacher to connect the head and heart of the listener to the central message of the text in a way that enables the hearer to understand what the passage is saying about the message of the text and to communicate appropriate ways to help the listener implement the proclamation point of the text to relevant aspects of their lives.

People want to hear a word from God. If our thoughts are not the thoughts of God as expressed in the text, then we have missed the essence of preaching. I have become painfully aware that my preaching must always be about "Thus saith the Lord!" not "Thus saith Joe!" When I was a student in seminary, Haddon Robinson often told our homiletics class, "When you are done preaching, if someone disagrees with you, your sermon should be so deeply rooted in the text that you can tell them that their disagreement is with Scripture, not with you!" That's great advice!

In 2 Timothy 4:1–2, Paul commands Timothy to, "Preach the Word!" The Greek term in the text translated "preach" is the word "herald." In the ancient world, a herald was one who took the edict of the king and declared it to the villagers of the kingdom. A herald who wanted to keep his life didn't go into the villages and say, "The king has a thought that he wants you to discuss and see if you think it is worthwhile." Or, "What I wish the king would have said . . ." He didn't dare. It would have been a breach of his calling and an abrupt end to his career. A herald simply declared, "The king says . . . !" He represented the will and wishes of the king and carried the authority of the king to communicate it without apology. This is the privilege and power of great preaching.

Preachers join the grand legacy of the prophets of the Old Testament, who for good or ill shamelessly and courageously served as middlemen in a divine informational transaction. Their message was aimed at repentance and the realignment of lives gone out of whack. Being a modern "prophet" is a good thing. People desperately need to hear from God!

Lots of voices are vying for the minds and hearts of God's people. Most of them are counterproductive and contradictory to God's voice. But no voice is as dangerous as the inner voice that responds to our own desires and shapes our decisions. We are fallen creatures. Too often our first instincts are wrong and destructive. We do not lean toward forgiveness and love for our enemies. We tend more toward greed than generosity. Our hearts rush to serve self instead of others. We believe we have an inherent right to joy and happiness in the here and now. We think suffering is unproductive and something to be despised. Is it any wonder our relationships fail, spiritual expectations are not realized, and we remain empty and disillusioned with life?

Thankfully God's Word helps us with these impulses. The preacher is an agent of transformation when he speaks the Word and will of God.

God's voice is counterintuitive and countercultural. Whether it's on talk shows or in self-help books, classrooms or chat rooms, from neighbor chatter to church folk sharing their thoughts, God's point of view is rarely expressed. He warns us that there is a way that seems right to a man, but in the end it leads to death (Prov. 14:12). I love the thought that when I preach, I am bringing God's voice back to center again. His voice desperately needs to be heard.

The prophet Isaiah speaks of the readiness of God to receive and restore those who have wandered from His thoughts and His ways when he writes: "'Seek the Lord while he may be found; call on him while he is near. Let the wicked forsake his way and the evil man his thoughts. Let him turn to the Lord, and he will have mercy on him, and to our God, for he will freely pardon. For my thoughts are not your thoughts, neither are your ways my ways,' declares the Lord" (Isa. 55:6–8).

If you visit Staunton Harold Church in Staunton, England, you will find an inscription praising its founder, Robert Shirley: "In the year of 1653, when all things sacred were throughout the nation destroyed or profaned, this church was built to the glory of God by Sir Robert Shirley, whose singular praise it was to have done the best things in the worst times. . . ."

In this godless age, preaching has to be among the best things you can do in what many believe to be the worst of times. I pray that the same will one day be said of my ministry and me.

2. Talking about the real, compelling Jesus

Through the years I have discovered how easy it is to tire of myself. I tire of the insecurities that hound me, of the sins that defeat me, and of the words I wish I could take back. I tire of the foolish decisions I have made, of being tempted to think too well of myself, and of my tendency to fail repeatedly.

Yet I never tire of Jesus. I find Jesus more compelling, more adventuresome, and more troubling (in the best sense of the word) than anyone I have ever known. Each day I serve Him He proves to be more worthy of my adoration than before.

And, I love to tell others about Him.

I love to help people wake up to the fact that when life is "all about me," it backfires. But, when it is all about Jesus, even our greatest accomplishments become like dung, compared to the surpassing value of knowing and experiencing Him (Phil. 3:1–11).

I love to lead people to the true Jesus—to the Jesus who is more than a meek and mild hero of history. I want them to know the Jesus who was a tough and determined revolutionary, who came to overthrow the regime of hell and set the captives free. I want them to see Jesus as He really is, intriguingly radical and truly authentic—to recognize that He had nothing but warning for religious hypocrites and scorn for Bible bureaucrats. This Jesus loved sinners. He came to heal the sick, to help the hurting, and to restore the lost. He made losers winners. Tough men dropped everything to follow Him, and women felt safe with Him. By observing His life and listening to His teaching, we too can learn how to really live, right side up in an upside-down world, and how to really die. By knowing Jesus, we can die to ourselves and live to God.

I love to invite others to care for the kind of people Jesus cared for—the marginalized, the weak, the despised, and outcasts of this world. I love helping people get their heads on straight and their hearts back in line. I love being a part of the process of allowing Jesus to dominate our thoughts and our ways, so that our broken lives can announce the reality of His kingdom and the radiance of His glory.

I love to ignite the spark of hope in the unbeliever's heart by telling them that Jesus loves them and died so they might be forgiven. I tell them that Jesus will liberate them from their sins and that Jesus alone is someone they can follow without disappointment.

3. Knowing that God will be at work through the preaching of His Word

It has happened many times. I am sure it has happened to you as well. After you have given birth to the sermon—in public for all to see—someone approaches you and tells you word for word what they heard. "It was just what I needed," they say. "Thank you so much! It was such a blessing." At this point most preachers press the rewind button only to discover that they never actually said that—something close perhaps—but not that! What does a preacher do in such a case? Does integrity demand we say, "Sorry, I never said that, so scratch the blessing?" Or, do we acknowledge that there is a supernatural dynamic to our preaching?

In a mysterious way, beyond our comprehension, the Holy Spirit takes our words and runs them through the grid of the listener's life, customizing the application to a needy heart in order to make a difference.

If it weren't for the Holy Spirit, who empowers us and energizes God's Word, I would quit today. There is no way I could stand before people Sunday after Sunday and talk to them for thirty to fifty minutes and expect them to listen to me, not after being stimulated all week by a high-tech, special-effects world. How can a preacher compete? A preacher can't. Not by himself.

But we can be assured that the supernatural work of the Spirit probes deep into hearts in a way that is "living and active." God's Word is "sharper than any double-edged sword; it penetrates even to dividing soul and spirit, joints and marrow; it judges the thoughts and attitudes of the heart" (Heb. 4:12). The preacher can know that in spite of the odds he is up against, God is at work.

I preach to see the light of discovery in the eyes of a listener . . . to see a tear of relief or repentance roll down a cheek . . . to see a genuine nod of understanding. I preach to have my listeners tell me that God has used my ministry to make a difference in their lives and then to hear how God used His Word for His glory and their gain.

good

I preach with the confidence that even when no one tells me what is going on in his or her heart, God knows and his Word meets listeners right where they are. I preach to hear what I have heard so many times before, that the passage I chose to preach was exactly what they needed.

Hearing that God has used our preaching to touch the lives of others is encouraging. We live for those affirmations. But I find it awkward to respond to such compliments. I could say something like, "Thanks, I really worked hard on that sermon and I'm glad you liked it." But that doesn't seem like a good plan. God doesn't take it lightly when we steal His glory. I remind myself that it is God and His Spirit who have been at work in spite of me. I remind myself of the gifts He has given me, the education He has permitted me to have, the opportunities He has granted, the wife with whom He has blessed me, the abundant mercy with which He covers my persistent failures—the list is long. If it weren't for all these things, my preaching would be in vain. I am nothing without Him. Really! I cannot take credit for the gain He brings to people when I preach.

Hence, my problem. What should I say when someone wants to tell me what God has done through my ministry?

I have learned not to reject my listener's words of appreciation. God has been at work in their lives, and it is important for them to express thanks for the impact my ministry has made. So I listen with a sense of appreciation and say something like, "Well, we know where all of that came from. But thanks, your words are a real encouragement to me."

I often tell them that I pray God will use me to make a difference in somebody's life and if that has happened with them, then God has answered my prayer. But my all-time favorite answer is: "See how much God loves you? I had no idea what you needed, and God laid that on my heart just for you. How good is it that He loves you that much! Thanks for telling me. It's a great encouragement!"

While I want to transfer the gratitude to its proper destination, my heart is overflowing with joy that God would see fit to use me in a divine connection between His heart and theirs. It's what I love about preaching!

WHEN THE PREACHER DISAPPEARS

Some time ago I sat in a congregation where people were going to microphones in the aisles to describe what God had done in their lives through the ministry of that church. One man addressed the pastor, "Bill, ten minutes into the sermon last week you disappeared and I heard from God." There could not be a more profound compliment for a preacher than that. When His Word is preached, God rolls up his sleeves and gets to work.

This is why I love to preach!

I don't understand the current climate that downgrades preaching to a brief closing thought at the end of extended worship. Nor do I understand those who say that preaching is "arrogant." If I am only preaching my own thoughts, then perhaps they are right. A sermon based on the authority of my own thinking is indeed arrogant. But if it is based on God's truth clearly seen in His Word, and carefully proclaimed by the prophet-preacher, it is not arrogant. What we preach is then strategically important. Truth is not found in community. Truth is found in the God who is true and in His Word, which is truth. For reasons best known to God alone, He has enlisted preachers to join in the enterprise of conveying His Word to His people.

I have preached enough to fully understand that getting God's Word to His people is a demanding task. I must extract God's ideas from the text and craft them into a sermon that speaks to the head and the heart.

I want my audience to know that I am in touch with their struggles. Delivering the goods while staying on top of my insecurities and short-comings requires an unshaken reliance on God. Preaching is a demanding assignment, but I love it just the same!

Amen

I love it when the light of exegetical discovery illuminates the text. I love sensing that I am, at last, emerging from the dark cave of wondering what I will say in the sermon.

Every preacher knows the excitement of feeling a sermon grow within, like an embryo developing cell upon cell. It is an excitement that flows from the increasing awareness that we have something to say from God for His people—an excitement that gives way to a sense of urgency and confidence. Urgency makes us passionate about the message of the text and confidence empowers us to preach that message with boldness and authority.

Simply put, good preaching is the art of bringing glory to God by delivering a word from God to His people in a way that touches them where they live and leads them to where they should be living. When I sense that I have found that word, it takes on a life of its own in my soul. It is then that I can't help myself. I must preach. At that moment, I know I am almost ready to preach. And when I am ready—almost ready—I love to preach!

JOSEPH M. STOWELL was president of the Moody Bible Institute for eighteen years (1987–2005). He has been a pastor for more than twenty years and is currently president of Cornerstone University in Grand Rapids, Michigan.

NOTES

1. Bruce W. Theilmann, *The Wittenburg Door*, no. 36 (April–May 1977).
2. *Chariots of Fire*, Warner Bros.,1981.

EVANGELISM

AND

PREACHING

by
George Sweeting

During my lifetime, I have had the special privilege of being exposed to the ministries of two world-famous evangelists: D. L. Moody and Billy Graham. Though I was not alive to meet Moody personally, from 1966–1971 I pastored the Chicago church that Moody began. Later I served as president, then chancellor of the school he founded. These two men, along with others, provide excellent examples of how evangelism relates to pastors.

Both of my parents were converted in Scotland through ministries that resulted from Moody's evangelistic campaigns of 1873–1875, 1883, 1888, and 1891. My layman father also attended an evening Bible school, called the Glasgow Training Institute, primarily inspired by D. L. Moody.

In 1923, both parents emigrated from Glasgow to the United States. Our family was raised on the sermons of Moody and the music of Ira D. Sankey. As I grew in my Christian faith and decided to prepare for the ministry, it was natural for me to travel to Chicago and enroll in the

Moody Bible Institute (1942–1945). My entire life has been lived under the sway of a man called by the *Encyclopedia Britannica* (1953), "one of the greatest of modern evangelists."

I have also been challenged and changed by the life of Billy Graham. I first heard and met Billy during my student days at Moody Bible Institute. He was in the early years of his evangelistic ministry and was speaking at Chicago Youth for Christ, which was a new organization in 1945.

In those days, Billy spoke at rallies and conferences in local churches, including my boyhood church in Hawthorne, New Jersey. Even then, it was clear that Billy was set apart for something extraordinary. Only eternity will reveal the enormous impact of his life and ministry.

In 1986, I had the privilege of introducing Billy to an audience of twenty thousand people for the centenary celebration of Moody Bible Institute. It was an unforgettable event. I began by saying, "D. L. Moody would have loved Billy Graham." I continued, "No evangelist in all of history has spoken to more people than Billy Graham."

EVANGELISM AND THE EVANGELISTIC SERMON

While attending the International Conference for Evangelists in Amsterdam, I heard Billy Graham define evangelism as "the proclamation of the historical, biblical Christ as Savior and Lord, with a view to persuading people to come to him personally and so be reconciled to God."[1]

The word *evangelism* is a beautiful word. *Evangel* means "glad tidings." The word *gospel* means "God's story." Evangelism is preaching God's story with the aim of calling the unconverted to repentance and faith in Jesus Christ.

In his book, *The History of Evangelism,* Paulus Scharff explains what an evangelistic sermon should include: "On the basis of Scripture, it affirms that without Christ, man is dead in trespasses and sins (Eph. 2:1) and enslaved by the power of darkness (Col. 1:13).[2] At the same time, it declares the saving love of God in Christ, with which the individual is to be confronted.

The evangelistic sermon proclaims objective, central biblical truths—particularly Christ's saving actions, the forgiveness of sins, assurance of salvation, and reconciliation to God the Father—which can lead to personal faith in Jesus Christ.[3]

Scharff reminds us that the evangelistic sermon calls attention to "the now and today."[4] Its primary purpose is not general but specific. Its goal is to awaken souls from spiritual death to life in Christ by the power of the Holy Spirit.

A BRIEF HISTORY OF EVANGELISM

Episode One: From Jerusalem to the edges of the Roman Empire

Beginning as members of an outcast faith, the early followers of Jesus witnessed in Jerusalem, Judea, Samaria, and to the ends of the known world. Despite being members of a minority, "the word of God spread. The number of disciples in Jerusalem increased rapidly" (Acts 6:7). By land and by sea, the disciples traveled preaching "that God was reconciling the world to himself in Christ" (2 Cor. 5:19). Evangelism was their passion. Some evangelism was done by preaching. Some was done through the witness of early apologists who winsomely answered Christianity's critics. Some of it took place as common people shared the good news at the marketplace or with loved ones in their social network.

Sometimes persecution propelled the early Christian witness. Often it was commended by the attractive lifestyle of ordinary Christians. The early Christians had a reputation for caring for others (e.g., unwanted children, the sick during epidemics).

The gospel also spread because the message was unique. It spoke of a personal relationship with God and His love for sinners. This was a unique message among the religions of the ancient world—a message that appealed to the poor, the slave, and even the wealthy from Caesar's household.

By the third century, a significant Christian minority existed in almost every province of the Roman Empire. By 312, even the emperor was identifying himself as a Christian. When he embraced the Christian faith, he made it the official religion of the Roman world. This is what people prayed for. But the answer to their prayers brought new challenges.

Episode Two: From Rome to early Europe

From the fifth to the sixteenth centuries, the gospel kept spreading, north, south, east, and west. During this era, the Christianization of Europe took place. The faith went from a Mediterranean religion to a European one. Sometimes it spread by mass conversions as people followed (or were pressured to follow) their king. Often it was missionary monks who brought the gospel to the Celts and early Germanic peoples of pagan Europe. God used evangelists such as Ulfilas (to the Goths), Martin of Tours (to the Franks), Patrick (to the Irish), Columba (to Picts and Scots), Boniface (to the Germans), Ansgar (to the Scandinavians), and Cyril and Methodius (to the Slavs). They were apostles of their age who preached, set up communities of light, taught the children of kings, helped establish languages, and taught literacy with the Bible.

When the institutional church grew corrupt in the late Middle Ages and the gospel got lost through multiplying traditions, it was itinerant preachers, such as Bernard of Clairvaux, Francis of Assisi, John Huss, John Wycliffe and his Lollard followers, and Savonarola, who pointed people to Jesus and His Word.

Episode Three: From Old World to New World

During the Reformation period, the gospel was rediscovered and proclaimed with great power by reformers like Martin Luther, John Calvin, John Knox, the Huguenots, and others. The printing press helped propel their influence. Calvin, himself, sparked an international movement of training pastors and church planting among the French and the Dutch.

This was also the period when the gospel was introduced to the new world by friars, clergy, pilgrims, and missionaries who followed the explorers. Sometimes they did it with more faithfulness than others, but they were the first to proclaim the name of Christ and set up missions in places like North, South, and Central America, Japan, the Philippines, Vietnam, etc. This was also the period of the first great awakening sparked by Zinzendorf and the Moravians. In the eighteenth century, the evangelistic preaching of George Whitefield, John Wesley, and Jonathan Edwards unleashed the gospel on two continents and led to massive social transformations. Many historians have said that their preaching kept England from the horrors of the French Revolution.

Episode Four: From the New World to Global Christianity

The last two centuries have seen the advance of the gospel from the new world to the poorer developing world (now referred to as the majority world). The nineteenth century has been called the great missionary century. William Carey argued for and then modeled the relevancy of the Great Commission in England. A generation of missionary evangelists brought the gospel to the coastlands of the world. Pioneer missionaries such as Adoniram and Anne Judson went to India. David Livingstone went to Africa. Jennie and J. Hudson Taylor (1832–1905) went to China. Many others followed, both men and women.

A second great spiritual awakening arose during the nineteenth century through the evangelistic preaching of Charles G. Finney, Dwight L. Moody, William and Catherine Booth, and Charles Spurgeon. The motivation of Moody, Robert Wilder, and John R. Mott ignited the Student Volunteer Movement. Their catchphrase was "the evangelization of the world in this generation." The ongoing legacy of this movement is seen in the Urbana student missionary conferences of this day.

By 1900, there was a gospel witness on every continent of the earth. The evangelistic seeds planted in India, Africa, China, and Latin America began to grow. Christianity became a worldwide faith. The church became a global church.

In the twentieth century, this movement continued. It was encouraged by the worldwide Pentecostalism movement and undergirded by the Bible translation movement, spearheaded by William Cameron Townsend. It was aided by new technologies of mass communication—radio, television, personal computers, and the Internet helped it; the unparalleled mass evangelism of Billy Graham strengthened it.

In 1974, the Lausanne Congress developed strategies for world evangelization. Graham and John Stott made it their mission to not only evangelize but to train a generation of itinerant pastors and evangelists in the developing world. Between 1983 and 2000 Graham organized three large training gatherings for the world's evangelists in Amsterdam. Nothing on this scale had ever been attempted. Most of these evangelists were nonwhite and non-Western.

By the end of the century, the gospel had spread to every nation of the world. But the challenge of reaching unreached people groups within the nations remained. Still, today we have the surprising prospect of there being more Anglicans in Nigeria than America, more Presbyterians in Korea than in Scotland or America, and more evangelicals in Brazil than in the whole of Europe.

In fact, some have noted that the center of Christianity, and evangelism, has shifted from the West to Africa, Asia, and Latin America. The map of the Christian world has been altered. We face a new era where non-Western missionaries and evangelists are on the move. We are seeing more partnerships between Western and non-Western churches. We are seeing Chinese evangelists who want to bring the gospel all along the Silk Road back to Jerusalem. We are seeing African evangelists preach in the streets of neo-pagan Western cities. Not only has the center shifted, but also there is a reversal in missions. Countries that were once considered Christian homelands are now mission fields. And the mission fields are Christian homelands. What an amazing time we live in.

THE ELEMENTS OF EVANGELISTIC PREACHING

The spread of the gospel, as given in the New Testament, was inextricably linked to preaching. Following the arrival of the Holy Spirit on the day of Pentecost, Peter stood up, raised his voice, and preached to the crowd (Acts 2:14). Though I enthusiastically believe in sharing the gospel on a one-to-one basis, personal evangelism cannot substitute or take the place of evangelistic preaching (1 Cor. 1:21). Peter stood up! Raised his voice! And addressed the crowd!

Peter's sermon focused on the life of Jesus: "Listen to this," Peter said, "Jesus of Nazareth was a man accredited by God to you by miracles, wonders and signs, which God did . . . through him" (Acts 2:22).

Peter's sermon also proclaimed the death of Jesus. He preached that even though Jesus was crucified according to "God's set purpose and foreknowledge," His listeners were guilty of Jesus' death: "You, with the help of wicked men, put him to death by nailing him to the cross" (v. 23). It's essential in evangelistic preaching to get to Jesus! Surprising as it seems, many sermons never do!

Philip, the evangelist of Acts 8, quickly got to Jesus. Philip told the Ethiopian "the good news about Jesus" (8:35). He probably reviewed the life, death, resurrection, and commission of Jesus. The message was all about Jesus. How else would the Ethiopian know to ask, "Why shouldn't I be baptized?" (8:37).

Peter's sermon included the resurrection of Jesus. He continued, "God raised him from the dead . . . and we are all witnesses of the fact. . . . Therefore let all Israel be assured of this: God has made this Jesus, whom you have crucified, both Lord and Christ" (2:24, 32, 36).

The conclusion of Peter's sermon was awesome. Luke says, " . . . they were cut to the heart and said to Peter and the other apostles, 'What shall we do?'" (v. 37). Evangelistic preaching, in the power of the Holy Spirit, enables people to ask, "What shall we do?"

The question of the three thousand at Pentecost is exactly the same as the Roman jailer at Philippi (Acts 16:30). Because of an earthquake, the jailer assumed that some prisoners escaped. However, Paul, led by the Holy Spirit, called out, "Don't harm yourself! We are all here!" (16:28). In response, the jailer "fell trembling before Paul and Silas . . . and asked, ' . . . what must I do to be saved?'" (v. 30). Paul not only told him to "believe in the Lord Jesus" (v. 31), but also followed with additional instructions. "Then they spoke the word of the Lord to him and all the others in his house" (v. 32).

Peter concluded his sermon at Pentecost the same way. After telling the seekers to repent, Peter gave specific instructions: "With many other words he warned them; and he pleaded with them" (Acts 2:40).

Evangelistic preaching is all about Jesus—his sinless life, atoning and sacrificial death, and triumphant resurrection and coming again. At least half of Peter's sermon was taken directly from the Old Testament Scriptures. The phrase made famous by Billy Graham, "The Bible says," is on target.

CALLING FOR A RESPONSE

It's enlightening to review some of the biblical invitations of the Old and New Testament. On one occasion Moses, in a time of national crisis, "stood at the entrance of the camp and said, 'Whoever is for the Lord, come to me.' And all the Levites rallied to him" (Exodus 32:26). Moses called for an open decision.

Joshua, the successor of Moses likewise invited Israel to make a public declaration of their intentions. Joshua appealed, "Choose for yourselves this day whom you will serve. . . ." (Joshua 24:15). The people responded, "We will serve the Lord our God and obey him" (v. 24). Then Joshua wrote out their decision in "the Book of the Law of God" (v. 26). This was followed by a decision carved in stone, as a continual reminder to future generations of their decision (24:26, 27).

Good King Josiah, after discovering the Law of the Lord and hearing what God required, "stood . . . and renewed the covenant in the presence of the Lord to follow the Lord and keep his commands . . . Then he had everyone . . . pledge themselves to it" (2 Chron. 34: 31–32). The audience openly went on record to serve the Lord.

The New Testament tells us, "After John was put in prison, Jesus went into Galilee, proclaiming the good news of God. 'The time has come,' he said. 'The kingdom of God is near. Repent and believe the good news'" (Mark 1:14–15). Jesus called for a decision to repent and believe. To Andrew and Peter he also said, "Come! Follow me!" Decide!

To the tired farmer, the money-minded merchant, and the weary worker, Jesus called, "Come to me . . . and I will give you rest" (Matthew 11:28).

How disappointing to bring an audience by prayer, study, and preaching to the door of eternal life and not allow them a chance to enter! This is as unnatural as a salesperson who carefully presents the needs and virtues of a product, only to leave without providing an opportunity to own the product. A thousand times I have sat through the closing minutes of a sermon, only to be let down by the conclusion. At times I've wanted to stand and ask, "So what?!" or lift a banner with one word: Application. Peter and Paul did not omit the application.

The methods of application are as diverse as people and situations. Once, while ministering at St. Giles Cathedral in Edinburgh, Scotland, I invited those who desired to make a profession of faith in Jesus Christ for the first time to remain in their seats until after the benediction. To my joy and surprise, over five hundred people waited to be instructed in the way of salvation after the congregation had dispersed.

I'm aware of the struggles that some have concerning any form of invitation. Yet evangelistic preaching calls for a decision. Jesus emphatically said, "Whoever acknowledges me before men, I will also acknowledge him before my Father in heaven. But whoever disowns me before men, I will disown him before my Father in heaven" (Matthew 10:32, 33).

The reasons for a public decision are many. First, we owe it to Jesus. Jesus died publicly on the cross for our sins, and we are required to publicly acknowledge Him. Secondly, we owe it to others. We are to confess Him "before men" (10:32). Both Nicodemus and Joseph of Arimathea tried to be secret disciples. It took Jesus' death to encourage them to beg and care for his dead body. Third, we owe it to ourselves. A public decision puts a person on record and brings out the best in them. It's a constant reminder of what we have decided and helps fortify our faith.

WHY WE FEAR TO CALL FOR A RESPONSE

The failure to call for a response may find its source in several areas. First, there is fear. Fear often exists because of uncertainty and inexperience. It is difficult to know what to do and how to do it. At times, the most seasoned pastor omits any kind of appeal simply because he fears no response! It's easier to close with a dramatic illustration than risk no response. This fear is very real. However, can we allow fear of perceived failure to rob us of an awesome opportunity?

After sixty years of preaching, I still prayerfully prepare the conclusion of the sermon. I do it best in the quietness of my study as I wait on the Holy Spirit for guidance. I write out key reminders to bring the message home to the heart, mind, and will. I have found that adequate preparation reduces fear and allows the conclusion of the sermon to be a moment of power!

Second, we may have misconceptions. Some of my esteemed friends do not give an opportunity for response because they feel an inconsistency between the truth of God's sovereignty and man's responsibility.

Theologian J. I. Packer speaks to this in his book *Evangelism and the Sovereignty of God.* He says there is an apparent incompatibility between these two truths, which we cannot solve. He urges us to live with these two doctrines. "Be careful, therefore, not to set them at loggerheads, nor to make deductions from either that would cut across the other."[5] The Bible clearly teaches God's sovereignty and human responsibility. The great Charles H. Spurgeon of London was asked to reconcile these two truths. He answered, "I wouldn't try. I never reconcile friends."

The life and ministry of Jesus has helped me in this area. To the man with a deformed hand, Jesus said, "Stretch out your hand" (Mark 3:5). He did, and his hand was completely restored. This man was incapable of responding from a human standpoint, and yet he obeyed, and he was healed. Jesus gave him the ability to respond.

John 5:5–9 records the story of a man who was an invalid for thirty-eight years. He was totally helpless. Then Jesus asked, "Do you want to get well?" He answered, "'I have no one to help me.' . . . Then Jesus said to him, "'Get up! Pick up your mat and walk.' At once the man was cured." The God who calls . . . is the God who gives the ability to respond.

Lazarus, in John 11, is an example of a dead man doing what he was incapable of doing. Jesus called, "Lazarus, come forth!" and he came forth. God did it! In the same way, those dead in sin are made alive, when God calls.

When we preside at the Lord's table to remember our Lord's death, we say on Christ's behalf, "Take, eat! Take, drink!" In the same way, we say on Christ's behalf, "Come, receive! Come, believe!"

3. Third, we may feel fatigue. It is possible to be so consumed with the body of the message that we have little strength left for the strategic closing moments of decision.

There is little in the ministry as draining as preaching for a verdict. It's the most difficult work I know, primarily because we're wrestling not only against flesh and blood. But as Paul reminds us: we are coming "against the . . . powers of this dark world and against the spiritual forces of evil in the heavenly realms" (Ephesians 6:12). All hell conspires to defeat us in this sacred moment of opportunity.

Occasionally, I've been asked, "Is it right to persuade people to make a spiritual decision?" Based on Paul's ministry in the book of Acts, the answer is an emphatic yes!

While at Thessalonica, Paul reasoned with the people, "explaining and proving that the Christ had to suffer and rise from the dead. 'This Jesus I am proclaiming to you is the Christ'" (Acts 17:3). The following verse answers the question, "Is it right to persuade people?" "Some were persuaded and joined Paul and Silas."

Later, Paul tried to persuade Governor Felix (Acts 24:24), then his successor Porcius Festus (Acts 25), and finally, King Agrippa (Acts 26).

Speaking about the judgment seat of Christ, Paul writes, "We know what it is to fear the Lord. We try to persuade men . . . " (2 Cor. 5:11). Paul was a persuader, compelled by Christ's love (2 Cor. 5:14).

PRACTICAL ASPECTS OF THE EVANGELISTIC SERMON

Moody spoke about the three R's of preaching: "Ruined by the fall; Redemption through Christ; Regeneration through the Holy Spirit." This is the heart of evangelistic preaching.

As we recall the three R's while we preach, we can also embrace these eight elements for an effective evangelistic sermon. As a pastor-evangelist:

1. Know beyond all doubt that you are divinely called. There can be no uncertainty here. With Paul be able to say, "I am compelled to preach. Woe to me if I do not preach the gospel" (1 Cor. 9:16).

2. Believe that men and women are lost, apart from the gospel. A lifeline is not needed unless people are perishing! "Whoever believes in him shall not perish" (John 3:16).

3. Believe that Jesus is the only Savior. Jesus clearly said, "No one comes to the Father except through me" (John 14:6).

4. Be a student of God's Word and the times. Philip, the evangelist, knew the Scripture so well that he was able to immediately answer the question of the Ethiopian and direct him to Jesus. We must also be aware of world conditions so that we can apply the unchanging gospel to a fast-changing culture.

5. Make the message clear. It's best to avoid long, run-on sentences and theological phrases for plain, understandable words. Jesus said, "Feed my sheep," not "my giraffes." If we must use a difficult word, follow it with several understandable synonyms.

6. Don't be afraid of illustrations. The most intelligent attendee will be helped when you use one. Jesus used them all the time, as did D. L. Moody and Billy Graham. As windows admit light to a house, an illustration or quotation brings clarity to the sermon. Illustrations are nail sinkers that drive home truth. It is a compliment of the highest order when teenagers tell me they understood every word. Don't mistake confusion for depth.

7. Seek a conversational style. An old preacher once said to me, "When I first began to preach, I thought it was thunder that killed, and so I tried to preach loud. After awhile, I discovered it was the lightning that did the work, and since that time, I've asked the Lord to help me thunder less, and lightning more."

Finally, practice loving your audience. If you sincerely love those to whom you speak, they will feel it, and they will love you back. In D. L. Moody's day, they called the church he founded, "a house of love." Mr. Moody said, "The churches would soon be filled if outsiders could find that people in them loved them when they came. This . . . draws sinners."[6]

Before I preach, I fervently ask God to display His love through my presence, voice, gestures, and primarily my words. Each time I preach, I claim Romans 5:5, "God has poured out his love into our hearts by the Holy Spirit." Never do I preach without thinking of the words of Paul, "We are . . . Christ's ambassadors, as though God were making his appeal through us. We implore you on Christ's behalf: Be reconciled to God" (2 Cor. 5:20).

Because of God's salvation, each believer is an ambassador of Jesus. The fact is that I may be a good one or a poor one, but I can't help being one. Paul clearly reminds us that God makes "His appeal through us." That's astounding!

What an awesome position we have! Think about it—our sovereign God makes His appeal through you and me. That's mind stretching. With 2 Cor. 5:20 in mind, I position myself when I preach. God's voice can be my voice. His eyes can be my eyes. His opened hands can be my hands. His love can be my love. His appeal can be my appeal. On Christ's behalf, I call, "be reconciled to God" (2 Cor. 5:20). *This* is the privilege and passion of evangelistic preaching.

GEORGE SWEETING served as president of the Moody Bible Institute for sixteen years (1971–1987) and twelve years served as chancellor (1987–1999). Prior to his ministry at MBI, he was an evangelist and later the pastor of the Moody Memorial Church in Chicago.

NOTES

1. As quoted in *The Work of an Evangelist*, J. D. Douglas, ed. (Minneapolis: Worldwide Publishers, 1984), 5. It was my honor to also address the Amsterdam conference that year.

2. Paulus Scharff, *The History of Evangelism* (Grand Rapids: Eerdmans, 1963), 3.

3. Ibid.

4. Ibid.

5. J. I. Packer, *Evangelism and the Sovereignty of God* (Downers Grove, Ill.: Inter-Varsity: 1961), 21.

6. Richard E. Day, *Bush Aglow: The Life Story of Dwight L. Moody, Commoner of Northfield* (reprinted by Crown Christian Publications, n.d.), 146.

HOW WOMEN

HEAR THE

SERMON

by
Pam MacRae

Since I was a child I have been interested in the differences in the way men and women communicate and relate to each other. When I had something difficult to discuss with my parents, I knew that my dad would become less upset than my mother. Maybe it was the other way around for you, but my mom and my dad often responded in completely different ways. Was it just their personalities? Perhaps, but as a child, I concluded that something was different.

My relationships with boys at school affirmed those early observations about my dad and mom. I encountered those differences again as I interacted with men at work, in church, and in dating relationships. Watching men talk to men, women talk with women, and then noting how they talked together, I realized that women and men have distinctive styles of communication.

These differences affect our closest relationships with the opposite sex. A puzzled husband asks, "Why don't you get this?" "How can you think that?" A frustrated wife asks, "Why can't you understand?" Clearly the way men and women communicate differs.

Such diverse communication styles between men and women raise a question for those preaching: Will the communication difference create the potential for conflict when a woman in the pew listens to a man in the pulpit? Or can he just speak as a preacher, and dismiss the gender issue? Most statistics indicate the majority of a church audience consists of women. Should the gender difference influence the way a pastor frames his message?

Some argue that God's Word does not need to be applied according to gender. To a degree that's true. Knowing that God says not to lie is a principle that is applied without regard to gender, age, culture, or any other distinctive. But there are times when application can be made or the sermon's form may be structured in a way that reaches the heart of a woman differently than a man.

In her New York Times bestseller *You Just Don't Understand,* Deborah Tannen says, "Pretending that women and men are the same hurts women, because the ways they are treated are based on the norms for men. It also hurts men who, with good intentions, speak to women as they would to men, and are nonplussed when their words don't work as they expected."[1]

WHY CONNECT WITH WOMEN LISTENERS?

What happens when a woman fails to hear preaching that is directed to her? For the most part, women have been in church long enough to "translate" sermons. Women can hear a sermon and readily work out the application to fit their own lives. But there are times when she longs to hear you acknowledge that she is even there. It helps when you speak directly to her.

Women make up 51 percent of the U.S. population. The percentage of women in a typical United States church is even higher at 61 percent.[2] If you do not directly address the women who make up more than half of your congregation, you will risk them feeling forgotten or ignored.

I can offer one woman's perspective on what women want or expect when they listen to a sermon. First, and foremost, I want to hear something about God. Please tell me, remind me, or refresh my soul with something true about God. I need to know about His greatness, because, particularly as a woman, I often feel powerless in my life. I need to know that His sovereign plan makes my life purposeful. My life, as yours, often feels routine and mundane. I want to know that He loves me. I need to hear that I am worth something in a world where I am often tempted to feel marginalized.

I want to know that what you are teaching means something to you. Are you convinced that what you are preaching about is important? If it means something to you, I will be interested in what it means to me. I want to know how what you are telling me has made a difference in your life. When I see that it has, I will look for God to work in my life too.

Indeed, most women want to know about God's love, their value in Him, and how the Scriptures apply to them. In Genesis 16:13 Hagar called the Lord, "the God who sees me." God saw she was in trouble and spoke directly to her need. This characteristic of God should be reflected in your sermons. Women want to be acknowledged, understood, and have you speak to the deepest needs of their hearts and lives.

Do you know what is happening in the lives of women who come to our churches and what factors influence their ability to hear the message? Everyone has filters through which they hear. The situations women come from influence how they hear what is said. Understanding their pain and struggle, as well as their accomplishments, helps you speak truth into their lives.

RESPECT YOUR AUDIENCE

The women who walk through the doors of your church are more highly educated than ever before. There has never been a time in history where women were so freely able to pursue higher education. Today more women than men are earning associate, bachelor's, and master's degrees. Between 1989–90 and 1999–2000, the number of bachelor's degrees awarded to men increased by 8 percent, while those awarded to women rose by 26 percent.[3]

Pastors need to respect the intellect of women. Women can hear in your voice when you address them on a condescending or simplistic level. We know that women are sharing the workplace in positions comparable to their male colleagues. They are engaged in homeschooling and higher education; they serve in positions of influence in their communities. If women who listen to you can grasp the complexities of today's most intricate scientific issues, you should not be afraid to excite their intellect with theological wonders. Challenge them to stand in awe of the complex nature of God. Yes, they will want you to speak to their hearts, but do not neglect their minds.

If a woman senses that you direct more complex theological teaching to the men in the congregation, or even have conversations outside the pulpit that direct theological questions and discussions to men, she will assume you believe women are either not interested in or incapable of understanding such truths.

Recently a pastor was speaking with my husband and me about his family. During that part of our conversation, I was very much included in what was being said. Then he began to talk about a theological question he was pondering, related to a topic that had been discussed in one of his seminary classes. At that point, the conversation shifted and was directed solely to my husband. Even his body turned slightly to shift away from me and more directly face my husband. Ironically, I was probably more interested in the particular topic he was discussing than my husband was. I would have enjoyed having a conversation with him about the subject, but was not included, nor expected to be included, in the discussion.

"TEACH ME!"

Women crave theological content. This is what they are asking for in Bible study. In the church I attend, we offer ten different women's Bible studies. If you find a church with a couple of women, you will probably also find a women's Bible study. The studies that are currently most popular tend to emphasize deep biblical study on a strong academic and intellectual level that is also high in application.

BSF International, which has more than one thousand classes worldwide, is an intensive, inductive Bible study that requires daily homework. Started by H. Wethrerell Johnson, a former missionary with China Inland Mission, BSF—better known as Bible Study Fellowship—

has had three female directors during its fifty years. It offers day and evening classes for men, women, and children, but most of the classes are populated with women hungry to better know God's Word. Those in the groups prepare by reading study notes on the passage that is taught equal to a good academic commentary. Women discussion group leaders do extensive homiletical analysis of the passage that will be discussed in the leadership training time (this training is done each week the day before the Bible study). This is not for presenting a message, but for training in how to study a passage.

I was in BSF for more than ten years and often heard women mourn the fact that their pastor did not bring an exegetical message on Sundays, the way they were used to hearing at Bible study on Thursdays.

Other examples of serious interest in Bible studies are the strong responses to ministries by authors and Bible teachers Beth Moore and Kay Arthur. They are just two of the many women who write quite rigorous Bible studies for women. These studies are not for the faint of heart or mind. Pastors would do well to sit in on these studies and hear what the women are learning and see what they are drawn to. The cry of women is, "Teach me!"

CONNECTING WITH WOMEN

Many women who walk into churches are mothers and wives. I often hear pastors try to relate to women with illustrations regarding mothering, homemaking, or being a wife. This is a good beginning, but this is not the only and may not even be the most common life situation for the women in your church. Being a wife and mother is an important aspect of many women's lives, but typically it is a limited part.

I have two adult children. The part of my life that was taken up with child rearing and homemaking is now greatly diminished. That was only about a twenty-year segment of my life. Naturally, I still am involved in the lives of my children, and I still like to create a warm environment in my home, but the days of that being my primary focus are gone.

Consider these statistics that compare women in 1967 to women in 2006:

MOTHERS IN AMERICA, THEN AND NOW[4]

Category	Then (1967)	Now (2006)
U.S. total population	200 million	300 million
Married moms (w/children age 18)	24.6 million	26.0 million
Single moms (w/children< age 18)	2.6 million	8.2 million
Births to unmarried women	0.3 million	1.47 million
Children per married couple w/kids	2.44	1.89
Children per single mom	2.42	1.73
Married moms in the workplace part time	35%	70%
Married moms in the workplace full time	15%	45%
Married moms who are college graduates	12%	33%

Notice the final three categories of women: Most mothers work, almost half on a full-time basis; and one of every three mothers has a college degree. Directing your application to women solely as mothers and wives means you may miss the normative life experience for most women. I have often heard pastors say to women that their *highest* callings are to be a godly wife and mother. Those are certainly high callings, but they are not a woman's only two callings. A woman's highest call is to be a godly woman in whatever circumstance of life God places her.

Of course, there are wonderful biblical examples of God using women as wives and mothers, such as Naomi, Mary, Hannah, and the Proverbs 31 woman. The way God used them informs and inspires women to be the wives and mothers we so desperately need today. But women also need to see that God used women in Scripture in other ways. Speak to the women in your congregation about the prophetesses in both the Old and New Testament who spoke God's truth with great impact. In Micah 6:4, Scripture says that Miriam, with Moses and Aaron, led the Israelites. God used Deborah as a judge and great military leader for the Israelites. Esther served God as a queen.

In the New Testament, influential businesswomen supported Jesus' ministry and the ministry of Paul out of their own means. These were intelligent women whose lives serve as great examples for today's audience. It is not hard for women to be encouraged when you preach about other women from Scripture and show how God used them in a variety of ways.

THE PROBLEM OF ABUSE

Sadly, we need not look far to find women who are suffering abuse at the hands of men. "For more cultures through most of history, the most serious deviation from biblical standards regarding men and women has not been feminism, but harsh and oppressive male chauvinism," writes complementarian Wayne Grudem.[5] This is the case within the church as well. Women often experience difficulties and oppression from men who take power over women intellectually, physically, sexually, economically, and emotionally.

Throughout the world, women make up the largest segment of the poor, neglected, abused, and forgotten. Their children suffer with them in their hardship. Physical abuse touches many women. Around the world at least one woman in three has been beaten, coerced into sex, or otherwise abused in her lifetime. Most often the abuser is a member of her own family or a friend.[6] Somewhere in America, a woman is battered, usually by her intimate partner, every fifteen seconds.[7]

Economic need is higher among women. It is not typical for most women to be supported by men. The inability to financially support their families is a greater problem for women, who overall bear this responsibility more often than men. Women are taught in church that men are to be their protector, provider, and the authority. Yet it is from the hands of men that some women experience disregard, suffering, and trauma.

Pastors need to realize that women who come into your congregation may feel unsafe, even when there is no reason to fear. Tannen notes that a woman may feel dominated even when there is no intention to dominate.[8] The pastor's role as an information provider creates a context where women who have been abused may feel vulnerable. Tannen explains, "The act of giving information by definition frames one in a position of higher status, while the act of listening frames one as lower."[9] This means that women who come to the church from abusive situations are at greater risk of feeling threatened—even abused—by the power of the pulpit. Pastors teach with authority. Even when the intention is not one of sinister power, women who have been injured may fear the pastor as a potential abuser.

God places leaders over men and women and gives those leaders authority. We should not reduce the structure of the church. But a pastor needs to show compassion toward female listeners who may fear him or struggle with his position because he is a man. A pastor is to be a godly man who carefully reflects God toward women.

A woman who has been hurt may respond to authority by withdrawing. That is, she may just leave and never come back to church. Or she may give the pastor more authority in her life than God ever intended him to have. She might respond with an inordinate attachment and inappropriate submission to his every word. It is hard for a woman to live unentangled if she is used to being entangled.

Women who have been abused feel powerless. Alice Matthews, in *Preaching that Speaks to Women,* says, "Women's general disbelief in their ability to change their circumstances ought to be of deep concern to pastors. A fundamental aim of preaching is to empower listeners to incorporate what they have heard from Scripture into solutions to the challenges of everyday life. Yet if women do not believe that as women they can act, they will not hear your message of empowerment in the same way the men might hear it."[10]

A WOMAN'S NEED TO BE UNDERSTOOD

Women typically have deep emotional waters and want to be understood. In the classic scenario, a woman wants to talk about a problem she is facing with her husband, only to get his quick response telling her how she should fix it. Her frustration and irritation shoots through the roof. She wanted him to listen to her and understand how she was feeling. He thought the best way to be helpful was to tell her how to fix it.

Generally, it is enough for her to feel heard and understood, which is of great value to her. She may *eventually* want help, but what she really wants is to feel validated in her experience and then perhaps hear something soothing and comforting.

Tannen notes that men are sometimes confused by the various ways women use conversation to be intimate with others. One of these ways she calls "troubles talk." She says, "For women, talking about troubles is the essence of connection. I tell you my troubles, you tell me your troubles, and we're close. Men, however, hear troubles talk as a request for advice, so they respond with a solution."[11]

Conversations with the pastor give a woman information about the level of understanding he has for women in general. Does he offer quick solutions, answers, or comments? Or, does he really listen to her? When a man offers an off-the-cuff solution, a woman may feel he is trying to diminish or dismiss her problem. He is communicating that he does not get her. This does not build trust and can profoundly affect how a woman hears the pastor in the pulpit.

A WOMAN'S PERCEPTIONS OF A PREACHER

A woman's need to be understood has a flip side that is generally revealed in her quick ability to size up and assess situations with surprising accuracy. She wants to be understood, but she also has a high need to understand. Typically this means that she can intuitively assess situations.

My husband, Bob, often wonders how I seem to just "know" things. Occasionally our daughters will say one thing, and I will subsequently tell him they really mean something entirely different. Often, he just gives me a baffled look, wondering how I could get that from what they said. Most of the time I read the situation right. How do I know what they really mean? I just do.

Indeed, one Stanford University study concluded that women catch subliminal messages faster and more accurately than men.[12] Nonverbal clues are not lost on women.

Meanwhile brain-scan studies have found those areas dealing with affective responses are larger on the female brain.[13] Analyzing those findings in her book, *The Female Brain*, Louann Brizendine concludes the female brain is uniquely gifted in its ability to assess the thoughts, beliefs, and intentions of others with minimal information.[14]

Thus you should realize that women in your congregation will naturally use this ability to "read" a pastor. Women assess the preacher. Of course, men do this too. Every listener draws conclusions about how much a speaker can be trusted and respected based on nonverbal cues. This does not diminish a listener's obligation to show respect and listen to the preacher as he teaches and preaches from Scripture. He is there with God's authority. But a pastor can make it unnecessarily difficult for a woman to hear the message because of what she senses from him. If a woman believes that you do not understand or value the needs of women, it will be hard for her to take your teaching seriously. An attitude of mutual respect creates a context where true communication can take place.

A woman will also take note of your reputation and watch what you do when you are not in the pulpit. What you say outside of the pulpit will impact how you are heard in the pulpit. How you relate to a woman, to your wife, to your children, to the needy, and to injustice will teach the women of your congregation who you are and how you understand or fail to understand women.

Pastors would do well to acknowledge and capitalize on the intuitive abilities of women. Aside from the value of helping discern strategic and sensitive ministry matters, this is an ability God gives that is meant to be of encouragement to the church.

Matthews says, "What are the messages the average woman may hear when she attends church on Sunday? She *may* hear the messages contained in the pastor's words. She may hear other messages in what the pastor does *not* say. She is likely to pick up nonverbal messages from the preacher's stance in the pulpit. She may receive unintended messages from the informal social interactions that occur before or after the service."[15]

Several years ago I was talking with a pastor who told me a joke that made fun of a woman in a stereotypical manner. I reacted lightly and asked him why he was telling me a joke that belittled women. He responded defensively, saying it *wasn't* demeaning to women, and joked about my being overly sensitive. If he had understood my point about demeaning women and acknowledged that it could be taken that way, rather than defending himself and pointing the finger at me, the conversation would have been quickly forgotten. Because of his response I really did become offended by the joke. I also became frustrated because he discredited my opinion and tried to turn the offense into my problem.

A short time later I had the opportunity to sit in a service where he was preaching. I immediately saw him in the context of our earlier conversation. It was understandably difficult for me to take his message seriously.

In her insightful book *Women, the Misunderstood Majority*, Gay Hubbard writes, "Women come to therapy with a lifetime of smiling politely at such jokes, having learned that if they object they will be publicly rated as a poor sport or, even worse, be suspected of dangerous feminist leanings."[16]

The relationship a woman has with her pastor is very important. That does not mean she must personally know a preacher to "hear" him. But his reputation, attitudes, and relationships as seen by others are often well known enough to mean something to those who hear him. The need for this sense of knowing is more important to a woman than to a man. In the book *Believing in Preaching: What Listeners Hear in Sermons,* the authors ask whether gender differences affect the way males or females respond to a preacher who has little relationship with his people. They note, "We found almost twice as many males as females reporting the relationship with the preacher did not affect their listening. This is particularly significant when it is remembered that there were almost one-third more women than men in the study."[17]

In many pulpits today pastors do communicate well to women. Yet others do not seem to be conscious of the women in their congregation. Still Bible colleges and seminaries should consider this as they prepare future pastors for their duties.[18] The pastor who has little or no formal training in understanding the needs of women may fall back on assumptions from his family life, other social relationships, or even crude locker-room jokes. We often are unaware of the paradigms that underlie our speech and relationships. The authors of *Believing in Preaching* give a key warning about how pastors should live out their faith:

> It is important to remember that when we preach we are not just telling the congregation about God; we are representing God. Preachers are teaching, but they are also demonstrating the faith. What we say in the pulpit and who we are on the streets are both being listened to. If congregants do not "hear" a consistency in our lives, our ability to engage the pew is lessened. And, unfortunately, our weaknesses and inconsisten-

cies can be seen as weaknesses in the faith. We represent the faith; our foibles become the foibles of the faith.[19]

SUGGESTIONS FOR THE PREACHER

Given these dynamics, what can the preacher do?

First, be a man who is respected by all—with a reputation of caring for all. Women are watching and forming an impression that will influence how they hear their pastor. The relationship you have with people outside the pulpit will open doors to be heard once you step into the pulpit. Where personal relationships are not possible, the impact you have from afar will serve to do the same. Because a number of women will come from situations where the relationships they have with men are hurtful, avoid speaking to a woman in a condescending, or patronizing way.

Jesus cautioned his disciples against using position and power for anything other than an open door to serve.

> "You know that the rulers of the Gentiles lord it over them, and their high officials exercise authority over them. Not so with you. Instead, whoever wants to become great among you must be your servant, and whoever wants to be first must be your slave—just as the Son of Man did not come to be served, but to serve, and to give his life as a ransom for many." (Matthew 20:25–28)

Second, never underestimate the influence and power you have as a pastor. God has given you authority in the body of Christ. Use it to encourage women to go to the heights of who they are in Christ. Many women need to hear from a pastor that they are valuable, that they are worthy of respect, and that God can use them in a mighty way in the body of Christ. For most churches the old adage applies, "As the pastor goes, so goes the church." Be known as a pastor who opens doors of ministry for women. Women need to see that you strongly and visibly affirm their gifts.

Third, acknowledge women in general. It is validating just to hear a reference to a woman in the message. I have listened to many sermons that never even mention a woman. I have heard illustration after illustration directed only to men. The Scriptures are full of biblical characters, but the women in the Bible are noticeably absent from many of today's sermons. Robert Howard, bibliographer in homiletics and liturgics at Vanderbilt, says, "Theologically, the exclusion of women's point of view in the imagery of sermons distorts the very Good News that preachers seek to proclaim. If women as well as men are to love God with all their souls, they will find powerful help to do so in biblical examples, illustrations, stories, and metaphors of women as well as men who are psychologically whole."[20]

Women in your congregation would be encouraged to hear a series of messages on the women of the Bible. Or, you could research what women have done in the church throughout history to use as illustrations for your sermons. (One helpful source is the book *Daughters of the Church*, by Ruth Tucker and Walter Liefeld.) As Matthews summarizes, "Preachers must preach in such a way that all women are valued and seen as worthy of love and acceptance regardless of the particular roles they do or do not have. To love others, women must also see others. Preachers, therefore, must preach in such a way that all women are visible in the life of the church."[21]

Fourth, value theology as part of the lives of women. The influence of a tradition that said that the study of theology was appropriate only for men may bind us even if we reject such a view. Such thinking may not substantially impact some younger women—they are the highly educated ones who do not question their ability to know. But you will have older women who struggle to believe they truly can think on a theological level. You will have certain women who are unsure of their own intellect. For years they have come to church and have been spoken down to. These women must know that it is reasonable and normal that they learn biblical truth and develop a theology to live by. Be the one who tells them differently and then watch what happens as they grow.

Finally, be careful not to preach to what you don't understand. Nothing is more discrediting for a pastor than to speak about the emotional life of a woman, try to relate to menopause and PMS, when we know they just don't get it. We don't expect you to get it. You don't have to over-relate—but you do have to be aware. When it comes to circumstances that are solely feminine, compassion is the key—not empathy. But a woman truly appreciates when a man at least acknowledges the truth of her experiences.

BEING AN EXAMPLE AND SPOKESMAN FOR GOD

One of the most worthwhile things you can do is to teach husbands how to love and respect women. You be the good example and leader for this too. You will be forever endeared to a woman if you teach her husband how to love her better. Her heart will be open to hear you if you have spoken truth to her husband.

Women want to hear from God. They struggle with huge questions and are often straining throughout the entire message just to hear something that will help. You are God's spokesman.

Finally, remember that there are *always* people like me listening to you. Challenge their intellects, reach their souls, answer their questions, and honor them as women. Never underestimate the power of your life and your message to bring words of hope, comfort, and truth.

PAM MacRAE is assistant professor of women's ministries at the Moody Bible Institute. She has M.A.Min. from Moody Bible Institute as well as a B.A. degree from Trinity International University, Deerfield, Illinois.

NOTES

1. Deborah Tannen, *You Just Don't Understand* (New York: Ballantine, 1996), 16.

2. Cynthia A. Woolever, "Generations of Women in Church. The US Congregational Life Survey." 2001.The study looked at data from the General Society Survey of 2000. Specific data can be found at http://www.uscongregations.org/pdf/sisr-cw-women.pdf.

3. *U.S. Department of Education, "Post Secondary Education Statistics in 2001," Almanac of Policy Issues, August 1, 2003.*
http://www.policyalmanac.org/education/archive/2001_Postsecondary_Education.shtml

4. "As U.S. Population Swells to 300 Million," Press Release of Johnson & Johnson Consumer Products Company, PRNewswire. http://www.prnewswire.com/cgi bin/stories.pl?ACCT=104&STORY=/www/story/10-16-2006/0004451976 &EDATE=

5. Wayne Grudem, *Evangelical Feminism & Biblical Truth* (Sisters, Oreg.: Mult-nomah, 2004), 524.

6. The abuser is an "intimate," i.e., family member, or a friend in 76 percent of rape cases. "Table 9: Victim and Offender Relationship, 2005," in, Shannan M. Catalano, "Criminal Victimization" *Bureau of Justice Statistics Bulletin*, U.S. Department of Justice, September 2006, as cited in http://www.rainn.org/statistics/index.html

7. *UN Study on the Status of Women,* 2000. Issued in 2001 by the UN Commission on the Status of Women; as cited in "Facts about Violence," Fact #27, at www.feminist.com/antiviolence/facts.html

8. Tannen, *You Just Don't Understand,* 18.

9. Ibid., 139.

10. Alice Matthews, *Preaching That Speaks to Women* (Grand Rapids: Baker, 2003) 49.

11. Tannen, *You Just Don't Understand,* 52.

12. As cited in Gary Smalley and Norma Smalley, *Hidden Keys of a Loving, Lasting Marriage* (Grand Rapids: Zondervan, 1988), 17.

13. Louann Brizendine, *The Female Brain* (New York: Morgan Road Books, 2006), 120.

14. Ibid., 120–21.

15. Matthews, *Preaching That Speaks to Women,* 18.

16. Gay Hubbard, *Women, the Misunderstood Majority* (Nashville: Nelson Reference & Electronic Publishing, 1992), 24.

17. Mary Alice Mulligan, Diane Turner-Sharazz, Dawn Ottoni Wilhelm, and Ronald J. Allen, *Believing in Preaching: What Listeners Hear in Sermons* (Atlanta: Chalice Press, 2005), 86.

18. Hubbard notes that most seminaries do not offer a single course aimed at helping men understand women; Hubbard, *Women, the Misunderstood Majority,* 2.

19. Mulligan et al, *Believing in Preaching,* 88.

20. Robert R. Howard, "Gender and Point of View in the Imagery of Preaching," *Homiletic* 23, no. I (summer 1999): 1; as quoted in Matthews, *Preaching That Speaks to Women,* 16.

21. Matthews, *Preaching That Speaks to Women,* 16.

Eight

PREPARING YOURSELF

SPIRITUALLY

FOR THE MESSAGE

by
Dan Green

A masterful preacher, Phillips Brooks served as rector of Trinity Episcopal Church in Boston in the 1870s. During his tenure there, he was invited to speak at the annual Yale Lectures, where he delivered the still highly respected *Lectures on Preaching*, later published in 1877. Brooks was a colleague of evangelist D. L. Moody and ministered effectively alongside him during evangelistic crusades.[1] When Brooks died in 1893, Boston mourned as if the entire city had been a member of his parish.

Perhaps the greatest hallmark of Brooks's preaching was the intimate tie between his personal spiritual life and his power in the pulpit. As he explained during one of his lectures: "Nothing but fire kindles fire; to know in one's whole nature what it is to live by Christ; to be His and not our own; to be so occupied by gratitude for what He did for us and for what He continually is to us that His will and His glory shall be the sole desires of our life . . . that is the first necessity of the preacher."[2]

Brooks characterized the preacher as a messenger—and a witness. These two poles marked the boundaries of his spiritual landscape when it came to sermon preparation. As a conveyer of truth, the preacher is responsible to communicate God's message, he explained. The preacher who faithfully executes this responsibility functions as a courier not a performer. "The minstrel who sings before you to show his skill, will be praised for his wit, and rhymes and voice," Brooks wrote. "But the courier who hurries in, breathless, to bring you a message will be forgotten in the message he brings."[3]

As a witness, the preacher must speak from experience. "It is to be a message given to us for transmission, but yet a message which we cannot transmit until it has entered into our own experience, and we can give our own testimony of its spiritual power."[4] Today we would probably use the word "incarnational" to describe his philosophy.

Brooks's approach to preaching reflected his view of the spiritual life. In an address on the best methods for promoting the spiritual life, he complained, "There is something almost like the creak of machinery about our subject."[5] Brooks steered away from abstract mysticism and the rote performance of ceremonialism to a more dynamic "method" that identified the home, the school, and the workplace as the primary context for spiritual development. Brooks found it significant that the final spiritual state of man is pictured as a heavenly city. "The training place of his spiritual life must be a city," Brooks concluded, "a place of many relationships as well."[6]

MAKING AN INTIMATE CONNECTION WITH GOD

His example points to an essential aspect of sermon preparation that stands alongside the disciplines of exegesis and homiletics: the spiritual preparation of the preacher himself. The experience of an ever-deepening relationship with God is critical for communicators of the Scripture. Those who wish to connect spiritually with a congregation must first be intimately connected with the Lord.

The preacher must engage God personally through the practice of spiritual disciplines, prayer for the message, and dependence on the Holy Spirit through the entire preparation process. He must also deal with "the critical interval," the time between message completion and delivery, preparing his heart and mind for the message and the audience.

This chapter will consider those issues and others as well, including greeting the congregation *before* the message as part of the messenger's personal commitment to his audience; and living out the just-preached message before family, friends, and congregation *after* the sermon.

THE SPIRITUAL DISCIPLINES

Personal Time with God

Expositors find themselves with a numbing assortment of responsibilities. Preparation for preaching, pastoral care, large-scale leadership, specific administration, and community outreach compete for time very sincerely intended for intimacy with God. Those who oversee a staff feel the pinch of this additional responsibility. People who pursue a deepening relationship with the Almighty think about prioritizing time for this pursuit.

Success in this area requires specific scheduling. Many find that the earliest part of the morning is best, before other duties press in. They mute their phones and turn off their e-mail. Their administrative assistant helps minimize distraction. Each preacher is now a child, leaving his duties for a time of relational joy with his Father. He may want to keep a Bible, journal, and songbook in a special place for this regular event. Perhaps he will play a CD to set the tone of the encounter. In some cases this will require substantial reeducation.

My own orientation to seminary included these never-to-be-forgotten words: "Seminary is not a spiritual retreat. No one is going to take care of your spiritual life for you. If one wants to be a doctor, he attends medical school, if he wants to be a lawyer, he attends law school, and if he wants to be a pastor, he attends seminary." True to the message, there was very little emphasis in the curriculum on the development of the spiritual life.

Many of the best preachers have extensive training. This may include biblical languages, a broad spectrum of theology, exposure to international missions, Christian education, homiletics, and pastoral theory. Literally thousands of hours have been spent in development—development of the mind, that is. The spirit, however, is often left to nurture itself. Attitudes and habits formed under admired mentors, at an impressionable time of life, strongly influence later ministry priorities.

Seminarians often study for years without taking a single course on developing the inner person.[7] While purists may argue that this should be one of the objectives of every class, such is hardly the case in terms of emphasis. So fine men and women who enter Bible college or seminary with great zeal of heart often leave with a cold intellectual approach to the Christian life. The new pastor thus enters service without a clear idea of how his own intimacy with God is necessary for effective ministry. It can take years for the mind and heart to meet in a mixture of rational and mystical theology.

The pastor needs to blend exegesis with piety, management with meditation, and evangelism with reflection. Perhaps some of the reason for the spiritual malaise[8] among many leaders lies in imbalance. The person may be well disciplined in sermon preparation, Bible reading, and administration but deficient in experiential passion for God. One way out of this spot is through an emphasis on an affective aspect of the devotional life. Just as objective study takes care of some of the essential learning required for meaningful proclamation and personal growth, the preacher and teacher needs to be just as intentional with the more experiential aspects of the walk with God. Thus the pastor must set aside special time in his own life to maintain the intimacy with God that Jesus wants wed with objective truth (John 4:24).

No doubt, the objective revelation of God's Word forms the core for Christian theology and spiritual development. This cannot, however, hide the sad truth that theologians and preachers can be quite unconnected with God in any deeply personal, experiential sense. The disciplines described below may aid the development of an affective life in the one who has heretofore approached Christ, in a large part, intellectually.

Journaling

A journal provides a visual reminder of the need to think about what is going on in the preacher's life. It allows the writer to meditate with pen in hand, and to mull over the thoughts that come. During this time the journaler can trace tendencies, record impulses of the Spirit, and note important passages of Scripture. Bruce Demarest, professor of Christian theology and spiritual formation, has said of journaling: "It is to us what history is to the world . . . it is a record of inner life, its emotions and graces. It is a spiritual and emotional context for life."9 Such a record may contribute to a positive outlook on life with God. It provides a place to praise God for His faithfulness, as well as a healthy context for complaint. The journal keeper may record passages of the Word that the Spirit has highlighted in the person's experience, or he may note counsel from trusted allies.

Journaling may also keep the expositor from fooling himself. Bill Hybels's comment bears this out: "Most of us . . . live unexamined lives. We repeat the same errors day after day. We don't learn much from the decisions we make, whether they are good or bad. We don't know why we're here or where we're going. One benefit of journaling is to force us to examine our lives."10

Preachers are not immune to the pitfalls of such lack of scrutiny. Many excellent exegetes of the Scriptures are woefully unaware of their psycho/spiritual immaturity, as attested by clergy burnout, moral failures, and broken marriages.11 Journaling offers a way for pastors to engage in valuable self-inspection and reflection. Entries may be made several times a month, and reviewed monthly and yearly to trace the flow of actions, attitudes, and emotions. Such reflection can help to develop spiritual depth.

Such thoughtful analysis of areas of immaturity and improper motivation not only promotes personal growth, it can also improve the effectiveness of your sermon. You may ask, "What events are taking place in the church that need to be addressed?" "How is my own attitude in communicating the Word helping or hindering the process?" "How do I come across personally in the pulpit? Am I riding a hobbyhorse?" And you may be able to answer the question of change: "What needs to change within me to be a more effective change agent?"

While this discipline is not prescribed in the Bible, the principle of remembering God's faithfulness is often described or commanded. Joshua memorialized, for future generations, the drawing back of the Jordan River (Josh. 4:1–7), and David enjoined Israel not to forget the goodness of God to His people (Ps. 103:2). Psalm 102:18 calls to mind God's faithfulness to Zion. Record keeping can aid the modern believer in the pursuit of God.

Journals can take numerous forms. Many bookstores carry formal ones. On the other hand, a simple ringed notebook, composition book, or computer file can do just as well. The point is to start getting in touch with God through written reflection. Then one will be more effective in getting others in touch with God through the sermon.

Practicing the Presence (Contemplation)

Sometimes referred to as *contemplation*, practicing the presence of God emphasizes the reality of God's omnipresence in the experience of the believer. By continual interaction with God through prayer, the believer comes to know God's presence in a more meaningful way.

God is present everywhere. The fleeing believer cannot escape him (Ps. 139:7–10). Positively, God is with all the members of the church via incarnation and commission as Matthew's *inclusio* demonstrates (1:23, 28:20). This truth extends to God's desire for personal intimacy. The Lord seeks close fellowship with His own, and those who would be close to Him respond in-kind (Ps. 27:7–8). It is God's will that His followers seek Him habitually, bringing all manner of praises and concerns into their conversation with Him (1 Thess. 5:17). This sort of activity helps the seeker live out at least some of the implication of this fundamental attribute of the Godhead.

The frequent gap between head and heart on this issue is expressed well by A. W. Tozer:

> The Presence and the manifestation of the Presence are not the same. There can be one without the other. God is here when we are wholly unaware of it. He is manifest only when we are aware of His presence. . . . On our part there must be surrender to the Spirit of God, for His work is to show us the Father and the Son. If we cooperate with Him in loving obedience, God will manifest Himself to us and that manifestation will be the difference between a nominal Christian life and a life radiant with the light of His face.[12]

This sort of relationship should characterize the preacher's entire life and ministry. Words flow freely to the Lord throughout the day. Prayers may be spoken for one's spouse, children, extended family, other church leaders, the sick, and the overall direction of the fellowship served. Concern for various aspects of the next sermon should be expressed all week long. Such interaction may take place while at home, driving in the car, calling in homes or the hospital, or at an athletic contest or concert. The potential venues and content of such interactions are myriad. This sort of hot-hearted interaction with God makes for a fervent follower of God, ready to proclaim messages reflecting spiritual reality.

Waiting/Listening

The teacher of the Bible is a professional talker. He has normally taken several public speaking or preaching courses. In most cases, God has gifted him verbally beyond the norm. Such assets help get the message of the text across, but can also result in unjustified self-confidence. The speaker must not get to the point where he believes that his is the only voice, or that his education and verbal skills are sufficient to control eternal outcomes. One who proclaims the Word needs to also have a willingness to listen for God's leading in his life. He should be ever open to the promptings of the Spirit of God. He often needs to humble himself, becoming quiet, so as to listen for God's probing and directing.

In other words, God sets forth an irony. If the preacher would speak for God, he must profit from silence before God. Silent waiting helps the minister to realign his thoughts, preparing him for service. As Donald Whitney says, "In silence we learn to rely more on God's control in situations where we would normally feel compelled to speak, or to speak too much. We find out that He is able to manage situations in which we once thought our input was indispensable. The skills of observation and listening are also sharpened in those who practice silence and solitude so that when they do speak there's more of a freshness and depth to their words."[13]

We should not misunderstand this as a call to silence. Rob Plummer is correct when he says that what many interpret as a biblical call to silence is actually an invitation to active waiting upon God.[14] Silence per se is not valued in Scripture. However, it often accompanies the submission, awe, and anticipation to which God responds (Hab. 2:20). It indicates a heart that is waiting for God's next move. Sometimes this takes place in the context of great suffering (Ps. 62:1–8; see especially vv.1, 5).

While Elijah was exhausted from spiritual conflict, God communicated with the prophet in a voice that was barely audible (1 Kings 19:12–13).[15] God spoke with the prophet as he stayed quiet and receptive.

A communicator of the Word today might approach a new passage in the following sequence. After praying for God's guidance for the process, he reads the text to be preached several times for familiarity, ideally in both his native tongue as well as the original language. While he employs good hermeneutics and consults high-quality lexicons and commentaries, he depends on God for insight. Anticipation is high for God to shed light on the passage. When a thought comes to him about the text, he writes it down for consideration.

There will be much interaction here. Hard work in exegesis and homiletics will be coupled with times of quiet hands and attentiveness to what God may want to communicate about the text at hand. He may bring to mind events in the preacher's background that provide helpful illustrations. The expositor will become aware of the needs of specific parishioners whose needs are addressed in the passage. Understanding that the preparation of the message is a week-long process, the cycle of active work and listening behavior may be repeated several times. The listening will take place not only in the study, but also in other contexts such as exercise, visiting a parishioner, and sitting quietly at home.

Sabbath Rest

Since a period of rest was implied before the Law was instituted (Genesis 2:2–3), the general principle of honoring God in practice is still advisable. This being so, there needs to be a plan of implementation. One day will be set aside from the normal rigors of ministry for rest and reflection on the goodness of God. Suffice it to say that this day will not be Sunday. Choose another day and closely guard it. Tell those in your sphere of ministry about that day so they will not disturb it except in the case of emergency. You will need to exercise discipline to keep that day restful. For example, don't engage in obsessive checking of e-mail or visits to the office.[16]

The activities of this day are in your hands; schedule them as you wish. They may include personal spiritual pursuits, family time, exercise, and hobbies. While this is a day away from the office, it is certainly not a vacation from the Lord. To bear any semblance of Sabbath rest *it needs to include God at the center*. Reflection and release should be its themes. Reflection on Scripture readings, prayer, and rejoicing in the kindness of God should all be present. Release from the toil of the normal schedule should also be evident. It may be valuable to think of this day in terms of change of pace. One may enjoy God in increased time with family and friends as well as in unbridled fun.

The person who neglects the Sabbath principle views his own work as indispensable and is living vainly, denying himself God's wonderful gift of rest (Psalm 127:2).[17] The higher way of life begins with trusting the Lord in your work.[18] God affords the preacher the luxury of time away from work to tend his soul and body. The one who accepts this gift and responsibility will be revitalized for the task of proclamation.

Prayer and Dependence on the Holy Spirit

In a survey of fifty-three homiletics textbooks,[19] about one-half mention prayer only in passing or not at all. There is but slightly more emphasis on the need to depend on the Holy Spirit. Why is this so?

Certainly the writers of such texts are people of prayer and also believe that it is important to the process of sermon preparation. Most, I suspect, would say that it is assumed that we should pray over any Christian endeavor, all the more for an event as sacred as preaching. Perhaps this should not be taken for granted. One might argue that prayer belongs in the fundamental outline of homiletical theory. Every aspect of the preaching event should be brought before the Lord.

The book of the Bible, or series, to be preached should be determined through prayerful consideration of present congregational needs, leadership counsel, and a concern for preaching both testaments. While in one sense any passage is a good passage to preach, God is well able to narrow the field for the preacher.

Once a passage has been chosen, the exegete should enlist God's help in interpreting its details and finding the central theme of the text. Training in hermeneutics and homiletics is necessary, but so is prayer. As the expositor, ask God to help you with outlining the text accurately. Also ask Him to help you find relevant illustrative material that validly applies and clarifies the text at hand.

Help from the Spirit of God should be requested for the entire preparatory process described above, as well as for the delivery of the message. The preacher needs to pray for personal strength for, and audience receptivity to, the sermon to be delivered. God the Spirit is able to do far beyond that for which any preacher, however gifted, could ever hope to accomplish through his own skills. In *Christ-Centered Preaching*, Bryan Chapell summarizes these concerns:

> Public ministry true to God's purposes requires devoted private prayer. We should not expect our words to acquaint others with the power of the Spirit if we have not met with him. Faithful preachers plead for God to work as well for their own accuracy, integrity, and skill in proclaiming his Word. Success in the pulpit can be the force that leads a preacher from prayerful dependence on the Spirit. . . . Neglect of prayer signals serious deficiencies in ministry even if other signs of success have not diminished. We must always remember that popular acclaim is not necessarily the same as spiritual success.[20]

THE CRITICAL INTERVAL

The critical interval describes the time between the completion of sermon preparation in the speaker's study, and the delivery of the message on the platform. A period of at least twenty-four hours best follows the divine model. A number of things may take place during this time, including meditation on personal application, preparation for spiritual warfare, adequate sleep, Sunday morning at the parsonage, engaging the audience prior to the message, and the prayer of submission before entering the pulpit.

Some preachers practice forms of abstinence during this period in order to seek God's favor for the message. One may set aside a meal in order to seek power for the delivery. Another might withdraw from human company to spend time alone in the sanctuary, praying for those who will inhabit the pews the next day. Still another may forego sexual relations the night before a message, in order to enhance spiritual preparation. If any of these alternatives is chosen, it should be with the Lord's clear leading and the full consent of the nuclear family. The New Testament strongly suggests that while such acts are not obligatory, God often chooses to bless the ministry of one who gives fullest attention to a spiritual duty.[21]

good

The importance of adequate sleep the night before the sermon should not be underestimated. Effective delivery of a message is taxing work. Thirty minutes or more of energetic monologue places demands on the mind for recall of material, reading the verbal and nonverbal responses of the audience, and filtering environmental interference. It usually takes place in a setting where much broader ministry expectations exist. People in the context of the speaker's environment will place demands on him from the time he reaches his ministry site—the last-minute announcement, burden of a new prayer need, and responsibilities associated with the overall worship experience all add stress. Even the presence of his own family may contribute to the stress. If the message will be delivered more than once on a given day, energy consumption will be multiplied.

The need for sleep applies to more than the night before the presentation. It calls for a lifestyle that includes adequate rest. Ministers who are not committed to such may be dealing with larger personal issues. Drivenness can originate from fear of failure, unresolved developmental issues, or lack of willingness to trust laity and professional staff with significant ministry responsibility. Eventually such a lifestyle will likely take its toll physically, psychologically, and spiritually.[22]

The preacher should be on the alert for various forms of spiritual attack the day the message is to be given, typically Sunday. Pastor Bill (not his real name), for instance, notices the pretty woman in the tight dress as she walks past on the way to the auditorium. She seems to be attracted to him. He resists the impure thoughts that race through his mind. *Why does this have to come my way right now?* he asks himself. The thoughts persist as he goes to sit in the pew. In fifteen minutes he will stand up to preach.

His home will also be a target for Satan who is ever mindful of opportunities to upset God's people (1 Peter 5:8). Few others have to think about taking their families to work with them, but the minister of God's Word does. He will need to be careful of the feelings of his wife and children as he heads into his most important ministry of the week. Flare-ups can weaken the family as well as the preacher himself. He should guard his attitudes and words. If he has a wife with young children to get ready, he should help. A family that leaves home together in peace, or departs in different vehicles in peace, is best prepared for ministry.

The pastor may want to request prayer from the leaders of the church and others for spiritual protection for this most challenging day. The speaker and his spouse should also pray together for spiritual discernment and vigilance.

His main approach to such temptation should be resistance. He is to take a stand on the spiritual ground that Christ won for him (Eph. 6:13–14, James 4:7, 1 Peter 5:9).[23] This means taking conscious control of his mind by faith, and refusing to let negative thoughts and attitudes linger. He need not address evil spirits with rebukes or verbal formulas.

THE CRITICAL INTERVAL . . . WITH THE PEOPLE

Just before the service, the communicator can spend significant time mingling with those about to hear the message. A few minutes of such contact can prepare positively dozens—and even hundreds—of listeners. Shake the hands of some attenders. Greet by name or with a warm general acknowledgment others who are seated but less accessible. Sometimes a wave and friendly smile can positively touch a whole section of the audience who notice those gestures. This, no doubt, increases the perceived credibility of the speaker. A friendly speaker always scores highly in the area of reliability in the eyes of the audience.

Such contact can be of great spiritual benefit to the preacher as well. It reminds him that he is ministering to flesh-and-blood people with deep spiritual needs. Think of it: You will be hearing concerns from some and be receiving personal encouragement from others. The audience is not present to advance your agenda but to be served by your ministry.

When undertaken sincerely, this practice heightens the messenger's own personal concern for the flock, reliance on God to use the Word for their welfare, and readiness for the preaching event.

RECOGNIZING DISTRACTIONS DURING THE FINAL INTERVAL

Congregational worship should be an uplifting time for the preacher. Instead the preacher may find the mechanics of the service distracting if he is not properly prepared. For instance, you may be interrupted by a person insisting on a last-minute announcement or wanting information about some aspect of the church ministry. Your own evaluation of the musical elements of worship or the adult Bible class you just attended the previous hour may distract you. A newly revealed burden of an attendee may occupy your thinking.

This does not excuse a pastor from the responsibility to engage with God. If he has prepared and rehearsed thoroughly, such a quality encounter will be easier. As preachers we should discipline ourselves to concentrate on worship until a couple of minutes before we begin to deliver the message. God will help the speaker who honors Him in worship before the sermon.

In a context where there are multiple services, the speaker may choose to be actively involved in certain parts of each service. This way he may truly join each group without overly taxing his voice.

A prayer of dependence may be silently uttered as the moment of delivery approaches: *Father, I am utterly dependent on You right now. Please do not let me fail You or those who depend on me so much for spiritual guidance. Help me to remember what I have prepared and give me the power of Your Holy Spirit for the delivery. Use me as You will. Amen.*

AFTER THE SERMON

Then you present the message, drawing upon the power and sensitivity of the Holy Spirit, as well as your spiritual and homiletical preparation. What happens after the sermon? Personal conviction often comes in the days that follow the delivery of the message. Hearing oneself exhort others during the live presentation, or later while reviewing the audio tape, CD, or DVD, can be an unnerving experience as you consider the application. While it is certainly necessary to think about personal change during the course of preparation, it is just as important to be working on it afterward. There will often be some aspect of the message that is not yet very well applied in your own life. You may want to write down what the Holy Spirit is targeting for change. This item, along with the biblical text from which it is derived may be written on a 3x5 card for meditation or entered in your journal for regular review and prayer.

There should never be a time in an expositor's life when there is not a self-awareness of the need for repentance and growth. This humbling knowledge should keep the messenger close to God as well as to his listeners. As the preacher engages in the struggle of applying the principles of the Word, he will be encouraged, as will those who observe his life.

KEEP A CLOSE WATCH

Preaching that most pleases God comes from a person intimately engaged with Him. God is consciously invited into the whole of life, including the whole of the sermon preparation process. Phillips Brooks argued that if only an incarnate God can speak of and convince another of the power of God, then only when that Word is incarnate in preaching can God's Word be spoken anew. He believed that more than just the preacher's words, the preacher's *very self* could be the medium and occasion for changing lives and making God present.

When this happens, the Lord's representative will fulfill the injunction: "Keep a close watch over yourself and your teaching. Persevere in them. For in so doing you will save both yourself and your hearers" (1 Timothy 4:16 author translation).

DAN GREEN is professor of graduate studies in the Moody Graduate School. He has earned the D.Min. degree from Trinity Evangelical Divinity School, Deerfield, Illinois, along with degrees from Dallas Theological Seminary and Michigan State University.

NOTES

1. Warren Wiersbe, *Walking With the Giants* (Grand Rapids: Baker, 1989), 81.

2. Phillips Brooks, *The Joy of Preaching* (Grand Rapids: Kregel, 1989), 47, as quoted by James Rosscup in *Preaching: How to Preach Biblically* (Nashville: Nelson, 2005), 48.

3. Phillips Brooks, *Phillips Brooks on Preaching* (New York: Seabury, 1964), 15.

4. Ibid., 14.

5. Phillips Brooks, *Best Methods of Promoting Spiritual Life* (New York: Thomas Whitaker, n.d.), 2.

6. Ibid., 30–31.

7. A survey of seminary catalogs shows that some schools have begun to include integration labs/small groups in their curricula. While such change is welcome, it is too late to benefit most present-day preachers.

8. The Ellison Research Group surveyed 868 Protestant pastors nationwide and found that 41 percent were somewhat dissatisfied or very dissatisfied with their prayer lives. The average minister surveyed spent thirty-nine minutes a day in prayer, with mainline Protestants praying slightly more than Evangelicals. Twenty-one percent of the respondents reported praying less than fifteen minutes per day. See *Facts and Trends,* May 23, 2005.

9. Bruce Demarest, unpublished lectures in the course DMN 880 "Theology and the Spiritual Journey: the Path of the Heart," Trinity Evangelical Divinity School, Deerfield, Illinois, winter, 1991.

10. Bill Hybels, *Too Busy Not to Pray* (Downers Grove, Ill.: InterVarsity, 1992), 103.

11. This troublesome fact is detailed in *Pastors at Greater Risk,* by H. B. London and Neil B. Weisman (Ventura, Calif.: Regal, 2003).

12. A.W. Tozer, *The Pursuit of God* (Camp Hill, Pa.: Christian Publications, 1982), 61,64.

13. Donald Whitney, *Disciplines for the Christian Life* (Colorado Springs:Navpress, 1991), 185.

14. Rob Plummer, "Are the Spiritual Disciplines of 'Silence and Solitude' Really Biblical?" a paper presented at the meeting of the Evangelical Theological Society in November, 2006.

15. English translations render the Hebrew words קוֹל דְּמָמָה דַק of 19:12b variously. The NASB is overly cautious, translating "a sound of a gentle blowing." More to the point are the ESV, "the sound of a low whisper," and NIV, "a gentle whisper." A very literal rendering is "a small whisper of a voice." See Francis Brown, S. R. Driver, and Charles A. Briggs, *The Brown, Driver, and Briggs Hebrew Lexicon of the Old Testament* (London: Oxford University Press, 1907), pp. 199A and 201A.

16. The question as to whether Sabbath prescriptions are still binding is beyond the scope of this chapter. It has been debated extensively without consensus. Nevertheless, most traditions consider the implementation of some form of Sabbath rest profitable. For extensive discussion of this and related issues see D. A. Carson, ed., *From Sabbath to the Lord's Day: A Biblical, Historical and Theological Investigation.* (Grand Rapids: Zondervan 1982), and Wayne Strickland, ed., *Five Views of Law and Gospel* (Grand Rapids: Zondervan, 1993).

17. The proper understanding of the last line of this verse is debatable. It is probably best to take the simple reading of the Hebrew text, "he gives his beloved sleep." Thus, we are to understand that God gives his followers the gift of sleep itself (NIV), rather than tending to all of their business for them while they sleep (NASB). See Leslie C. Allen, "Psalms" in the *Word Biblical Commentary*, vol. 21 (Nashville: Nelson), 234, 239.

18. Willem A. VanGemerren, "Psalms" in *The Expositor's Bible Commentary*, vol. 5 (Grand Rapids: Zondervan, 1991), 794.

19. My faculty assistant, Liviu Ursache, did the lion's share of this work and presented me with a summary chart with which I have worked.

20. Bryan Chapell, *Christ-Centered Preaching: Redeeming the Expository Sermon* (Grand Rapids: Baker, 2005), 33.

21. Solitude, fasting, and sexual abstinence variously accompanied prayer by Jesus and the early church in contexts related to ministry tasks and personal needs (Matthew 4:1–2, 14:22–24; Mark 1:38–39; Luke 6:12–19; Acts 13:1–3; 1 Corinthians 7:1–5).

22. For an excellent discussion from a medical doctor, see Richard Swenson, *Margin: Restoring Emotional, Physical, Financial, and Time Reserves to Overloaded Lives* (Colorado Springs: NavPress, 1992).

23. The chiastic structure in the Ephesians passage is particularly convincing. It centers on back-to-back uses of the verb "to stand," in the infinitival and imperatival states (στῆναι, στῆτε).

Part Two

MINING

THE

TEXT

PREACHING

HISTORICAL

NARRATIVE

by
Michael Rydelnik

"Our response to life is different if we have been taught only a definition of faith than if we have trembled with Abraham as he held a knife over Isaac."[1] In one sentence, Flannery O'Connor captures the benefit of reading, studying, and preaching the historical narrative literature of the Bible. Yet despite their value, the stories of Scripture are often relegated to children's Sunday school classes, while pastors teach adults the "mature" propositional truths of epistolary literature in their sermons. As a result, people in our pews rarely encounter God's most popular means of communicating truth: the story.

Why do so many pastors neglect preaching historical narrative? It is not for lack of material, but for some it is for lack of confidence, because many pastors have received virtually no instruction in interpreting and preaching narrative literature. For example, when I was in seminary, the one required Hebrew exegesis course focused on Psalms and never addressed historical narrative. The required Greek exegetical method courses revolved around Philippians, Ephesians, 1 Corinthians, and

Romans, never touching the Gospels or Acts. We spent hours diagramming sentences, a practice with little significance for stories. On top of all this, the preaching courses were aligned with the exegesis of Ephesians and 1 Corinthians, failing to address the preaching of stories. This approach is typical of seminary education, so it is no wonder pastors are reluctant to preach narratives.

Besides lacking confidence, pastors often overlook narrative literature because didactic literature is just so much easier to preach. Finding the exegetical idea is simpler in the epistles than in stories. Also, building an application bridge from Ephesians or Colossians to church members requires less thought and effort than it does in Genesis or 1 Kings. Moreover, universities teach us to think propositionally and logically. Learning from stories, while common around the world for millennia, is foreign to our thinking. All this makes the epistles the favorite choice of most preachers.

VALUING HISTORICAL NARRATIVE

Yet we neglect the stories of Scripture at our, and our congregation's, peril. One reason for preaching narrative literature is that those sermons, if done well, will have greater impact on hearers, because the truths revealed in stories will reach the emotions of listeners far better than mere propositions. The truth of God must influence the entire being of a person: mind, heart, and will. Stories are effective in teaching the heart as well as the head, with a greater likelihood of effecting change in the will. Speaking from didactic literature exclusively can result in truth bypassing the heart while going straight to the head.

Another reason to preach the stories of Scripture is that so much of God's Word is in the narrative genre. About three-fourths of the Hebrew Bible is narrative, while fully one-half of the New Testament is in story form. Neglecting the stories of the Bible has caused God's people to view the timeless truths of the Old Testament as mere Sunday school stories.

Overlooking the gospels has produced congregations who understand the doctrine of Christ without ever encountering the person of Jesus. With so much of the Bible presented as story, we cannot fully communicate the truth of God without preaching narrative literature.

We should also preach narrative texts because contemporary culture is increasingly story-oriented. Entertainment and information demonstrates that we now live in a story society. For example, the Harry Potter novels, mere English boarding school stories with a twist, have sold millions of copies and have made author J. K. Rowling richer than Queen Elizabeth. J. R. R. Tolkien's epic trilogy of *The Lord of the Rings*, when made into movies drew massive audiences around the world. Teenagers buy extended versions of the films and spend days watching *Ring* marathons. On television, continuing stories of Mafia families, desperate housewives, singles in New York City, even those with stories about nothing, draw millions of television viewers on a weekly basis. Such is the power of story.

The story society is the fruit of postmodern thought, which has abandoned reasoned argumentation in favor of personal narratives. This kind of thinking emphasizes learning through stories and experiences as opposed to carefully argued logical propositions, one built upon another. The stories of the Bible would be especially meaningful for an audience trained, intentionally or inadvertently, in postmodern modes of thinking. If we are to communicate eternal truth in the contemporary world, we must do it with the ancient stories of Scripture.

Since preaching biblical historical narrative is so vital, our responsibility is to communicate the truths of these stories well. Preachers must grow toward capable communication of the historical narratives of Scripture, focusing on accurate interpretation and effective exposition.[2]

Understanding Historical Narrative

What is meant by historical narrative literature? One helpful definition is "the re-presentation of past events for the purpose of instruction."[3] Biblical authors understood that they were not writing fiction but recording actual historical events. Some interpreters mistakenly conclude, therefore, that the purpose of recording these events was merely to inform readers about the past, making biblical narratives no different than a high school history book. Although it is plain that these texts are indeed historically accurate, the authors of Scripture had a purpose deeper than merely recording facts. Biblical authors selected events and framed them in such a way as to instruct readers about the truth of God and His relationship with people. Their purpose was instruction. Paul exhibited this perspective when he wrote that the events included in the narratives of the wilderness wanderings recorded in Numbers, "happened to them as an example, but they were written down for our instruction" (1 Corinthians 10:11 ESV).[4]

Readers of historical narrative must note that no text completely recounts every event or every aspect of the event recorded. Rather, authors operated selectively, choosing and arranging the events in the narrative accurately, but with the intention of communicating the theological meaning of those events. A good example of this principle of selectivity is seen in the book of Genesis. The first eleven chapters deal with primeval history and encompass thousands (millions according to some) of years. The next thirty-nine chapters deal with four generations of one family. Even in those chapters, selectivity is evident. For example, chapter 16 closes by relating that Abraham was eighty-six years old when Ishmael was born, and chapter 17 opens by stating that Abraham was ninety-nine years old when the events in this chapter took place. Thirteen years passed in the span of one verse. What happened in the intervening years? Obviously the author did not believe those events were significant to his narrative, so he excluded them. Therefore, when we read biblical narratives, we are not asking, "What really happened?" but rather, "What does the author want us to understand about what really happened?"

This last question gets at the heart of what interpreters are asking when approaching a narrative text. This is so because, to preach a narrative text, preachers need to understand the author's meaning to his original audience. So how do we go about getting at the meaning of these texts? The following are some helpful steps for interpreting narratives.[5]

To begin, *individual narrative texts should be read holistically*. Every story fits into a greater whole. In fact, biblical authors were careful in their selection of stories, placing them within a particular story line. Thus to understand a specific narrative text, it would be helpful to read it in connection with the stories that surround it. The levels that should be observed are as follows:

Top level: The story's placement within story line of the Bible.

Higher middle level: The story's placement within its particular book.

Lower middle level: The story's placement within its compound narrative.

Bottom level: The story's features within its own individual narrative.

Too often preachers interpret stories from the bottom level alone and thereby misinterpret and misapply its message. For example, when studying the story of David, Nabal, and Abigail (1 Samuel 25), it would be a mistake to read the text atomistically, without understanding its situation within the surrounding narratives. At the top level, in the story line of the Bible, it relates to David's place as the ideal king of Israel. As the ideal king, he is the one against whom all others are measured and only the Messiah would surpass. At the higher middle level, the story is found in 1 and 2 Samuel, which tells the story of the beginning of the Davidic dynasty. It is David who would receive a covenant containing the promise of a future Son who would have an eternal house, kingdom, and throne. At the lower middle level, the story is found in the compound narrative of David's flight from Saul, when he lived life on the run. The purpose of this compound narrative is designed to show David's preparation by God to serve as the ideal king.

At the bottom level, the narrative is surrounded by two narratives of David choosing not to exact vengeance on Saul, showing his greater virtue than Saul and exemplary character. But what would David do with someone who takes advantage of him, but unlike Saul, is not anointed by the Lord? How will David respond to a petty, cheap, ungodly fool of a man? Here David learns that to be the ideal king, he must not be one to exact vengeance on his enemy. Without reading holistically, or from the top down, we might miss the point of this individual narrative.

Second, in order to interpret narratives, *carefully observe the literary features of the individual story.* Remember these narratives are products of literary artistry and use the normal components of good storytelling. Therefore, answering Rudyard Kipling's six questions (who, what, when, where, why, and how?) will open the details of a narrative. As you read, follow the plot, note the various scenes, identify the characters, observe the tension, recognize the climax, and detect the resolution. In other words, read the narrative as you would any other story.

A close reading of 1 Samuel 25 would show that Nabal, whose name meant "fool," took advantage of David and his men. Tension rose as David resolved to exact vengeance against Nabal. The climax took place when Abigail convinced David not to participate in bloodshed but rather to trust God to take vengeance. The story is resolved when Nabal, after a night of drunken stupor, was struck with perhaps a seizure, stroke, or heart attack, and died ten days later. David thanked God for the lesson that he learned and took wise Abigail as his wife. Each character in the story played a special role: David as the learning protagonist, Nabal as the wicked antagonist, and Abigail as the wise heroine.

A third way to derive meaning from a narrative is to *be alert to repetition in the story*. Biblical authors frequently repeat words, phrases, themes, events, and motifs as clues to the essential meaning to a text. To illustrate, the gospel of John uses the word *pisteuo* (believe, trust, commit) no less than ninety-eight times. The story of the disobedient prophet in 1 Kings 13 repeats the phrase "the word of the Lord" seven times in one chapter. Judges reiterates the saying "In those days there was no king in Israel; everyone did what was right in his own eyes" (21:25, cf. 17:6 NASB). Moses consistently highlights themes like reversal of primogeniture in Genesis or rebellion in the wilderness stories. Events tend to replicate like Abraham and Isaac saying that their wives were merely their sisters. These are not mere coincidental repetitions but deliberate compositional strategies that authors use to communicate theological meaning.

In 1 Samuel 25, the phrase "shedding blood and avenging" repeats three times (although slightly different in the English versions, the Hebrew uses the same words in verses 26, 31 and 33). Plainly the author is concerned with David's lesson about not avenging himself with bloodshed and wants his readers to understand the evil of such behavior.

Yet another step in gathering the meaning of biblical stories is *to note carefully both narration and dialogue as clues* to the theological meaning. Present in most biblical narratives is an omniscient narrator who guides the plot of the story. Robert Alter has noted that the primary purpose of narration is to form a bridge between larger units of dialogue through which the story is told.[6]

Nevertheless, the omniscient narrator at times does reveal God's perception of the story. For example, in Genesis 6:5–6, when observing humanity's wickedness, "The Lord was grieved that he had made man on the earth, and his heart was filled with pain," laying the foundation for the following flood story. Another omniscient insight into the Lord's mind is in the narrator's comment at the conclusion of the story of David's adultery with Bathsheba and murder of Uriah: "But the thing that David had done was evil in the sight of the Lord" (2 Sam. 11:27 NASB). This insight bridges the story of David's sins to the story of the Lord's discipline through Nathan's message and the death of David's baby. Observing the omniscient narrator's comments will sometimes give a clue to the Lord's perspective on the matters in a narrative.

In 1 Samuel 25:3 (NASB), the author uses narration to guide readers in understanding the nature of two of the new characters. Abigail is characterized as "intelligent and beautiful" while Nabal is described as "harsh and evil in his dealings." Almost immediately, readers identify both the villain and the heroine in the story.

But biblical stories most often find their overall meaning in the words of the characters. While speech may be used merely to transmit the details of a story, even more importantly, biblical authors use dialogue to get at what Alter calls the "essence" of a story.[7] The writers of Scripture will deliberately select speeches that communicate the true perception of the events described. As such, they get at the authorial intent and guide readers to the actual meaning of the story. The point is that often preachers who are mining texts to discover the essential message of a story will find gold through careful observation of key speeches.

To return to 1 Samuel 25 as an example, David's speech at the conclusion of the story clarifies the essence of the passage. When hearing of Nabal's sudden death, David exclaims, "Praise be to the Lord, who has upheld my cause against Nabal for treating me with contempt. He has kept back his servant from doing wrong and has brought Nabal's wrongdoing down on his own head" (1 Sam. 25:39). This is the heart of the leadership lesson David was to learn: A godly king should not take personal vengeance on those who wrong him but rather allow God to carry out any judgment necessary.

The struggle to discover the exegetical idea and meaning of a biblical narrative is only the beginning of the preaching process—there is still much more to do. Preachers must then concentrate not only on an accurate retelling of the story and its message but also effective communication of its relevance and application to a contemporary audience.

COMMUNICATING HISTORICAL NARRATIVE

The general essentials of good preaching apply to every genre: It is always accurate, clear, relevant, and practical. Nevertheless, there are some special steps preachers must emphasize for effective exposition of narrative literature.

The Timeless Principle

To begin, effective communicators of historical narratives will relate the timeless principle of the biblical story to their contemporary audience. They do not merely allegorize the story or retell the tale and stop to moralize at certain points. Rather they link the exegetical message of the story to their audience by discovering the timeless principle inherent in the biblical tale. This, in turn, forms the basis for valid application.

The timeless principle is the theological idea at the foundation of the message to the original audience. The preacher needs to build a bridge from the original audience to the contemporary one by recognizing what the passage teaches about God and our relationship with Him. By climbing a ladder of abstraction, preachers will find the parallel between a text's theological message to the ancient audience and its message for the modern one. As a result, preachers will be able to relate a timeless principle to their audience in the twenty-first century.

Using the example of 1 Samuel 25, the narrative shows how David became the ideal king of Israel: David learned several lessons of kingship by fleeing from Saul. It might be said that David needed to live life on the run in order to learn how to sit on the throne. But the exegetical idea of 1 Samuel 25 is about only one of those lessons and might be expressed: "When a foolish man takes advantage of him, David learns not to seek vengeance but to trust the sovereign God to defend him."

The preacher, having discovered the exegetical idea, will then start climbing the abstraction ladder to find the similarity with the message about David, the ideal king, and the message for a contemporary audience. Perhaps if the sermon were to be preached to a group of leaders, the first level of abstraction would be to see the parallel between David's leadership and that of the audience. Then the timeless principle might be, "When foolish people take advantage of leaders, godly leaders do not seek vengeance but trust God to defend them." But if the preacher is addressing a more general audience it might be necessary to take yet another step up the ladder of abstraction beyond leaders to general believers who want to serve God. Then the timeless principle might be, "When foolish people take advantage of God's servants, the servants are not to seek vengeance but to trust the sovereign God to defend them."

By climbing the ladder of abstraction, preachers can move from an exegetical idea to a timeless principle that can be applied with validity to a modern audience.

The Homiletical Idea

Additionally, effective communicators of historical narrative make their messages memorable by having a homiletical idea for their sermons. Although this is true for all preaching, communicators of historical narrative sometimes emphasize telling the story and fail to relate a main idea. While just having a main idea is essential, preachers should also strive to make the idea memorable. Additionally, the homiletical idea should not be about the characters in the text (God chose David to battle with Goliath because he was a man of faith) but rather address the audience directly. As Haddon Robinson has said, "Ultimately, we are using the Bible to talk to people about themselves. We're not talking to them about the Bible."8

Using 1 Samuel 25 as an example, the clear timeless principle, as stated above might be, "When foolish people take advantage of God's servants, they are not to seek vengeance but to trust the sovereign God to defend them." While stating this timeless principle is helpful, it is important to communicate the idea in a catchy or memorable way. To help an audience retain the timeless principle it would be better to relate the homiletical idea as "When foolish people take advantage of you, don't get mad, let God get even." It captures the message for the contemporary audience in a succinct, pithy, and easily remembered way that is also true to the text. Note also that the homiletical idea is not about David or even a generic servant of God. Rather, the homiletical idea is about the audience and their relationship to God.

A Relevant Introduction

Also, effective communicators of historical narrative highlight the relevance of their message through introductions that raise need. Too often people think the Bible is not relevant to their lives because preachers introduce mere exegetical lectures rather than biblical sermons that have bearing on the lives of real people. Preachers of biblical narratives sometimes become irrelevant by introducing their messages with ancient Near Eastern history as a background for a particular text or with a statement of the context of the narrative that will be under discussion. Rather, preachers of historical narrative should use the introduction to engage listeners by relating the message of the sermon to their lives. In other words, discussing an ancient Suzerain treaty for a sermon may be informative or the context of events before and after David's battle with Goliath might be significant exegetically, but neither would make an audience want to listen.

An effective introduction has three components: It must create interest, raise need, and orient to the text. Of these three, in preaching stories, the most important is raising need because it shows listeners that the ancient story being discussed is important to their lives; therefore, they ought to pay attention to the sermon. In order to be relevant, the introduction should raise the need that the timeless principle will answer, even if it will not be answered until later in the sermon. Preachers may use a variety of approaches for introducing this topic—perhaps a meaningful quote, a personal anecdote, or some recent statistics that would raise the need of the message.

As an example, in 1 Samuel 25, the subject of the narrative is vengeance. Therefore, the introduction must not be about ancient Near Eastern practices of protecting flocks nor should it be about the biblical context of the story. It should be about how we want vengeance when we are mistreated.[9] Therefore, this anecdote about a former University of Texas basketball coach might be a good start. "At times we're a lot like Abe Lemons who was fired as the basketball coach of the University of Texas Longhorns in 1982. When asked if he was bitter at Texas Athletic Director Deloss Dodds who fired him, he replied, 'Not at all, but I plan to buy a glass-bottomed car so I can watch the look on his face when I run over him.'"[10]

Preachers should then move from the anecdote to some real-life situations to which listeners can relate—the behavior of a divorced spouse, the demanding nature of a boss, and/or the difficult and insensitive actions of a neighbor. Then, and only then, is it possible to transition to the text, explaining, "Today we'll be examining what David learned when he was mistreated and wanted revenge." At this point it would be fine to discuss the historical and/or biblical context because the listeners will want to know what the Scriptures say to them about vengeance.

An Inductive Structure

Additionally, effective preachers of historical narrative retain the interest of their audience by using a form of inductive structure.[11] Preachers frequently use a deductive structure in their sermons, stating the homiletical idea at the outset of a message for the sake of clarity. This is problematic with historical narrative literature because most of the time the resolution does not come until the end of the story. So stating the main idea at the beginning of a sermon would be clear but boring, like telling one of Aesop's fables with the moral of the story at the outset rather than the end. Why bother listening to the story if the point is already known? It is far more compelling to tell the story as it unfolds in Scripture. Only after telling the story and seeing the resolution in the text does it make sense to state the homiletical idea. So in 1 Samuel 25, a preacher would only express, "When foolish people take advantage of you, don't get mad, let God get even" at the end of the story, when David learned that lesson. He would not reveal the key idea at the beginning of the sermon, when the audience is unaware of the circumstances of the situation.

A Clear Outline

Yet another important element for effective communicators of historical narrative literature is that they must have clear outlines. That is not to say that preachers need to hit their audiences with a sledgehammer of points. The outline is for the communicator to use, not for the congregation to memorize. Nevertheless, a clear outline functions like a roadmap for the message, showing the way from departure to arrival. The message starts with an introduction that is interesting and raises need. Then the body of the historical narrative sermon is fairly simple: *story, principle,* and *application.* The preacher tells the *story,* explaining the elements of the tale. When the story resolves, preachers should declare the *principle,* or homiletical idea. Then the message should be driven home with concrete and relevant *applications.* Finally, preachers should use a conclusion that brings the message to a clear and memorable ending. 1 Samuel 25 is a good example of a sermon that should be developed as story, principle, and application. After an introduction that raises need about vengeance, the preacher would tell the story of David, Nabal, and Abigail, relate the homiletical idea (see above), and apply it in a variety of ways.

A variation of this structure should be used with extended stories or a narrative with multiple complements for its subject. In that case, preachers should use repeated cycles of story, principle, and application. In other words, tell part of the story, state the partial principle or the first of the multiple complements, and then give an application. This cycle can be repeated several times until the story is finished.

An example of this would be a sermon on the entire Joseph narrative. Rather than tell the whole story at once, relate the story in parts, each one including a partial principle and then an application. So the introduction might raise the question, "How should we respond when people deliberately hurt us?" The body of the sermon would then have multiple story cycles—how Joseph responded in faith to his brothers' betrayal, to the false accusation of Potiphar's wife, and to being forgotten by the butler—each one followed by a partial principle and an application. Finally, the preacher should show how the story resolves with Joseph as the deliverer of Egypt and ultimately Israel. At last Joseph tells his brothers, "You meant evil against me, but God meant it for good"

(Genesis 50:20 NASB). At this point the homiletical idea is clear: When people deliberately try to hurt us, we should respond by knowing that God is with us and has a good plan for our lives. The story is too long to wait for the end to present principles and application without losing interest. By telling the story in parts, the speaker is able to retain the interest of his audience and to build to the main idea.

A Creative Approach

Another element of preaching historical narrative is to use a creative approach. Since the art of storytelling is intrinsically imaginative, the exposition of stories should make use of creative communication. Innovative presentations could include using video presentations that retell the biblical story, recasting the ancient story as a modern tale for a contemporary audience, or a drama, which places the story set in a different era. One imaginative way to communicate a biblical story is with a first-person narrative. With this method, the entire sermon is presented as a monologue, usually through the perspective of one of the characters. Some expositors dress up in Bible robes and attach long beards to play a variety of roles, from Jonah the prophet to Herod the Great. However, a first-person narrative can be just as effective without props, costumes, or makeup.[12] An effective communicator can "become a character" and tell the story just as believably without the production values of a play. In fact, that can be more effective, since it is the actual story that communicates and not the staging.

PART OF THE WHOLE COUNSEL OF GOD

So how important is preaching historical narrative? Since some two-thirds of the Bible is written in this genre, any preacher who neglects it will never preach the whole counsel of God. Indeed, God loves stories so much that He communicated much of His revelation about Himself through them. Ancient Jewish sages understood this. They used to explain a portion of the biblical text during synagogue services emphasizing the moral and practical values of the passage to the entire congregation. They were able to reach their audiences, from the unlearned to the learned alike, by using parables and tales to enhance interest in their audience.

There was even a Rabbi from Nazareth whose favorite method of communicating the truth of God was through stories. Preachers would do well to follow His example.

MICHAEL RYDELNIK is professor of Jewish studies at the Moody Bible Institute. An alumnus of MBI, he has earned the D.Miss. degree from Trinity Evangelical Divinity School, Deerfield, Illinois, along with degrees from Dallas Theological Seminary and Azusa Pacific University in Azusa, California. Dr. Rydelnik has served as a pastor for fifteen years.

NOTES

1. Flannery O'Connor, "The Catholic Novelist in the Protestant South" in *Flannery O'Connor: Collected Works*, ed. Sally Fitzgerald (New York: Library of America, 1988), 858–59.

2. I am presuming a basic understanding of exegesis and homiletics, particularly expository preaching as described in Haddon Robinson's *Biblical Preaching*, 2nd ed. (Grand Rapids: Baker, 2001). Also, I expect readers to understand the most basic aspect of preaching, namely, that preachers should have a main idea or the big idea of a text.

3. John H. Sailhamer, *The Pentateuch as Narrative* (Grand Rapids: Zondervan, 1992), 25.

4. Gordon Fee and Douglas Stuart have argued that God alone is the hero of all biblical narratives. They maintain that the point of the stories of Scripture is solely to teach about God and not to use the characters as moral examples. Therefore, they assert, quite correctly, that the ultimate point of the Joseph narrative is God's providential protection of the people of Israel. Thus, they conclude, less correctly, "Joseph's lifestyle, personal qualities, or actions do not tell us anything from which general moral principles may be derived. If you think you have found any, you are finding what you want to find in the text—you are not interpreting the text." (See Fee and Stuart, *How to Read the Bible for All Its Worth: A Guide to Understanding the Bible*, 2nd ed. (Grand Rapids: Zondervan, 1993), 80. They go too far in limiting the message of Scripture stories. Although God is indeed the hero of biblical tales, how His people respond to Him, whether in obedience or disobedience, is also part of the message of the biblical narratives. That is Paul's point when he wrote that these things were written for our instruction.

5. In recent years, a number of works have been written that give insight to the artistry and meaning of biblical narratives. Although not always accepting the historicity and accuracy of the stories, they are helpful in determining the meaning of

narrative texts. Robert Alter's *The Art of Biblical Narrative* (New York: Basic Books, 1981) is especially useful. Interpreters would also do well to consult Shimon Bar-Efrat's *Narrative Art in the Bible* (Sheffield, England: Sheffield Academic, 1997) and Meir Sternberg's *The Poetics of Biblical Narrative* (Bloomington, Ind.: Indiana Univ. Press, 1987).

6. Alter, *The Art of Biblical Narrative,* 65.

7. Ibid., 70.

8. Robinson, *Biblical Preaching,* 172.

9. My favorite introduction about vengeance is from Judith Viorst's children's book, *I'll Fix Anthony* (New York: Harper and Row, 1969), 5, 15, 26–27, 29–30, in which the younger brother complains about the way his older brother Anthony treats him: The younger brother plots vengeance on Anthony: "When I'm six I'll fix Anthony . . . When I'm six I'll float, but Anthony will sink to the bottom. I'll dive off the board, but Anthony will change his mind. I'll breathe in and out when I should, but Anthony will only go glug, glug . . . When I'm six my teeth will fall out, and I'll put them under the bed, and the tooth fairy will take them away and leave dimes. Anthony's teeth won't fall out. He'll wiggle and wiggle them, but they won't fall out. I might sell him one of my teeth, but I might not . . . Anthony is chasing me out of the playroom. He says I stink. He says he is going to clobber me. I have to run now, but I won't have to run when I'm six. When I'm six, I'll fix Anthony."

10. See "Abe Lemons's Glass-bottom" at http://www.Mysanantonio.com. Lemons, often good for a colorful quotation, won 599 games in his thirty-four years coaching college basketball, including an NIT championship in 1978. (He died in 2003.)

11. For an extended discussion of the different ways to develop sermons, including deduction, induction, and semi-induction, see Robinson, *Biblical Preaching,* 116–31.

12. An excellent example of a first-person narrative presented in contemporary garb (the story of Esther), is Donald Sunukjian's "A Night in Persia," *Biblical Sermons,* ed. Haddon Robinson (Grand Rapids: Baker, 1989), 69–80.

PREACHING FROM

DIDACTIC

LITERATURE

by
David Finkbeiner

In the broadest sense, didactic literature is literature whose intent is to teach. In a similarly broad sense, then, all of Scripture could be considered didactic. After all, every part of Scripture does, in fact, teach us theological truth—truth about God, His work, His will, and His interaction with us.

Every major genre of Scripture likewise has an element of instruction to it. For example, *biblical narratives can teach us* about the ways of God (2 Kings 17:7–23); illustrate important theological truths (John 3:14); foster theological reasoning (Rom. 4:18–25; 1 Tim. 2:11–15); or set an example to follow or to avoid (1 Cor. 10:6–11). *Biblical poetry in the psalms can be considered instructive* (Ps. 32:1–2 in Rom. 4:4–9; Ps. 110:1 in Acts 2:32–36), *as can the wisdom literature* (the proverbs of Solomon are considered the "instruction" of a wise man to his "son," [see Prov. 1:8ff]. The speeches of Job's friends seek to inform Job on the proper perspective on his suffering; and Ecclesiastes records the words of Qoheleth, the "Teacher"). Similarly, *the commands of biblical law were given for Israel's instruction* (Exod. 24:12), *and the biblical prophets con-*

tinue to instruct Israel with God's words in accordance with the Mosaic covenant (Deut. 18:14–22). Finally, *the Gospels record Christ's teaching* (e.g., the Sermon on the Mount, Matt. 5–7).

FOUR TRAITS OF DIDACTIC LITERATURE

But even if all of Scripture could be considered broadly instructive, only certain sections of Scripture might be categorized as didactic in a more narrow sense. Didactic literature, narrowly construed, has at least four characteristics. First, its *primary* purpose is to instruct the reader in theological truth and godly living. Second, didactic literature has a second-person point of view. That is, it is a direct address by the author to his audience. Third, didactic literature displays logical structure and development. In other words, generally in didactic literature the author is making an argument; even exhortations come within the context of a larger argument.

Finally, didactic literature favors prosaic language. Leland Ryken describes what prose is by comparing it to other forms of language.

> Poetry differs from ordinary prose by its reliance on images and figures of speech, and by its verse form. Poetry is heightened speech, far more compressed than prose. Whereas expository prose uses the sentence or paragraph as its basic unity, and narrative the episode or scene, the basic unit of poetry is the individual image or figure of speech. Thus in the New Testament epistles we might get a paragraph or chapter that explains godliness. In a historical narrative we get a story in which a character displays godliness in action. But the poet compresses godliness into an image or picture: 'He is like a tree planted by streams of water, that yields its fruit in its season' (Ps. 1:3).[1]

Of course, didactic literature might include elements of poetry and narrative. Indeed, because the line between prose and poetry is not always sharp, some prose can have a rather poetic feel to it.[2] Nevertheless, didactic literature is largely prosaic.

Given these characteristics, what portions of Scripture might be considered didactic in this more narrow sense? The discourses of Jesus in the Gospels and the sermons in Acts, though embedded within a narrative, would basically fit within these parameters. In addition, some portions of Scripture, while perhaps not meeting all of these criteria purely or precisely, still have a strong didactic feel to them. Sections of Old Testament legal material, wisdom literature, and the prophets come to mind here.

But the quintessential example of didactic literature is the New Testament epistle, which will be the focus of this chapter. Concentrating on the epistle makes sense because the epistle is a dominant genre in the New Testament (twenty-one out of twenty-seven NT books are epistles) and so tends to be prominent in our preaching. In fact, many of our general principles of preaching and interpretation most naturally fit the epistle.[3] But more importantly, the principles for preaching epistles discussed here can also be applied, with only minor adjustment, to other didactic sections of Scripture as well. What are those principles?

LITERARY DISTINCTIVES OF DIDACTIC DISCOURSE

First, *didactic preaching should recognize the literary peculiarities of a didactic discourse.* Even if all didactic materials share similar traits, they also may differ significantly from one another. For example, a discourse of Jesus in Matthew is both similar to and significantly different from a Pauline epistle. Consequently, the preacher not only must be cognizant of characteristics shared by all didactic texts, but he must also pay attention to relevant literary features characterizing the particular didactic discourse he is preaching. These peculiarities involve literary features of context and content.

Peculiar literary features of *context* are largely associated with the literary characteristics of the genre in which the didactic text appears. Consider, for example, a didactic text in a Pauline epistle. Paul's epistles, following a format adapted from typical first-century letters in the Greco-Roman world, have an opening, a body, and a closing. The opening includes the identification of the sender and addressee, a greeting, and prayer (usually a thanksgiving). The body, of course, is the main part of the epistle, conveying Paul's message to the addressees. Its most prominent features are doctrinal teaching and exhortations. The letter's closing contains various elements, including travel plans, commendations and greetings, prayers and prayer requests, final instructions, and a benediction.[4]

Anyone preaching in the epistles should pay attention to the epistolary form. If nothing else, it reminds him that epistles are writings of occasion; they directly address specific people at a specific time for specific purposes. Fee and Stuart are probably right to say that their occasional nature is the single most important feature to consider when interpreting epistles.[5] Furthermore, the epistolary form encourages the preacher to compare each epistle to other epistles. This will give him insight into the message and structure of that particular epistle.

It is therefore helpful to compare Paul's epistles both to Greco-Roman epistles and to each other. Sidney Greidanus maintains that, when comparing Paul's epistolary form with the standard Greco-Roman form, the changes in Paul's format serve to make his letters both "God-centered" and "relevant"—characteristics that ought to be reflected in our preaching on these texts. This can be seen, for example, in the fact that Paul's opening and closing greetings highlight the grace of God, or the fact that Paul regularly includes sections of exhortations that are rooted in the indicative.[6] It is similarly helpful to compare the structure of Pauline epistles to one another, because this will often help us see the particular emphases of each epistle. Take Galatians, for example. In the opening, Paul's description of himself highlights the divine origin of his apostleship and his message. And then he skips the typical thanksgiving section to chide the Galatians immediately for being quick to abandon the gospel message. Features like this serve to highlight the concerns that Paul has in Galatians to defend the gospel to people who were all too ready to abandon it and its apostolic defender.[7]

Distinctive literary features of *content* will be tied both to the genre of the text as well as the style of the author. To use the Pauline epistles as our example again, we find that Paul regularly makes use of certain literary features. These would include exhortation sections (Rom. 12:1–15:13), the dialogue or diatribe style (frequently in Romans; e.g., 6:1–2), hymns and creeds (Rom. 1:3–4; Phil. 2:6–11), household codes (Eph. 5:22–6:9), and other rhetorical structures like chiasm and repetition (e.g., Eph. 4:4 –6).[8]

Obviously the peculiar literary features of a didactic discourse of Jesus in Matthew would differ considerably from many of these features in a Pauline epistle. In terms of the differences of *context*, the preacher would have to consider, for instance, not only the audience of Jesus, but also the purpose of Matthew in recording the discourse and placing it where he did within his narrative. And in terms of the differences of *content*, the preacher would, for instance, expect to see a regular use of parables in Jesus' discourse, unlike Paul. Consequently, didactic discourse cannot be flattened out; each text has its own peculiarities of context and content that affect the meaning of the text and its communication.

OCCASION OF THE DIDACTIC DISCOURSE

Second, *didactic preaching should consider the occasion of the discourse.* By its very nature, didactic literature is second-person address and, as such, is already sermonlike. This is an obvious advantage for the preacher, and it is why preachers are so often intuitively drawn to didactic texts first. And yet it is this very sermonlike characteristic of didactic literature that gives it a historical distance from the modern sermon. After all, the didactic text addresses a particular group of hearers at a particular time in particular circumstances far removed from today. The second-person point of view in didactic address thus highlights the centrality of the occasional nature of all didactic discourse.

Once again consider Paul's epistles. Thomas Long has pointed out that Paul's epistles are sermonlike because they rhetorically function to establish a friendly atmosphere between Paul and his audience, to make Paul present to his readers (even though they are separated from him physically), and to invite them to respond to him and his message.[9] But it is precisely this sermonlike quality of his epistles that makes their occasional nature so important.

When considering the occasional nature of Paul's epistles (or of didactic literature in general), the preacher must set out to do three things. First, he must *understand* the occasion of the epistle. Fee and Stuart believe the occasional nature of epistles is so important for interpreting them because reading the epistles is a little like listening to one end of a phone conversation and trying to figure out what the other party is saying. We are hearing the answers, but what are the questions? They go on to point out that while the epistles are undeniably theological, they display "task theology," theological truth directed toward a specific situation.[10] It is therefore critical for the preacher to seek to reconstruct the historical-cultural background and situation of the epistle.

But how do we reconstruct the occasion of the epistle? Clearly secondary resources like Bible dictionaries, general historical reference works, book introductions, and commentaries are all essential to the task. But we cannot forget that a reconstruction of the specific situation of any text reflects an interpretation of that text. That is, there is a certain chicken-egg relationship between the meaning of the text and its occasion. The more we understand the text, the better we can understand the background, which, in turn, better helps us understand the text. Still, Scott Hafemann is right to maintain that the preacher should *begin* by becoming thoroughly acquainted with the text itself before considering the occasion.[11]

Second, the preacher must *communicate* the occasion of the epistle. Of course, the preacher must avoid becoming so enamored with the historical background that the sermon is little more than a history lecture. After all, the primary concern of the preacher is to communicate God and His truth to his audience.[12] But too often preachers fall prey to the opposite error, namely, a failure to acknowledge and communicate the occasion of the text. While historical-cultural reconstruction does not have to be a lengthy part of the sermon, it ought to be a clear element of the sermon. For this element not only elucidates the argument and message of the text, but it also helps the preacher apply the text to his audience.

Finally, the preacher must *make a bridge from* the occasion of the epistle. The epistles are at once both ancient documents and God's Word to us. They therefore demand that we bridge the gap from their time to our time. Numerous texts on hermeneutics have offered helpful principles for bridging the gap, but the procedure outlined by Klein, Blomberg, and Hubbard is particularly helpful:

- Determine the original application(s) intended by the passage.
- Evaluate the level of specificity of those applications. Are they

transferable across time and space to other audiences?

- If not, identify one or more broader cross-cultural principles that the specific elements of the text reflect.

- Find the appropriate applications for today that embody those principles.[13]

As this procedure implies, sometimes the gap is quite narrow (Rom. 5:1), and other times it is quite wide (1 Cor. 8). But preaching that is able clearly to demonstrate how that gap has been bridged—to show how our occasion is like their occasion—can be very effective and powerful. God's Word to them becomes God's Word to us![14]

A FOCUS ON THE BASIC UNIT OF THOUGHT

Third, *didactic preaching should focus on the basic unit of thought.* Every literary genre can be broken down into more basic units that make up the larger work. For example, in narrative it is the episode; in poetry, it is the stanza; in prophecy, it is the oracle. The basic unit of thought in much of the didactic literature is the paragraph. This is certainly the case for the epistles.

Why is the paragraph—or the corresponding basic thought unit in any other literary genre—so important? Any interpreter worth his salt recognizes that you cannot properly interpret a text apart from its literary context. But to understand the literary context of didactic literature, the interpreter must pay attention to the paragraph. For one thing, the paragraph is crucial in understanding the *larger* literary context. Epistles present an extended argument or series of arguments, and the paragraph is the basic building block of the extended argument(s) of the epistle as a whole. Consequently, it is important to distinguish each paragraph and its basic point. Otherwise, you cannot follow the flow of thought of the epistle as a whole, nor can you understand the structure and outline of the work as a whole.

In addition, the paragraph is important for understanding the *immediate* literary context. Words, phrases, clauses, and sentences can only be interpreted accurately when understood in their immediate context. And the paragraph is that immediate context. Hafemann writes, "Within discursive literature, due to its style of argumentation, even individual propositions express very little meaning apart from the paragraph to which they belong. The discursive nature of the Epistles therefore demands that we take as the smallest unit of meaning to be interpreted, not the word or the proposition, nor even a compound sentence, but the *paragraph*."[15]

How does one delineate each paragraph in an epistle? In one sense, our Bible translations make that easy, for most of them are printed with paragraph divisions. Still, these paragraph divisions are not inspired. Nor, in fact, do the translations always even agree with each other in delineating paragraphs. In the end, then, the paragraph divisions are an interpretive decision. To make that decision, the preacher should obviously consult the standard translations and commentaries. But, especially when there is no consensus, he must make that decision by looking for "changes in the text as clues to a shift in the author's flow of thought."[16] The most important of these is a transition to another major idea.

How does the importance of the paragraph affect the preacher's choice of sermon text? As a general rule, in didactic literature the preacher should preach paragraph by paragraph.[17] But this is only a *general* rule. If, for instance, a preacher wants to do careful exposition, some paragraphs are so dense theologically that they will require multiple sermons to do them justice. Or if a preacher is more interested in an expositional survey, he may choose to cover several paragraphs in one sermon. In other words, a paragraph-centered approach does not *demand* that each sermon cover only one paragraph (even if it often will). It does demand, however, that each sermon's text be explicitly tied to the paragraph divisions.

DEVELOPMENT OF THE PASSAGE'S PROPOSITION(S)

Fourth, *didactic preaching should think in terms of propositional development*. We have seen that the didactic literature favors prosaic language and logical development. This is another way of saying that it largely involves propositional communication. For our purposes here, a proposition can be defined as "an assertion or statement about something," which requires a subject and predicate (stated or implied).[18] So an epistolary paragraph, for example, is made up of a series of assertions that are logically interrelated. The key to understanding what the biblical writer is communicating in a paragraph is to delineate each proposition in the paragraph and determine its relationship to the other propositions in the paragraph. In this way, the preacher can trace the flow of thought in the paragraph, discovering its main idea and what the author is saying about it.

The propositional nature of didactic literature in general, and the epistles in particular, highlights the need for grammatical analysis. For tracing the argument in an epistolary paragraph, Thomas Schreiner has suggested a three-step method that is rooted in grammatical analysis.[19] First, one must isolate each proposition in the paragraph. Usually, a paragraph's propositions are to be identified with grammatical structures that contain a subject and verb.[20] Second, one must determine how all the propositions in the paragraph relate to one another. This at least involves distinguishing the primary propositions in the paragraph (which convey the paragraph's main assertions) from secondary and tertiary propositions (which further clarify the main assertions). One useful tool in this connection is called block diagramming, which in various ways seeks to represent visually the relationship between propositions in a paragraph.[21] Third, one must explain the exact nature of the relationship between each proposition. These clausal relationships are most often indicated by connecting words. For instance, James 3:1*b* ("*because* you know that we who teach will be judged more strictly" [emphasis added]) gives a *reason* for James 3:1a (Not many of you should presume to be teachers, my brothers"). In addition to providing a reason, other types of clausal relationships include contrast (words such as *but*), continuation (*and*), concession (*even if*), means (*by*), purpose (*in order that*), result (*consequently*), and timing (*when*).[22]

Why is it so important for the preacher to be able to trace the argument in didactic literature? Hafemann says it well:

Only when one is able to trace the actual way in which the argument develops within a paragraph has the text been understood well enough to preach it. To preach in the Epistles does not mean to remove one of its propositions (not to mention concepts!) out of its literary and/or historical context in order to interpret it against a context foreign to it (whether a biblical context or the preacher's context). Nor does it mean to focus in on the "big ideas" in the passage, as if these ideas stand alone apart from what is said concerning them, why it is said, and for what purpose it is said. Instead, preaching in the Epistles means to construct a sermon which is faithful to the author's original intention as expressed in the various assertions in the text *in their original context*, which is first and foremost the *literary* context of the argument in which they "live and move and have their being."[23]

Having traced the argument, the preacher is then able to determine the paragraph's main idea. The paragraph's main idea "is that *one* assertion, which is supported by *all* of the other propositions in the paragraph, and which itself supports *no* other proposition in the passage."[24] As we will see below, ascertaining the main point of the paragraph will be crucial for the preacher when he formulates the purpose of his message.

APPROPRIATE DESIGN FOR THE SERMON

Finally, the didactic preacher should design the sermon appropriately.
The principles we have considered so far tend to have a direct impact on how the preacher *interprets* the didactic literature. But the nature of didactic literature also directly affects how the preacher *designs* the sermon.

Consider, first of all, how didactic literature affects the sermon's *purpose*. Didactic preaching shares the same broad goal as any other type of preaching. John Piper has rightly said that for all types of preaching the overall goal "is the glory of God reflected in the glad submission of the human heart."[25] This is certainly the case in didactic preaching. After all, didactic literature communicates *theological* truth, i.e., truth about *God*. And this theological truth exalts the glorious God about whom it teaches and, in turn, calls His people to respond appropriately to Him in light of who He is.

But beyond this broad purpose for every sermon, the specific purpose of each sermon ought to be shaped by its didactic text in at least two ways. First, the didactic text should set the agenda for the *content* communicated by the didactic sermon. It is not enough that the sermon and the text simply deal with the same topic.[26] Preaching James 1:13–15, for instance, requires more than just preaching a sermon on the topic of temptation. The didactic sermon needs to communicate the main idea of the paragraph and the propositions in the paragraph supporting that main idea. After all, that is exactly what the didactic text is doing!

This does not necessarily mean that the sermon's theme will always be a restatement of the paragraph's main idea (though that is often the best thing to do). Sometimes the preacher's context will require him to focus on certain propositions within the paragraph rather than the paragraph's main idea. But even in these cases, he must never isolate that proposition from the larger argument and main idea of the paragraph. The preacher's audience should know that he is *focusing* on a proposition, not *ignoring* the paragraph as a whole.

Nor does the need to communicate the main idea and argument of the paragraph mean that the preacher should ignore wider theological considerations. That is, the preacher is not *limited* only to the theological propositions in a paragraph. It will often be helpful to bring in the writer's teaching on the same topic in other passages, to deal with significant cross-references in other parts of Scripture, and to remind the audience where this teaching fits into redemptive history. In fact, dealing with wider theological considerations is sometimes necessary for accurate communication of the truth. For example, Greidanus maintains that anyone preaching about the believer's relationship to government in Romans 13:1–7 should also refer to passages like Acts 5:29 and Revelation 13:1–10 lest Romans 13 be misunderstood.[27]

Second, the didactic text should set the agenda for the *goal* of the didactic sermon. Having understood the occasion, the main idea, and the argument of the paragraph, the preacher is better able to discern the author's goal in writing the passage to his audience. This in turn helps the preacher set the goal for his sermon. So even if, as Greidanus points out, the writer's and preacher's goals "cannot always be identical," the two should always "at least be in harmony" with each other.[28] To help establish that harmony, the preacher should ask the question posed by Long: "How may the sermon, in a new setting, say and do what the text says and does in its setting?"[29] Sermons whose goals reflect a suitable answer to this question create an impact on their hearers similar to the impact on the original audience. And those sermons most certainly will be "relevant." For they will reflect the didactic texts themselves, where the indicative moves to the imperative and the imperative is rooted in the indicative.

Consider also how didactic literature affects the sermon's *form*. If the preacher wants to create an impact on his audience similar to the impact of the text on the original hearers, then his sermon's structure will probably need to reflect the structure of the text.[30] But this hardly means that all sermons on didactic literature will have a similar structure. Greidanus points out that sermons can be developed deductively or inductively (or some combination of the two) and have a didactic or narrative form.[31] But none of these will always be required of a sermon on a didactic text. For didactic texts themselves are not always developed in one of these ways.

Furthermore, even when the preacher wants to maintain "such respect for the textual form that its spirit is not violated by the sermonic form," this does not mean that his sermonic form needs to be a "slavish imitation of the form of the text" to accomplish the same effect. In fact, a sermon may be faithful to its text with a very different outline.[32] Hence, the preacher of a didactic text has a great deal of room to develop his sermon creatively while still being faithful to the text. For example, the preacher might structure his sermon on an epistolary passage with a problem-solution form. That is, before tracing through the argument in the text, he could recreate the situation or problem to which the text is responding (i.e., the other side of the phone conversation). That in turn creates interest in the argument of the text itself. Many other possible sermon forms could also be used fairly with didactic passages.[33]

The importance of Scripture's didactic literature cannot be underestimated. It is Scripture, and a common form of Scripture at that. It is preached at least as often as any other type of literature in Scripture. And it directly teaches truth about the living God who shapes His people. The preacher should therefore treat this material with the respect that it deserves. Keeping these five principles in mind can help him do that.

DAVID FINKBEINER is professor of theology at the Moody Bible Institute. He received his Ph.D. degree in systematic theology from Trinity Evangelical Divinity School, Deerfield, Illinois. He also holds degrees from Biblical Theological Seminary, Hatfield, Pennsylvania, and Bob Jones University, Greenville, South Carolina.

NOTES

1. Leland Ryken, *Words of Delight: A Literary Introduction to the Bible* (Grand Rapids: Baker, 1987), 159.

2. William W. Klein, Craig L. Blomberg, and Robert L. Hubbard Jr., *Introduction to Biblical Interpretation* (Dallas: Word, 1993), 216.

3. Grant Osborne, *The Hermeneutical Spiral* (Downers Grove, Ill.: InterVarsity, 1991), 252.

4. Thomas R. Schreiner, *Interpreting the Pauline Epistles* (Grand Rapids: Baker, 1990), 25–36.

5. Gordon D. Fee and Douglas Stuart, *How to Read the Bible for All Its Worth*, 2nd ed. (Grand Rapids: Zondervan, 1993), 48.

6. Sidney Greidanus, "Preaching from Paul Today," in *Dictionary of Paul and His Letters*, ed. Gerald F. Hawthorne, Ralph P. Martin, and Daniel G. Reid (Downers Grove, Ill.: InterVarsity, 1993), 738–739.

7. Ibid.

8. Ibid., 739; Schreiner, *Interpreting the Pauline Epistles*, 36–41.

9. Thomas G. Long, *Preaching and the Literary Forms of the Bible* (Philadelphia: Fortress, 1989), 111–116.

10. Fee and Stuart, *How to Read the Bible*, 48.

11. Scott Hafemann, "Preaching in the Epistles," in *Handbook of Contemporary Preaching*, ed. Michael Duduit (Nashville: Broadman and Holman, 1992), 364.

12. Ibid., 364–5.

13. Klein, Blomberg, and Hubbard, *Introduction to Biblical Interpretation*, 407. This procedure is explained in greater detail on 407–426.

14. To use the terminology of Fee and Stuart, *How to Read the Bible*, 65.

15. Hafemann, "Preaching in the Epistles," 366.

16. J. Scott Duvall and J. Daniel Hayes, *Grasping God's Word*, 2nd ed. (Grand Rapids: Zondervan, 2005), 128–29. They suggest that the interpreter look for five items that mark a transition to a new paragraph: "conjunctions (e.g., *therefore, then, but*)," "change of genre (e.g., from a greeting to a prayer)," "changes of topic or theme (main idea)," "changes in time, location or setting," and "grammatical changes (e.g., subject, object, pronouns, verb tense, person or number)."

17. See, for example, Haddon Robinson, *Biblical Preaching: The Development and Delivery of Expository Messages* (Grand Rapids: Baker, 1980), 54–55. He maintains that in the epistles, sermon "texts will usually be selected by paragraph divisions, since paragraphs delineate the building blocks of thought." This is consistent with a more general principle for expositional preaching in all genres: "Base the sermon on some unit of biblical thought."

18. Schreiner, *Interpreting the Pauline Epistles*, 99.

19. Ibid., 113–26.

20. This is only a general rule. Schreiner, 109–111, points out that he often does not isolate relative clauses (which do have a subject and verb) as separate propositions, and sometimes he will treat exegetically significant grammatical structures that do not contain a subject and verb (such as a prepositional phrase) as separate propositions. Hafemann, 366, makes a similar point, though his method seems, on balance, to elevate a greater number of grammatical structures to propositional status than does Schreiner's.

21. Some block diagramming schemes are simple, while others can show the complex interrelationships between propositions. For some examples, see Schreiner, *Interpreting the Pauline Epistles*, 113–26 and Osborne, *The Hermeneutical Spiral*, 27–35.

22. For a more comprehensive list of clausal relationships, see Schreiner, *Interpreting the Pauline Epistles*, 100–108; Klein, Blomberg, and Hubbard, *Introduction to Biblical Interpretation*, 212.

23. Hafemann, "Preaching in the Epistles," 368.

24. Ibid.

25. John Piper, *The Supremacy of God in Preaching*, rev. ed. (Grand Rapids: Baker, 2004), 29.

26. Hafemann, "Preaching in the Epistles," 370–71.

27. Greidanus, "Preaching from Paul," 742.

28. Ibid.

29. Long, *Preaching and the Literary Forms*, 122.

30. See Sidney Greidanus, *The Modern Preacher and the Ancient Text: Interpreting and Preaching Biblical Literature* (Grand Rapids: Eerdmans, 1988), 154. See also Hafemann, "Preaching in the Epistles," 369.

31. For a description of these, see Greidanus, *The Modern Preacher*, ch. 7.

32. Ibid., 154–55.

33. For a list of these, see Fred B. Craddock, *Preaching* (Nashville: Abingdon, 1985), 176–77.

PREACHING

FROM THE

POETIC BOOKS

by
Andrew J. Schmutzer

The poetic books of the Old Testament just might be the easiest part of Scripture to preach poorly. The reasons are understandable, including the scant historical context behind many poetic texts; an avalanche of metaphors; frequent "raw" language; lack of story line; and the illusive definition for biblical poetry.[1] Couple this with postmodern notions of what poetry is *not*, and communicating the message of this biblical genre is truly daunting. However, simply avoiding the poetry of the Bible is not an option.

In his book *Seeing the Psalms*, William P. Brown sheds insight on the sober status of biblical poetry today:

> The need for conducting an iconic analysis of biblical poetry is all the more pressing in light of our contemporary context. More than ever before, Western culture is awash with manipulated images spawned from the corporate world's "imagination," images that, in the words of the female protagonist of a children's classic, "leave so little scope for

imagination." We live in an age of media saturation in which an infinite array of competing images circulate for our personal entertainment, fulfillment, and ultimately our enslavement. Such is the iconography of consumption, and it has not left the medium of the text unscathed. Religious reading has become a lost art, reduced to "extract[ing] what is useful or exciting or entertaining from what is read, preferably with dispatch, and then [moving] on to something else." To read religiously, however, is to read the text "as a lover reads, with a tensile attentiveness that wishes to linger, to prolong, to savor, and has no interest . . . in the quick [thrill] of consumption." To read theologically is, in part, to linger over the metaphor.[2]

Like no other biblical genre, Old Testament (OT) poetry reveals astounding literary creativity, daring human honesty, powerful community ethic, and theological insights into the heart and mission of God.

To develop a workable procedure for preaching poetry, the preacher should consider the following elements: 1) the distribution of biblical poetry; 2) the nature of OT poetry; and 3) studying and "packaging" (i.e., preaching) poetic texts. Here we will illustrate with an example from Psalm 1 (and conclude with sample exegetical and homiletical outlines of the psalm).

DISTRIBUTION OF POETRY

Before exploring the nature of poetry, it's important to note where poetry is found. Poetry occurs in almost every OT book, making one-third of the OT poetic. In fact, only seven books contain little or no poetry: Ruth, Ezra, Nehemiah, Esther, Haggai, and Malachi. The books of Psalms, Song of Songs (Song of Solomon), and Lamentations are entirely poetic. The standard collection of "poetic books" includes Job, Proverbs, and Ecclesiastes, and is considered "Wisdom Literature." Yet because the book of Psalms contains the largest concentration of poetry, and the most common book found among the Dead Sea Scrolls,[3] it stands as the prime example of poetic expression at every level. For this reason, the psalms will serve as the basis for our analysis and illustration.[4] Moreover, the psalms are quoted in the New Testament more than any other OT book—especially Psalms 2, 22, and 110—adding to their theological significance that has been cherished throughout church history.[5]

While poetry is concentrated in specific books, it is also important to recognize that poems and poetic language are strewn throughout the canon of Scripture (Jonah 2), and the New Testament (Phil. 2:6–11). In fact, the nativity hymns and Mary's song of praise are prime examples of poetic expression (Luke 1:46–55, 68–79), with Jesus' teaching often reflecting Hebrew poetic style (Matt. 11:3–11; Mark 2:27).[6] Beyond the Gospels, early Christian hymns can be found in many of the Epistles (Rom. 11:33–36; Eph. 1:3–14).[7] Such distribution of psalmic texts requires that the preacher skillfully communicate poetic literature *wherever* it appears, not just where it's traditionally expected.

NATURE OF OT POETRY

Defining Old Testament poetry is notoriously difficult, with experts often fixating on one aspect to the exclusion of others. To move beyond this impasse, we will identify some distinguishing characteristics of Hebrew poetry, draw out the significance of genre, and then summarize by isolating poetry's "boil-down" features with a definition of our own.

Moving from the known to the unknown, it may be helpful to consider some standard conventions of Western poetry in order to better grasp biblical poetic practices. Without knowing it, peoples' expectations of what a biblical poetic sermon has to offer is largely driven by their exposure to Western poetry.

Unlike Western Poetry

Biblical poetry is not Western poetry. Classic Western poetry is built around the conventions of meter, rhyme, and rhythm. Meter refers to the cadence of stressed and unstressed syllables forming a regular rhythmic pattern called a foot. The type of pattern combined with the number of feet produces the meter.[8] Rhyme is the use of similar or identical sounds to conclude (most often) lines of poetry. Finally, rhythm refers to regularizing combinations of stressed and unstressed syllables.[9] To illustrate this, carefully consider these and other conventions in an anthem by Isaac Watts:

Awake, my heart, arise, my tongue, prepare a tuneful voice;
In God, the life of all my joys, aloud will I rejoice.
Awake, my soul, awake, my voice, and tunes of pleasure sing;
Then hallelujah shall address my Savior and my King.
Hosanna! Let the earth and skies repeat the joyful sound;
Let hills and vales reflect the voice in one eternal round.[10]

The stressed [/] and unstressed [x] syllables are the same in every line above. For example:

```
x  /    x   / x / x     x  /   x   x /
```
In God, the life of all my joys, aloud will I rejoice.

Not only is this an iambic beat (unstressed and stressed), but its rocking cadence also produces a rhythm that is easy for us to memorize and sing. The personal imperatives ("Awake, my") in the first half (i.e., cause) conclude with the grander cosmic effect ("Then . . . earth/skies") in the second. Each set of poetic lines employ end-rhyme (e.g., "sing/king"), with the last line creating an inclusion by reiterating Watts's theme of "voice" begun in the first line.

In the medial bicola (i.e., two lines), "voice" is used again, and finally is modified by a prepositional phrase of temporal extent ("in one eternal round"). That praise is indeed the overall theme is validated by the musical terms (nouns and verbs) used throughout (e.g., "tongue," "joys," "rejoice," "tunes," "hallelujah," "sound," "round").[11] Observing the elements in Watts's anthem illustrates the basic kind of things, poetic and rhetorical, we look for when studying and communicating poetic texts. The *how* of structure is always tied to the *what* of meaning.

That said, most of these familiar Western poetic conventions are not found in Hebrew poetry. Whereas Western poetry employs an identifiable meter, Hebrew is better described as having "flexible rhythm." While Western poetry employs classic rhyming techniques, Hebrew poetry amounts to a "rhyming of ideas," not words. So, in the following verse, God is praised, whether in religious memory or temporal honor:

"All your works praise you, Lord;
your faithful people extol you" (Ps. 145:10 TNIV).[12]

"Works" and "praise" (10a) are matched by "people" and "extol" (10b). In each line, the nominal subject is followed by its verb. Both lines, however, emphasize divine relationship, as "*your* works" (10a) and "*your* faithful people" (10b) express devotion.

Thus, while there are major differences between Western and biblical poetry, the two forms both have an *oral* quality.[13] Remember, personal study Bibles are a recent phenomenon in church history! Poetry, such as the psalms, was not read so much as chanted or sung by the congregation. This is significant, since the poetic texts, by their very nature, fostered religious enactment. A standard "enactment" was the antiphonal expression, in which one group chanted the initial line of a psalm and the second group responded with the subsequent line. It is the nature of Hebrew parallelism (to be discussed) that both fosters and reflects this dynamic.

Psalm 24 illustrates this liturgical "call" and "response" pattern:

Call: "Who is the King of glory?"
Response: "The Lord, strong and mighty;
              the Lord, invincible in battle." (v. 8 NLT)

A unique "performance" occurs in Jesus' triumphal entry into Jerusalem when the crowds were shouting: "Hosanna! Blessed is he who comes in the name of the LORD" (John 12:13). Though largely uneducated, the exuberant people were familiar enough with Psalm 118 to *collectively chant* desired texts (vv. 25–26), prompted by the occasion of the Passover when Psalms 113–118 were commonly used (cf. Matt. 26:30; Mark 14:26).[14]

Unique Characteristics of Biblical Poetry

There are, however, several unique characteristics or descriptive "rules" that distinguish Hebrew poetry, particularly from prose. They are:

- *Personal involvement*—poetry represents the world through contrasts and associations, differences and likenesses in which the psalmist participates; significantly, commitment to God always works within spiritual community.

- *Heavenly stage*—poetry by its very function operates in a heavenly arena, "engaging" God's realm whether by petition (i.e., lament) or praise (i.e., hymn).

- *Gnomic trait*—poetry portrays life with an air of timelessness, concerned with the ongoing theological truths and ethical patterns that span the past, present, and future.

- *Linguistic selectivity*—poetry is compressed expression, omitting incidental details and particular words common to prose,[15] stressing instead, ideals and impressions commonly held and liturgically useable.

Clearly, OT poetry has its own literary personality. While the above characteristics may not be apparent in every poem, one can still objectively recognize a poetic profile.[16] After all, as Wilson suggests, "a poem is still a poem and not a grocery list."[17] With practice then, the preacher will increasingly recognize these key characteristics and value them as "signposts" to the author's meaning. Poetry not only exposes the spiritual commitments of the writers, but the psalm's poetic performance expresses its message in patterns and imagery the preacher must be open to explore and then able to explain.

Genre and Communicative Competence

Poetry emerges at one end of a linguistic spectrum as a specialized genre. Why does this matter for the preacher? If poetic texts are going to be accurately and meaningfully communicated to people, the preacher must understand how the poetic genre (and its subcategories) works and the unique requirements that a given genre places on the communication process. For the preacher, there is both a literary and communicative competence that must operate together. A passage must be adequately read (i.e., preacher and text) if it is to be properly heard (i.e., audience and message).

When an intricate genre is communicated appropriately, the listening (i.e., "submitting") audience is now equipped to both understand and ethically perform that message—both literary and communicative competence have done their jobs. Much like a key for a door, genre recognition correctly reads and "unlocks" the interpretative possibilities necessary for the preaching and audience-performance of that text. The diagram "The Three Genres of OT Writing" highlights poetry's station within the broader genres of the Old Testament.[18]

THREE KEY GENRES OF OT WRITING

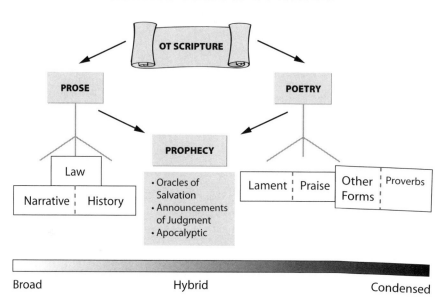

A working knowledge of genres prevents "blind alleys," and may be the preacher's single most important element in the interpretative process. Poetic genres such as: hymns, laments, love poems, victory songs, wisdom instruction, and prophetic speech were written in a basic framework that any reading must respect. Literary competence has been ably defined as the ability to examine the text to discover what type of literature you are reading and to then understand what to expect from it.[19] Some define literary competence, like John Barton, as primarily *"the ability to recognize genre."*[20] For example, if prose is speech organized to inform, poetry is speech framed for contemplation.[21] As noted above, when we recognize traits like: (1) personal involvement, (2) heavenly stage, (3) gnomic trait, and (4) linguistic selectivity, we realize we are entering the realm of poetry. Although prophecy is a linguistic hybrid of prose and poetry, poetry is the most "condensed" at numerous levels, thus the darkening scale toward poetry (see above chart).

A genre can be defined by form, content, and function.[22] In terms of poetry, *form* refers to the "language of measured lines." Such measured line length is a crucial signifier of poetry and can be quickly identified. Modern Bible translations do a good job laying out the "measured lines" of poetic texts for readers. But no translation can do all the work.

Following the recognition of formal poetic features, a genre is further determined by a close read of its *content*. This step distinguishes, for example, a lament psalm from a praise psalm, two of the Psalter's most common types yet stunningly different in substance.[23]

Function is the third mark of genre and discloses intentionality; that is, how a psalm (in our case) is intended to work or operate. For example, it is no mistake that each of the five "books" of the Psalter closes with its own doxology:

> **Book I**—(Psalms 1–41)
> *Closing doxology:* "Praise be to the LORD . . . Amen and Amen" (41:13)
>
> **Book II**—(Psalms 42–72)
> *Closing doxology:* "Praise be to the LORD God . . . Amen and Amen" (72:18–19)[24]
>
> **Book III**—(Psalms 73–89)
> *Closing doxology:* "Praise be to the LORD . . . Amen and Amen" (89:52)
>
> **Book IV**—(Psalms 90–106)
> *Closing doxology:* "Praise be to the LORD . . . all the people say, 'Amen'" (106:48)
>
> **Book V**—(Psalms 107–150)
> *Final Doxology:* (146–150)

However, when one arrives at the closing five psalms (146–150), the brief doxologies are laid aside for a portrait of praise psalms that reverberate together as the *Final Doxology*—fifty-nine verses![25] Any exposition of one of these psalms must also acknowledge its function within the larger culminating doxology. There are circles of context the communicator must be aware of, and uniquely so when preaching any given psalm. Many psalms are a part of a larger group. So, while Psalm 148 is the cosmic anthem at the center, a powerful note is struck with the climactic declaration: "Let everything that has breath praise the Lord" (Ps. 150:6; cf. 145:21). Obviously, function can be multilayered within a psalm and the psalm's larger unit (e.g., the Psalms of Ascent, 120–134). Ultimately, the whole Psalter and the entire canon comprise the "boundaries" for any given psalm. Therefore, preaching any psalm must take in the "literary environment" of psalms that surround it, since the Psalter was edited this way, like a patchwork quilt.

In sum, literary competence occurs when the preacher interacts with the genre *signals* (e.g., terms, mood, structure) that the authors used consciously to guide readers in the proper understanding of their composition. The poetic genre is only one of many "public contracts" authors used to guide their readers. Genres, then, are a historical form of communication that can present a timeless theological message within a contemporary context.[26] Additionally, communication occurs when the hearer grasps the intention of the text, encounters it as divine truth, and experiences God's voice anew.[27]

DEFINITION AND FEATURES OF OT POETRY

Having considered some of poetry's broad characteristics, we're now ready to isolate its "boil-down" features and offer a working definition. *Biblical poetry is intensified discourse, marked by 1) terse lines, 2) overt parallelism, 3) frequent figures, 4) and formal structure.*[28] If the audience is to truly engage poetry as a vehicle of God's voice, the communicator must be able to interpret and interact with these key features, not ignore or tolerate them.

Poetry behaves differently than prose, expressing firm belief even while living through vivid pain.[29] Elements of prose like "plot" and "character development" are simply not required for the powerful expressions of poetry. However, alongside the characteristics and features listed above, the reader will find in psalmic poetry: 1) a stated topic, 2) development of thought and emotion about that topic, and 3) a resolution of emotion at the end.[30] In other words, the audience should understand that they are hearing rich theological impression in the craft of poetry, not merely an existential "journal entry" and certainly not a discourse of propositions in linear argument. The nature of the poetic text should affect the nature of the sermon.

Terse Lines

Terseness refers to the "telegraph style"[31] of poetry's "lines" (*cola*; singular is *colon*) that are clearly more condensed than the prose sentence.[32] Though three (tricolon) and four lines (quatrain) can be found, two lines (bicolon) form the standard verse:

> "You-give to-them, they-gather; (colon a)
> You-open your-hand, they-are-satisfied well." (Ps. 104:28)
> (colon b)

This example shows that terseness is achieved by placing short lines side-by-side with few, if any, connectives (e.g., *and*, *but*).[33] Instead, the phrases are joined by a paratactic style; that is, linked without subordinate relationships, unlike the style of the New Testament epistles. So, the exact relationships between Hebrew cola is hardly explicit, even when the conjunction "and" is present, as a survey of translations often reveals (i.e., *when, even, or*, etc.).[34] What biblical poetry does have, however, is contour and movement; a repetition and echo of key terms that make an art form.

In poetry, each colon only contains three or four Hebrew words, a denseness that distinguishes the poetic line from the far longer prose sentence. Inserted hyphens in the above example precisely illustrate the individual Hebrew words in the verse. Taken as a whole, biblical poems average only thirty verses—a workable quantity that should commend their more frequent preaching.[35]

OVERT PARALLELISM

Deceptively simple, the most dominant feature of poetry is the pairing of lines called "parallelism." The traditional categories of synonymous, antithetical, and synthetic parallelism[36] are too simplistic to address the vast amount of biblical poetry. With great variation and nuance, some form of "equivalence" is formed between the lines through an interplay of sound, syntax, grammar, and lexemes (key words). So actually, numerous linguistic elements combine to produce parallelism.[37] The net result is that the second line is reshaping, extending, contrasting, sharpening, and intensifying the first. In other words, some form of development occurs in the second line. To illustrate the sophistication and aesthetic beauty of parallelism, consider the following example from Job 5:14, given in (literal) English.

(14a) "[In] daylight they *encounter* darkness,
(14b) And as in the night they *grope* at noon."

The contrasting word pairs drive the parallelism. While "day" and "night" begin both lines, "darkness" and "noon" close the lines, holding opposite places. Lexically similar, the four nouns function as temporal descriptors of a basic day. The fixed rhythm of creation itself is used to highlight an opposite spiritual reality. The very syntax emphasizes this by placing these nouns at opposite ends of the cola ("day/night . . . dark/noon," 14 a,b). In the middle are the verbs "encounter" and "grope." The more aggressive verb "groping" underscores their mounting desperation. In this case, a semantic chiasm of word pairs illustrates the power of parallelism for antithetic expression:

The description of God thwarting the schemes of the crafty is high-

A *day*		(colon 14a)
	B *dark*	
	B' *night*	(colon 14b)
A' *noon*		

lighted by the chiastic U-turn in the verse. Functioning as the "skeleton" of the verse, this chiasm shows the economy of words (three in each colon) typical of poetic verse. The very poetic presentation is part of what communicators must be alert to. So, parallelism not only weds paratactic cola, it creates a balance between them.[38] While grammatical and semantic equivalence account for most forms of parallelism, each expression is molded to fit its unique context.[39] For our purposes, the types of parallelism can be viewed in the following way.[40] One should be alert for these basic types of parallelism.

---

1. When a colon A and B are interchangeable (A=B):
- *Echo* (Mt. 11:30)
- *Contrast* (Prov. 11:20

2. When a colon A and B qualify each other (A>B):
- *Subordination of means* (Ps. 111:6)
- *Subordination of reason* (Ex. 15:21)
- *Subordination of time* (Ps. 137:1)

3. When a colon A and B expand each other (A<B):
- *Continuation* (Isa. 40:9)
- *Comparison* (Ps. 103:13)
- *Specification* (i.e., spatial [Isa. 45:12], explanation [Isa. 48:20b–21], dramatic effect [Ps. 72:9], purpose [Prov. 4:1]
- *Intensification* (Ps. 88:11–12)

Remember that these labels are not an end in themselves. These terms are merely meant to stimulate thought, sharpen skills of observation, and trace the movement of the poetry.

Studying poetry, however, does not stop with the standard bicolon (A, B). Similar to paragraphs, larger subdivisions are called strophes (two or three verses) and stanzas (two or more strophes). Strophes and stanzas are found by observing structural and lexical repetition in a passage and then dividing that text accordingly.[41] Because these units of measure move the author's argument, they must also shape the preacher's sermon. Modern Bibles try to divide poems in their various thematic units to help readers; nevertheless, no two Bibles will look alike.[42]

Frequent Figures

Preachers probably struggle more often with imagery than with any other element of poetry. A figure, or image, uses nonliteral language to express a realistic idea, but biblical poets did not limit themselves to modern notions of nature, spirituality, or relationships. Because of this potential disconnect, the modern preacher must attempt to (1) identify, (2) interpret, and (3) explain the poetic figures encountered in a given text. Poetic imagery creates a picture in the reader's mind.

Poetry's figures function to compare, substitute, amplify, and omit ("gap") key ideas or terms within a verse.[43] For example, when David says:

> "Many bulls have surrounded me;
>   powerful bulls of Bashan hem me in!" (Ps. 22:12 NET)

he uses a figure (*hypocatastasis*) that compares his wicked enemies to lethal "goring" animals. Extending the use of animal imagery, David goes on to say:

> "Yes, wild dogs surround me;
>   a gang of evil men crowd around me." (22:16a, b NET)

In this example, the second colon clearly identifies just who (or what) David is referring to: "evil men." This imagery accomplishes his purpose well since the opportunistic and "pack mentality" of dogs provides vivid imagery.

These are "ready" illustrations for the preacher. People can be taught to listen empathetically to this language. For their part, preachers must learn to interact with figures and not sidestep or ignore them. Preachers must realize that not only is the figurative the *means* of communicating the literal, but the figurative *is* the literal in its chosen means of expressing that truth. These are indeed "thick" truths that include the intellectual, emotional, and allusion elements (i.e., "sounds").

As a preacher, you should recognize four truths as you use poetic figures and their imagery. First, realize that "poetry communicates truly but not precisely. What it gives up in detail of information, it makes up for in intensity of expression."[44] Preaching poetry, then, should help people to identify with the author's experience, not dispense more "content." Second, poetry operates at the level of imagination, "often swiveling the universe on the hinges of single image."[45] With poetic figures there is a concealing and revealing dynamic operating in the biblical verse that calls on the power of imaginative insight as much as "objective" study.[46] Third, recognize that when the Bible speaks of God, it uses metaphorical terms out of necessity. Images of shape, color, and size "incarnate" God for a world defined by shapes, colors, and sizes. So, at times, biblical language will even compare God to natural elements (Deut. 32:11; Ps. 36:5–7).

Finally, and most significantly, realize that the imagery of poetry will foster theological expression. Gillingham insightfully states,

> The language of theology needs the poetic medium for much of its expression, for poetry, with its power of allusion, reminds us the more hidden and mysterious truths which theology seeks to express. Poetry is a form which illustrates our need for a sense of balance in our study of theology. On the one hand, good poetry still testifies to the need to be properly analytical in our pursuit of knowledge, but on the other, it illustrates the importance of being open to the possibility of mystery and ambiguity in our pursuit of meaning.[47]

Formal Structure

Whereas figures decorate a text with rich color (e.g., Ps. 42:1–2), they do not structure the poem in which they occur. Formal structuring refers to the shape or "skeletal form" evident through the poem's sense units (i.e., stanzas and strophes).[48] In addition to the syntax of sentences, there is also "syntax of the discourse." Like describing a house comprised of various-sized rooms, observing the sense units of a psalm is crucial because it is a vital clue to the theological movement of that text. Beyond basic genre forms (e.g., lament), formal structure is the poem's unique literary contour (see Psalm 73). Aside from acrostic psalms that follow the letters of the Hebrew alphabet (see Psalm 145), larger and smaller units, like stanzas and strophes, naturally shape poetic texts.

The sense units that structure a psalm are detected through: (1) changes in content, grammar, literary form, and speaker; (2) the concentration of key words in a section; and (3) the use of refrains or repeated statements.[49] At a simplified level, these are the paragraphs visible in an English translation. For example, Psalm 32 can have five sense units (1–2, 3–5, 6–7, 8–10, 11). Next to each sense unit, concise labels can be written describing each unit's form, content, and function. Describing a poem's literary form through sense units enables one to grasp the points of thematic shift and climax in a passage. The following are diagnostic questions one can ask of a psalm to find its sense units.[50]

1. What comes first in the poem? Why?

2. What comes last in the poem? Why?

3. What comes in the middle? Why?

4. How does each sense unit contribute to its thematic development?

5. What is the poem's main theme?

The formal structure of a psalm can justifiably be viewed in several ways, depending upon which structural "signs" one decides to focus. Modern Bible translations, for example, attempt to show their read of sense units in the numerous ways they break up poetic texts into paragraph-like sections, yet not one of these translations are the same in word or structure. So one structural reading need not exclude all others, though some may be better than others. Instead, it is appropriate to observe that the structure and contour of a poetic text can operate at more than one level[51] (see Psalms 62, 87, 101, 122, 129, 146). Understanding how such elements as parallelism and figures work in a poetic text is absolutely vital for both sound interpretation and meaningful communication. Alongside the occasional pointers for interpretation and presentation, we can now focus on "packaging" a poetic text for presentation.

STUDYING AND "PACKAGING" POETIC TEXTS

Obviously one cannot adequately jump into the packaging of poetic texts without developing some degree of literary competence—sensitivity to genre, theme, and structure. Given our above discussion, here are six steps, offered as a general "checklist" for preaching poetry. As you work through each point, follow the illustrations on the next page.

Step 1: Approaching the Parade. Copy the text onto a computer document that can be thoroughly manipulated. Start making a semantic layout of the text, looking for its broad sense units.

Step 2: Entering the Parade. Identify the type of parallelism used in each verse. Draw out the rest of the semantic layout at the verse and clause level.

Step 3: Joining the Parade. Study syntactical constructions, clauses, nouns, verbs, prepositions, etc. Scrutinize eight different translations, read three to four quality commentaries.

Step 4: Enjoying the Parade. Determine the precise genre of psalm and what your text emphasizes. Determine how the figures and other images are functioning.

Step 5: Leaving the Parade. Make an exegetical outline, stating the essence of each verse in the sense unit. State the essence of each sense unit observing its relationship with others around it. (A sample follows based on Psalm 1.)

Step 6: Pondering the Parade. You can ponder two ways. First, form a homiletical outline in contemporary language. (A sample follows.) Second, formulate several "abiding" theological principles clearly rooted in the text.

A SAMPLE EXEGETICAL OUTLINE OF PSALM 1

Exegetical Statement:

The psalmist describes the blessed person who leads a pure and thriving life in accord with the Word of the Lord, in contrast to the ungodly who will perish.

Structure:

I. The psalmist describes the blessed one who leads a pure and thriving life in accord with the Word of the Lord (vv. 1–3).

    A. He describes the pure life of the blessed individual (1).
    B. He describes his delightful meditation in the law of the Lord (v. 2).

C. He describes the vitality of the blessed individual with the image of the fruitful tree (v. 3).

II. By contrast, the psalmist describes the ungodly antitype (vv. 4, 5).

A. He pictures the worthlessness of the ungodly with the image of the chaff (v. 4).
B. He anticipates the final separation of the ungodly from the righteous (v. 5).

III. The psalmist concludes that the ungodly will perish because the Lord "knows" (= protects) the way of the righteous (v. 6).

A SAMPLE HOMILETICAL OUTLINE OF PSALM 1
"LIVING OUT WHAT WE MEDITATE ON"

Homiletical Statement: The righteous person is thoroughly rooted in God's instruction, enabling perseverance in the present and hope for the future.

I. Encouragement: Righteous Profiled by Character and Outcome (vv. 1–3).

A. What We Must Avoid—Negatively (v. 1).
B. What We Must Affirm—Positively (v. 2).
C. Illustration #1 (v. 3).

II. Discouragement: Wicked Profiled by Outcome (vv. 4, 5).

A. Illustration #2 (v. 4).
B. The Final Outcome for the Wicked (v. 5).

Motivation: The Lord's Perspective in Promise and Warning (v. 6).

ANDREW J. SCHMUTZER is associate professor of Bible at the Moody Bible Institute. He has earned the Ph.D. degree from Trinity Evangelical Divinity School, Deerfield, Illinois, and degrees from Dallas Theological Seminary and the Moody Bible Institute.

NOTES

1. While this essay does not presume knowledge of biblical Hebrew, many elements of this discussion will be appreciated and used far better by those with at least one year of Hebrew.

2. William P. Brown, *Seeing the Psalms: A Theology of Metaphor* (Louisville, Ky.: Westminster John Knox, 2002), 13; also citing L. M. Montgomery, *Anne of Green Gables: 100th Anniversary Edition* (New York: Putnam, 2008); Douglas P. Ottati, *Hopeful Realism* (Cleveland: Pilgrim, 1999); Paul J. Griffiths, *Religious Reading* (Oxford: Oxford Univ. Press, 1999).

3. Among the Dead Sea Scrolls a total of thirty-nine copies of Psalms have been found, with Isaiah coming in second with twenty-four. C. D. Elledge, *The Bible and the Dead Sea Scrolls.* Archeology and Biblical Studies, ed. A. G. Vaughn, vol. 14 (Atlanta: Society of Biblical Literature, 2005), 87.

4. Important psalms also occur outside the Psalter: Moses and Miriam's Song of the Sea (Exod. 15), Moses' song (Deut. 32), Deborah and Barak's victory song (Judges 5), Hannah's song of praise (1 Sam. 2), David's lament (2 Sam. 1), and Habakkuk's song of praise (Hab. 3); similarly, Gen. 4:23–24; ch. 49; 1 Kings 8:12–13; Ruth 1:16–17, etc.

5. The Gospels also contain numerous poetic quotations from the prophets (Matt. 4:15–16; 12:18–21; Luke 3:4–6; 4:18–19).

6. The book of Revelation also contains several doxologies construed poetically (4:8, 11; 5:9–10, 12, 13; 15:3–4).

7. Other embedded hymns and hymn fragments include: Col. 1:12–14, 15–20, and 1 Peter 1:3–5.

8. Basic types of poetic rhythm include: iambic (alternating pattern of unstressed and stressed syllables [x /]); dactylic (single stressed syllable followed by two unstressed [/ xx]); trochaic (stressed and unstressed syllables [/ x]); anapestic (two unstressed and one stressed syllable [x x /]).

9. Gerald H. Wilson, *Psalms*, vol. 1, in *The NIV Application Commentary* (Grand Rapids: Zondervan, 2002), 32–33.

10. "Awake My Heart"; in public domain. For a good example of a modern hymn written in this tradition, see "My Heart is Filled with Thankfulness," by Keith Getty and Stuart Townsend (© 2003, Thankyou Music).

11. Though a noun, "tongue" functions here as a metonymy of cause (= "tongue") for effect (= "tuneful voice"), a literary technique frequently used in Hebrew poetry.

12. The future tense ("will") reflected in some English translations (NASB, NIV) and the gnomic in others ("praise you" TNIV) are two standard ways of construing imperfective aspect in Hebrew poetic genre.

13. On the highly debated issue of Hebrew meter, see Adele Berlin, *The Dynamics of Biblical Parallelism* (Bloomington, Ind.: Indiana Univ. Press, 1985); S. E. Gillingham, *The Poems and Psalms of the Hebrew Bible* (Oxford: Oxford Univ. Press, 1994).

14. Psalms 113–118 form the *Hallel*, the Hymns of Praise, which were sung at the three greatest festivals: the Feast of Passover, Pentecost, and the Feast of Booths (or Tabernacles). "*Hosanna*" (Heb. "O Lord, save!") was an expression that by Jesus' day functioned as an Aramaic liturgical praise formula. Beyond the commitments of the crowd, soon to demand his crucifixion, John presents Jesus as *the* victor over enemies, adding a "procession of humility" to his messianic portrait of sign-working (Andreas J. Köstenberger, *Encountering John: The Gospel in Historical, Literary, and Theological Perspective* [Grand Rapids: Zondervan, 1999], 136). All four evangelists use Ps. 118:25–26, with John and Mark adding "the King of Israel" (John 12:13) and "the kingdom of our father David" (Mark 11:10).

15. Specifically, the Hebrew definite article ("the," *ha*), accusative marker (*'et*), the conjunction ("and," *waw*), personal suffixes ("my/I"), and the relative pronoun ("which/that," *'asher*) are generally rare in poetic expression.

16. Wilson, *"Psalms," The NIV Application Commentary*, 34.

17. Ibid.

18. Adapted and modified from Ronald L. Giese Jr., "Literary Forms of the Old Testament," in *Cracking Old Testament Codes: A Guide to Interpreting the Literary Genres of the Old Testament*, ed. D. Brent Sandy, Ronald L. Giese Jr. (Nashville: Broadman & Holman, 1995), 18.

19. William W. Klein, Craig L. Blomberg, and Robert L. Hubbard Jr., *Introduction to Biblical Interpretation*, rev. ed. (Nashville: Nelson, 1993), 324.

20. John Barton, *Reading the Old Testament: Method in Biblical Study* (London: Darton, Longman and Todd, 1984), 16; emphasis original.

21. A. Fitzgerald, "Hebrew Poetry," in *The New Jerome Biblical Commentary*, ed. Raymond E. Brown, Joseph A. Fitzmyer, and Ronald E. Murphy (Englewood Cliffs, N.J.: Prentice Hall, 1990), 201.

22. Ibid., 11. His analysis is reflected in our brief observations of form, content, and function. For further discussion of OT genres, see also Klein, Blomberg, and Hubbard Jr., *Introduction to Biblical Interpretation*, 323–98.

23. The lament psalm typically contains: (1) invocation, (2) plea to God for help, (3) complaints, (4) confession of sin or assertion of innocence, (5) curse of enemies, (6) confidence in God's response, (7) statement of trust; and the praise psalm typically contains: (1) call to praise, (2) cause for praise, (3) renewed call to praise. For further discussion, see Bruce K. Waltke, "Psalms: Theology of," *New*

International Dictionary of Old Testament Theology and Exegesis (Grand Rapids: Zondervan, 1997) 4:1100–115.

24. While Psalm 72 closes out Book II, the psalm itself ends with a colophon (72:22), noting that: "The prayers of David son of Jesse are ended." Since other Davidic collections are found later in the Psalter (e.g., Pss. 138–145), 77:22 is evidence that various "editions" were compiled in stages, which is also indicated through "duplicates" (see Psalms 14 = 53; 40:13–17 = 70; 108 = 57:7–11 + 60:5–12; Brevard S. Childs, *Introduction to the Old Testament as Scripture* [Philadelphia: Fortress, 1979], 516–17).

25. On these doxologies, see P. C. Craigie, *Psalms 1–50*, Word Biblical Commentary, vol. 19 (Waco, Tex.: Word, 1983), 30–31; G. H. Wilson, *The Editing of the Hebrew Psalter*, SBL Dissertation Series 76 (Chico, Calif.: Scholars, 1985), 157.

26. Craig C. Broyles, "Interpreting the Old Testament: Principles and Steps," in *Interpreting the Old Testament*, ed. Craig C. Broyles (Grand Rapids: Baker, 2001), 34.

27. G. R. Osborn, "Genre," *Dictionary for Theological Interpretation of the Bible* (ed. Kevin J. Vanhoozer; Grand Rapids: Baker, 2005), 253.

28. The elements of terseness, parallelism, and imagery define biblical poetry for numerous scholars. See Adele Berlin, "Parallelism," *ABD* 5:155–62; Tremper Longman III, "The Analysis of Poetic Passages," in *Literary Approaches to Biblical Interpretation*, Foundations of Contemporary Interpretation (Grand Rapids: Zondervan, 1987), 119–34.

29. For an in-depth analysis of psalmic theology, see Hans Joachim Kraus, *Theology of the Psalms*, trans. by K. Crim (Minneapolis: Fortress, 1992).

30. "Psalms, Book of," *Dictionary of Biblical Imagery*, ed. Leland Ryken et al. (Downers Grove, Ill.: InterVarsity, 1998), 684.

31. James L. Kugel, *The Idea of Biblical Poetry: Parallelism and Its History* (New Haven, Conn.: Yale Univ. Press, 1981), 77.

32. Terseness is also defined by ellipsis (omission) or "gapping" (cf. Ps. 47:2–5). This occurs when the second line omits the verb used in the first line:

> "May the Lord *cut off* all flattering lips,
>
> the tongue that makes great boasts." (Ps. 12:3; emphasis on verb added)

33. Adele Berlin, "Poetry, Biblical Hebrew," *The Oxford Companion to the Bible*, ed. Bruce M. Metzger and Michael D. Coogan (Oxford: Oxford Univ. Press, 1993), 598.

34. Some translations insert English connectives where the Hebrew has none. So departing from the above translation and scantion (verse format) of Ps. 104:28, the NLT reads:

> "*When* you supply it, they gather it.
> You open your hand to feed them,
> *and* they are richly satisfied.

35. Psalm 119 is the longest poetic text with 176 verses. Similarly, the poetic core of Job (3:2–42:6) is actually a succession of poems fit into a narrative frame (cf. Judg. 5:25).

36. That is, parallelism in which the second line reproduces the first (*synonymous*), the second line contrasts with the first (*antithetical*), the second line extends the thought of the first (*synthetic*).

37. Types of parallelism include: *morphological* (nouns, tense, gender), *syntactical* (types of clauses, mood, subject-object exchange), *lexical* (word pairs, associations), *semantic* (lines with progression of thought), and *phonological* (sound, assonance). Working knowledge of the biblical languages is necessary to appreciate these expressions.

38. Berlin, "Poetry," 598.

39. Ibid.

40. See the discussion of Gillingham, *The Poems and Psalms of the Hebrew Bible,* 78–86.

41. For example, Psalm 103 can be construed with three stanzas (1–8; 9–16; 17–22), with numerous strophes in these stanzas.

42. Oriented around syntactic or thematic units, these divisions can be shown differently. For example, the NIV divides Psalm 148 into three stanzas (vv. 1–6, 7–12, 13–14), while the NRSV sees 7 bi-cola (vv.1–2, 3–4, 5–6, 7–8, 9–10, 11–12, 13–14), and no literary divisions appear in the *Tanakh* (or *TNK*, the Hebrew Bible; from the acronym for the Torah ["Law"], Nevi'im ["Prophets"], and Ketuvim ["Writings"]).

43. Examples of figures that compare include *simile* (resemblance, Ps. 1:3), *metaphor* (representation, Ps. 23:1), *hypocatastasis* (implication, Ps. 22:16), and *personification* (ascribing, Psalm 114). Figures that substitute include *metonymy* (change of noun, Ps. 23:5) *synecdoche* (transfer, Ps. 44:6), *merism* (the whole referred to by two major parts, Ps. 139:2), *hendiadys* (two approximate words describe one thing, Ps. 148:13). Among figures that amplify are *inclusion* (discourse marked off by similar word or phrase, Ps. 8:1, 10), *chiasmus* (literary device forming an "x" pattern, Ps. 2:9), *anabasis* (gradual intensity, Ps. 1:1), and *hyperbole* (overstatement for emphasis, Deut 1:28). Figures that omit ("gap") include *ellipsis* (dropping a word, Ps. 21:12), *erotesis* (rhetorical question, Ps. 2:1), and *asyndeton* (relating clauses by dropping linking conjunctions or prepositions, Gen.3:16).

44. Tremper Longmann III, "Literary Style," in August H. Konkel and Tremper Longmann III, *Job, Ecclesiastes, Song of Songs,* Cornerstone Biblical Commentary, ed. P. W. Comfort (Carol Stream, Ill.: Tyndale, 2006), 343.

45. Thomas G. Long, *Preaching and the Literary Forms of the Bible* (Philadelphia: Fortress, 1989), 47.

46. Gillingham, *The Poems and Psalms,* 277.

47. Ibid., 278.

48. David L. Petersen and Harold Richards Kent (in *Interpreting Hebrew Poetry*, ed. M. Tucker Gene 60–63) refer to "sense units," while Fokkelman uses "stanza" and "strophe" (*Reading Biblical Poetry*, [Louisville: Westminster John Knox, 2001], 117–140).

49. Klein, Blomberg, Hubbard, *Introduction to Biblical Interpretation*, 316.

50. Questions drawn from Klein, Blomberg, Hubbard, *Introduction to Biblical Interpretation*, 319.

51. J. C. McCann Jr., "The Book of Psalms," in *The New Interpreter's Bible*, vol. 4 (Nashville: Abingdon, 1996), 654.

Twelve

PREACHING

FROM THE

PROPHETS

by
Walter McCord

Ask the average church member how many messages he or she has heard preached from the prophets, and the answer will be few, if any. In the past five years, I have asked this question of hundreds of students. Fewer than 20 percent of my students remember ever hearing a sermon series from one of the prophetic books. Most pastors do not preach through the prophetic books of the Bible. Why is this true?

THE CHALLENGE OF PROPHECY

Narrative literature conveys its message in story with a flow of thought and interesting individuals. Wisdom literature communicates with short pithy statements that ring true to life and pack a punch. Poetry has heightened speech expressing intensified feelings or insights, which connect to human emotion. But prophecy is different and frequently difficult. Many biblical preachers and teachers struggle to understand prophetic literature. Prophecy, with its symbolic imagery, communicates historical realities through ideological symbols rather than explicit statements.

However, the prophets ministered in a time surprisingly similar to our own. They faced national intrigue and uncertainty, moral ambivalence, unchecked materialism, and a general disregard for God and His standards. This is an excellent time for Bible students to read, understand, and teach the prophets.

IMPORTANCE OF THE PROPHETS

Almost one quarter of the entire Bible is classified as prophetic. Traditionally "the Prophets" refers to the sixteen writing prophets and their Old Testament books. Although there are prophetic sections found in the New Testament, such as Matthew 24 and most of the book of Revelation, for our purposes, we will focus on the Old Testament writings classified as the Prophets. Although portions of these prophetic writings contain narrative (for example, the historical interlude of Isaiah in chapters 36–39), the majority of these critically important biblical books are composed primarily of prophetic material. The sheer volume of prophetic material warrants that every serious preacher intending to preach "all the counsel of God" (Acts 20:27 KJV) be comfortable with and adept at preaching from the Prophets.

The sixteen writing prophets and their seventeen Old Testament books have commonly been divided two different ways. The canonical presentation in English Bibles has the Major Prophets first: Isaiah, Jeremiah, Lamentations, Ezekiel, and Daniel. These writings are considered the Major Prophets either because of their volume of writings (Isaiah, Jeremiah, and Ezekiel) or their perceived prophetic importance (Daniel). The Minor Prophets follow with Hosea through Malachi. These last twelve books of the Old Testament were known by the rabbis from ancient times as "The Twelve."

The prophetic writings of the Old Testament have also been divided into three categories chronologically. The *preexilic prophets* writing from about 850 through 586 B.C. are comprised of Obadiah,[1] Joel, Jonah, Amos, Hosea, Micah, Isaiah, Nahum, Zephaniah, Habakkuk, and Jeremiah. The *exilic prophets*, writing from about 605 through 535, include Daniel and Ezekiel. Finally, the *postexilic prophets*, writing from about 520 through 400, include Haggai, Zechariah, and Malachi. This categorization of the prophets is especially helpful in considering the cultural and historical settings and the messages of each of the individual prophetic books.

BACKGROUND OF THE PROPHETS

The most common word in the Old Testament for prophet is *nābi'*. Used more than three hundred times, it characterized the prophet as one who was authorized to speak for God. The emphasis of this term seems to be on what the prophet did, namely the proclamation of divine revelation. Moses is a good example. Exodus 6:28–29 explains that God spoke to Moses, and then Moses was to tell Pharaoh everything the Lord had told him. The prophets spoke for the Lord. The English term *prophet* is derived from the Greek *prophetes,* meaning one who speaks forth.

God's prophets received their messages directly from God (Num. 12:1–2, 6). The prophet had to speak in the Lord's name (Deut. 18:18–20). When a true prophet said, "Thus saith the Lord . . ." there was an expectation that the prophet and his message could be authenticated (Deut. 13:1–5; 18:15–22). In addition, the prophet's message had to conform to previously certified revelation (Deut. 13:1–5). If this was not the case, the punishment was to be death (Deut. 13:5). Finally, the prophet's message was accompanied by authenticating signs (Deut. 18:21–22, but cf. Deut. 13:1).

Another dimension of the prophet's ministry is reflected in two different Hebrew words translated "seer." The emphasis of these terms seems to be on how the prophet knew what he communicated. One word is *rō'eh*, which comes from the Hebrew word meaning "to see." It is used twelve times to refer to a prophet. The prophets usually received their messages through dreams or visions. 1 Samuel 9:9 indicates that the earlier name of "seer" had in Samuel's time changed to "prophet." A second word translated "seer" is *hōzeh*. It is used to refer to a prophet at least sixteen times and is virtually synonymous with *rō'eh*. One interesting passage uses all three terms (1 Chron. 29:29). Here the life of King

David is said to be recorded in the chronicles of Samuel the seer (*rō'eh*), Nathan the prophet (*nābi'*), and Gad the seer (*hōzeh*).

Three other expressions are found in the Old Testament related to the prophets. "Man of God" is used to describe some prophets and identifies them as ones who knew God and were sent by God on a particular mission. This term is used of Moses (1 Chron. 23:14), Shemaiah (1 Kings 12:22), Elijah (1 Kings 17:18), Elisha (2 Kings 1:7–13), and two unnamed prophets (1 Kings 13:1; 2 Chron. 25:7). "Servant of the Lord" is an expression stressing the relationship between God and His faithful messengers. It is used of Moses (Deut. 34:5), Ahijah (1 Kings 14:18), and the prophets generally (2 Kings 9:7; 17:13; Jer. 7:25; Ezek. 38:17; Zech. 1:6).

A "messenger of the Lord" was sent as God's messenger to deliver His word. This term focuses more on the mission and message than it does on the man. It is used of Haggai (Hag. 1:13), John the Baptist (Mal. 3:1), and the prophets generally (2 Chron. 36:15–16; Isa. 44:26).

Prophets were divided into two classifications. One group is commonly called the *speaking prophets*. These men and women delivered messages from a sovereign God with supernatural insight. Individuals in this group include Miriam (Exod. 15:20), Deborah (Judges 4:4), King Saul (1 Sam. 10:9–11), Gad (1 Sam. 22:5), Nathan (2 Sam. 7:2), Elijah (1 Kings 18:22), Elisha (1 Kings 19:16) and numerous other individuals in the Old and New Testaments. Moses (Deut. 34:10) and Samuel (1 Sam. 3:20) are also confirmed as prophets, and they authored biblical books, but their writings are not among the prophetic corpus. The second group of prophets is more commonly referred to as the *writing prophets*. These individuals are all men, and their books are commonly referred to as the prophetic books.

TIMES OF THE PROPHETS

It is critical to understand the times of the writing prophets in order to interpret their works. The prophets wrote during a period of transition between world powers. The preexilic prophets wrote of the turmoil between Egypt, Syria, and Assyria (which was to become the world power of note for almost two hundred years). Around 734 B.C., the southern kingdom, Judah, and her king, Ahaz, joined with Assyria and her king, Tiglath-pileser III, to defeat the Arameans and Israel (2 Chron. 28:5), who were attacking. For more than a century, Judah would pay heavy and burdensome tribute to the Assyrians for that kingdom's aid. Meanwhile Israel was saddled with an even heavier tribute.

The Fall of Israel

Seven years after Israel's disastrous defeat to Judah and Assyria, Tiglath-pileser III died (in 727 B.C.) and Shalmaneser V came to the throne. Israel's King Hoshea used this as an opportunity to stop paying tribute. It was a fatal choice. The conquest of the northern kingdom of Israel and destruction of its capital Samaria by Assyrian siege from 725–722 was the result of this rebellion. Sargon II came to the throne of Assyria in the same year, and there is some question as to whether Samaria was captured by Shalmaneser V or Sargon II as he claimed in later inscriptions. In any case, Israel ceased to exist as a nation and a large influx of war refugees joined their relatives in Judah.

The Fall of Judah

In 705 Sargon II died and Sennacherib came to the throne. Judah's king Hezekiah used this as an opportunity to stop paying tribute, and triggered the resulting invasion of Jerusalem in 701. Sennacherib mentions taking forty-six strong and walled cities and 200,150 people into captivity.[2] Sennacherib sent his general to Jerusalem to demand surrender (Isa. 36:1–22). At the same time a combined army from Egypt and Ethiopia came against the Assyrian forces (Isa. 37:9–13). Sennacherib split his army leaving some at Jerusalem to maintain the siege while the rest traveled south to near Eltekeh (allotted to the tribe of Dan in the Sorek Valley) to battle the army coming from Egypt.

Although he boasted of a great victory against the Egyptian/Ethiopian army and claimed to have "personally captured alive the Egyptian charioteers with their princes and also the charioteers of the king of Ethiopia,"[3] his victory was less than total. Sennacherib made no mention of spoils, other than the capture of chariots. The Bible reports the miraculous defeat of the Assyrian army and the loss of 185,000 troops to the angel of the Lord (2 Kings 19:35). This miracle is not mentioned in the Assyrian document (the Prism of Sennacherib, or sometimes called the "Taylor Prism"), which records the other events from this invasion. Instead, in the midst of recording the destruction of numerous nations that opposed him, all Sennacherib says of Hezekiah and Jerusalem is "a prisoner in Jerusalem, his royal residence, like a bird in a cage."4

Impact of Assyrian Rule

The major development during the period of Assyrian domination, which ruled the Jewish people into the time of Christ, was the Assyrian policy of forced intermingling of the nations that they defeated. This intermingling was intended to cause racial, political, and religious dilution of national loyalties and eventual assimilation into the Assyrian nation. Through the removal of all known native leaders and their families, and the introduction of nonnative refugees, the stage was set in the northern kingdom of Israel for the intermingling of races (2 Kings 17:24–41) which would result in the Samaritan people with their deviations from traditional Judaism (John 4).

Assyria continued to dominate the land of the Bible until the last quarter of the seventh century B.C., while at times sharing the stage with the corresponding Egyptian dynasties. During this time, the second great world power for the period of the prophets arose. With the death of the last great Assyrian king Ashurbanipal in 627 the Babylonians moved to assert their independence. Nabopolassar (626–605) defeated the Assyrian army and took control of the city of Babylon and the whole southern region of the former Assyrian empire.

Following the defeat of Egypt in the second battle of Carchemish (605 B.C.), Judah came under the domination of Babylon in fulfillment of Isaiah's prophecy (Isaiah 39:1–8). At this time the first deportation of Jews under Nebuchadnezzar (605–562) to Babylon occurred, including Daniel and the three Hebrew youths (Daniel 1:1–6). The second wave of deportation took place in 597, when Jehoiachin (598–597) rebelled and led to his family's deportation (2 Kings 24:6–16).

Finally, Mattaniah/Zedekiah came to the throne (597–586), rebelled against Nebuchadnezzar against Jeremiah's advice, and joined Egypt (Jeremiah 37:5–8) in an attempt to defeat Babylon. This time

Nebuchadnezzar came and besieged Jerusalem for nearly two years (2 Kings 25:1–21) ultimately destroying Solomon's temple, the palace, and the whole city of Jerusalem. This final deportation and destruction of the temple city led to seventy years of desolation and captivity (Jer. 25:11–12; 29:10–14) and nearly one hundred fifty years that the city walls of Jerusalem would lie in ruins (Neh. 2:11–6:16, about 444 B.C.). The time of the exilic prophets was now begun.

Impact of Persian Rule

During the period of the Babylonian captivity, the Judaism of the New Testament began to take form. At least three major developments from the period of Babylonian domination greatly influenced Judaism through to the time of Christ. First was their policy of forced expatriation of defeated peoples, contrary to the intermingling policy of the Assyrians. This deportation of many of the brightest and most powerful from their homelands was to have rendered their home countries leaderless and less likely to rebel, while at the same time adding to the talent pool of Babylon the "best and brightest" of all other countries (Daniel 1:3–4). This began what would later develop into the *diaspora* of Jewish peoples into many nations (see Acts 2:5-11 for the first-century result).

The second lasting impact was because of the destruction of the temple. Sacrifices and offerings could no longer be made. Jewish exiles needed to reorganize religiously around new gathering places and develop worship without temple sacrifice. Thus the stage was set for the development of religious "parties" and leaders outside the prescribed priestly system, and places of gathering outside the temple.

Third, the leadership in captivity reflected on the theological reason for the defeat of Yahweh at the hands of the Babylonians came to the conclusion that the prophets Isaiah and Jeremiah were correct in giving idolatry as the main cause. Thus it seems from a Jewish point of view that the Babylonian captivity was used by God to remove the idolatry from His chosen people.

The postexilic prophets wrote following the demise of Babylon and during the time of the Persian Division (539–332) which began when Cyrus II (559–530) conquered Babylon in 539 (described in Daniel 5) and ended with the Persians' defeat by Alexander the Great at Tyre.

Contrary to the intermingling policy of the Assyrians and the forced expatriation of the defeated foes of Babylon, the Persians practiced repatri-
ation. This policy was designed to foster gratitude and goodwill in those
refugees who were allowed to return to their historic lands and rebuild
their nations and religious practices under the guidance and control of
the Persians (Ezra 1–4). Due to this policy the Jews in the land became
semi-independent and the high priest was given increased civil power.
The attitude of tolerance toward the returned remnant remained until
increased rivalry over the high priest office resulted in a partial destruction of Jerusalem once again by the Persian governor.

The Persian policy resulted in the rebuilding of the temple during
the time of Darius the Great (521–486) under the combined religious
leadership of the prophets Haggai, Zechariah, and the political leadership of Zerubbabel (Ezra 5–6). This "second temple" built in 516–515
was eventually enlarged by Herod the Great (John 2:20). Artaxerxes I
(465–424) permitted the walls of Jerusalem to be rebuilt (445–444)
under the leadership of Nehemiah (Neh. 1–2). The Persian policy also allowed freedom for the establishment of the Samaritan temple on Mount
Gerizim (John 4:20). This would develop into social and religious segre-
gation between Jews and Samaritans by the time of Christ (John 4:9).

The religious freedom of dispersed Jews led to the rise of the synagogue as the local place of worship and the scribes as the interpreters of
Hebrew Scriptures. Though scribes as writers and copiers had already
been an important part of Jewish society (2 Kings 12:10; 1 Chron. 2:55)
they grew in importance to be interpreters of the Law during this period
of exile (Ezra 7:6–26; Neh. 8:1–9). Some trace the rise of the synagogue
movement to the time of the Babylonian captivity, and the seeds of this
development do trace their origins to that period. It was with the increasing latitude of the Persian Empire that this fledgling institution
could become overtly public without fear of being considered as a political threat to the government.

During the period of the Persian domination, Nehemiah completed
the rebuilding of the walls of Jerusalem and the prophet Malachi wrote
the final prophetic book of the Hebrew canon. Thus about 420 B.C. the
prophetic period, which had begun with Moses over one thousand years
earlier, was over.

FORMS OF BIBLICAL PROPHECY

One major reason for our reticence to preach from the prophets is a lack of confidence in handling prophetic material. The main form of prophetic material is the oracle. The oracle, or message, from the prophet usually takes one of two forms: messages of judgment and messages of salvation. These messages, if properly explained, resonate well with contemporary listeners.

A brief example of both forms can be easily seen in the book of Obadiah. In the first fourteen verses the prophet announces a coming day of judgment for Edom. The certainty of God's coming judgment is proclaimed in verses 2 through 4, where God says He will make her small and bring her down in spite of her arrogance and pride. Obadiah goes on to say everyone will, "be cut off from the mountain of Esau by slaughter" (v. 9 NASB). Illustrations of the completeness of the judgment are given in verse 5. The destruction will be more thorough than robbers coming into a home, or than gleaners cleaning out the remnants of a vineyard. Robbers and gleaners would each leave a little behind, but Edom's destruction will be complete. The destruction will be accomplished by individuals the Edomites believed to be their friends (v. 7). The reason for the judgment is the harm perpetrated against her brother nation Judah. In verses 10–14 the violence is spelled out as beginning with Edom's indifference as Jerusalem was attacked by others. This indifference developed into verbal gloating (v. 12) and eventually degenerated into aggressive participation in direct harm (vv. 13–14).

The hinge of this book is found in the principle of sowing and reaping stated by the prophet Obadiah. "The day of the Lord is near for all nations. As you have done, it will be done to you; your deeds will return upon your own head" (v. 15). The rest of the book is a message of God's salvation. It tells of a time when Judah will be restored even as Edom is destroyed. God's people will someday possess all of Edom's territory. The final summation is "the kingdom will be the Lord's" (v. 21).

Preaching the prophet Obadiah could employ a summary of lessons from the exposition of these twenty-one verses of judgment and salvation. God opposes the proud but gives grace to the humble remnant. Pride ultimately deceives and leads to destruction. Judgment and blessing are sure to eventually occur, but only in the Lord's timing. The prediction and fulfillment pattern of the promises of judgment on Edom in the past should serve as the model for the prediction and eventual fulfillment of the promises for the Lord's coming kingdom.

PRINCIPLES FOR INTERPRETING PROPHECY

Bible prophecy should be interpreted using the same literal, grammatical, historical rules of interpretation one would apply to the rest of the Bible. While this allows for visionary and symbolic images employed by the prophets, the symbolic writings were meant to communicate historical realities that would be understandable for the readers. When a vision or symbol is given and then interpreted, as in Daniel 2, readers should understand God's stated interpretation as it is given without additional embellishment.

Prophecy has only one true interpretation. In Deuteronomy 18 the mark of a true prophet was that what he predicted would come to pass and would be verifiable. Thus, prophecy and its interpretation must make sense in its original setting. Daniel emphatically stated that only the God of his fathers could make such things known ahead of time even as he gave Nebuchadnezzar's dream and its interpretation.

The exact interpretation and fulfillment of prophetic passages will become clearer as their time of fulfillment arrives. Of the four kingdoms described in Dan. 2:31–45 only the first one is given a clear interpretation for the original audience. The head of fine gold is Nebuchadnezzar (Dan. 2:36–38). But, Daniel's original audience would clearly have understood that three other significant kingdoms were to follow the Babylonians. The specific fulfillment of this prophetic vision became clear as the Medes and Persians, Greek, and finally Roman kingdoms succeeded one another on the biblical stage over the following five hundred years.

Prophecy often may describe events which are still future but still have significance for each generation. Past prophecies fulfilled like the specific birthplace of the Messiah (Mic. 5:2; Matt. 2:4–6) should encourage and motivate believers and provide biblical hope that all God's words will fully come to pass. God has declared His intentions, and He will bring to pass all His prophets foretold in order for the whole world to know He is truly God and be glorified (Isa. 48:3–7, 11). As we study and teach the prophets, our people should be aware of the imminence of fulfillment for the next great prophetic events of God. This should give them hope and motivate them to purity of life.

THE USE OF THE OT PROPHETS BY NT WRITERS

OT Prophecy Is Sometimes Prophetic . . .

The Old Testament prophets are referenced in a number of ways by the New Testament writers, and not always as purely prophetic. This is a difficult and debated topic and can be clearly brought into focus with one specific example. In Matthew 2:15 the escape of Joseph, Mary, and Jesus to Egypt is recorded. Matthew states this is a fulfillment of the Lord's prophecy spoken through the prophet that, "Out of Egypt I called my son." This prophecy is from Hosea 11:1. As one examines the context of Hosea the son spoken of is Israel. Even more troubling, the son of Hosea 11 is wayward (11:2), idolatrous (11:2), and insensitive to the Father's care (11:3). Because of this the son will be disciplined by being judged by Assyria. Most readers would agree that Jesus is not in view in the original context of Hosea 11. What is Matthew doing?

The way readers of Scripture normally desire to see NT writers use the OT prophets is purely prophetic. An OT passage predicts an event that is easily seen fulfilled in the New Testament. Matthew does this in 2:1–6 as he gives the quote from Micah 5:2 predicting the Lord's birthplace. Other examples would include the virgin birth (Isaiah 7:14, Luke 1:30–35), of a son whose character would be divine (Isaiah 9:6–7, Matthew 1:21–23).

. . . Sometimes Applicational

However, New Testament writers also quoted Old Testament passages for applicational use. In 1 Corinthians 10:1–11 instances from the nation of Israel's Exodus failures are given as examples and applied to the Corinthian audience in warning. This seems to be the way Matthew employs Hosea 11:1. Here the nation of Israel as God's perpetually wayward son who came out of Egypt is contrasted to Jesus as God's fully obedient Son who returned from Egypt. The contrast is intended to force the readers to consider how they plan to relate to God and His gracious dealings in their lives.

. . . Sometimes Illustrative

A third way New Testament writers utilize prophecy is as illustrations. In Matthew 2:18 the prophet Jeremiah 31:15 is quoted as being fulfilled when the infants in Bethlehem are slaughtered by Herod. The wailing and heartache displayed at the time of Israel's Babylonian exile is used by Matthew to illustrate the depth of the anguish experienced by the residents of Bethlehem.

APPLYING LESSONS FROM BIBLICAL PROPHECY

God intended His prophetic messages to be a blessing to all believers throughout all time. Though certain prophecies have been, or will someday be fulfilled at specific times, the application to contemporary readers is still very real. Believers today should receive hope from exposition to the prophets. We should have confidence knowing God's ordained outcome for all of history is sure. Prophecy provides a strong argument for the veracity of all the Scriptures. In the midst of life's uncertainty, we can trust God's Word. This is one practical aspect of preaching the prophets that cries out for application.

The prophets see the ultimate purpose of God in history as the establishment of the kingdom of God on earth. Isaiah 60 and 62 speak of the coming glory. Daniel 2:43–44 speaks of a coming kingdom which the God of heaven will set up, "which will never be destroyed, and that kingdom will not be left for another people; it will crush and put an end to all these kingdoms, but it will itself endure forever" (Daniel 2:44 NASB). The final summation of Obadiah is "the kingdom will be the Lord's" (21). God is going about doing a great work preparing for the coming kingdom. As we preach the prophets, our goal should be for believers to align their lives and our churches with the Lord's plan.

Finally, Christians should be living expectantly, believing that the Lord's kingdom is coming at any moment. This expectation should motivate believers to lives of faithfulness as they hear God's messages of judgment and messages of salvation in the prophets. The clear preaching of these messages should ring a clarion call for personal holiness in light of the soon return of the Lord.

NOTES

1. The dating of Obadiah is most commonly given as either approximately 840 B.C., or exilic in the sixth century B.C. The dating is dependent on which invasion of Judah is in view in verses 11–14. This author sees the invasion in reference to 2 Chronicles 21:16–17 and thus Obadiah is the first writing prophet.

2. James B. Pritchard, ed. *Ancient Near Eastern Texts: Relating to the Old Testament* (Princeton, N. J.: Princeton Univ. Press, 1969), 288.

3. Ibid., 287.

4. Ibid., 288.

USING BIBLICAL

HEBREW IN SERMON

PREPARATION

by
Andrew J. Schmutzer

People have Word-shaped souls, says Robert C. Roberts, distinguished professor of ethics at Baylor University.[1] The ability of Holy Scripture, then, to indict and instruct, save and salve, is a cherished truth of the church. This ministry of Scripture is evident in every biblical book and continues to animate our evangelism and teaching. Scripture is powerfully *receptor*-oriented.

Its innate power aside, the "sword" of Scripture is most effectively wielded and commissioned in the hands of those appropriately trained (Ezra 7:10; 2 Tim. 2:15). One prominent Hebrew teacher laments:

It's easy to "go with the flow," assume that Hebrew is a luxury, not an essential, and rely on the opinions of others when preaching and teaching the Old Testament. However, I challenge you to reevaluate the current trend. After all, we who preach and teach the Bible have an awesome responsibility (James 3:1). God's people look to us for insight and direction, often assuming that our education and experience give us the credibility and competence needed for the task . . . One cannot preach credibly and competently from the Old Testament without a working knowledge of Hebrew and basic exegetical skills.[2]

This discussion, then, is not a "recast" of exegetical lectures you may have heard; it's more like a "fireside chat" containing encouragement to persevere, key points to cultivate, core values to hold, warnings to heed, and some recommendations to adopt. In fact, I am not even defending the need for Hebrew exegesis and an understanding of biblical languages—although renowned preacher Charles H. Spurgeon has declared that "a man to comment well should be able to read the Bible in the original."[3]

The following discussion will assume the need of the Hebrew interpretative craft and a substantive knowledge of biblical Hebrew. The skill of preaching the "older testament" presumes a working knowledge of Hebrew grammar, lexical semantics, textual criticism, syntax, Old Testament (OT) genres, and discourse analysis. The "how-to" and "why-we-should" manuals of OT interpretation and preaching are available and plentiful enough.[4]

By addressing some particulars of what lies before the preacher of OT Hebrew texts (e.g., stories, ancient culture) and some pointers (positive and negative), we wish to point the preacher toward a lifetime of Hebrew learning and communication. Unfortunately, hard training in biblical languages has fallen on hard times. Think about it; just as surgeons undergo years of intense training and then enter medical practice where they must hone existing skills and learn new ones, so it is in the study and use of biblical Hebrew. Like the surgeon, the preacher's use of biblical languages requires a lifetime of development and refinement. The work isn't over when language training is; next comes methodological maturity and practice. Although the combined difficulties of church culture and personal effort might make Hebrew seem hardly worth it, in the end the better OT preachers are ongoing students of the Hebrew language. The goal is proficiency, not perfection.

THE HEBREW TEXT: HOW DID THE AUTHOR DO THAT?

In an effort to explain and illustrate the use of Hebrew in the preacher's craft, a reminder of some Hebrew linguistic "building blocks" is helpful. Straddling the technicality of exegesis (which is *not* heard or seen) and the performance of preaching (which *is* heard and seen) is the skill of sympathetic "engagement" with the text, or the text as it can be *re*-presented to others. Thus both the preacher and the audience encounter the text. As the preacher deciphers the "anatomy" of the OT discourse (i.e., "building blocks"), he gains an understanding of the biblical author's techniques. Through awareness of Hebrew grammar, literary genre, historical context, and so forth, the discourse is laid bare. So the craft of preaching includes a study of the following:

- an important Hebrew word (e.g., *nasah*, "to test")
- a literary genre (e.g., disputation)
- a theological theme (e.g., retribution)
- a particular clause (e.g., syntax)
- a rhetorical technique (e.g., flashback)
- a cultural practice (e.g., betrothal)
- or an historical period (e.g., Persian/Hellenistic)

This gives the preacher a well-stocked "toolbox," and he is prepared to address what any given passage may require.[5]

The Need for a Multivalent "Toolbox"

If the preacher is going to interact with the text, he must be ready to go where the text goes. The meaning of a passage is best gathered from the combined strength of a multivalent method rather than from one or two approaches (such as discourse analysis) pursued in isolation from others. Behind an emphasis on a text-dominant approach lie two core presuppositions: 1) the genetics of (Hebrew) language are determinative and accessible, and 2) the role of literary context is vital and discernable. So while language enables meaning, context enacts it; language is largely conventional, while context is amazingly dynamic in its interaction with its world. Adele Berlin asserts that we must first know *how* a text means before we can know *what* it means.[6] In other words, form communicates content. As the oral is celebrated in the written, so the linguistic dynamic is preserved in the recital of the liturgical community.

Additionally, the relationship of language to context further illustrates the role of genre, forming a "contract" between the author and his audience. Context forms the historical horizon for receiving the language; yet the particular socioreligious context may be difficult for modern interpreters to reconstruct.

AN EXAMPLE FROM JONAH 2

As one example of the difficulties of socio-religious context, consider Jonah 2. This is a difficult passage to preach. Its genre is "declarative thanksgiving," and practically every line can be found somewhere else in the psalter. Shifting from narrative to poetry, the story line of the book of Jonah modulates to expressive language. Poetry *replays* events in a different key, just as the Song of Miriam (Exodus 15) rises out of the deliverance of Moses (Exodus 14).

Three paragraphs, called stanzas in poetry (vv. 2b–4, 5–7, 8–9), are framed by narrative (2:1–2a, 10). In these three stanzas are four key motifs of thanksgiving psalms: 1) statements of unanswered prayer; 2) personal crisis; 3) divine rescue; and 4) a vow of praise.

What poses the most difficulty for preachers is the figurative language of Jonah's prayer, not the least because the prayer cuts into a chronological sequence of events that is typically more suited to our thinking and preaching. In chapter 2, Jonah describes his drowning in theological terms. The great fish is God's deliverance, not punishment (another common misconception)—thus the Thanksgiving Psalm. The summary in verse 2 gives way to a report using water imagery in verse 3, which will switch to "land" (v. 6). Notice that it is God who "hurled me into the deep" (v. 3). Issues of marine biology (the fish) and instrumental causes (the sailors) are hardly the point! When Jonah claims to be "Banished from your sight," a theological shoe drops—*he views himself as exiled from God!* (cf. Ps. 31:22). Whether literal or not, "your holy temple" stands for the presence of God in his prayer. Both the first and second stanzas close with this key phrase (cf. vv. 4,7).

The desperation of his plight is resumed in water imagery that almost extinguishes his life (v. 5). The imagery of severity serves to amplify God's deliverance. His "exile-journey" ends when he finally arrives at "the roots of the mountains" (v. 6). An understanding of ancient Near Eastern cosmology of the underworld is necessary to understand this prayer. Further, "Sheol" and "the pit" (vv. 2, 6 NASB) are not hell or death. Because of Jonah's three-day journey into the heart of earth (1:17), early Christianity capitalized on the symbolic parallel to Jesus' death, entombment, and resurrection. But that should not be "downloaded" into the story, especially before one has grasped the essence of Jonah's prayer!

At the point of utter despair, his plea came to God's "temple" (v. 7). The theological center of Jonah's prayer comes in verse 8 with his unsettling distinction between those who appeal to "worthless idols" and his own access to the real God. The Hebrew *hesed* (v. 8b meaning "loyalty" and translated "faithfulness" in NASB) would require a word study. The prayer closes with his vows to sacrifice to God, a required step in Israelite faith when God delivers someone. There is great irony in Jonah's (future) promise to make sacrifices, when in fact the "pagan" sailors have already completed (just recently!) their vows and sacrifices (cf. v. 16).

Now we can appreciate the literary organization of this chapter, the rhetorical "spine" holding Jonah's prayer together. Observe the following chiasm:[7]

A	"to your holy temple" (v. 4)	
	B	"life" (v. 5)
		C "I went down" (v. 6)
		X "pit/sheol" (v. 6; cf. v. 2)
		C' "you brought up" (v. 6)
	B'	"life" (v. 6)
A'	"into your holy temple" (v. 7)	

This chiasm shows the *inclusion* of "temple" (A, A') that envelopes the chiasm. Jonah's *descent* (C) in spiritual banishment is brilliantly countered by his *ascent* (C') in standard pilgrimage language, now in return movement to the "temple." Brought to the brink of destruction, Jonah's "life" (B, B') has been rescued by God—there is a "syntax of the discourse." The first-person report of his "sinking" (= "I went down") is also overturned through the active voice (= "you brought up") in second-person address. The threat of death in the "pit" (x) has been averted. This verbal centerpiece all occurs in the same verse! Review the various strategies we've noted in this discourse, comparing them to the chiasm chart above. This is how the author chose to communicate his message. This type of interpretation takes hard work and sympathetic reading.

Ironies remain. Jonah does not immediately set out for Nineveh; nor, in fact, do we ever hear a "confession." Preachers can affirm the difficult mysteries of contemporary life by acknowledging the mysteries in the biblical text. Practically, this chapter holds some great truths of God and insights into biblical literature that people need to hear. Literarily, through this poetic aside of chapter 2, we can enter more fully into the experience and attitudes of Jonah. Historically, Amos and Hosea are his contemporaries. Jonah did not want to extend "grace" (cf. 3:8–9; 4:2) to the mighty Assyrian empire, and, in turn, be party to the very nation instrumental in Israel's demise. Theologically, Jonah was all about the justice of God, but struggled with grace. Today, our struggle is the reverse.

Yet, if *Veggie Tales* can "juice" this story for children, preachers can help adults take the plunge into this rich text, and the brutal ironies surrounding Jonah's character and our own antics with God.

When was the last time you heard Jonah 2 preached well?

PRIVILEGE AND RESPONSIBILITY

To effectively use biblical Hebrew, it's important to keep in mind the exegesis you've been trained to do and the informed preaching the audience is entitled to receive. In other words, with a working knowledge of biblical Hebrew, the preacher is responsible for *both* the "map" (i.e., biblical text) and the "ocean" (i.e., culturally informed communication). Using this seaworthy metaphor, let's consider the preacher's privilege and responsibility.

The Hebrew text has its own personality, a unique profile of characteristics that are the preacher's joy to engage. That's not to say these elements are easily expressed, or always sound politically correct, but that's a different issue. Here's what biblical Hebrew delivers—some of its characteristics and thoughts on preaching them.

Riveting Stories

From the gut-wrenching drama of Abraham's sacrifice (Gen. 22) to the seductive power plays of David (2 Sam. 11) and the fiery dispute between Amos and Amaziah (Amos 7:10–17), there is a drama to engage the imagination and reenact—for good or ill—every experience of modern life. These are "paradigm" stories, stories in which we do not lose ourselves; we come home.

The Old Testament worldview took story form. In a way, the Old Testament *shows* us what the New Testament *tells* us. The transcendent theological message is there if we have the humility to see the best and worst of ourselves replayed through the protagonists of these stories. While postmodernism may be waning, it still finds relevance within storied frameworks.[8] OT stories come alive within current narrative modes of thought. Standard elements of plot, characterization, tension, resolution, etc., have been resuscitated in a modern culture that sharpens its moral compass on *The Lord of the Rings* and its instructive mythology. Preachers must capture and relate the passion and drama of OT stories.

Vivid Imagery

The Old Testament is hardly "G-Rated" (Num. 25:1–9). Frankly, its violence is, at times, unbearable (Judg. 19). But imagery not only animates sin, imagery also helps to explain the depth of married love (Prov. 5:15–23) and the pathos of a call to repentance (Isa. 1:18). Its vibrancy moves the hearer to ethical action, social empathy, and spiritual loyalty to God that extends beyond cognitive "belief" (see "Frequent Figures" in chapter 11). Preachers should communicate these texts in a way that vividly shows how sin destroys relationships, confession cleanses, and joy rejuvenates. Rahab's faith was stunning before the New Testament ever extolled it (Josh. 6:25; cf. Heb. 11:31; James 2:25).

"Strange" Cultures

No Hebrew text is written in a theological vacuum. The text is culturally "situated," just like the hearers (or readers) themselves. So, neither full objective "understanding" of the biblical cultural context nor the "overstanding" of imposed preconceptions is appropriate. The preacher should model a "hermeneutic of humility" where God's theocentric values and teaching help define people's particular and temporal viewpoints. From the outset, the books note their own cultural distinctions (Genesis 29:26; 43:32). When the preacher models this, the people can accentuate the ongoing redemptive mission of God, by placing food laws (Lev. 17:10–16), purification rites (Lev. 14), and religious rituals (Lev. 16) in their rightful place within the divine theodrama.

Dramatic Perspectives

Dramatic perspective is the precise angle at which the narrator positions the "movie lens" for dramatic effect. Here the narrator is *showing* the reader rather than telling. One key character can capture a specific view of the action. The Hebrew word *hineh* ("behold!") is often used with verbs of "perception."[9] As the narrator has exploited a particular viewpoint, so too, the preacher should alert people to this pulsating drama in the text, highlighting the words: "And when morning came, *Look!* It was Leah!" (Gen. 29:25); "And he said to them, *Listen* to this dream I had. *Look!* We were fastening sheaves . . . and, *Look!* My sheaf arose . . . and *Look!* Your sheaves . . ." (Gen. 37:6–7).[10]

The first example (29:25) reflects Jacob's shock. Circumstances have indeed come full circle as the deceiver is deceived! Like Isaac, Jacob was plied with food and wine (cf. 27:25), deprived of sight in the darkness (cf. 27:1), baffled by clothing (cf. 27:15), and left with misleading touch (cf. 27:23). In the second example, a self-absorbed Joseph says "Look!" *three* times. Demanding an audience of the half brothers he's just tattled on fuels the fire (cf. 37:2–4). Confirming our suspicions, the narrator notes that the brothers hated Joseph before *and after* his dreams (cf. 37:8). Of course, then checking up on the "gang of ten" wearing his garment of royalty (!) confirms his insensitivity, and is the final straw for the slighted brothers (cf. 37:23–28). The irony could not be thicker, and, like tour guides, preachers should point out these key sights or words to people.

Explosive Dialogue

When interpreting dialogue in Old Testament texts, the significance lies not just in *what* is said, but *who* is speaking and the *nature* of their exchange.[11] Dialogue joins together the triad of author, text, and reader.

Hebrew dialogue is essentially an irreducible community of two and offers a "complementary vision" of meaning by grafting together two social elements. The preacher must learn to "listen" to the interchange for the timeless moral thrust of the discourse. Studying dialogue then, is taking people seriously, not just "concepts." Propositional literature, such as the didactic epistles, has created impatient Old Testament readers. But dialogue reminds us that we cannot collapse one person's perspective into the other or distill a theological imperative—there remains a "call" and "response" that draws us into the fray, personalizes ideas, and creates responsibility in relationship.

Hebrew dialogue is both a literary genre (e.g., Song of Solomon) and a technique of style (e.g., Job).[12] Its words do not come *at* us to be accepted or rejected; as God's revelation, the words are gifted *to* us as persuasive discourse we chew, digest, and enact. Many examples are found in prophetic literature, where the prophets as covenant preachers are calling the Israelites back to covenant fidelity (e.g., Jer. 15:10–21; 14:11–15:3; Micah 4–5; Isa. 3:6–7). The significance may lie, for example, in the fact that the prophet quotes the words of his audience *precisely to refute them* (Ezek. 12:22–23). The preacher must be attentive to the stylistic "road signs" to discover how an author has structured the text. When dialogue is *lacking*, as in a question unanswered, there is typically a key theological point being made. The prophets often dramatize the silence from idols/false gods, mocking their "nothingness" (cf. 1 Kings 18:26–28). In haughty protest, Jonah refuses to answer God's question about his anger, abandoning the city instead (Jon. 4:4–5; cf. v. 9).[13]

A REPRESENTATIONAL STORY

The combined weight of these several literary characteristics is a *representational story*. This is sobering for the preacher. It is the *representational* nature of Hebrew texts that have a unique capability of drawing the hearer (and reader) into a transformational dialogue in ways that transcend propositionally phrased truth claims.[14] The *story* humanizes a medium, making it accessible to us all. Trained to listen to the "map" (or Hebrew text) for direction, the preacher then charts the best course to take in the "ocean" (or contemporary culture) to communicate particular *significances* of that text.

The task of the preacher, then, is to wed the horizons of the map and ocean, leading the people of God into a participatory understanding of the redemptive theodrama.[15] Such preaching helps believers think biblically and live Christianly.

TIPS FOR USING HEBREW

Using biblical Hebrew in preaching is a skill one develops. Language class teaches the key questions to ask in exegesis (i.e., the "map") but using Hebrew is the journey of navigating in the "ocean" of contemporary culture. Read a few quality journals and commentators who exemplify the exegetical skill and the pastoral craft of communicating to the people of God.

Preach Large Portions

Preach larger rather than smaller portions. In so doing, the "relevant" topics will inevitably be covered, but they will be done so in a way that situates them in the larger theodrama of God's Word. Larger portions reflect the large characters themselves that live in the text. A given discourse can be broken down further into thematic units preached at a later time addressing different contemporary concerns. Detailed analysis promotes detailed ability in application.

Look for and Declare the Big Picture

Help your listeners see the "big picture." The goal is to help people understand how any given text flows from what preceded and contributes to what follows in God's redemptive plan. Far and away this is one of the greatest needs in the church today. We have particularized our sermons completely out of any historical context. What enables us to preach texts connecting one to the other is biblical theology. Biblical theology forms the ligaments that make all of Scripture cohere, so that Jesus' temptation (Matthew 4) is clearly seen to flow out of Israel's historical testing in another wilderness. Every year a pastor should be reading through a significant biblical theology text as a part of their regimen of study.

Prepare Fully

As you work with the Hebrew text, consult multiple translations. There are more than fifty translations in the English language. The vast majority of translations are the product of enormous skill and theological insight, increasingly of a literary nature. Translations can be compared to cars—each gives you a different feel for the road. Use them in your own exegetical work.

One of the greatest advantages in referring to biblical Hebrew in study is that it slows us down. Our problem is not that we preach too little. Rather, we preach too much without adequate passion or preparation. Analyzing the passage in the original language enables the preacher to be saturated with the text and dialogue with its message. What people hear in the sermon is the distilled impact of a story that has already washed over the heart and mind of the preacher. It is essential that those who feed the sheep must themselves drink at deep wells. Feeding deeply includes deeply facing one's own needs.

The point is not necessarily more study. Rather, take all necessary measures to more intimately acquaint yourself as the vessel of God's message.[16] Embrace your gifts; face your fears; exalt the work and person of Christ even as you face your humanity in all its brokenness.

With an eye to Hebrew discourse and bridging the "map" and "ocean," we can illustrate some particular observations using Genesis 39.[17] The next page displays a visual diagram of Genesis 39. (All Hebrew translations are the author's.) In contrast, the following "Written Notes on Genesis 39" will walk the reader through the entire discourse in its context, using the *New Living Translation*. The NLT is a common version in churches today, and it illustrates how various translations can aid one's reflection and presentation. At the outset, 39:1 functions as a *janus*, or hinge, which thematically links texts of exaltation with humiliation (37:2–36). *Theological narration* (exaltation over Potiphar's house, vv. 2, 6) alternates with *phenomenological narration* (incarcerated in prison, vv. 7–20), returning again to *theological narration* (exalted over the prison warden's house, vv. 21–23).

THE DISCOURSE STRUCTURE OF GENESIS 39

I. INTRODUCTORY NARRATIVE FRAME (39:1–6) [=SETTING]

> ** Narrative Description*
> - ⮥ **LORD's Presence:** "the LORD was with Joseph" (2, 3)
> - ⮥ **Location:** "in the house" (2)
> - ⮥ **LORD's Blessing:** "[LORD] gave him success . . . he did (3b)
> - ⮥ **LORD's Support:** "found favor in his eyes" (4a)
> - ⮥ **Made Overseer:** "Potiphar put him in charge" (4)
> - ⮥ **Comprehensive Duty:** "all that he owned" (5a)
> - ⮥ **Complete Delegation:** "he [Potiphar] did not concern himself with anything" (6b)

II. TEMPTATION & AFTERMATH (39:7–19) [=CLIMAX]

> ** Narrative With Contrastive Dialogue*
> - ❖ Narrator—(6c)
> - ❖ *Dialogue*—"wife" > Joseph (7; 8–10)
> - ❖ Narrator—(11–12a)
> - ❖ *Dialogue*—"wife" > [Joseph's reaction] (12b–13)
> - ❖ Narrator—(14a)
> - ❖ *Dialogue*—"wife" > "his master" (17b–18)
> - ❖ Narrator—(16–17a)
> - ❖ *Dialogue*—"wife" > "his master" (17b–18)
> - ❖ Narrator—(report of dialogue, 19)

III. CLOSING NARRATIVE FRAME (39:20–23) [=OUTCOME]

> ** Narrative Description*
> - ⮥ **LORD's Presence:** "the LORD was with him" (21, 23)
> - ⮥ **Location:** "in the prison-house" (20b)
> - ⮥ **LORD's Blessing:** "[LORD] gave him success . . . he did (23b)
>   - ○ LORD . . . showed him mercy [21a, a new element]
> - ⮥ **LORD's Support:** "granted him favor in his eyes" (21b)
> - ⮥ **Made Overseer:** "warden put Joseph in charge" (22a)
> - ⮥ **Comprehensive Duty:** "all that was done there" (22b)
> - ⮥ **Complete Delegation:** "the warden paid no attention to anything under Joseph's care" (23a)

RESUMPTION

WRITTEN NOTES ON GENESIS 39

39:1–47:31 The narrative arrangement balances Joseph's three employments (Potiphar, 39:1–20; prison, 39:21–40:23; palace, 41:1–57) with his family's three trips (42:1–38; 43:1–45:28; 46:1–47:31). Joseph begins as a slave assistant and ends as Pharaoh's viceroy; he encounters ten bowing brothers on their first trip and ends their third by reuniting with Jacob and his still-bowing family.

39:1–23 Joseph serves in Potiphar's house. Joseph's integrity is contrasted with Judah's moral failure (ch. 38). The story's opening and closing (38:1–6; 20–23) frame the temptation scene (38:7–19). The narrator highlights Joseph's connection with the patriarchs by using the covenant name *Lord* seven times in chapter 39. By about age eighteen, Joseph's bio includes a father's favoritism (37:3), his brothers' hatred (37:8) and betrayal (37:27–28), and a slave's life as chattel (37:36; 39:1).

39:1–6 The narrative opening highlights the Potiphar-Joseph relationship: *Potiphar* (see 37:36); the Hebrew only mentions his name here, stressing the slave-master relationship elsewhere. *LORD was with Joseph*: the crucial theme of chapter 39 is stated four times by the narrator but has to be discovered by the characters (39:2, 3, 21, 23; see Acts 7:9). The Lord's presence (39:2, 3; see 21, 23), blessing (39:2; see 23), and support (39:4; see 21) enable Joseph's oversight (39:4; see 22), tasks (39:5; see 22), and delegation (39:6; see 23). *Master*, a term that is used seven times to emphasize Joseph's social accountability. *Put in charge* (literally, *in his hand*) is an idiom soon to be enacted (see 12b). *LORD began to bless*. God applies Abraham's blessing (12:3) to the property of Potiphar (see 30:27–30). *Kind of food to eat!* There were ritual food laws and ethnic separation during meals between Hebrews and Egyptians (see 43:32; 46:34). *Very handsome . . . well-built*. A similar phrase is used of Rachel's beauty (29:17; see 1 Sam. 16:12).

39:7–9 The scene shifts to Joseph and Potiphar's wife, who is known by her actions rather than by name: *Look . . . my master trusts*. Joseph first emphasizes practical stewardship (8–9a), then spiritual relationship (9b). For Joseph, her outrageous proposition is foremost a breach of responsibility to his master. Our integrity in sexual matters depends on the strength of our nonsexual relationships. Biblical sexuality is tied to the entire web of human relationships. *How could I . . . sin against God* [?] Ultimately Joseph's management is watched over by God. Joseph's horizontal relationships were guided by an acute vertical consciousness of a God that neither Judah nor his other brothers (chapters 37–38) have even mentioned.

39:10–12 *Day after day* acknowledges that this is a daily proposition (39:10), tied to employment (39:10), in the midst of racial tension (39:1, 14, 17), to a slave with no rights (39:1, 19), for a young man with a horrific past. This is an astounding scenario. *Grabbed him by his cloak.* Words become actions as his *running* counters her *grabbing*. Integrity does not depend on our circumstances but on a righteous character that sees beyond them. *Left . . . in her hand:* It will weigh against the master's trust *in his hand* (see 39:4). This is the second garment Joseph has lost; it also will be used as deceptive evidence that will land him in another prison, harsher than the first (see 37:23, 24, 32).

39:13–19 *Hebrew slave . . . make fools of us.* She deputizes slaves as witnesses, appealing to their Egyptian solidarity (*us*), though *no one else was around* (39:11). *Hebrew* is an insulting term among Egyptians (see 39:1). *But I screamed.* Actually, Joseph fled and then she screamed (see 39:14, 18). *Behind with me.* Saying *in my hand* would have incriminated her! *Kept the cloak with her.* The master is given an illustrated story. A garment was also used by Tamar (chap. 38) with a different son of Jacob. In both stories, a woman entices the main character, keeps personal tokens as condemning evidence, and an innocent party is falsely accused (see 37:31–33). *Tried to come in and fool around.* Joseph must be cast as the perpetrator.

39:20–23 In the closing frame (see 39:16) with Joseph and the chief jailor, God's presence with Joseph is reaffirmed (39:21, 23, see 2, 3). *Into the prison.* Joseph has gone from estate house to prison house; he will now rise to *assistant* again (see 37:2; 39:4, 9a). *King's prisoners:* This anticipates the cup bearer and the baker (see 40:1). The LORD . . . *showed him his faithful love* (literally, *granted . . . covenant kindness . . . favor;* see Exod. 3:21). Everything is restored (see 39:1–6) through God's *covenant kindness* (*hesed,* see 32:10) as Joseph is delivered from his adversaries. Joseph's reward for faithfulness is God's continued presence (see James 1:3–4; 1 Peter 2:19–21), which does not guarantee the absence of temptation. God's blessing is the privilege of those who guard their steps with Him.

FINAL CAUTIONS

Keep "Hebrew speak" to a minimum. Avoid the temptation to pepper your sermons with Hebrew words and phrases. There is a time and place for the essential term to be used, but as a rule, people need to understand what they've read in English. Adding another layer of Hebrew terms rarely clarifies or advances the message being developed. Better to spend your energy in the creative presentation of biblical truths than to recite to all what was learned in your personal study. Those in your audience who know the biblical languages are able to recognize when your exegetical homework has been done.

Don't abuse or ignore language software. It is almost impossible to underestimate the contribution of biblical software to scholars and pastors alike. But a "loaded" laptop does not a preacher make. Remember that all biblical data one gathers with these marvelous tools still needs to be interpreted, prioritized, and, if necessary, relayed to the people of God. Preaching has far more to do with suffering and relationships than parsing capabilities and gigabytes. Thank God for these technological tools, but remember that proficiency in the language can never be limited to software.

Don't preach the silences or problems of the text. Many texts have problems. However, there is always the danger of creating an imaginary world from tantalizing silences in the text; be it Moses' years in Egypt or Paul's in Arabia. People are naturally inclined to search out such holes in the narrative but speculation about these 'silent years' will ultimately distract from the Word that has been revealed to us. *good*

When Paul wrote, "All Scripture is inspired" (2 Tim. 3:16), he had in mind the "older" testament. In another place, Paul exhorted Timothy based on the Scriptures he heard at his grandmother's knee. The truth is that two-thirds of the Bible is comprised of the older testament. At least 20 percent of the New Testament is quotation of the Old. In other words, by the time we reach the New Testament, those biblical writers are assuming we know the Old. Thus, pastors should regularly preach from the Old Testament books that reveal the mission and mind of God.

NOTES

1. Robert C. Roberts, *Taking the Word to Heart* (Grand Rapids: Eerdmans, 1993), 293.

2. Robert B. Chisholm Jr., "Credibility, Competence, and Confidence: Why You Need to Buck the Trend," in *From Exegesis to Exposition: A Practical Guide to Using Biblical Hebrew* (Grand Rapids: Baker, 1998), 10–11.

3. As quoted by Thomas Lyon, "A Plea for the Study of the Scriptures in the Original Languages," *Banner of Truth* 474 (2003), 4.

4. Helpful sources on exegesis and preaching could include: Elizabeth Achtemeier, *Preaching Hard Texts of the Old Testament* (Hendrickson); John Barton, *Reading the Old Testament: Method in Biblical Study* (Westminster); Craig C. Broyles, ed., *Interpreting the Old Testament: A Guide for Exegesis* (Baker); Robert B. Chisholm Jr., *From Exegesis to Exposition: A Practical Guide to Using Biblical Hebrew* (Baker); Stanley Greidnaus, *The Modern Preacher and the Ancient Text* (Eerdmans/InterVarsity); David M. Howard Jr. and Michael A. Grisanti, eds., *Giving the Sense: Understanding and Using Old Testament Historical Texts* (Kregel); Tremper Longmann, III, *Making Sense of the Old Testament* (Baker); David Parker, *Using Biblical Hebrew in Ministry* (UPA); D.B. Sandy and R. L. Giese, *Cracking Old Testament Codes* (Broadman and Holman); Douglas Stuart, *Old Testament Exegesis*, 3rd ed. (Westminster John Knox); Willem A. VanGemeren, ed., *A Guide to Old Testament Theology and Exegesis* (Zondervan); Hans W. Wolff, *Old Testament and Christian Preaching* (Fortress).

5. It goes without saying, "If all the preacher has is a 'hammer,' then every text will look strangely like a 'nail.'" I think most people have had enough exposure to this "pet theology" approach to readily see the value in having numerous interpretative tools in their toolbox. So neither the arid wind of intellectualism nor the literalism of naïve fundamentalism will do. The need for hermeneutical sensitivity in biblical preaching ministry has been missed by both extremes.

6. Adele Berlin, *Poetics and Interpretation of Biblical Narrative*, Bible and Literature Series 9 (Sheffield: Almond, 1983), 15. Written for the interpretation of narrative, the point holds equally true for poetic literature.

7. Author translation; cf. English Standard Version.

8. For an insightful overview of postmodernism's interface with the biblical text, see C. G. Bartholomew, "Postmodernity and Biblical Interpretation," in *Dictionary for Theological Interpretation of the Bible*, ed. Kevin J. Vanhoozer (Grand Rapids: Baker, 2005), 600–607. For an in-depth analysis, which pastors should also engage, see G. Hyman, *The Predicament of Postmodern Theology: Radical Orthodoxy or Nihilist Textualism* (Louisville: Westminster John Knox, 2001).

9. See *Introduction to Biblical Hebrew Syntax* (*IBHS*) §37.6d; Joüon-Muraoka (J.-M.) §167 *l*, noting that it "is used especially to attract attention" (cf. §105 d). The

exact emphasis *hineh* contributes is based on the context. God's seventh and climactic evaluation (Gen 1:31) follows the creation of humankind where we read: "and look! It was exceedingly good." Here, we do not witness divine "surprise," instead, the *hineh* particle (with *waw*) "draws attention to the marvelous" (M. Futato, *Beginning Biblical Hebrew* [Winona Lake, Ind.: Eisenbrauns, 2003], 190).

10. Author's translation. Style editors tend to exclude such translations of the Hebrew text because they're too "awkward." However, in these exegetically based discussions, I do not assume any one translation. Instead we're going "behind the curtain."

11. Susan M. Felch, "Dialogism," *DTIB*, 174. Her observations (173–75) are reflected throughout our discussion.

12. Alonso Schökel, *A Manual of Hebrew Poetics* (Rome: Pontificio Istituto Biblico, 1988), 170.

13. For other examples of powerful dialogue, see Isa. 28:7–13; 37:21–29; 51:9–52:6; Jer. 3:14–4:4; Zech. 1–6; and Malachi. A significant subcategory is *interior dialogue*. Here a character breaks into an interchange with a reflection directed to themselves, creating a "doubling" of an individual (cf. Deut. 32:19–20, 26–27; Pss. 42–43; 73:16–18). It is a stunning technique when used in narrative as well (cf. Gen. 20:11–13). Used in the psalms, this technique can expose interior struggles concerning the presence and absence of God.

14. Thorsten Moritz, "Critical Realism," *DTIB*, 149.

15. See especially Kevin J. Vanhoozer, *The Drama of Doctrine* (Louisville: Westminster John Knox, 2005).

16. A meaningful and substantive resource for spiritual input of pastors is D. A. Carson, *For the Love of God: A Daily Companion for Discovering the Riches of God's Word.* 2 vol. (Wheaton, Ill.: Crossway, 1999).

17. Genesis 39 is an easy text to preach poorly. Rather than using it as an illustration of Paul's injunction to "flee youthful lust" (2 Tim. 2:22), it is well worth the effort to uncover its rich truths that go far beyond the "sexual purity" talk.

good

Fourteen

THE USE AND

ABUSE OF GREEK

IN PREACHING

by
Gerald W. Peterman

Life-giving preaching engages the Word of God firsthand. Good preaching from the English text and good preaching from the Greek text are as different as instant and brewed coffee. Both are enjoyable; but one really sings. Preaching from the Greek text is like reading the New Testament in color; without, it is black and white.[1]

If you desire to use the Greek effectively for preparing sermons, you need to be in Greek systematically, using a scheduled reading program that allows you to read the Greek New Testament on a regular basis.[2] Assuming you already have one or two years of Greek from Bible college or seminary, the most important next step you can take is to make a habit of reading a small portion of Greek daily. Remember, an athlete trains daily but competes occasionally. In the same manner, a preacher must read daily and put the knowledge gained into practice, that is, preach or teach, occasionally (e.g., weekly, biweekly, or monthly).

TOOLS AND PRACTICES

One way to begin to read from the Greek text on a daily basis is to select a book. Choose a book appropriate to your level of ability. For example, the Greek of First John or John's gospel suits the beginner rather than engaging the more difficult Greek of Matthew, Romans, or the especially challenging Hebrews. It is critical to set aside an uninterrupted block of time. Of course more time is better, but, as A. T. Robertson concludes, "It requires only a half hour a day and the determination to stick to it steadily, and one will win out and be glad of it all his life. So will his hearers."[3] The important thing is to commit to consistent daily study, not to a set number of minutes or verses. Even one or two verses a day will yield fruit over time.

Tools especially designed for reading the Greek New Testament are a great help, such as Sakae Kubo's *Reader's Greek-English Lexicon of the New Testament* (Zondervan) or *A Grammatical Analysis of the Greek New Testament* (Rome: Biblical Institute) by Max Zerwick and Mary Grosvenor. These helpful tools will minimize the need for page-turning to look up words and paradigms. In addition, they parse the more difficult or rare forms. For those who are more technically savvy, the functions of Kubo and Zerwick can also be performed by software tools like *Logos* or *BibleWorks*.[4] While there are advantages and disadvantages to both paper and electronic tools, the choice is up to you.

As you read, you will need to review or relearn the forms (endings, verb principle parts) that are unfamiliar. Very few of us can become experts in the language; constant review is a must. In addition, the function of every word in each verse must be clarified. While English usage is largely determined by word order, Greek usage is determined by morphology. Pondering the function of each word goes hand in hand with reviewing forms.

As one becomes more proficient, more verses can be read and more complex questions can be asked. Such questions include how a noun case is used, what adverbial nuance a participle has, and how subordinate clauses are related. For these kinds of questions and their answers, one can dip into Wallace's *Greek Grammar* or Brooks and Winberry's *Syntax*.[5]

The study of the Greek text may require that more tools be added to your library such as a good lexicon and an exhaustive concordance. Reading a few minutes might require dipping into one or both of these in order to explore the significance of particular words or phrases.6 Though it requires mental effort, this program is not just an intellectual exercise. By the grace of God, daily reading of the Greek New Testament can become a time of rich personal blessing, prayer, and meditation.

It can be very difficult to establish and stick to this habit of daily Greek reading. For most of us, it requires great amounts of dedication and perseverance. But there is no other way. As Robertson warned more than seventy years ago, let it not be said of us that "the chief reason why preachers do not get and do not keep up a fair and needful knowledge of the Greek New Testament is nothing less than carelessness, and even laziness in many cases. They can get along somehow without it, and so let it pass or let it drop."7

USING GREEK IN SERMON PREPARATION

Interacting with the Greek text can provide insight for preaching. This interaction occurs at four different levels: the whole document, the paragraph, the phrase, and the word.

The Whole Document

Paul's use of the second-person pronoun in his letter to Philemon shows how analyzing the use of language in an entire book can be helpful. In modern English, the pronoun "you" does duty for both the singular and the plural. That is, one can use "you" when speaking to a crowd or when speaking to an individual. King James English has the ability to distinguish between these two with its use of *thou* (singular) and *ye* (plural). But beyond the King James, it's rare that an English translation will alert the reader to a change. Of course, the Greek distinguishes between the singular and the plural of the second-person address. Knowledge of such a change gives us insight into what is happening in the text. Is Paul writing his letter to Philemon or to many readers? The answer is the apostle varies between the singular and the plural second-person pronoun, having the singular in verses 2, 4, 5 (twice), 6, 21 (three times), and 23 and the plural in verses 3, 6, 22 and 25.

The English reader has no idea that such variation occurs. Those who can read the original Greek text will realize that Paul addresses Philemon primarily in this letter—but not exclusively. As he speaks directly to the slave owner, he also speaks to the church that meets in the slave owner's home. So, is the letter to Philemon private or public? The answer is both. Paul makes Philemon's relationship with Onesimus into a church-wide affair by addressing the whole church. But, while most of the letter is addressed to the slave owner, the specific comments are not applicable to all of his hearers.

When preaching on Philemon, because Paul varies between the singular and the plural, we might emphasize that Paul considers Philemon's personal relationship with Onesimus to be church business. We might consider: What relationships in our lives might the apostle also consider to be church business?

The Paragraph

Ephesians 2:1–10 shows the importance of analyzing the entire paragraph. The paragraph's first three verses open with the accusative case (the case of direct object). But those verses go by without a main verb and without a main subject. In verse 4 we have the subject, God. Paul describes God, but he still does not provide the verb. Finally, in verse 5, we find what serves as the main verb for verses 1–5: "made . . . alive." In other words, the structure becomes: *God* (subject) in verse 4, *made alive* (verb) in verse 5, and *you/us* (object) in verses 1 to 3.

English translations do not clarify what is happening in Ephesians 2. Some (e.g., NIV, NASB, ESV) make verse 1 into a complete statement by changing Paul's participle in 2:1 (*being* dead) into a finite verb (you *were* dead). Others (e.g., KJV, NKJV) bring the subject of verse 4 and the verb of verse 5 into verse 1, putting these words in italics: "And you *hath he quickened*" (KJV). Both of these approaches are understandable, making verses 1 to 3 comprehensible in and of themselves. But both of these approaches also eliminate part of the anticipation caused by Paul's structuring of the paragraph. Paul's statements, being incomplete statements, create suspense. They look forward to and anticipate closure.

Ephesians 2 highlights for us the need to diagram a sermon from the Greek text. For if one, in order to create a sermon outline, diagrams verses 1–10 using the English text, the suspense and the anticipation of closure is also lost.

The Phrase

The phrase is also important. After Peter fails to walk on the water, Jesus asks, "Why did you doubt?" (Matt. 14:31). A similar but slightly different construction is often translated *why* in the New Testament (e.g., Matt 9:11, 21:25; Mark 7:5; Luke 24:38; John 12:5; 1 Cor. 6:7; Rev 17:7). Although both are translated *why*, these two constructions have different nuances. The phrase in Matthew 14:31 asks for the goal or purpose of an action (see also Matt 26:8; Mark 15:34). The second phrase asks for factors that led to the action.

Both nuances can be found in the English word *why*, but only knowledge of the Greek tells us what kind of information Jesus asks for. D. A. Carson comments: "Jesus does not ask 'because of what' Peter doubted (any fool can see that!) but for what purpose, to what end: what was the point of his doubt, having come so far?"[8] When preaching this text on the basis of this phrase, we can ask our listeners such questions as: "Have you thought about your goals when you doubt?" or "What are you trying to accomplish when you doubt the Lord?" or "Does doubting the Lord help you stay in control of your own life?"

Those with a year or two of Greek studies will have been taught about the difference between the objective and subjective genitive. Two English phrases demonstrate the difference between the objective and the subjective genitive: "the betrayal of Jesus" and "the betrayal of Judas."

Although it is a noun, "betrayal" has a verbal idea (to betray). The Greek genitive is very often approximated by the English preposition "of." So in both these instances, the final word (Jesus or Judas) is the genitive noun. But what do these two phrases mean? From what we know of the Gospels, Judas, and Jesus, the first phrase means: "the betrayal directed against Jesus" or "Jesus was betrayed." The second means: "the betrayal committed by Judas" or "Judas betrayed someone." So in the first phrase Jesus is the object of the action (thus the objective genitive). In the second phrase Judas is the subject of the action (thus the subjective genitive).

With these preliminary observations in mind, we might consider Galatians 2:16. In the phrase διὰ πίστεως Ἰησοῦ Χριστοῦ (literally, "through faith of Jesus Christ"), what type of genitive is "Jesus Christ"? If objective, it would be understood to mean trust directed toward Christ. If it is subjective, it would be understood to mean Christ's faithfulness or the faithfulness that Christ demonstrated.

Pondering this question is important, since the TNIV, although giving an objective translation ("by faith in Jesus Christ"), contains a marginal note giving the subjective alternative ("through the faithfulness of Jesus Christ"). Consequently, some of the people in our congregations, if they are the thoughtful Bible readers we want them to be, may be exposed to the subjective rendering and require an explanation from us as to how the different translations arise.

The Word

Robert L. Thomas states, "Elaboration on Greek and Hebrew words in pulpit exposition is by far the most frequently encountered homiletical use of exegesis. . . ."[9] Indeed most preachers find they can easily bring into their messages reflections on particular word meanings. Conversely, we must be careful not to make too much of words isolated from context.

For example, all English translations render Romans 15:26 with the phrase "make a contribution" or with a virtual equivalent (see ESV, NASB, NIV, KJV, and NLT). But "make a contribution" is a questionable translation. The word translated "contribution" is κοινωνία (koinōnia). Those with some knowledge of Greek will recognize this as the common word for fellowship in the NT. But the translation "contribution" gives koinōnia a rare, if not unknown, concrete sense. As of this writing, no English translation even alerts the reader to an alternative. Furthermore, most commentators on the book of Romans do not alert the reader to an alternative.[10] So the bottom line is this: Hidden treasures await us, but we must be reading the Greek text.[11]

In their book, Greek for Preachers, Joseph Webb and Robert Kysar rightly encourage the use of Greek for preaching, noting that in John 21, when Jesus asks Peter if he loves Jesus, Jesus uses ἀγαπάω, but Peter uses φιλέω. Webb and Kysar assert that since ἀγάπη love is divine and φιλία love is brotherly, Peter has refused to answer Jesus' thrice-repeated question.[12]

While an appeal to the Greek text is welcomed, this assertion about the difference between ἀγάπη and φιλία is faulty. A student with the Greek New Testament and a concordance can discover the fault easily. Luke 11:43 says, "Woe to you Pharisees, because you love (ἀγαπᾶτε) the first seats in the synagogues and greetings in the marketplaces." Certainly this love of the Pharisees was not a godly love. Similarly John 3:19 says, "Men loved (ἀγάπησαν) darkness rather than light," and Paul says, "Demas has deserted me, loving (ἀγαπήσας) this present world" (2 Tim 4:10, author's translations). A particularly telling example may be taken from the Septuagint, the ancient Greek translation, of 2 Sam. 13:1–19, especially vv. 1 and 15. After Amnon rapes Tamar, it says that he hated her more than he loved her (ἀγαπήσεν αὐτήν). Certainly this love of Amnon was not a godly love.

On the other hand, regarding φιλία love, John's gospel says, "the Father loves (φιλεῖ) the Son" (5:20) and "the Father himself loves (φιλεῖ) you" (16:27; cf John 20:2). In these last two examples, should we reach the conclusion that Jesus is speaking about an inferior kind of love?[13]

You do not need to be a scholar to discover these truths about κοινωνία and ἀγάπη versus φιλία. You only need a rudimentary knowledge of Greek, a Greek New Testament, an exhaustive concordance, and the desire and motivation to keep looking for the riches of God's Word. When doing word analysis, preachers should ponder the comments made by D. A. Carson in his chapter on Word Study Fallacies.[14]

USING GREEK IN SERMON DELIVERY

While teaching at a college in South Florida, I attended a church that was looking for a senior pastor and so had a variety of men doing pulpit supply. One morning our preacher, speaking from Titus 3:1–2, took a moment to analyze the word "obey" (3:1). "The word," he said, "is ὑπακούω. It means to 'hear under.'" And so, our preacher spent a few minutes drawing conclusions about the necessity for believers to "hear under." Since I was following his message in the Greek text, I could see that the word for obey in Tit. 3:1 is not ὑπακούω, but πειθαρχεῖν. Afterward, I met the preacher, gave him encouragement about the good parts of his message and mentioned the difference in the Greek words for "obey." He was speechless. I asked if he had read Titus 3:1–2 in Greek and, to his credit, he admitted that he had not. He had assumed the word for obey in Titus 3:1 was ὑπακούω.[15] Obviously, this is the kind of Greek to avoid in sermon delivery.

In his "Exegesis and Expository Preaching," Robert Thomas has several helpful suggestions for the preacher's presentation, some dealing specifically with bringing exegesis and Greek into the sermon.[16] Here, in the space allowed, I will mention a few guidelines considered most important. We will categorize these as *Greek to Avoid* and *Greek to Include*.

Greek to Avoid

First, as a general rule, we should shy away from using Greek words from the pulpit.[17] It is especially needful to avoid references to Greek that are redundant. Such references are ubiquitous in today's preaching. A preacher simply says, "The Greek word here is σώφρων and it means 'prudent' or 'temperate.'" From this point he goes on to define the English words "prudent" and "temperate." Since it is extremely likely that most English translations will already have the rendering "prudent" or "temperate" in the verse (e.g., 1 Tim. 3:2), how has the listener been helped by the preacher's display of Greek language knowledge? The preacher's comment is at best redundant and at worst a waste of everyone's time.

Certainly the preacher with knowledge of Greek has a valuable tool that most of the congregation does not have. But, secondly, he should avoid references that make the listener feel inadequate in his or her own reading of Scripture. For example, using κοινωνία, the preacher might say, "The NIV wrongly translates the Greek of Philemon 6 with 'be active in sharing your faith,' because the Greek word translated 'sharing' is κοινωνία, which does not mean 'sharing' but 'fellowship.'" Here, the preacher is basically correct. But, after hearing such a comment, his listeners might leave the sermon believing that Scripture is only comprehensible to those with specialized knowledge in Greek.

Greek to Include

The preacher, based on his knowledge of Greek, can take the listener from the known to the unknown. For example, referring back to Matthew 14:31, we saw that the NIV text's "Why did you doubt?" translates the construction εἰς τί in contrast to the phrase διὰ τί. The first phrase (εἰς τί) asks for the goal or purpose of an action, the second (διὰ τί) asks for factors that lead to the action. Either one of these nuances can be contained in the English word *why*.

Further, our listeners know this fact about English: that *why* can have different meanings. We can take them from this known example of the English word to the unknown Greek word. Similar are the earlier comments on the English use of the word "of" in comparison with the Greek genitive. The two English phrases "the betrayal of Jesus" and "the betrayal of Judas" give easily comprehensible, known categories from which to start when taking the listeners to the unknown category of the Greek genitive.

Through this type of careful explanation, the preacher can share some of his exegesis. Admittedly, guides to exegesis and delivery debate this question: Should the preacher communicate to the congregation the process of his exegesis or only the results of it? Robertson asserts that, "Results and not process suit the pulpit."[18] I am of the view, however, that carefully selected references to process can be helpful, for they implicitly teach the listeners how to study and find insight on their own. In order to avoid alienating listeners, preachers can show them how to discover the same results.

In our earlier example of Philemon 6, the preacher can introduce listeners to several translations of the verse. In this particular text, the NASB, NIV, NLT and The Message differ greatly. Any serious layperson can now see that translators were struggling to bring out the meaning of this difficult verse.

At this point you can lead your congregation by saying, "If you get out your *Strong's Exhaustive Concordance*[19] you don't need Greek to discover that the difficulty partly lies in how to translate the word typically rendered 'fellowship' in the New Testament. Here in Philemon the NIV renders it 'sharing.' That's not bad. The word *can* be used to talk about financial sharing. The word also has that meaning in Hebrews 13:16.

But the phrase 'sharing your faith' is an English idiom that means 'doing evangelism' not 'sharing financially.'"

Some assert that we should be slow to correct the translation we preach from, saying that too many criticisms will shake the hearers' confidence in Scripture. They suggest that corrections should be limited to two or three.[20] In general, this is sound advice. But when our comments are similar to those given above on Philemon 6, we bring the listener in to the process of exegesis. Their confidence need not be shaken. Instead we have demonstrated that they can also examine Scripture using the capability or tools of the serious layperson (various English translations, *Strong's Concordance*, knowledge of English).

In order to skillfully employ the Greek text in preaching we must be in it daily. Reading Scripture in the original language is not just something we should employ for message preparation, but something we should read as a habit, as a joy. Studying the Greek text can yield insights on various levels. These insights can be missed when reading the English text, even if this text is found alongside an interlinear Greek text. As preachers of the Word, it can be profitable for our hearers to hear what we have gained from study of the original language. Such gains can be brought into our messages without referring to the word "Greek" or in terms the congregation can easily understand.

Clearly, the methods presented here for studying and preaching from the Greek text of the New Testament require mental concentration, diligence, finesse, and sensitivity. It is a difficult task, but one we can be glad to undertake, for, as Robertson says, "No amount of toil is too great for the lover of the truth of God."[21]

GERALD W. PETERMAN is chairperson and professor of Bible at the Moody Bible Institute. He holds the Ph.D. degree from King's College, London, and academic degrees from Trinity Evangelical Divinity School, Deerfield, Illinois, and the University of Florida.

NOTES

1. Bart Ehrman attributes this comparison to Jeff Siker, professor of New Testament at Loyola Marymount University, Los Angeles. Bart Ehrman, *Misquoting Jesus* (New York: HarperCollins, 2005), 219.

2. Twenty-two verses per day will take the reader through the Greek New Testament yearly.

3. A. T. Robertson, *The Minister and His Greek New Testament* (New York: Doran, 1923), 25.

4. *Logos* (Bellingham, Wash.: Logos Research Systems), and *BibleWorks* (Norfolk, Va.: BibleWorks LLC).

5. Daniel B. Wallace, *Greek Grammar beyond the Basics* (Grand Rapids: Zondervan, 1996); James Brooks and Carlton Winberry, *Syntax of New Testament Greek* (Washington, D.C.: Univ. Press of America, 1978). Such works are also accessible through *Logos* and *BibleWorks*.

6. For the lexicon, Walter Bauer's *A Greek-English Lexicon of the Greek New Testament and Other Early Christian Literature* (Chicago: Univ. of Chicago, 2000) is highly recommended. For the concordance, see *The Exhaustive Concordance to the Greek New Testament* by J. R. Kohlenberger III, E. W. Goodrick, and J. A. Swanson (Grand Rapids: Zondervan, 1995).

7. Robertson, *The Minister*, 16.

8. D. A. Carson, "Matthew," in *The Expositor's Bible Commentary*, vol. 8, ed. Frank E. Gaebelein (Grand Rapids: Zondervan, 1984), 346.

9. Robert L. Thomas, "Exegesis and Expository Preaching," in John MacArthur Jr. and the Master's Seminary Faculty, *Rediscovering Expository Preaching*, ed. Richard Mayhue (Dallas: Word, 1992), 142.

10. Exceptions are L. T. Johnson, *Reading Romans* (Macon: Smyth & Helwys, 2001), 230; Katherine Grieb, *The Story of Romans: A Narrative Defense of God's Righteousness* (Louisville: Westminster/John Knox, 2002), 141; Ben Witherington III, *Paul's Letter to the Romans* (Grand Rapids: Eerdmans, 2004), 365; and Thomas R. Schreiner, *Romans* (Grand Rapids: Baker, 1998), 777.

11. For further discussion of Romans 15:26, see G. W. Peterman, "Romans 15:26: Make a Contribution or Establish Fellowship?" *New Testament Studies* 40 (1994), 457–63.

12. Joseph M. Webb and Robert Kysar, *Greek for Preachers* (St. Louis: Chalice, 2002), 3.

13. See further the analysis of Stephen Voorwinde, "Ἀγαπάω and Φιλέω—Is There a Difference?" *The Reformed Theological Review* 64 (2005), 76–90; and D. A. Carson, *Exegetical Fallacies* (Grand Rapids: Baker, 1984), 31–32.

14. Carson, *Exegetical Fallacies*, 25–66.

15. The assumption is reasonable, as ὑπακούω appears 21 times in the NT and πειθαρχεῖν only 4 times.

16. Thomas, "Exegesis and Expository Preaching," 148–52. See also similar suggestions in Terry G. Carter, et. al., *Preaching God's Word: A Hands-On Approach to Preparing, Developing, and Delivering the Sermon* (Grand Rapids: Zondervan, 2005): 76–79.

17. In Thomas's view they should be used sparingly ("Exegesis and Expository Preaching," 148).

18. Robertson, *Minister*, 82.

19. James Strong, *Strong's Exhaustive Concordance of the Bible* (Peabody, Mass.: Hendrickson, 1988).

20. Thomas, "Exegesis and Expository Preaching," 150.

21. Robertson, *Minister*, 85.

Part Three

ILLUSTRATING

TRUTH

THE POWER

OF

COMPARISON

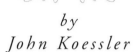

by
John Koessler

Science fiction author Douglas Adams once wrote, "*It is no coinci-dence that in no known language does the phrase 'As pretty as an airport' appear.*"[1] His statement may tell us something about the aesthetic quality of airports. But of greater import is its commentary on the nature of metaphor and simile. Sometimes they just don't work. When they do, however, metaphors and similes are some of the sharpest implements in the preacher's toolbox.

The use of metaphor and simile in human language is intuitive. We employ these comparisons because they make sense. Indeed, the nature of human language is such that we could make little sense of it without metaphors and similes. Human understanding is wired to think in com-parisons. George Lakoff and Mark Johnson note: "Our ordinary concep-tual system, in terms of which we both think and act, is fundamentally metaphorical in nature."[2] We come to understand that which we do not know by using that which we do know as a point of reference. This is the essence of metaphor and simile. When we use metaphors and similes, we hold the unknown before the listener while pointing to that which is known and say, in essence, "This is that."[3] The strength of verbal comparisons is in their power to evoke personal experience and make the abstract concrete.

PREACHING IS METAPHORICAL

It should come as no surprise, then, that preaching is also inherently metaphorical in nature. It must be, since it is an oral experience. In oral communication sounds are used to represent ideas that can be either concrete or abstract. Likewise, in written language a set of symbols is used to convey ideas. Some alphabets began as ideograms—systems that use pictures of the thing the symbol represents. In other cases the images represent the sounds of language. Both systems are symbolic and referential in nature. Donald K. Smith notes that some languages tend to be concrete while others are abstract. They use analogy to take the abstract and make it concrete. In a particularly beautiful example he cites the Dutch word for hydrogen, which is literally *water dust*. Smith explains the meaning behind the metaphor this way: "Hydrogen is a gas that remains when water is broken down to its components—the 'dust' left behind when water is demolished."[4]

It is this capacity to convey meaning in a striking manner that makes metaphoric language such a powerful ally to the preacher.

It is tempting to view the use of metaphoric language as only a rhetorical flourish—a stylish embellishment of the sermon rather than a statement of substance. However, the place of metaphor in preaching is more than ornamental. Metaphor has the potential to shape behavior and illuminate meaning. When it comes to metaphoric language, "what you say is what you get." Our choice of language defines the nature of a statement and may even influence the parameters of behavior that takes places within the context in which it is used.

Lakoff and Johnson offer the metaphor "argument is war" as an example. Arguments are not wars. They are not armed conflict and do not involve the shedding of blood (though they may lead to both). Yet argument is war to the extent that it "is partially structured, understood, performed, and talked about in terms of WAR. The concept is metaphorically structured, the activity is metaphorically structured, and, consequently, the language is metaphorically structured."5 When we argue we "take sides" and sometimes begin by "throwing down the gauntlet." We argue with an "opponent" and the one who is successful in the argument "wins." It's not surprising that experts in handling conflict see word choice as an important element in resolving disagreements. Ken Sande, a Christian lawyer who specializes in helping churches and individuals resolve their disputes, emphasizes the need to plan our words when talking to others about their faults. In particular, he advises readers to use metaphors and analogies, " . . . that the other person will understand and value."6

It is true that simile, metaphor, and analogy can be used to clarify ideas. But their real power is the capacity they possess to speak the dialect of the heart. Northrop Frye notes that the connections being made when we use associative language are not always logical. "In descriptive writing you have to be careful of associative language," Frye warns. "You'll find that analogy, or likeness to something else, is very tricky to handle in description, because the differences are as important as the resemblances. As for metaphor, where you're really saying 'this *is* that,' you're turning your back on logic and reason completely, because logically two things can never be the same thing and still remain two things."7

The most compelling metaphors often employ a kind of nonlinear logic, comparing apples to oranges. The effect is like walking into a room that a decorator has painted with two colors one normally wouldn't put together but which somehow "work." Suddenly, we see shades of color and features of the room that we otherwise would have missed. Powerful metaphors juxtapose unrelated ideas in ways that surprise us.

Obviously, this places a burden on the preacher to be thoughtful when utilizing comparisons in the sermon. Poorly selected metaphors can set the wrong tone and may mislead the listener. Well-chosen metaphors not only define the response called for in the text but help in providing a proper emotional context for it to take place.

A THEOLOGICAL NECESSITY

The value of using comparative language in preaching is more than pragmatic. There is also theological warrant using this kind of language.

The biblical ideas that the preacher hopes to convey in the sermon are often bound to metaphor in a way that goes beyond style.[8] The concepts themselves cannot be understood apart from the metaphor. In this case, the metaphor is not merely an accommodation to human limitation but a component of revealed truth. To paraphrase Marshall McLuhan, the metaphor is the message.

Consequently, the Scriptures teach that God is "the Shepherd, the Rock of Israel" (Gen. 49:24). Jesus is the "Word" (John 1:1). He is "the Lamb of God who takes away the sin of the world" (John 1:29). He is "the bread of life," "the bread that came down from heaven," and "the living bread" (John 6:41, 48, 51).

We understand ourselves, too, through the Bible's use of metaphor. We are the "salt" and "light" of the world and are like a "city set on a hill" (Matt. 5:13–14). We are "God's fellow workers," "God's field," and "God's building" (1 Cor. 3:9). We are "God's temple" and the "body of Christ" (1 Cor. 3:17; 12:27).[9] The use of metaphor is so prevalent in Scripture that almost nothing significant about God and our relationship to Him has been revealed without it.

Metaphoric language may be "nonliteral" but its meaning is ultimately rooted in literal truth. Gordon Clark has pointed out, for example, that the metaphor of the lamb employed by John the Baptist was based on the literal directives of the Mosaic law. According to Clark, without the background of the books of Leviticus and Romans modern readers would "have no basis for understanding what John the Baptist meant."[10] Consequently, metaphor is not a replacement for literal, propositional language. Nor is it necessarily superior to it. Each is the handmaid of the other. If metaphorical language helps me to understand the propositions made by the biblical author, it is by way of the literal connection made through the image.

SIMILES AND ANALOGIES

Similes function like metaphors. The chief difference is the presence of "like" or "as" in the comparison. The metaphor says that one thing *is* another. A simile says that it is *like* something else. Consequently, the metaphor equates the two, while the simile falls short of doing so. For example, God promised to make Abraham's offspring "like the dust of the earth" (Gen. 13:16). Abraham, however, when he bargained with God for the preservation of the righteous in Sodom, said, "I am nothing but dust and ashes" (Gen. 18:27). If there is a conceptual difference between the metaphor and the simile, it is that there is greater distance implied in a simile. Metaphor is the stronger of the two.

To speak of the use of analogy as a separate category is somewhat redundant. Metaphors and similes are analogous in nature. When analogy appears as a separate literary device, the comparison is extended and developed. One of the best models of this was the Christian apologist C. S. Lewis. He was a master not only of concise writing, but of analogy. Consider, for example, his explanation of what he calls "the law of human nature" in *Mere Christianity*. Lewis's goal is to make a rather subtle and technical theological point for a theologically unsophisticated audience. From a theological perspective, he is explaining the concept of divine general revelation. Specifically, he wants to show that all people share a common sense that there is a moral law and they have broken it.

He makes his point by appealing to common experience. Everyone, Lewis points out, has heard people quarrelling. Even though his point is self-evident, he goes on to provide concrete examples: "They say things like this: 'How would you like it if anyone did the same to you?'— 'That's my seat, I was there first'—'Leave him alone, he isn't doing you any harm'—'Why should you shove in first?'—'Give me a bit of your orange, I gave you a bit of mine'—'Come on, you promised.'"[11]

It is not hard to visualize the circumstances that Lewis describes and to hear the tone in which these objections are made. Their effectiveness, however, is not merely a function of their universal quality but the fact that when we read these examples we inevitably identify with the one who has been wronged. This serves a dual purpose. First, it enables Lewis to make his point that the person who says such things appeals to a standard that he expects others to know about. "Quarrelling means trying to show that the other man is in the wrong," Lewis writes. "And there would be no sense in trying to do that unless you and he had some sort of agreement as to what Right and Wrong are; just as there would be no sense in saying that a footballer had committed a foul unless there was some agreement about the rules of football."[12]

More importantly, because Lewis frames his examples in a way that puts us on the receiving end of wrongdoing, he enables us to see ourselves as God sees us. This was precisely what Nathan did when he confronted David regarding his sin with Bathsheba. Nathan's parable was an extended analogy. Although the prophet ultimately wanted David to see that he was the rich neighbor in the story, the story was framed in a way that insured that the king would identify with Uriah. David had spent his youth watching over his father's sheep and knew what it was like to be attached to the flock. What David had closed his eyes to in his own life, he could not help seeing once he looked at his behavior through the eyes of the one he had offended (2 Sam. 12:1–14).

Illustrations are the primary tools the preacher uses to shape the analogies in the sermon. Whether the purpose is to illuminate a biblical principle or to help the audience "put a face" on the application, the illustration like the metaphor and the simile say, "This is that."[13]

PAINTING A PICTURE

In some cases, comparative language is used by the preacher to help explain the truth of the text. Just as a prism bends the light and exposes its different bands, metaphor, simile, and analogy expose different facets of the truth for the listener by refracting it through the lens of common experience. In some cases this is made easy for us by the text itself. In a sermon by Timothy Keller entitled "Why Sin Makes Us Addicts," he uses a vivid sexual image to help his audience understand both the nature and offensiveness of idolatry: "What God says is that when you worship idols, you're spreading your legs."[14]

Although the picture Keller paints is intentionally disturbing, it is not gratuitous. The image is suggested by an even stronger metaphor embedded in Jeremiah 2:23–24, a text which condemns Israel's love of Baal worship: "You are a swift she-camel running here and there, a wild donkey accustomed to the desert, sniffing the wind in her craving—in her heat who can restrain her?"

In a sermon on the sovereignty of God, Jonathan Edwards uses a commonplace metaphor to underscore his point that because God is great, He is infinitely above our comprehension and it is unreasonable for us to question the way He orders the universe. Edwards begins with an analogy: "If little children should rise up and find fault with the supreme legislature of a nation or quarrel with the mysterious administrations of the sovereign, would it not be looked upon that they meddled with things too high for them?"15

He goes on to state an explicit metaphor and apply it to his audience: "And what are we but babes? Our understandings are infinitely less than those of babes, in comparison with the wisdom of God. It becomes us therefore, to be sensible of it and to behave ourselves accordingly."16

The force of Edwards's comparison may be blunted somewhat for the modern reader because of differences in perspective regarding children. His goal is not merely to make an intellectual point (we cannot really understand how God has ordered the affairs of the world) but to make an emotional one as well. Edwards wants his hearers to recognize that their challenge to divine sovereignty is "unbecoming." He hopes that they will be abashed, like a child who has been discovered after they have somehow managed to climb to a high shelf, and has grasped some valuable or delicate thing that has been intentionally placed out of their reach. Notice that Edwards not only employs an explicit metaphor, he frames his explanation using "parental" language.

Perhaps like no other preacher, Edwards is a master of using analogy to speak to both the mind and the emotions of the listener. It is this device that gives his most famous sermon, "Sinners in the Hands of an Angry God," its emotional force. Edwards overwhelms the listener with visual images of helplessness and peril, many of them involving fire and falling. It is easy for us, Edwards says, to crush a worm that is crawling on the ground or to cut the thread of some loathsome insect. In the same way, it is just as easy for God to cast His enemies down to hell. In making such a comparison, Edwards succeeds in helping us emotionally connect with the loathsomeness of sin from God's point of view.

Elsewhere in the message he describes the fiery pit of hell with its glowing flames and tells his listeners that there is nothing between them and hell but the air; only the power and pleasure of God holds them up. What is worse, he says, they are insensible to their own danger, and their wickedness makes them as heavy as lead. If God should let them go, they would immediately sink: "and your healthy constitution, and your own care and prudence, and best contrivance, and all your righteousness, would have no more influence to uphold you and keep you out of hell, than a spider's web would have to stop a falling rock."[17]

USING COMPARATIVE LANGUAGE

Most of us, of course, would not consider ourselves to be in the same league as Edwards. How, then, do ordinary mortals like us learn to use comparative language in the sermon? Where do we find the most effective metaphors, similes, and analogies for preaching? The best starting point is the passage itself. Mine the biblical text for its metaphors, similes, and analogies. The biblical writer may employ explicit comparisons that can be taken up and developed by the preacher. This is what Timothy Keller does in the example cited above.

In cases where there is no explicit simile or metaphor, the text may provide an implicit comparison that can be developed. In the case of biblical narratives, these are often revealed through the actions of the characters in the story. The events recorded in the gospels are historical in the sense that they actually happened the way the authors say they happened. But these writers were both selective in the details they chose to emphasize and often intentional about their placement in the gospel, framing their accounts of the words and works of Jesus with theological intent. Consequently, the events they record often have metaphorical significance.

The miracles of Jesus are a good example. Craig Blomberg encourages biblical interpreters to see the miracles of Christ not only as proofs but as parables: "The miracles both reveal and conceal, acting as signs for believers while repelling unbelievers, just like the parables."[18]

The preacher's own life experience is another valuable resource when looking for analogies. In the preface to *Eat This Book*, author Eugene Peterson tells of the day his wife picked up their seven-year-old grandson Hans for a trip to the museum. The two of them stopped at the park to eat lunch. As they were about to leave, Hans, who had not yet learned to read, took a New Testament from his book bag and held it in front of him and carefully scanned the page. The incident amused Peterson. But he also saw in it a parable of the way we often approach the Bible: "Hans on that park bench, his eyes moving back and forth across the pages of his Bible, 'reading' but not reading, reverent and devout but uncomprehending, honoring in a most precious way this book but without any awareness that it has anything to do with either the lettuce and mayonnaise sandwich he has just eaten or the museum he is about to visit, oblivious to his grandmother next to him: Hans 'reading' the Bible. A parable."[19]

Our days are filled with experiences that have symbolic significance. Like the light that shines through a stained glass window, when our experiences are used as analogies and illustrations, they have the potential and reveal shades and nuances in biblical truth that otherwise might have been hidden from our view.

Literature is also a treasure-house of metaphors, similes, and analogies. Classic literature not only teaches us how to see the world around us in a different light, it provides us with a more vivid vocabulary for talking about biblical truth. (For more on the use of classic literature in preaching, see chapter 16.) The best communicators read widely.

AN ELEMENT OF STYLE

The place of metaphor in preaching is more than ornamental, yet it does have a kind of "decorative" function in the sermon. The use of comparative language enables the preacher to bring the point to life. Master preacher-teacher Haddon Robinson modeled this in a sermon based on the book of Ecclesiastes, which he began by saying: "As I look back in my life over the last several years, there was a period in which I lived in the dark night of the soul. I spent several months of my life on the sloping back of a question mark."[20]

It is obvious to the listener that Robinson is not speaking literally. He could have just as easily made the same point without the metaphor. Robinson might have said, "I spent several months of my life struggling with doubt." However, the metaphor communicates the same idea in a way that gets our attention and conveys the disorientation Robinson obviously felt during this period of his life. Not only did he struggle with questions, he rode out those months on the "sloping back" of those versations have also helped me review my scene selections and in some cases to stop using scenes that an audience might find objectionable or unclear. The ultimate goal of such film application should always be to edify and not to offend or confuse (Ephesians 4:29).

FILM AS METAPHOR

In some cases, the film scenes I use are metaphors for biblical truths after the teaching traditions of the biblical prophets, Jesus, and other New Testament authors. For example, I regularly teach an assimilation workshop for new members in my church. I generally close the three-hour-long workshop with the final scene from a film titled *The Family Man* (Universal 2000), starring Nicolas Cage and Tea Leone. The scene takes place at Kennedy Airport where Leone's character, Kate, is leaving for Paris and Cage's character, Jack, is trying to convince her to stay and try to restart their relationship. I close with Jack's statement, "I know we could go on with our lives and do fine but I have seen what we can be together and I choose us."

I make the application that so many Christians have given up on the church and have, like Kate, chosen instead a flight to Paris (or their own need for personal fulfillment). Then I challenge these new members to remember the vision of church and community we have tried to present to them in the workshop and encourage them to choose the church as a way to glorify God to a watching world.

I have watched people emotionally respond to the challenge and tell me they had almost given up hope for the church as a place to serve. The film clip acted as a renewed call to bring them back to church service. Some of those people are now strengthening the ministries of our church while others are starting new ministries with encouraging success.

A PERSONAL AWAKENING FOR AUDIENCE MEMBERS

Earlier I named four typical responses to film viewing: rejection, discernment, discussion, and application. I would suggest one final response: personal awakening. This response is more individualistic and subjective in nature. But, from my experience, it has proven to have lasting impact questions. It is not hard to imagine him holding on for dear life, afraid that he might slide off.

Comparative language, however, is more than a matter of style. It is elemental to the sermon. We cannot really understand God's truth without it. C. S. Lewis has noted: "Heaven is, by definition, outside our experience, but all intelligible descriptions must be of things within our experience." It is the preacher's impossible task to speak of heavenly realities to those whose experience is limited to the earth. We cannot hope to do so in a meaningful way without using metaphors, similes, and analogies to make comparisons to earthly experience.

NOTES

1. Douglas Adams, *The Long, Dark Tea-Time of the Soul* (New York: Pocket, 1988), 1.

2. George Lakoff and Mark Johnson, *Metaphors We Live By* (Chicago: Univ. of Chicago, 1980), 3.

3. As Lakoff and Johnson explain, "The essence of metaphor is understanding and experiencing one kind of thing in terms of another." Ibid., 5.

4. Donald K. Smith, *Creating Understanding: A Handbook for Christian Communication Across Cultural Landscapes* (Grand Rapids: Zondervan, 1992), 240.

5. Lakoff and Johnson argue that activities as well as concepts are metaphorically structured: "It is not that arguments are a subspecies of war. Arguments and wars are different kinds of things—verbal discourse and armed conflict—and the actions performed are different kinds of actions. But ARGUMENT is partially structured, understood, performed, and talked about in terms of WAR. The concept is metaphorically structured, the activity is metaphorically structured, and, consequently, the language is metaphorically structured." Ibid., 5.

6. Ken Sande, *The Peacemaker* (Grand Rapids: Baker, 2004), 176.

7. Northrop Frye, *The Educated Imagination* (Bloomington: Indiana Univ. Press, 1964), 32.

8. Peter Macky brought this to light in his helpful comparison of Gordon Clark and C. S. Lewis on the role of metaphor in Christian thought. According to Macky, Clark considered metaphor and analogy to be ornamental to truth and inferior to proposition. Lewis held that we cannot know the reality of God apart from the metaphors He has chosen to reveal Himself through. See Peter W. Macky, "The Role of Metaphor in Christian Thought and Experience as Understood by Gordon Clark and C. S. Lewis," *Journal of the Evangelical Theological Society,* 24:3 (September 1981): 239–50.

9. This is by no means an exhaustive list. Warren Wiersbe has included a helpful

index of major biblical images in *Preaching and Teaching With Imagination: The Quest for Biblical Ministry* (Grand Rapids: Baker, 1997).

10. Gordon H. Clark, "A Reply to the Metaphorical Dr. Macky," *Journal of the Evangelical Theological Society* 25:2 (June 1982): 202.

11. C. S. Lewis, *Mere Christianity* (New York: Macmillan, 1943), 17.

12. Ibid., 17–18.

13. "Stories function like metaphors. Just as a metaphor states 'a' is 'b' (God is a rock), so stories imply that 'individual experience is universal experience' (Moses struck the rock when angry—we act like that too." John Koessler, "View From the Pew" in *The Art & Craft of Biblical Preaching*, ed. Haddon Robinson and Craig Brian Larson (Grand Rapids: Zondervan, 2005), 125.

14. Timothy Keller, "How Sin Makes Us Addicts," *Preaching Today* (258) CD recording, tr. 17.

15. Jonathan Edwards, "The Sole Consideration, That God is God, Sufficient to Still All Objections to His Sovereignty," reprinted in *Classic Sermons on the Sovereignty of God*, comp. Warren W. Wiersbe (Grand Rapids: Hendrickson, 1994), 102.

16. Ibid.

17. Jonathan Edwards, "Sinners in the Hands of an Angry God," in *Developing a Christian Imagination* comp. Warren W. Wiersbe (Wheaton, Ill.: Victor, 1995), 88–89.

18. Craig Blomberg, "New Testament Miracles and Higher Criticism: Climbing Up the Slippery Slope," *Journal of the Evangelical Theological Society*, 27:4 (December 1984): 426–427.

19. Eugene Peterson, *Eat This Book* (Grand Rapids: Eerdmans, 2006), xii.

20. Haddon Robinson, "The Message of Ecclesiastes," *Preaching Today* (248), CD recording, tr. 3.

Sixteen

FELLING

THE

DEVIL

by

Rosalie de Rosset

In the movie *Walk the Line*, which recounts the career of music legend Johnny Cash, a key interchange occurs between Johnny and studio manager Sam Phillips. Longing to break into country music, Johnny buys an audition and, with his small band, sings a shaky rendition of the gospel song, "I Was There When It Happened." Within a minute, Phillips, obviously irritated, demands that he stop.

"I don't do gospel," Phillips says. "This stuff doesn't sell. People want something honest, something felt."

Johnny, hurt and angry, snaps back, "You listen to me sing for a minute and tell me it won't work?"

The manager looks Johnny in the eye and says, "Do you *believe* it? I've heard that song sung exactly that way five hundred times. If you got hit by a truck and you only had time to sing one song before you died, what would it be?"

Taken aback, Johnny pauses, looks down at his guitar, then proceeds to sing, hesitantly at first, then powerfully, a riveting rendition of

"Folsom Prison Blues," a song that later mesmerized prison audiences.

That manager was right in saying that unless Johnny Cash's singing could do things to the people listening, it was just the *same old-same old*. Unless he could be more than a peddler of a tired sentiment, he might as well quit.

The same could be said for preachers who hope to break into the lives of their congregations. The language we use to tell our stories, to teach and preach our faith, the content of the illustrations we select have the ability to dull or enliven the listener.

WHY STORIES?

Imagine for a moment the Old Testament without narrative or the New Testament without the Gospels (including the parables) or the book of Acts. The largeness of those stories commands our attention; their characters from Abraham to Habakkuk, from the Twelve Disciples to Paul, are replete with complex dilemmas, foolish sins, and good questions, and engage our senses and souls as well as our reason. And, of course, the incarnated Christ—acting among the people, healing them, teaching them, seeking to make them see through analogy and metaphor, suffering their disregard, and dying and rising from the dead—is the center of our faith.

Each biblical narrative is classic, an illustration of God's sovereignty and merciful work in history.

Great literature, then and now, enables us to see the connectedness of life. We cannot always rise above present circumstances to see the completeness of our story. The better the story, meaning the more skilled the language and the more complex the characters, the more vision we receive. Fiction, as narrative, incarnates theology into the stuff of humanity.

Of all people on earth, Christians have the most reason to value the arts and imagination and to use these rich resources as a means of grace, a way to compel people into the kingdom and to obedience, wooing them with a kind of holy seduction instead of hitting them with a propositional hammer. Illustration well used never upstages the teaching of Scripture; instead, it brings its message home concretely and eloquently, gripping the heart and enlarging the understanding.

THE ROLE OF IMAGINATION

C. S. Lewis believed that when humans are converted, their memories, fantasies, imaginations, and dreams are the last to be entirely healed. In *The Screwtape Letters*, Screwtape tells Wormwood to think of human beings as a series of concentric circles—will as the innermost, next the intellect, and finally the imagination, all of which must be won for Satan or for God. "For me," Lewis proposed, "reason is the natural organ of truth; but imagination is the organ of meaning. Imagination, producing new metaphors or revivifying old, is not the cause of truth but its condition."[1] Warren Wiersbe, well-known preacher and author, describes the balance this way: "Right brain religion generates a lot of heat and left-brain religion generates a lot of light. . . . Preaching that involves the imagination as well as the mind and the emotions will encourage balanced spiritual growth."[2]

In other words, a healthy and complex imagination is essential to understanding how one truth relates to another and how both of them relate to life. Alan Jones, writer and theologian, explains what happens without it:

> For many the Christian story no longer bears the mystery. It seems to trivialize it. The Christian way of looking at, interpreting, understanding the world has lost its power, its fragrance. It has become sterile, dead, lost behind a mountain of custom, habit, and convention. We have the outlines of the story, but there are precious few living characters in its half-forgotten and emaciated plot.[3]

American society seems to have early forsaken the poetic and embraced the pragmatic. According to sociologist Robert Bellah, this step "dried up" the American imagination. He points out that Jonathan Edwards was "the last Protestant theologian before the twentieth century to have in his control the entire imaginative resources of the Christian tradition. Edwards' use of imagery was unparalleled."[4]

In the thirty-six years I have been teaching and speaking, the single most important thing I can do by God's grace is to somehow, in Lewis's words, "water the deserts of parched imaginations," to find a way to help the listener come alive in his or her soul discovering that Christianity walks hand in hand with the richest kind of imagination.[5]

The mental, spiritual, and emotional awakening Lewis speaks of can and has often come through the vehicle of classic novels, which are inseparable from my growth in faith and understanding, and which underpin the best of everything I do.

When I was a little girl living on the mission field in Peru, reading was my primary source of entertainment. My mother read energetically to us from *King Arthur and His Knights, Robin Hood and His Merry Men, Pilgrim's Progress*, teaching me, and my siblings, to love classics. Our early lives were saturated with great literature—a reality that undergirds my Christian faith, my respect for language and good writing, and for any success I have had as a professor and speaker.

With themes that transcend time and place, with elegant and poetic language and complex characters, the classics marked my life and choices in specific ways; they heightened my imagination, filled me with longing for ideas and things bigger than myself, and ultimately, along with Scripture, gave my theology and Christian experience backbone.

The best writers, teachers—and preachers—may be those familiar with the greatest texts, texts that illuminate the breadth of human experience and its consequences, which engage spirit, mind, and heart, whose language becomes theirs, whose themes provoke reflection. Great literature challenges shallow, clichéd ideas, something that is true of the biblical narratives as well.

WHATEVER HAPPENED TO LITERATURE?

But such preaching is not mainstream. One has to ask why more preachers do not both talk about the importance of great texts in their congregation's lives and model those choices in their use of illustrations. Could it be that the same people who so reverence Scripture are careless in the choice of what they read, watch, and do in their leisure? After all, as T. S. Eliot argues in his essay "Religion and Literature," very little affects one's mind and spirit more than what one does at leisure. Sermons—and congregations—would be well served by illustrations that include not just personal stories and popular culture elements like film clips and the omnipresent sports story but also the force of great novels and plays and the texts of great poems.

The difference between popular literature and classic literature is, after all, the difference between the ephemeral and the eternal, the difference between a light bulb and the sun, or as Garrison Keillor says in the introduction to his collection of favorite poems called *Good Poems*, "writing that makes people stop chewing their toasted muffins and turn up the radio and listen and later zip into the website and get the dope on the poet or author" even fifty years after its initial release.[6] We need to be witnesses who make people stop chewing their toasted muffins and turn up the radio and listen and later zip into the Bible to get the dope on God.

"A great novel is a kind of conversion experience," wrote the great children's writer Katherine Patterson. And novelist Walker Percy described the prophetic novelist (and certainly preachers as well) as not only a wounded soldier but also as the sacrificial canary that coal miners "used to take down the shaft to test the air. When the canary gets unhappy, utters plaintive cries and collapses, it may be time for the miners to surface and think things over."

Along with my mother and other teachers, Warren Wiersbe—under whose ministry I sat for ten years at Moody Church—deepened my love of literature. He taught a seminary course I took, The History of Preaching. His wide knowledge, both in fiction and nonfiction saturated his sermons and teaching over and over. Wiersbe suspects that "the people in our churches suffer from starved imaginations." He wrote, "It takes more than a dictionary and a grammar to grasp the message of *King Lear* and it takes more than Robertson's *Shorter Greek Grammar* to see the meaning in the images given to us by John in the Book of Revelation."[7]

The Power of Literature on a Life

Literature exerted its power over me once again at a time when I was feeling the kind of spiritual lethargy that comes from overexposure to endlessly repeated concepts. At Trinity Evangelical Divinity School in the winter of 1979, I took my first theology course: Sin and Salvation.

Having started just six months earlier, I was progressing slowly, taking a course a quarter since I was also teaching full-time.

That course changed my life. Or, should I say, God, through that teacher's vision, changed my life. I read seven or eight classic theology volumes twice. I missed only one class despite traveling long distances during a hard winter. What I remember most, however, is not a theological outline. I could not rehearse today exactly what Berkouwer or Warfield say, although I cannot see those volumes on my shelf without feeling a warm rush of affection. What I do remember is the aura, the atmosphere, the fragrance, as it were, of the class, an aura I can recall instantly. What I also remember is the longing the material and lectures filled me with, a longing that many have spoken of—the longing for God—not to be confused with nostalgia (as Lewis notes) or romantic feelings or intellectual stimulation alone, but a longing that makes the demands for Christian living not only worthwhile but *necessary*.

What that professor did was to make sin concrete, to fit it into my personal history. He made sin real and grace a living thing. For the first time in my life I knew who I was, past and present. He did this by taking theological tenets and fleshing them out in ways that applied to me and to my culture, often through the venue of classic fiction.

In an early discussion of sin, he reminded us of the Gollum scene from *The Lord of the Rings*. Gollum finds the ring—an instrument of terrifying power symbolizing perverseness, arrogance, and the flesh. The ring's power infects him; he is tormented by the promises of the flesh and his own emptiness. The ring offers what it never delivers—it is only seductive and destructive. And Gollum is slimy and secretive, speaking in distortions, conniving, wanting to devour whatever comes in his path.

Sin is so much more, said my professor, than the absence of God— it is active hostility to God—deeply, intensely personal evil that distorts us. I could see myself as Gollum, not just as a person who had made mistakes, but as someone who had personally offended God, who in the midst of sin was slimy and corrupt. I could see my temptations as that ring, allurements that offered what they could not deliver, which gave one the feeling of temporary empowerment only to disappoint later. I remained shaken a long time, ready to understand grace in a new way, as more than a word easily spoken or an abstraction discussed repetitively in a Christian book. I could also understand anew the power of redemption that, in Martin Luther's magnificent poetry, says:

> And though this world with devils filled,
> Should threaten to undo us,
> We will not fear, for God has willed
> His truth to triumph through us.
> The Prince of Darkness grim—
> We tremble not for him;
> His rage we can endure, For lo! his doom is sure.
> One little word shall fell him.

"A MIGHTY FORTRESS"

The imaginative approach with which this professor taught, his use of literature along with theology to illustrate the old, old story (Jean-Paul Sartre's *Nausea*, Jonathan Swift's *Gulliver's Travels*, John Bunyan's *Pilgrim's Progress*) was like a hand grenade thrown into my heart, explosively invading the numbness, even the coldness that comes from too much unillustrated, unintegrated, or droned-on propositional information, from too much cliché, happy talk, and predictability. I have never been the same. That professor was the fragrance, the aroma of Christ in my life, pungent, moving, and compelling.

THE SMELL OF THE ALMIGHTY

Consider 2 Corinthians 2:14–17, in which Paul, who also models the use of imagination in teaching, uses the powerful language of the senses to express his point. He conjures up the splendor of a Roman triumphal procession in which the victorious general has led his captives as a public spectacle before the crowd of onlookers. We, who were God's enemies, have been overcome and taken captive by God and are displayed to the world every day and everywhere. As redeemed sinners, we are on exhibition as trophies of divine grace. We are an aromatic perfume to God.

If Christ is in our testimony, in our lives, in our language, we will exude this aroma. To the unsaved we will be, Paul writes, the smell of *great*

death, bringing them to see their choice between life and death. To the saved we are the smell of life—a living invitation to the dulled and lethargic Christian, persuading that Jesus makes a difference. Metaphorically, Paul calls us to have the power of smell: pungent, seductive, refreshing, mysterious, expensive, a power unable to be boxed or controlled once it is released. Is it any wonder that verse 16 asks, "And who is equal to such a task?"

That is my concern today. We too seldom prove equal to the task. Never has our world been so glutted with sermons, CD's, books, seminars, courses, conferences, educational options, and Christian talk of all kinds, much of it from skilled speakers. And never in recent history have there been so many dulled, lethargic, bored customers, resulting, of course, in disobedient customers: Christians whose experience with faith has produced no longing in them and who, therefore, find the answer to their longings in sin.

Perhaps one reason obedience seems so absent or thin even in the face of theological or biblical knowledge is that those of us who teach and preach are not fragrant. Our fragrance does not leave an expensive, memorable odor. We are instead accurate, prepared, but odorless leaders. It is not enough to know what we ought to say and teach; we must also say it and teach it, as we ought.

It seems to me that every Christian's (not to mention every teacher's and preacher's) greatest desire must be to avoid being either trivial or boring in their expression of faith to themselves and to others—both Christians and non-Christians. The truth we teach must be so enthralling that it compels listeners to want to make the sacrifices necessary to being a Christian, one who makes a difference in his or her world, one who helps people see God.

THE POWER OF THE WORD

The Christian's words must fell the devil through the capture of the listener's imagination for Christ who is the creative, enlightening, and powerful Word of God to us. God sent Christ, the Word, to fell the devil. How are we representing that Word, capital W, to fell the devil? As one theologian wrote, the average person on an average day is less interested in the doctrine of justification than in his torment over the last visit he made to a porn parlor or why he or she cannot get his or her prayers above the ceiling to God.[8]

The consequences of this drought of imagination may be much darker than we realize. Wiersbe suggests that "one of the symptoms of the starved imagination malady may be the success of pornography in our country—both the hardcore kind and the more sophisticated varieties . . . ." "It is possible," he continues, "to be pregnant with evil (Psalm 7:14), and the womb is the imagination impregnated by temptation";[9] a pregnancy, I might add, that leads to stillbirth as Scripture predicts.

In his wise, comic novel *Holy Fool* about a preacher who punches his assistant in the nose, an act which leads to his temporary undoing and subsequent redemption, modern novelist Harold Fickett writes,

> A preacher is the epic poet of his people, for in telling the old, old story, he also tells of present history, besides what has passed and is to come. . . . Our age, don't we know it by now, is an age of poetry—not the good poetry of the bard, but the bad poetry of the caption and accompanying photograph: we deal in images but without any depth of imagination, and so the more readily appealing the picture, the better.[10]

The preacher cannot afford to be a caption writer. In an editorial that addresses this, Mike Yaconelli suggests that the first thing our culture does is to steal the mystery and wonder from life. It takes away "risk, danger, spontaneity, intuition, passion, chance, threat, and peril. We become slaves of predictability, of rules, of policies, of uniformity, and of sameness. We learn to teach, but we're not really teachers." We learn to preach, but we're not really preachers. We have the credentials, the titles, the training, the lectures, and the sermons. "But what is gone," he adds, "is the sense of passion, the pleasure, the joy, the sense of calling."[11] At the root of all this, at least partly, is the loss of the sense of imagination and of good reading habits which when used make our words come alive.

Preaching and teaching the Bible and theology must catch hold of the intellect and the soul in order to manifest itself in the student's or the parishioner's practical reality. Bryan Chapell claims, "widespread dissatisfaction with preaching has invaded our churches." He goes on to say that the reasons for these complaints appear to be that the preaching is "lost in abstraction and buried in jargon, incapable of forging a clear path for an age in the midst of unprecedented change." He cites Reuel Howe's catalogue of familiar complaints about preaching:

> Sermons often contain too many complex ideas.
> Sermons have too much analysis and too little answer.
> Sermons are too formal and too impersonal.
> Sermons use too much theological jargon.
> Sermons are too propositional, not enough illustrations.
> Too many sermons simply reach a dead end and give no guidance to commitment and action.[12]

Some of the problem comes from the way many preachers (as well as teachers) approach their task. In his excellent book *Preaching and Teaching with Imagination,* Warren Wiersbe addresses what he calls the "wrong thinking" we may fall into, particularly subscribing to the "conduit metaphor." We "envision ourselves as fountains of knowledge and our listeners as empty receptacles ready to receive what we know . . . our words build[ing] an invisible conduit between us and our listeners." We imagine that the information automatically moves from us to them."[13]

This approach to preaching and teaching, Wiersbe contends, is more prevalent than we realize. Anytime we say, "I hope this isn't going over your head," or "I trust this idea is coming across," it implies that we are wedded to the conduit method. It's the conveyor belt idea. You work hard all week, do your exegesis faithfully, apply the rules of hermeneutics and come up with great biblical material that you think your congregation should know. You organize it on what he calls the "homiletical conveyor belt and as soon as the choir finishes its anthem [worship team, its final praise chorus], you throw the switch and start the belt moving. The receptors are supposed to gather it up and make it their own. But it just doesn't work that way."[14]

FAITHFUL PERSUASION

Christian theology and teaching is best understood as what author David S. Cunningham calls "persuasive argument."[15] Theologians, teachers, and preachers are involved, not just in the exchange of propositions or even in edifying conversations, but in debates, disputes, and arguments. They are seeking to *persuade* others and themselves of a particular understanding of the Christian faith. The goal of Christian theology is what Cunningham calls "faithful persuasion . . . to speak the word that theology must speak, in ways that are faithful to the God of Jesus Christ and persuasive to the world that God has always loved."[16] Or in Paul's terms: "Therefore, knowing the fear of the Lord, we persuade others" (2 Cor. 5:11 ESV).

Faithful persuasion involves close attention to what will both teach and move an audience, not in sentimental or superficial ways, but in ways that will engage their intellects and leave them thinking. We must not, as Craig Dykstra, Christian educator, puts it, "use language simply for its own self-perpetuation" or we will "capture God as the god of the religious cults . . . no longer the God of all life," a kind of "self idolatry."[17] We cannot lobotomize the relationship between God and ourselves and between ourselves and other people by throwing truth at them at its most obvious, clichéd level.

Emily Dickinson, one of the great American poets, has written a poem that addresses the way truth must be presented: indirectly and gently. She understood that truth can dazzle, even blind the listener if not carefully handled.

> Tell the truth but tell it slant—
> Success in circuit lies
> Too bright for our infirm Delight
> The Truth's superb surprise
> As Lightning to the Children eased
> With explanation kind
> The Truth must dazzle gradually
> Or every man be blind—[18]

Religious language, as John Newman, Horace Bushnell, C. S. Lewis, and others have suggested, is at heart the language of poetry and literature and metaphor, a language which in its subtlety contains an evanescence which stirs and surprises, which does not, finally, numb and bore. Language is not, after all, so much the dress of thought as the incarnation of thought. The Word is truth become flesh. Language is the body of the idea, and it is only in the body that we become aware of it.

We tend, however, to dismiss the importance of the body, the dress, by presenting unadorned how-to lists of principles and theological points, admonitions, "sharings," and details of popular culture with little classic touch or respect for language. Or we present theological outlines and terms, the omnipresent word study, unrelated to the life the theology seeks to change. There is no incarnation happening in such presentation. Then we wonder why people don't remember or why we, and they, aren't changed. As poet John Leax puts it in a poem called "The Fire Burns Low," "The living word reduced/to monosyllables,/the gospel cut like hash/for middleclass consumption. . . ."[19]

Such use of language has led to a trivialization of God, what Donald McCullough thinks may be the worst sin of the church at this time in history.[20] And Pulitzer Prize winner Annie Dillard puts it wryly when she writes:

> Does anyone have the foggiest idea what sort of power we blithely invoke? Or, as I suspect, does not one believe a word of it? The churches are children playing on the floor with their chemistry sets, mixing up a batch of TNT to kill a Sunday morning. It is madness to wear ladies' straw hats to church; we should all be wearing crash helmets. . . . For the sleeping God may wake some day and take offense, or the waking god may draw us out to where we can never return.[21]

LOVING OUR NEIGHBORS . . . AND OUR AUDIENCE

In a handout prepared by Brad Baurain, former adjunct literature instructor at Moody Bible Institute, he notes the functions literature fulfills:

Literature and the imagination may be thought of in terms of the greatest two commandments: to love God and to love our neighbors. If we are to love God with our whole selves—all our minds, hearts, souls and strength—we must do so with the imagination as well. If we designate the imagination as unnecessary, or childish, or for recreation only, we have in effect said to God, "There's a part of human nature that you have created that we are going to set aside." Since we do not want to find ourselves in such a position, it becomes our Christian responsibility to seek ways in which our imaginations can be part of obeying the commandment.[22]

As for loving our neighbors, literature helps us do so with insight and compassion, showing, not telling, the human experience it presents in concrete settings: people choosing, events happening, objects becoming symbols, communities developing. A significant part of loving our neighbors is understanding who they are.

Great preachers, like great writers, must cast a spell. The greatest preaching must cost the preacher something. It is demanding. It respects language, tells old stories in new and dimensional ways. It is lightning and sun. Its vision and ethos linger powerfully in the senses and spirit. It demands the reading of tried and true novels that make the soul stand on tiptoe and stimulate hearers to delight, conviction, and transformation.

ROSALIE DE ROSSET is professor of literature and communications at the Moody Bible Institute. She holds the Ph.D. from University of Illinois at Chicago, and has earned degrees from Trinity Evangelical Divinity School, Deerfield, Illinois; Northeastern Illinois University, Chicago; and Bryan College, Dayton, Tennessee.

NOTES

1. Colin Duriez, *C. S. Lewis Handbook* (Grand Rapids: Baker, 1990).

2. Warren Wiersbe, *Preaching and Teaching with Imagination* (Wheaton, Ill.: Victor, 1994), 62.

3. Alan Jones, *Journey Into Christ* (New York: Seabury, 1977), 24.

4. Robert N. Bellah, *The Broken Covenant* (New York: Seabury, 1975), 75.

5. Two resources that explain the power of class literature to apply imagination to

the Christian life and ministry are Vigen Guroian, *Tending the Heart of Virtue: How Classic Stories Awaken a Child's Moral Imagination.* New York: Oxford Univ. Press, 1998; and "On Literature and Ministry," *Theology, News and Notes* (December 1991): 3–23.

6. Garrison Keillor, *Good Poems* (New York: Penguin, 2002), xxvi.

7. Weirsbe, *Preaching and Teaching with Imagination,* 26.

8. Donald McCullough, "What Does Literature Have to Do With Ministry?" *Theology, News and Notes* (December 1991): 3.

9. Wiersbe, *Preaching and Teaching with Imagination,* 69.

10. Harold Fickett, *Holy Fool* (Westchester, Ill.: Crossway, 1984), 69, 71.

11. Mike Yaconelli, "When Our Souls Stand On Tiptoe," *The Wittenburg Door* (1976), 36, as quoted in *The Reformed Journal,* 21 (January 1977): 25.

12. Bryan Chapell, *Christ-Centered Preaching: Redeeming the Expository Sermon* (Grand Rapids: Baker, 1993), 168.

13. Wiersbe, *Preaching and Teaching with Imagination,* 19.

14. Ibid.

15. David S. Cunningham, *Faithful Persuasion: In Aid of a Rhetoric of Christian Theology* (Notre Dame, Ind.: Univ. of Notre Dame Press, 1990), 5.

16. Ibid.

17. Craig Dykstra, "Youth and the Language of Faith," *Religious Education,* 81, no.2 (Spring 1986): 163–179.

18. Emily Dickinson, "Tell the Truth But Tell It Slant," *The Complete Poems of Emily Dickinson,* ed. Thomas H. Johnson (Boston, Mass.: Little, Brown and Company, 1960), 506–07.

19. Lorraine Eitel, ed., *The Treasury of Christian Verse* (Old Tappan, N.J.: Revell, 1982), 156.

20. McCullough, "What Does Literature Have to Do with Ministry?" 13.

21. Annie Dillard, *Teaching a Stone to Talk* (New York: Harper and Row, 1982).

22. Brad Baurain, "A Christian Approach to Reading and Teaching Literature at Moody Bible Institute" (Department of General Education Handout, 1995), 1–2.

Seventeen

HISTORY:

THE HIDDEN

GOLD MINE

by
Thomas Cornman

A cartoon on the bulletin board in the faculty lounge shows a schoolteacher in front of her bleary-eyed class, distributing papers for a history lesson. The caption reads: "This may be boring to you, but at one time it was breaking news!"

Typically, historical illustration of a Scripture text suggests anything but a riveting, emotionally charged, or intellectually stimulating response. For a variety of reasons, some consider the past as irrelevant, boring, or a waste of time. In our Western, modern thinking with its worship of progress, we have come to believe that there is precious little we can learn from the past. It is impossible, we think, to gain perspective or enlightenment by the ideas and actions of primitives. After all, haven't we moved well beyond their limited understanding?

Yet some would dare to disagree. After all, the History Channel is incredibly popular and novels based on history sell well. For some, history is a curiosity. But in the general scheme of things, the current generation doesn't look for a usable past.

During my seminary days, I joined the staff of a midsized church in a suburb of Los Angeles. One day while talking with the senior pastor, he exclaimed that he wished he had realized the importance of history in general and church history in particular. Because he hadn't spent as much time studying the past, he had to relearn the history he had neglected because it was essential for the preparation of his sermons. Not only did he now understand the essential nature of history to provide critical background to his study of the Scriptures, he now realized the wealth of the past and its stories in illuminating the text. Good illustrations serve two useful purposes in the sermon. They provide clarity of the text and they provide a means of application. Historical illustrations serve both ends.

Later, as a fledgling church history instructor, I considered that pastor's foundational statement time and again. History not only informs us of where we've been, but also helps bring to life the lessons of Scripture as we seek to communicate the truth of God's Word. Many of us learn through the use of the story. Christ Himself presented much of His theology through the use of story. The rich history of the Christian church and the broader account of the human experience provide fertile ground for illustrations that speak to the human condition and stir the heart.

Just as we know that our personal stories and the story lines of great literature provide gripping illustrations for our listeners, so too the stories of our collective past help us to see clear examples of the scriptural concepts. It is never appropriate to preach history. Rather the correct use of history as illustration is to expose the text by bridging the idea of the text to the mind of the listener through calling upon the imagination. Historical illustrations give a reference to the meaning of Scripture.

Historical illustration comes in four primary varieties. *Human history* expounds on the common human experience. While the epoch may be different and the exact events may be unrepeatable, the rich illustration of the basic human condition can boldly illustrate a portion of Scripture. *Church history* presents the unique vantage point of the Christian past as illustration. Both the positives and the negatives of the life of the church can be used to illuminate the message of the Bible. *Biographies* of Christians and non-Christians alike can inspire and create a strong sense of identification. Finally, *personal histories* allow the listener to peer into our hearts, see who we really are, and how we struggle with making the Word of God a reality in our daily lives.

HUMAN HISTORY

Thousands of years of recorded history offer seemingly limitless examples of the human condition, which illustrate the precepts of the Word. As we mine the biblical text, we need to have an historical awareness; then an obscure text becomes clearer, taking the audience out of our limited present understandings and back to the time and understanding of the original readers. Often the preacher will assume that he knows what a word or concept means. Yet without getting back to the meaning of that era, he can come to very wrong conclusions.

For example, how many times have sermons suggested that in Ephesians 6 all elements of God's armor are defensive except one? The sword, we have been told, is the offensive weapon in the mix. Much has been written about the heavily armored soldiers of Greek and Roman times. God's armor in Paul's imagery is borne out of his knowledge as a first-century Roman citizen of both how they were outfitted and also how they fought.[1] If we peer into the past and examine the actual armor of the hoplite soldier on which Paul modeled his idea of God's armor, we find that the sword mentioned in Ephesians 6:17 was a *dagger* designed to provide for the soldier's *defense* rather than his offensive actions.[2] Thus the Word of God becomes a defense for us to withstand in the evil day and to stand firm against the cosmic forces arrayed against us. While we imagine the swords of King Arthur or Shakespeare's era, Paul had something else in mind. Thus, the reference to the history of Greek and Roman warfare, perhaps illustrated with pictures of discovered first century "swords," allows for a more accurate picture of Paul's point about the armor of God.

The book of Habakkuk was written around 600 B.C. Little is known about the prophet whose words we read, but we can all relate to his message. Habakkuk is concerned with evil in the world, especially as practiced by the people of Judah. They are God's people, and Habakkuk wonders aloud how God can allow such sordid behavior to go unpunished. God's answer is less than satisfying and Habakkuk and God engage in a dialogue about evil in the world and God's judgment, power, and goodness. This is a discussion of theodicy.

The Limits in Applying History

History provides a plethora of nations and individuals who could illustrate the story line of Habakkuk. The danger is that we will overstep the text in the selection of our illustration. History is the study of the record of the past left by human beings and speaks of their interaction with the world around them and with each other. This creates an important set of limits when using history to illustrate the sermon. It is essential to grasp the role of God within the context and limits of the record and my ability to discover it. It can be problematic to declare God's specific involvement in the world beyond biblical history. The trap of providentialism must be avoided as the quest for choice sermon illustrations progresses. The problem is not our belief in God's providence, but rather the assumption that you or I can discern that providence unambiguously in the historical record.

When we think of the context of Habakkuk and potential illustrations out of the record of the past, we find no scarcity of villains. Should we use Adolf Hitler? After all, he used his position to attack and massacre millions of Jewish men, women, and children. In the end, he too was destroyed and the nation he ruled was brought to its knees. Surely God can be seen in all of this. Yet, in doing so, the preacher may draw conclusions that are untenable. Were the Jewish people in the days before Hitler's rise to power guilty of the same types of sins as sixth-century B.C. Israelites? Did God raise up Hitler for the expressed purpose of judging the Jewish people? These are questions beyond our ability to determine. To use the rise of Nazis to power in Germany and the events of World War II to illustrate the story line of Habakkuk creates great difficulty. And, we may even bring great distress to Jewish believers in the process.

Perhaps the illustration of Idi Amin would work. The evil and debauched former dictator of Uganda serves as a clear example of a more wicked individual oppressing those who are less wicked. Yes, he was evil personified and many suffered under his brutal rule. But we really don't know the answer to the questions of why God allowed Idi Amin to rule.

Generally we can speak of God's sovereignty—no one rules without God's permission. That is a very different thing than to say that God placed Idi Amin in a position of rule to humble a nation and punish wrongdoing.

A providential approach to the book of Habakkuk that works is sticking with what we know to be true. In Habakkuk (as well as in the books of Jeremiah and Daniel) God shows us the means by which He would judge Judah for her sin and work to bring about the judgment of the nation He used as his instrument. The history of Nebuchadnezzar and the Babylonians illustrates exactly what God is doing. The text gives the entrée into the use of this story, because it is the story of the text. Providing details of the life of Nebuchadnezzar and the history of the Babylonian juggernaut helps to illuminate the text for the hearer, while keeping us firmly within the known providence of God.

Fallacies of the Historian

On a cautionary note, we must avoid the attempt to use the past to prove points not found in Scripture. There is a temptation to springboard from a text to make a statement about our present political or social context, which may not be the point of the passage and may not be an accurate representation of the situation. Preachers can be guilty of some of the same fallacies to which historians are known to succumb.[3] There is the fallacy of *exceptionalism* or ethnocentricity, which can mar the use of historical events as illustration. We can run into trouble when we assume by use of illustration that the American nation or church is unique or special in God's plan. The human condition is far more universal and our past far less unique than we would like to imagine. When we use the past as illustration we must not fall into the temptation of seeing our nation as the perfect positive illustration of a point in Scripture that is really about the people of God, or we are in dangerous territory. Daring to compare historic examples from the United States to historic events of Israel for illustrative purposes (e.g., comparing the American Revolution to early Israel's exodus from Egypt) puts us on shaky ground.

A clear example of this exceptionalism is found in a favorite hymn often sung around the Fourth of July. "The Battle Hymn of the Republic," by Julia Ward Howe was written in 1862, the second year of the American Civil War. In it we see the mingling of Christian truth with American exceptionalism. The final stanza reads,

> In the beauty of the lilies Christ was born across the sea,
> With a glory in his bosom that transfigures you and me;
> As he died to make men holy, let us live to make men free,
> While God is marching on.
> Glory! Glory, hallelujah! . . . His truth is marching on.

Notice where Christ was born—across the sea—He is a foreigner. In this hymn the locus of that which is viewed as central to the message of the hymn is in the western hemisphere and specifically the United States. In addition, the American Civil War is viewed as a battle of religious proportions. While it is clear that many on both sides of the battle were Christ-followers, it is dangerous when one side declares that God has chosen sides when we cannot know that for sure. One group becomes the unique friends of God while others, which may include believing Christians, become the enemies of God because they are not on our side.

It is also easy to slip into *presentism*—reading the past or a text of Scripture through the lens of our present situation or the backward projection of present phenomena.[4] Doing so can trivialize the importance of the text as we fail to grasp its significance within the historic framework of when it was written. Language and culture change can alter the meaning of an object or concept over time. If we attempt to illustrate, assuming that there has been no change, we can interject a serious change of thought through our illustration. Further, we must carefully avoid using what we believe to be a present positive reality to explain the past or the text. In the use of history closer to the present to illustrate a text from the first century A.D., it is quite possible to fall into the fallacy of making the more recent the clarifier of the more distant.

One of the ways presentism has shown itself in the church has been the way we understand pronouns and then draw conclusions about what their use means. Even though the King James Version is absent in most settings, when it is used, we struggle with the use of the familiar and polite pronouns in the English language. Many of us are not even aware that the English language has both a familiar and a polite set of pronouns. In 1611, when the King James Version was translated, such terms of address were a reality. In translating the second-person singular pronoun found throughout the Psalms and even in the New Testament, the translators chose to use "Thee" and "Thou" when the second-person singular pronoun referred to God, as opposed to the more acceptable "you" and "your" of today. Because the "thee" and "thou" sound more formal to the ear, the assumption has been that King David used these pronouns to show reverence toward God. The result has been to establish a sense of the distance of God toward man. In the seventeenth century, however, "thee" and "thou" were not the formal pronouns but the familiar. Therefore, we know that David was speaking to God in a more intimate sense rather than the reverential sense that we normally ascribe to Him.

How do we know this? The literature from the time of the translation provides the answer. There is an apocryphal story in which Samuel Pepys, a well-known diarist of the period, discusses his friendship with William Penn senior and junior. In his diary, he tells the story of William Penn Senior's annoyance with his son. He sent him to the king's court with a message and discovered that in the Quaker habit, the younger Penn addressed the king with the familiar "thee" and "thou" rather than the formal "you" and "your." According to Pepys, the elder Penn declared that if his son ever showed such disrespect to the king again, he would box his ears![5]

Reading our present understanding of the English language into the past, we persist in perceiving King James language as showing deference and reverence with its formality. Without the clarification from history, we might erroneously conclude from King James language that God is distant and unapproachable.

THE HISTORY OF THE CHURCH

Listening to an Established Community

We are part of a community that stretches back more than two thousand years. From Pentecost to the present, the people of God have struggled with the meaning of Scripture and the application of its truth to their daily lives. At times the church has struggled to find its way, veering off course for a time only to have some courageous members redirect her steps and bring her (sometimes kicking and screaming) back to the core beliefs. At other times, great leaders in the church have been able to crystallize an important but difficult truth in such a way as to give it greater clarity.

Evangelical historian Mark Noll notes, "We may view the Christian past like a gigantic seminar where trusted friends, who have labored long to understand the Scriptures hold forth in various corners of the room. There is Augustine discoursing about the Trinity, here St. Patrick and Count von Zinzendorf comparing notes on the power of light over darkness. . . ."[6]

Those who have grappled with the deep truths of Scripture and applied them to daily life must not be ignored. To ignore the hard work and significant insights of these saints would be foolishness.

In other cases, esteemed members of the Christian community have failed to live according to the standards established in the pages of Scripture. They have struggled to maintain cordial relationships centered on the unchanging common experience in Christ. We must learn from their failures.

Learning from Our Failures

Two eighteenth-century giants of the faith, George Whitefield and John Wesley, once had a dreadful disagreement. The depth of the animus that enveloped them led to many years of discord and lack of communication. Both of these men were great evangelists. John Wesley began open-air preaching at the invitation of Whitefield. When Whitefield left for America after years of itinerant ministry throughout England, he had asked Wesley to travel his open-air preaching circuit to continue to spread the gospel of Jesus Christ to the lower classes in English society. What led them to the point of broken relationship when they had been co-laborers for the cause of Christ?

Paul discussed two coworkers in his letter to the Philippians. The case of Euodia and Syntyche, recorded in Philippians 4:2–3, presents a familiar dilemma. Two people who loved the Lord and who labored side by side with Paul were now at odds. Paul doesn't let us know what the nature of the conflict was. Yet he calls upon a trusted leader in the church to help these women to resolve their differences and "agree in the Lord."

Like Euodia and Syntyche, Whitefield and Wesley allowed something other than the gospel to tear at the very fabric of their relationship in Christ. In this case a difference regarding a point of peripheral theology, not core or central to the faith, had driven a wedge between them, isolating them and in the process diminishing the ministries of both men. Although both were called to preach the gospel, they had allowed their views concerning free will and divine election to separate them. Their personal theological differences made it into print and divided evangelicals in Great Britain. It was not until just before Whitefield's death in 1770 that a rapprochement was accomplished. Numerous British Christians had attempted to aid in bringing the two together. Finally, after years of acrimony it was accomplished. Wesley preached Whitefield's funeral sermon. Despite the eventual union, their years of enmity seriously injured the evangelical cause.[7]

John MacArthur bases his book *The Truth War* on the Letter of Jude. In his exposition of the epistle, MacArthur frequently turns to church history to drive home the truth of Jude's words. He explains the issues surrounding Jude's words, "I found it necessary to write appealing to you to contend for the faith that was once for all delivered to the saints. For certain people have crept in unnoticed who long ago were designated for this condemnation, ungodly people, who pervert the grace of our God into sensuality and deny our only Master and Lord, Jesus Christ" (vv. 3–4 ESV).

Who were these people? What were the doctrines that were destroying the church? MacArthur goes on to catalog the groups at the time of Jude's writing who exhibited the doctrinal and behavioral deficiencies described. Judaizers and Gnostics were claiming to be part of the church and presented views that confused and led astray many young Christians. The church continued to struggle with those from within who challenged orthodoxy denying the deity of Christ. Modalists and Arians began to have such a presence in the church that they outnumbered those who believed Christ was fully and completely God. MacArthur recounts the story of Athanasius who, against great pressure from the church and the political powers of that day, contended for this cardinal doctrine to the point of exile from the Roman Empire.[8] The continuing significance of Jude's text is revealed in these examples from church history.

BIOGRAPHIES

Learning from the Saints

Those who have preceded us in this community of faith provide a rich tapestry of experiences to illustrate the meaning and application of Scripture. We can learn from men and women of faith who have demonstrated unswerving commitment to the God of the Bible. We can find powerful illustrations in the intersection between the lives of the saints and the text of Scripture.

In the process we must be careful to avoid hagiography, literally "holy writing." The saints who have gone before us and thus who share the journey must be portrayed accurately as those with both God-derived virtue and human foibles. We do no great service to God or our congregants when we present a picture wholly inaccurate in its inflated representation of the person we use to illustrate. We must avoid trying to find a place to insert a biographical illustration simply because we found a good one and need a place to use it. The text should draw us to the illustration rather than the other way around.

Five years before he died, R. A. Torrey, evangelist and early president of Moody Bible Institute, set about to answer a question that had been posed to him frequently over the years. Why had God so mightily used D. L. Moody? Torrey was quick to point out that he felt secure in answering the question because it would not be an attempt to glorify D. L. Moody, but rather a means of glorifying God.

I have heard a number of sermons on Micah 6:8 in recent years. Many have used Old Testament history for illustrations. Yet Torrey's *Why God Used D. L. Moody* provides another option for illustrating this verse. Micah 6:8 reads, "He has told you, O man, what is good; and what does the Lord require of you but to do justice, and to love kindness and to walk humbly with your God" (ESV). The fourth point in R. A. Torrey's treatise is that God used D. L. Moody because he was a humble man. Of Moody he wrote:

One day, speaking to me of a great New York preacher, now dead, Mr. Moody said: "He once did a very foolish thing, the most foolish thing that I ever knew a man, ordinarily so wise as he was, to do. He came up to me at the close of a little talk I had given and said: 'Young man, you have made a great address tonight.'" Then Mr. Moody continued: "How foolish of him to have said that! It almost turned my head." But thank God, it did not turn his head, and even when pretty much all the ministers in England, Scotland and Ireland, and many of the English bishops were ready to follow D. L. Moody wherever he led, even then it never turned his head one bit. He would get down on his face before God, knowing he was human, and ask God to empty him of all self-sufficiency. And God did.[9]

D. L. Moody's humility so beautifully illustrates the final statement of Micah 6:8. His humility was borne out of his walk with God. He was dependent on God to maintain a true sense of humility rather than the false humility, which sometimes characterizes those who claim to speak for God.

Using Biographical Stories Properly

There are times when a book or an article seems to present us with the perfect illustration. If only we had a text with which to use it! The urge to use what we've discovered can lead us to the prospect of shoe-horning a good illustration into the wrong text. Several years ago I read the amazing biography of Brother Yun called *The Heavenly Man.*[10] His account contained many nuggets that were just waiting to be told. I have yet to use any in a sermon as illustration. Why? Because I've never preached a text where any part of his life story would serve as a meaningful illustration.

But should I ever preach from Luke 21:12–19, I have an illustration. The context is Jesus' prophecy concerning the destruction of the temple. His disciples ask when this will happen. Jesus provides an answer that both anticipates the end of the age and warns the disciples of those things they will experience. Verse 12 begins a brief section on the persecution of the disciples.[11] The text says:

But before all this, they will lay hands on you and persecute you. They will deliver you to synagogues and prisons, and you will be brought before kings, and governors, and all on account of my name. This will result in being witnesses to them. But make up your mind not to worry beforehand how you will defend yourselves. For I will give you words and wisdom that none of your adversaries will be able to resist or contradict. You will be betrayed even by parents, brothers, relatives and friends, and they will put some of you to death. (vv. 12–16)

Spoken in the first century A.D., the words of this text are illustrated by the life of Brother Yun of China. Brother Yun had been imprisoned once more for preaching the Word of God within China. He was to be tried, and the outcome was almost certainly life in prison or death. At a pretrial hearing, his cousin was the judge. The cousin tried to secure information from Brother Yun with the promise of leniency. Brother Yun stood firm and did not give the names of fellow believers.[12] Instead this is what he told his cousin: "Although we are cousins, you work for the communist party and I serve Jesus Christ. I insist on practicing my beliefs. What you've said about me is true, but I know nothing about the activities of other people."[13]

His cousin responded with stunned silence.

Brother Yun was returned to his cell and when the trial took place, he was handed a lighter sentence than expected—four years! God gave him the words to say and confounded those who sought to judge him.

How precious are the feet of those who preach the gospel (see Isaiah 52:7), and how compelling are their biographies. God continues to work through His choice servants and they continue to illustrate the importance of key texts of Scripture for our lives. Whether dead for hundreds of years, or alive and continuing to live out the gospel, we must not ignore the lives of dedicated Christ-followers in our illustrations.

PERSONAL STORIES

Using Personal Stories Properly

The role of the personal story in the sermon is a point of contention. Although heavily used, its critics challenge its effectiveness. Richard

Eslinger of Duke Divinity School argues that most personal stories will not accomplish the task of connecting the reader to the point. Instead it can distance the preacher and the audience by highlighting and setting the preacher apart from the congregation, thus losing the impact of the first-person story.[14] This appraisal can be true if the purpose of the illustration is to make the preacher to be either a hero or a victim. I can recall *good* the preacher who used himself as an example in a sermon about prayer by mentioning that his only problem in praying is that he prays too long!

Using oneself as an example of God's work within the believer's life should have a different effect on the congregation. Used correctly, the homiletician is not glorifying his own actions or thoughts, but rather using himself as an example of how God applies the precept of the text in the life of the believer. The story is compelling when it focuses on the work of God in the experience of the individual.

Illustrating Our Journey as Co-Followers of Christ

An honest assessment of our lives reveals moments of failure and moments of obedience, which highlight the grace and goodness of God in relation to specific truths of His Word. There are other times when we are the observers of His goodness. These moments, expressed as part of the journey of co-followers of Christ, can serve as powerful illuminations of the text.

A few years ago, I was in the process of interviewing for a new position. I was feeling a significant amount of stress about the possibility of the change and its impact on my family, especially my teenaged children. For some strange reason, I couldn't get the worship song "Open the Eyes of my Heart" out of my head. It played over and over again. Was God trying to tell me something? At a critical point in the interview process, I was given a note saying that my son had been taken to the emergency room and was in serious condition with an infection. It didn't look good. In an instant, I had to come to grips with why I wanted the position, where my value and worth came from, and whether my identity was really in Christ. Was the position more important than my God-given responsibilities as a husband and a father? Not long after those events, I was preparing a sermon on Ephesians 1:15–23. Verse 18 begins "having the eyes of your heart enlightened . . ." The passage goes on to state that the reason Paul was praying that this would happen was so that the Ephesians would know three things: the hope to which God had called them, the riches that accrued to them as God's inheritance, and the greatness of His power toward believers. Paul wanted those eyes of the heart opened so that the Ephesians would know who they were in Christ—the source of their identity and value. God was doing the same thing in my life. He was opening the eyes of my heart, or enlightening them, so that I too could know from where I derived my identity. And once more, I was the recipient of His grace.

The honest unvarnished expression of our experiences can serve as powerful illustrations for the texts of the Bible. These personal histories, when presented with a focus on the work of God may not make us larger than life in the minds of our congregants, but they should point them to the one who desires their best and has called upon us to help them in that quest.

HIDDEN TREASURES OF THE PAST

The past with its hidden treasures is waiting for us. The richness of human experience can help us to explain and apply the Scripture for our audience. The time and effort of the search will be worth it. As we work to make the text central and then provide illustrations to drive the point home, our listeners will have real-life examples to better comprehend the meaning of God's communication with them.

So, read those history books, spend some time watching the History Channel. Pick up that biography you have always wanted to read. Explore the history of the Christian past. As you journey through the world of history, file away the nuggets you find. At the proper time, you will be working through a text and the appropriate illustration, seemingly made for the text, will be ready to help your audience better understand or apply the truths.

THOMAS H. L. CORNMAN is dean of the undergraduate school at the Moody Bible Institute. He holds the Ph.D. degree in United States history from the University of Illinois, Chicago, as well as degrees from Philadelphia Biblical University, Talbot School of Theology, La

Mirada, California, and Temple University, Philadelphia.

NOTES

1. See Chester G. Starr, *A History of the Ancient World* (New York: Oxford, 1965), 210.

2. The word used in Ephesians 6:17 is *machaira*: a short (around fifteen inches or less) sword or dagger used in close-in fighting. See John Childs, ed., *A Dictionary of Military History and the Arts of War*, English edition (Cambridge, Mass.: Blackwell, 1994), 81; and John Howard Yoder, *The Politics of Jesus* (Grand Rapids: Eerdmans, 1994), 149.

3. This idea is borrowed from David Hackett Fischer, *Historians' Fallacies: Toward a Logic of Historical Thought* (New York: Harper, 1970). Fischer includes in his list of fallacies both ethnocentricity (exceptionalism) and presentism.

4. Fischer, *Historians' Fallacies*, 136.

5. While the story cannot be documented, it does ring true to William Penn the Younger's habits as a Quaker. See *The Journals of George Fox*, vol. 1 (London: T Sowle, 1694), preface written by William Penn the Younger.

6. Mark A. Noll, *Turning Points* (Grand Rapids: Baker, 2000), 16.

7. Ian Murry. Ian Murray on Whitefield and Wesley found at http://www.spurgeon.org-phil/wesley/murray.htm; and John Giles, ed., *Memoirs of the Reverend George Whitefield*, vol. 2 (Hartford, Conn.: E. Hunt, 1853), 466.

8. John MacArthur, *The Truth War* (Nashville: Nelson, 2007), 85–94, 100–115.

9. R. A. Torrey, *Why God Used D. L. Moody* (n. p. 1923); see also www.whatsaiththescripture.com/Voice/Why.God.Used.D.L.Moody.html

10. Brother Yun and Paul Hattaway, *The Heavenly Man: The Remarkable True Story of Chinese Christian Brother Yun* (Grand Rapids: Monarch Books, 2002).

11. I. Howard Marshall, *Commentary on Luke* (Grand Rapids: Eerdmans, 1978), 765–66.

12. Yun and Hattaway, *The Heavenly Man*, 159.

13. Ibid., 159–60.

14. Richard L. Eslinger, "Story and Image in Sermon Preparation," *Journal for Preachers* (Decatur, Ga.) vol. 9 (1986) 2:19.

Eighteen

LEARNING

TO TELL

THE STORY

by
William Torgesen III

W hether it's a child listening in her bed or a group of friends shar-ing stories around a campfire, everyone loves a good story. A good story engages our sense of adventure, stimulates our curiosity, and develops our capacity to see beyond the words of a page or the lips of a speaker and into the drama of the story itself. Stories bring the past into the pres-ent, they build bridges from one life to another, and they help to expand our ability to understand and relate to the world around us. Everyone loves a good story!

More than anyone, God loves stories. God loves to share stories, and He loves to share them with us. The Bible is filled with hundreds of sto-ries focusing upon real lives filled with real drama as people wrestle with issues of what it means to live with a genuine faith. When we look at the entire Bible we find that it tells the story of redemption and God's in-credible love for humanity. After all, we confidently declare that history is "His Story." Since we believe that the Bible is inspired by God and there-fore written by the divine penmanship of God, then we must realize that

God is telling us much about Himself and about humanity through the use of story. While the story of our ultimate redemption awaits its final culmination, it is yet a complete and finished story.

God loves to tell a good story, and He calls us to tell them as well. When we study the Old Testament we realize that faith was nurtured and protected through the means of story. The nation of Israel depended upon the spoken story in order to keep their faith alive and well. Much of what the people knew of God's power, God's promises, God's protection, and God's presence was learned as each generation passed on the story of God's redemption. In fact, we see Moses reminding the nation of Israel to never forget the stories of their faith, and to share these stories with their children from generation to generation lest they forget and forsake their God (Deut. 6:1–15). It was vital to the welfare of the nation that they remembered to share their stories of faith with one another.

We see that same example in the New Testament. The disciples told the story of Christ and the story of the cross before those stories were ever recorded in Scripture. Paul used the art of storytelling throughout his ministry. His greatest means of evangelization was the story of his own salvation. It's hard to argue against a life that has been changed by the work of Christ upon the cross.

One of the greatest tools the Christian can develop is the ability to share the story of one's own salvation. Our own unique experiences provide a platform for declaring God's grace in our lives. Ultimately, Christ's life and ministry tell the greatest story ever told, and we share the story of Christ every time we share the gospel with another human being. We do the same thing when we share in the ordinance of Communion. As we share of the elements we are reminded of Christ's death and the story of the cross. We all have a story to tell.

LEARNING FROM THE MASTER STORYTELLER

When it comes to the art of telling a story, there is no one better than our Lord and Savior Jesus Christ. Throughout His ministry Christ used the power of the spoken story to connect biblical truth to the hearts and minds of His listeners. In some cases He spoke in parables using portraits from life to point to a deeper truth within the story. At other times Christ pointed to everyday events to explain extraordinary truth. Our Lord knew that there were times when the Word alone was what was needed to change hearts and minds, but there were other times when biblical truth was best presented through the use of illustrations. Therefore, in Luke 15 when Christ wanted to demonstrate the Father's grace and mercy, He didn't begin by stating, "Thus says the Lord," but He began by saying, "There was a man who had two sons" (v. 11) Then through the story of the prodigal son Christ drove home the truth of divine forgiveness and restoration.

Christ was a master storyteller because He could bridge the world of biblical truth into the lives of His hearers, and He could build a bridge from the lives of His hearers into the world of biblical truth! Both are needed and both must be included in the sermon.

DEVELOPING VITAL CONNECTIONS

Today people still love stories and people still long for truth. They long to better understand the pages of Scripture and how the Scriptures apply to their lives. People need to hear the truth of Scripture and that should never be debated, but they also need to hear the stories of faith and the illustrations of life to help them to better understand how truth affects their individual lives. We make a major mistake in preaching when we preach void of truth, but we make a similar mistake when we proclaim truth void of any connection to life. While truth is vital for our faith, it must be delivered in a way that is understandable and applicable for the listener. In his classic book *Between Two Worlds*, John Stott addresses this crisis in the pulpit today by stating that "a major reason for the contemptuous dismissal of some sermons is that people perceive them to be unrelated to real life as they know it."[1] In other words, people dismiss the message because the message misses them. We need to work hard at connecting with the congregation, and helping them to connect to the sermon. Illustrations can help to provide that vital connection.

It is often said that the pendulum swings to extremes, and such is the case when it comes to preaching. While illustrations are vital to the sermon, they must always be subordinate to the passage and not the other way around. Illustrations are just a tool to aid in the communication of God's Word and must never serve as a replacement for the truth. The danger today is that there are many times when the story becomes the driving force of the sermon at the expense of Scripture. People may weep at a well-told story, but they need truth to bring about eternal change. Both of these extremes are tragic mistakes. One leaves the listener with truth but no relevance, and the other leaves the listener with relevance but no truth. The end result is that listeners are left in the same place as when they entered into the sermon in the first place. The goal of all preaching is to bring glory to God and to change lives for God's glory! We need to work hard at transforming our sermons so that they build bridges from the words of biblical truth, to the world of our listeners.[2] The question is how do we do this without the pendulum swinging so wide we miss the mark when it comes to preaching?

FINDING A STORY THAT FITS

Anyone who has preached for any length of time knows that it's not always what is included in the message that makes or breaks the message, but it's what is left on the editing floor that often matters most. In other words, what you put into the message will make it very good, but what you leave out will make it even better. We need to be very selective when it comes to the supporting content we place within the sermon.

So when do we choose to include a story? The answer: Use a story when it fits the message, fits the audience, and is fit for telling.

First, *the story must fit the message*. Too often illustrations are found that fit the topic we need for the moment, such as the topic of grace, but they don't fit the context of the message or the specific point we're trying to make. As a result, we tend to force the story into the sermon. While an illustration may look great on paper, if it doesn't connect with the context of the passage, then the listener won't make the connection to the purpose of the sermon. In fact, more than likely people will remember the story and forget the rest. As we select illustrations, they must fit into the biblical truth that we are trying to highlight. If they don't then they should be left on the editing floor, and we continue to press on.

Second, *the story must fit the audience*. This would include culture, gender, age, and race. It's critical that we know the people who make up our congregations. Too often we're worried about what we will say instead of being concerned with how it will be received. There are many illustrations that will offend women. There are illustrations that will leave our children and youth in the dark. There are illustrations that will confuse those with cultural differences. Still others will divide us rather than unite us. But some will ignore race or ethnicity, and instead create tension and turmoil in the life of the listener. We must be sensitive to the work of the Holy Spirit in our lives, and sensitive to the life of the church in terms of its diversity as we prepare.

Third, *the story must be fit for telling.* Some illustrations have no place in a sermon. While humor at times might have its place, some humor is nothing more than distasteful. Some illustrations and stories are so archaic and out-of-date that the listener simply cannot relate to them. Many of the illustration books themselves seem to fit that category. They were written years ago and the illustrations contained within are no longer relevant. Such books can be scanned in a library for the few nuggets one might find, but it wouldn't pay to purchase them for one's shelves. Many illustration books published in the past decade do provide a far greater resource for the speaker—but remember, a day will come when these too will be out-of-date.

Still, contemporary resources are always available. Many preaching publications, such as *Leadership Journal*, contain current illustrations that can be adapted to the sermon. Today there are online resources such as Preaching Today.com and SermonCentral.com that provide a storehouse of illustrative material at the click of a button.

The best place by far to find illustrations is from life itself. We need to learn how to look for stories that are being told around us every day. Stories that describe the struggles of life, and illustrations that tell of our victorious faith—stories that tell of our doubts and fears, and our trials and temptations. We need to become students of life. We need to learn to observe more carefully, and as we do we will find that life is filled with stories.

Most of all, we need to listen to people's stories. To remember what life is like apart from God, and then to reflect upon what God is doing in the lives of the people that we preach to! Most important, write them down. For the sake of preaching, write them down. For years I've used a thin digital recorder so that as illustrations come to mind, or I see a story unfold before my eyes, I can enter the details into the recorder and edit them at a later date. If I don't have the recorder handy, I find any piece of paper I can find and I write the illustration down.

The key to finding illustrations can be found during our study times. If the goal of preaching is transformation, then we need to make it our goal to focus on two very important aspects of our study. We need to focus upon the exegesis of the text and upon the exegesis of the congregation. This means that we need to spend a tremendous amount of time poring over and through the passage that we will be preaching, but also pondering deeply over the lives of those who will be listening. I've come to call this season of study the process of saturation. As we dig into the depths of God's truths, His truth begins to saturate our souls. Words and phrases begin to take priority and precedence in the understanding of the passage. Soon the main points begin to take shape, and the sermon itself begins to unfold. It's during this time of saturation that the speaker needs to saturate their soul with the lives of the congregation. It's here that we need to take time to consider the condition of our listeners.[3]

What struggles do they face, what difficulties do they endure, what trials do they encounter? What are their concerns and worries? For example, when Scripture tells us in Philippians 4:6 that we should "not be anxious," we need to consider the various ways in which anxiety paralyzes the faith of many. Not just at the surface level, but at every level. In what ways are husbands anxious today? They're anxious about their careers, anxious about their health, anxious about their retirement. What do mothers worry about? They worry about their children, worry about their husbands, and worry about the fact that they worry too much. What do parents fear today? They fear that their children might be using drugs, they fear because this world is no longer a safe place to live, and they fear for their children's future. As we contemplate the various levels that anxiety takes place in the life of a congregation, soon an illustration comes to mind, or the perfect story finds its way into the study notes. If the sermon is going to transform lives then we need to become experts in understanding the human soul.

Once we've slowed down to saturate ourselves with Scripture, the congregation, and the context of our culture, we will find that we have more than enough material to fit the sermon.

PAINTING PICTURES

It has been said that a picture is worth a thousand words. I've never been an avid photographer, but I do love to take pictures. Others love to paint pictures! When taking a picture what we are really trying to do is capture the essence of the moment, or the essence of a human being. And so we try to capture the perfect sunset, or we try to capture a certain smile. What we capture in the lens of the camera we're hoping will eventually capture the imagination of the person looking at that photo years later and hundreds of miles away. When we communicate we're trying to capture that same effect and capture the same results.

Haddon Robinson describes this process well in his classic book *Biblical Preaching* when he writes, "As pigments define the artist's picture, so words capture and color the preacher's thoughts."[4] When we speak, we want people to literally "live in the moment." We want them to sense the surroundings, to see the colors, to hear the sounds, and to feel the breeze upon their face.

One of the greatest reasons that we depend so heavily upon multimedia today is because we've lost the fine art of rhetoric.[5] We forget that it has only been in the last fifty years that we've had multimedia available to us. Prior to that, if pictures were painted they were painted on canvas, or in the theatre, or through the use of words on radio or in person or in books. The great preachers throughout history knew how to captivate the listener with their words. When we read through the sermons of Chrysostom, Augustine, Whitefield, and Spurgeon, we will quickly discover that each one of them knew the art of rhetoric, and they knew how to make their words speak. George Whitefield is a great example of a preacher who knew how to use his words wisely. It is said that he was once preaching and began to describe a man who was nearing the edge of a cliff, and as he was speaking his words were so descriptive and vivid that Lord Chesterfield rose up and shouted, "He's gone, He's gone!"[6] His words were so colorful that the listeners could visually see the person falling over the cliff, and so powerful were his words that they could feel the emotion of the tragedy.

We have to always keep in mind that what we lack visually we have to create verbally in order for the listener to hear what they need to see. Good communicators play the role of the projector, and their words become the screen upon which the audience connects with the sights and sounds of the story!

Good communication doesn't happen by accident. It takes hard work to prepare a sermon, and it takes hard work to prepare the components of a good sermon. We pore over text, we pore over the grammar, and we pore over the commentaries as we gather our notes for the sermon. Much of our labor is spent mining the gold that we hope to deliver to the listener. Unfortunately, we don't spend nearly the same amount of time when it comes to illustrating and applying the text. If we did, our preaching would be far more penetrating. We must take painstaking effort to craft our introductions, illustrations, applications, and conclusions so that they are not simply additions to our sermon notes, but become part of the very fiber of the sermon itself. In order to accomplish this we need to learn to be artists and craftsmen when it comes to preaching.

BECOMING ARTISTS AND CRAFTERS
OF WORDS AND STORIES

First, we need to learn the art of crafting words. The way in which we tell the story will make all the difference in the world. If we don't create suspense, if we don't enter into the world of our listeners, they won't want to follow us to the text. Every illustration needs to be written in such a way that every word has a purpose and a meaning. Gardner Taylor, often referred to as the dean of black preachers, sums it well by stating, "I think our preachers ought to seek to cloth the gospel in as worthy a language as they can find . . . it should have an added sense of the majesty of life, the glory of its possibilities, and the greatness and the glory of God."[7]

Too often illustrations are simply copied from a book and pasted into the sermon, or written verbatim on an index card and carried into the pulpit. Stories should be told in our own voice and in our own unique manner. Therefore, it is prudent to rewrite the illustration making the stylistic changes needed for the illustration to flow smoothly within the sermon. This assumes that the preacher is writing a manuscript of the sermon. While it's not recommended that the manuscript be taken into the pulpit, the writing out of the sermon including the illustrations allows the speaker to gain a sense of the delivery. It's important that we take as much time to prepare our words as we do in our study of the Word. We need to work at eliminating words that distract or confuse, and replace them with words that attract and provide clarity. The words we select matter, and they should be chosen and crafted in such a way that they capture the imagination of the listener, and draw *great* them into the passage we are proclaiming.

Once we craft our words, we need to weave the story within the sermon. Too often illustrations are randomly placed within the sermon without thought of the flow or movements of the sermon. As a result, the illustrations appear to be awkward and out of place. As the sermon is being formed the story needs to be placed in the most strategic position within the sermon as possible. Sometimes the illustration sets the stage for a key aspect of the passage, other times the illustration reinforces and highlights the truth already spoken. Where we place the story matters. Illustrations need to be placed within the sermon with a sense of purpose and precision.

Once the story is positioned properly, we stitch it into the message. Key transitions are prepared for the introduction and conclusion of the story so that it fits neatly within the sermon. One of the weaknesses in preaching today is in this vital area of sermon preparation and delivery. Since so many find their introductions-illustrations-conclusions at the latter stages of sermon development, the vital transitions needed to move the listener through the movements of the message are neglected or ignored. Transitions should move the listener from the passage to the present and back into the heart of the passage. If we plan to tell a story to illustrate a key concept from Scripture, then the illustration needs to be set up by a transition, or even a series of transitions that move us from the passage to contemporary world the listeners live within. In this sense the story is woven into the fabric of the sermon.

Next, we need to learn the art of storytelling. There is indeed an art to telling a story. One of the best ways in which we can develop this skill is simply listening to good storytellers. Listen to great preachers, or read their sermons. Read with the eye, but listen with the ear and the heart. Watch how they move into the story and how they set the stage. Listen for the ways in which they create the suspense or the tension within the story and how it connects the listener to the passage. Look for words of emotion, intensity, and drama and pay careful attention to how they are placed. Listen to their cadence and their rhythm as they tell the story. When do they pause, and why? When do they repeat themselves, and why?

Another way we can improve in our ability to tell a story is by reading great stories. Great writers have a great writing voice. What are they doing that draws you into the story line? What are they doing that seems to force you to keep reading on toward the finish? How do they move from one scene to another scene? We can learn much from those who have the skill to tell stories well. Every story needs to have an introduction, a body, and a concluding point.[8] I like to think of these movements in terms of setting the stage, presenting the play, the finale, and then the curtain call.

In setting the stage we are preparing the listener to hear what we are about to describe for them through the story. This would include transition from the passage to the relevant information such as when the story took place, those involved in the story, and where the event was held. The play itself is the body of the story and includes the content or the heart of the illustration. Here is where the drama takes place and the tension in the illustration occurs. In Christ's illustration of the prodigal son this is where we find him squandering his inheritance, feeding on the husks of the swine, and wondering if it's at all possible to head back home (Luke 15:3–32). The finale is just what it sounds like; it's the conclusion of the story. Only here the finale highlights the grand theme or truth in such a way that it can't be missed. The prodigal son was lost, but now he is found!

Finally, the curtain call—we place the transition back to the passage, but as we transition we look for the opportunity to repeat or reframe the key concept or idea that the story was meant to illustrate. Each aspect of the story should be crafted with considerable detail and precision. David Larson reminds us,

> The preacher is not simply a technician, but a craftsman and an artist in the handling, ordering, and expressing of God's truth. . . . In one sense creativity is doing what other people don't. There are those so adept at creative expression that they can preach about Noah's ark and their listeners can hear it rain! . . . Aristotle maintained that the soul never thinks without pictures."9

LEARN TO TELL THE STORY WELL

Ultimately, the point of the story is to point us to the Scripture. We tell stories simply to help people to better understand the truth of God's Word. The priority of the story is to provide a clearer picture of what Scripture is declaring to be true. People should remember the story, but only so far as they can remember how the story points them to truth. Illustrations should be designed to enhance and enforce the message and tie into the point we're making from the passage itself. Therefore the story must always be secondary to the passage itself.

God loves a good story, especially when those stories magnify Him. Sermons should never be boring, and it's equally important that the stories we share are never boring either. That's why it is essential that we as preachers learn to tell the story, and learn to tell the story well.

WILLIAM J. TORGESEN III is assistant professor of pastoral studies at the Moody Bible Institute. He is completing studies for the Doctor of Ministry at Trinity Evangelical Divinity School, Deerfield, Illinois. He holds degrees from Trinity Evangelical Divinity School and Moody Bible Institute.

NOTES

1. John Stott, *Between Two Worlds: The Challenge of Preaching Today* (Grand Rapids: Eerdmans, 1982), 59.

2. Ibid., 137.

3. Wayne McDill, *The 12 Essentials Skills for Great Preaching* (Nashville: Broadman and Holman, 1994), 211.

4. Haddon W. Robinson, *Biblical Preaching*, 2nd ed. (Grand Rapids: Baker, 2001), 184.

5. Timothy Turner, *Preaching to Programmed People* (Grand Rapids: Kregel, 1995), 22.

6. David Larson, *The Anatomy of Preaching* (Grand Rapids: Kregel, 1989), 111.

7. Gardner Taylor, *Communicate with Power*, ed. Michael Duduit (Grand Rapids: Baker, 1996), 208–210.

8. Bryan Chapell, *Christ-Centered Preaching: Redeeming the Expository Sermon* (Grand Rapids: Baker, 1994), 182.

9. Larson, *The Anatomy of Preaching*, 106–107.

Nineteen

FILM AS A MEANS

FOR WORSHIP AND

ILLUSTRATION

by
Michael Orr

During 2006, two films gained the attention and response of American evangelicals: *The Chronicles of Narnia: The Lion, The Witch, and the Wardrobe* (Disney) and *The DaVinci Code* (Sony). One received the church's enthusiastic support; the other received well-deserved critical scrutiny. Both films demonstrated not only how we as Christians are becoming more familiar with contemporary film offerings, but also how the church can use and react to film in a way that teaches and promotes meaningful discussions.

For C. S. Lewis, author of the Narnia series, fantasy and story were a preferred means to present biblical characters and virtues to a mass audience. Perhaps, as never before, the church is also acknowledging the use of story as an effective way to present God's truth to postmodern audiences. In his book *Windows to the Soul*, Ken Gire explains that stories have the power to incarnate values by fleshing out universal principles.[1]

As a churchgoer, movie buff, and professor of communications, I have seen how films can be used to teach, inspire, and convict worshipers in congregational and small group settings. In this chapter, we will explore how pastors can effectively use film in the worship setting. We will see how pastors can help church audiences engage in a meaningful dialogue about film content in order to reinforce and clarify biblical truths, and how film clips and film references can be effectively selected and used for sermonic illustrations and theological clarification. Finally, we will offer some cautions about bringing film into the worship experience.

Some may ask, Why bring films into the worship setting at all? You might risk confusing church audiences. You could encourage inappropriate viewing of films by congregants or you might distract or diminish the worship experience from its proper focus on God and His Word.

Part of our hesitancy to use films in a worship setting is based upon misperceptions about our church audience. The Barna Group's research reveals that in 2004, 95 percent of all adults saw at least one movie in the previous year, and the median number of movies watched in that same year was 38, or approximately three per month. In addition, an increasing number of viewers watch films at home. According to Barna's 2006 study, 84 percent of born-again Christians own DVD players in contrast to 85 percent of non-born-again Christians, making no distinguishable difference between the two groups.[2] Also, researchers at MarketCast, a leading Hollywood marketing firm, found religious and nonreligious people indistinguishable in their film and television viewing habits.[3] The question is not whether churchgoers will be confused or discouraged by the use of film content in their worship experience, but, rather, will the church step in to demonstrate and teach its members and seekers how to appropriately interpret or evaluate film? Can we demonstrate how to see film through a Christian lens?

JEREMIAH AND EZEKIEL:
DRAMATIC AND VISUAL PERSUASION

For those who are still doubtful about the use of film in the worship context, we should remember that ours is a God who has often used unusual and unconventional ways to teach and reprimand His people. The prophets were often led by God to demonstrate truth with dramatic and visual persuasion. Jeremiah was commanded to bind a yoke on his shoulders and to warn the people of Judah not to rebel against the Babylonian conquest of their land (Jer. 27). Ezekiel was commanded by God to use multimedia messages as a way to convince Judah to submit to Babylonian captivity. God directed the prophet to draw Jerusalem on a clay tile, to act out the siege of Jerusalem, and to acquire an iron plate and put it up between him and the city.

All those actions by Ezekiel were attempts to visually dramatize the inevitability of Judah's capture and deportation. And these three acts together formed only one of ten "signs" that Ezekiel was directed to present to God's wayward people (Ezek. 4:1–3).

In the New Testament, Paul stands before the "men of Athens" and references pagan religious practices and quotes from secular poets in order to context the reality that God is calling all people everywhere to repent (Acts 17).

If it is true that God directs the writers of Scripture to address their audiences in contemporary, relevant ways and that our Christian audiences are regularly exposed to popular media, it would seem wise for church leaders to use a biblical style of visual and dramatic proclamation. With appropriate direction, church audiences can understand popular media texts as appropriate material for worship, instruction, and evangelism.

Of course, not all popular media elicit a response that is appropriate in a worship setting. By exploring how Christian audiences respond to film, and other popular arts, we can better examine how to interpret and use film content in worship.

In his book *Eyes Wide Open*, Bill Romanowski contends that though the believer should not fall prey to the naive influences of popular culture, the popular arts *can* be used to enrich worship, to affirm statements of faith, and to encourage believers in a more active faith. Romanowski encourages us to study popular culture in general and film in particular, discerning both its positive and negative aspects in a fulfillment of our call to subdue and redeem all of God's culture.[4]

RESPONSES FROM THE CONGREGATION

For our purposes, I will suggest that the preacher consider the most typical responses to films:

Resistance

The first critical response to film often made by Christians is resistance. This is a position often held by conservative viewers who distrust the motives of the film industry and/or deny the values that seem to dominate film culture (i.e., materialism or libertarianism). Others may resist watching films because they feel participating in this form of entertainment might lead others astray. They fear that attending films or certain films will have negative influences on their lives or the lives of others to whom they feel responsible.

So in selecting film clips as sermon illustrations, a preacher should carefully consider the appropriateness of the film's values and content. While valuable in terms of content, the preacher should realize that some films will simply not be appropriate for general church viewing. The preacher will also need to place the film in context. The listening audience should be helped to understand and embrace the theme of the film if they are going to appreciate the application that the film suggests.

In 1 Peter 4, the apostle Peter makes it clear that in the stewardship of our spiritual gifts, whether preaching or teaching, the ultimate goal is that in all things God may be glorified (vs. 10, 11). So it would be wise for the reader to keep in mind that whatever is used to illustrate a sermon, whether an anecdote, a quotation, or a film clip, the fundamental question should be how will the illustration material contribute to authentic worship?

Discernment

A second critical response that a church audience might have to films is literary discernment. Much has been said in recent decades about the importance of teaching audiences viewing skills or visual literacy. Paul Messaris of the Annenberg School of Communication has written extensively and thoughtfully about the need for visual literacy by audiences who view film, television, and print advertising. He claims that visual literacy is a prerequisite for an adequate understanding of all visual media. He further contends that when audiences have a better understanding of the principles of filmmaking, they will have a richer appreciation of the film itself.[5] For example, one of the devices film directors and editors employ to create a meaningful and continuous story and help to piece together an intentional sense of the world in front of the camera is the placement of the subject.

Gillian Dyer explains it this way, "We derive meanings from kinds of shots and other filmic techniques because we have learned the codes and conventions of television and film. We unconsciously compare high angle with low angle shots and know how to distinguish between the two and what both indicate."[6]

Those preaching or teaching at religious institutions often concentrate primarily on the language of film. However, we should also be mindful of the other modes of visual communication. Visual literacy should be a particular focus to anyone who wishes to guide the values and convictions of the evangelical worshipers. Anyone who uses film clips to illustrate biblical concepts should be aware of the power of film techniques to impact a viewer's perspective and interpretation of the dramatic scene.

Discussion

A third critical response to visual media viewing, and a very useful one to encouraging learning, is discussion. I had the privilege of studying with Dr. Francis Schaeffer at Swiss L'Abri in the early 1970s. It was there that I was first introduced to a serious approach to cultural criticism. Dr Schaeffer often made reference to significant contemporary films. After lecturing on the philosophical and theological implications of a specific film, he would caution us never watch a film alone and never watch a film without discussing its underlying message and cultural significance. I continue to model that same admonition with my students and friends. The proverb that encourages us to seek counsel for the sake of safety and wisdom applies I suspect to media exposure as well.

Numerous authors who view films also acknowledge the help of colleagues and students who have stimulated them to come to a better understanding of the spiritual significance of popular films. Roy Anker does so in his book *Catching Light* (Eerdmans) by thanking "stalwart students" who joined him in watching films and dissecting their meaning.

Each year I invite my students in media classes to join me in watching a carefully selected film together to discuss its social, cultural, and theological implications. On several occasions I have selected the science fiction film *Gattaca* (Sony 1997) for such group discussions. The film explores the potential harms of genetic engineering and the capacity of the human spirit to overcome physical limitations. Students often comment that such discussions have helped them not only to better understand that specific film but also to better apply the values of the film into their own life experiences.

Application

I have already pointed out the value of responding to films with resistance, discernment, and discussion. There is a fourth response, and it has already become common in American worship settings: application.

Increasingly I find chapel speakers and pastors using film quotations or movie clips as a way to illustrate biblical principles or applications. During a recent phone conversation with my pastor I discovered anew this role of film. He quoted a line from a film that we both appreciate. He was seeking to give me counsel, and that quotation so perfectly captured his advice that it helped me more than anything else he could have said to navigate through that difficult time. His application of that film proved powerful in my life.

As pastors, we should realize that audiences often find personal applications for films they watch. A 2004 Barna Research Group survey found that four out of ten people had viewed a movie within the last two years that had caused them to think more seriously about their religious faith.7 In any discussion I have had with friends or students, I commonly hear how favorite films are valued because of personal associations with character settings or themes.

Having taught college students for more than twenty years, I find the films they identify with most are ones that display characters who struggle with the same issues and disappointments that my students share. The popularity of films like *American Beauty* and *Garden State* are examples of how films help young people observe and work through their personal issues.

However, there are certain films that have the ability to identify with all ages. Classic films often illustrate universal themes like the courage to overcome difficult circumstances and personal discouragement. Films like *Amistad, It's a Wonderful Life,* or *North Country* have become favorites and award winners because they touch so many people in multiple ways.

When used appropriately, film clips from these types of films can be powerful in underscoring the central message of the sermon. Bryan Chapell in his book *Christ-Centered Preaching* underscores the need for excellence in sermonic illustrations when he reminds us that merely dispensing well-worn information as predictable arguments or descriptions may fulfill academic expectations, but Scripture admonishes us to do better (1 Peter 4:10). One aspiring student was quoted by Chapell as saying, "How can we communicate how seriously people must regard the truth of God if all we have to tell them is silly little stories."[8] Effective illustrations, whether through film or otherwise, are stories whose details allow the listener to identify with the experience and elaborates the biblical principle being presented. Maurice Meleau-Ponty contends that, "The live-body details flesh out the illustration in such a way that the listener can vicariously enter the narrative world of the illustration."[9] Films with their sensory and emotional description have the unique ability to provide these "live-body details" while inviting the viewer into the experience.

From his experience, Chapell concludes that no other aspect of expository preaching is less troublesome for conscientious pastors than illustrations.[10] Congregants seldom complain about illustrations and often cite them as the part of the sermon they appreciate the most.

In their book *Preaching That Connects,* Mark Galli and Craig Larson insist that effective preachers are like great NFL quarterbacks; they enjoy a full compliment of receivers and running backs and need not fear being sacked as they connect with a rich variety of illustrations.[11] As research indicates, our contemporary congregations are already familiar with films; thus they would welcome a pastor's attempt to help them apply biblical principles to this contemporary art form.

FILMS AS POWERFUL ILLUSTRATIONS OF TRUTH

Film screenwriter Brian Godawa, in his book *Hollywood Worldviews*, explains to his reader that film stories often present prevailing myths and cultural values that may not be immediately apparent to the viewer. He then demonstrates how movies are primarily not about dialogue, character, or action but fundamentally about redemption. Pastors can help audiences critically discern these redemptive myths in order to understand and speak truth to their contemporary audiences.[12]

Galli and Larson suggest six types of illustrations that can be used in sermons to explain or embellish: true stories, fictional stories, generic experiences, images, quotes, or facts.[13]

In reviewing this seemingly comprehensive list, five of the six are categories in which films can be used effectively. For example, many films like *Amazing Grace* and *Cinderella Man* are based on true stories or historical events and characters. Filmmakers have long understood the appeal true stories have for mass audiences including biblical stories like *Nativity* and *A Night With the King*.

As Galli and Larson suggest, fictional stories also have great motivational appeal in illustrating a point. It has been said that Alexander the Great read *The Iliad* to kindle his military passions, placing a copy of Homer's myth under his pillow at night alongside his dagger. I would suggest that screen images, quotations, and dramatic facts also have the ability to inspire and warn many film audiences. I am impressed by popular Christian writers like John Eldridge and Andy Stanley, who often refer to film scenes and dialogue to illustrate spiritual concepts.

Is it possible to take these films with worthy values and appealing characters and apply them to church settings for worship, education and evangelism? In my own experience, I have found Christian audiences very receptive and responsive to film segments used to illustrate or underscore a biblical principle. In some cases I have watched a movie clip bring clarity to an idea. In other situations, I have observed deep emotional responses from audiences who viewed a film clip after or before a truth is presented. In a very few cases I have had individuals respond negatively to the use of a film clip. Even then, this reaction led to further dialogue and helped us to listen to a differing perspective. Such rare con-

on my thinking and behavior. By personal awakening, I mean film viewings that have altered my view of reality, enlightened the darkness in my own soul, and persuaded me to take the appropriate redemptive action. At times film content can awaken the audience's minds and hearts in ways they may least expect, ways that are particular to each member's life experience.

Let me illustrate how specific films have affected my own life in transforming ways. More than a decade ago I saw the film *Field of Dreams* and was awakened to a hope that I continue to entertain (Universal 1989). Kevin Costner's character meets a young baseball catcher who, during the course of the film, he comes to realize is his father. Costner's character tells us at the beginning of the film that his father had been a ballplayer but had become ill and by the time he wanted to relate with his father, he was "all worn out."

I vividly remember sitting in a darkened theater and realizing that much of the frustration with my own father was due to his becoming chronically ill when I was thirteen and his dying when I was a college senior. I realized how during many of my formative years, I longed to interact with my father as a friend and mentor but he too often was preoccupied with the symptoms and emotions caused by his illness. It was at that cinematic moment when I contemplated for the first time the hope that in heaven I might enjoy a friendship with my father as two redeemed and physically renewed men free from the ravages of our earthbound natures.

Films have also acted as a convicting stringent that helps me see the darkness I have allowed to shadow my psyche. Some time ago I viewed *At First Sight* (MGM 1999), a film that dramatizes the true story of a man who regains his sight after being blinded as a child. As this blind but virtuous young man regained his sight, a new burden of self-awareness and self-absorption diminished his personal honesty and self-acceptance. I can remember weeping as I realized that though I had never been blind, I had spent much of my life trying to escape the perceived limitations of my own personal appearance and circumstances. At that moment in the theater, I repented of the false hope of winning human approval and thanked God again for the person He created me to be.

Films have convicted me of personal failure, but their influence has also energized me to live out my life in more responsible ways. When my children were very small I saw the film *Dead Poet's Society* (Touchstone 1989). I'm sure many would not consider it a great film, but, like many school genre films such as *The Emperor Club* and *Mr. Holland's Opus,* it captures the struggles and influences of adolescence. I viewed the film from the perspective of a young father who too often was distracted by the call of career to hear the immediate needs of my children. I saw the film the week before our family was scheduled to go on a three-week road trip to the West Coast. I determined after that viewing to "seize the day" and try to see the trip not from my own perspective, but to view the world through my children's eyes and to join them in the wonder of childhood adventures. That commitment changed the way I interacted with my family and continues to impact my behavior with my children.

Film can bring about personal enlightenment. Admittedly my subjective responses to movies will not apply to everyone, but they illustrate how film can be effective in awakening the viewer to hope, conviction, and repentance. Romanowski believes movies offer a common experience for most people by "addressing widespread concerns, fears, and prejudices and nurturing aspirations."[14] These shared experiences can give us a sense of belonging to a common community of faith.

SELECTING AN APPROPRIATE FILM SEGMENT

Viewers react and respond to film in powerful ways. Pastors can use the power of film content to aid audiences in worship.[15] However, it would be wise to suggest some criteria that might be useful in film content selection. First, be sure that the film scene or quotation is able to stand alone to sufficiently apply or illustrate the truth that is presented. We live in a postmodern age when audiences are increasingly asked to view drama with little or no context, but it is important when presenting Scripture or film to provide an adequate contextual setting for worshipers.

Second, ask whether the film content is appropriate for a specific audience. A *Veggie Tales* film clip may be very appropriate for a young audience or teacher training session, but may not be the best selection for an adult audience during a Sunday morning worship service. Likewise, a film with serious adult content also might not be appropriate for general viewing.

Some audiences will find subject matter and dialogue objectionable, while other audiences will be able to relate to them because they see them as consistent with their own experience. Worship leaders must take seriously the responsibility to use film material that edifies without offending. Generally, I find that films that move me deeply have the potential of affecting others in similar ways. Good literature examines experiences that are shared by humanity as a whole.

Finally the preacher should determine whether the medium of film is the best way to exemplify or underscore the specific sermonic principle. All media have their biases. For example, films tell stories and are constantly in motion, but a photograph or a painting allows the viewer to focus and ponder a specific subject or emotion in greater detail. A worshipful leader must decide which medium will best accomplish the goal desired.

In making such decisions, the preacher or teacher should ask what is the appropriate response to the biblical truth being presented. If the response is individualistic in nature, perhaps a still image can best encourage such a response. If, however, the appropriate response demands interaction, a scene from a film may be the best choice. On the other hand, if the listener needs to better understand the relevance or currency of a truth, a familiar quotation from a popular film may prove more effective.

ENGAGING THE HEARTS AND MINDS

I began this chapter by stating that during 2006 two films gained the attention of evangelical audiences. The second film released was the much promoted, *The Da Vinci Code.* Unlike *The Lion, The Witch, and the Wardrobe,* this film was not recognized for its quality or loyalty to its fictional source. It did, however, gain the attention of the American evangelical church because it made claims that attacked the accuracy of the Bible and the divinity of Christ. The church responded with an outpouring of books, videos, and instructional material that sought to practically inform the church and the world about the fallacies within the film.

The church's reaction to *The DaVinci Code* is a positive example of how Christian leaders can help their congregations respond to the cultural media in ways that engage their hearts and minds. We dare not put our heads in the sand and deny the influence of the film industry on churchgoers. Instead, we must take the opportunity to use contemporary film literature in ways that aid meaningful worship. If we are serious about doing this, we will train a generation of worshipers to effectively engage in film viewing. The long-term result may be that future generations of evangelicals will write, direct, and produce films that proclaim eternal truths to contemporary audiences.

G. MICHAEL ORR is professor of communications at the Moody Bible Institute. He previously chaired the electronic media department at Waldorf College, Forest City, Iowa. He earned the Ph.D. degree in communication from the University of Missouri and holds degrees from the University of Saint Thomas in St. Paul, Minnesota, and the Moody Bible Institute.

NOTES

1. Ken Gire, *Windows of the Soul* (Grand Rapids: Zondervan, 1996), 76.

2. Barna Group, "Americans' On-the-Go Lifestyles and Entertainment Appetites Fuel Increasing Reliance Upon Technology." http://www.barna.org.

3. Sharon Waxman, "The Passion of the Marketeers" *New York Times,* July 18, 2005: C3.

4. Bill Romanowski, *Eyes Wide Open* (Grand Rapids: Brazos, 2007), 13–22.

5. Paul Messaris, *Visual Literacy* (San Francisco: Westview, 1994), 1–40.

6. Gilian Dyer, *Advertising as Communication* (New York: Routledge, 1989), 131.

7. Barna Group, "New Survey Examines the Impact of Gibson's Passion Movie." http://www.barna.org.

8. Bryan Chapell, *Christ-Centered Preaching* (Grand Rapids: Baker, 1994), 165.

9. Maurice Meleau-Ponty, *The Phenomenology of Perception*, trans. Colin Smith (repr. New Jersey: Humanilas, 1981), 122.

10. Chapell, *Christ-Centered Preaching*, 165 .

11. Mark Galli and Craig B. Larson, *Preaching That Connects* (Grand Rapids: Zondervan, 1994), 57.

12. Brian Godawa, *Hollywood Worldviews* (Downers Grove, Ill.: InterVarsity, 2002), 30–41.

13. Galli and Larson, *Preaching That Connects*, 9.

14. William R. Romanowski, *Eyes Wide Open* (Grand Rapids: Brazos, 2007), 15.

15. For a more thorough discussion of how film conveys God's truth and leads ultimately to worshiping Him, see such works as Roy Anker, *Catching Light* (Grand Rapids: Eerdmans, 2004); Robert Johnston, *Reel Spirituality* (Grand Rapids: Baker, 2000); Matthew Kinne, *Reflections for Movie Lovers* (Chattanooga: CLW/AMG, 2004); and Kevin J. Vanhoozer, *Everyday Theology* (Grand Rapids: Baker, 2007). For facts on specific films, including plot lines and themes, see the Web site http://www.IMBD.com; for reviews of films, see http://www.metacritic.com.

Twenty

DRAMA

AND THE

SERMON

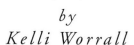

by
Kelli Worrall

My husband, Peter, and I attended our first Good Friday service in 2006 at our new church. We entered the dimly lit, thousand-seat auditorium and found a place near the front because, as expected, it was crowded. This being the last of five well-attended Good Friday services held at the church, I imagined how tired the leaders must be.

But when the service began, regardless of possible fatigue, the worship leader and his band led the congregation in a beautiful series of hymns and songs. Not unlike other Good Friday services we had attended in past years, the worship—solemn, reverent, and Christ-centered—was followed by a brief and moving sermon on, as anyone might guess, the Passion of our Lord. But then, as the pastor finished his message, this service departed from the typical Good Friday program. Our pastor began to walk the congregation through a dramatic worship event—one I won't soon forget.

He began by inviting the members of the congregation to locate slips of paper and pencils given to them as they entered the auditorium. As the band reassembled and began to play quietly, he instructed us to write on our slips of paper our most grievous sins, those that plagued us most—all the transgressions from which we needed cleansing. As I made a record of my own battles, I could see the bowed heads and hear the quiet sniffling of the men and women around me. The attitude of repentance was palpable.

Our pastor returned to the front. "Now, we will continue to worship with singing, and images of the Passion will appear on the screens. As we worship, we will form two lines," he explained. "At either side of the auditorium you will find a beam of a cross. You will also find hammers and nails. Tonight I invite you to nail your sins to the cross. This is a physical and tangible representation of the fact that Christ died for *your* sins."

Within minutes, as the worship music continued and images of Christ's broken and bloodied body were projected on the large screens, the room rang with the sound of hammers hitting nails—the sounds of sins being hung on the cross.

When Peter and I got to the front of the line, the sight was remarkable. Each section of the cross had been used at all five services, so thousands of slips of paper were already nailed there. Very little bare wood was still visible. Peter and I pounded our nails into the beam, adding our sins to Christ's judgment, requiring his atonement.

Making our way silently back to our seats, we ran into Vicki and Jim. Vicki hosts the women's small group I attend. We exchanged a silent smile and a hug and returned to our chairs.

The worship through music continued, and as we sang the classic words "When I Survey the Wondrous Cross," several ushers carried the now assembled, ten-foot cross down the center aisle.

> When I survey the wondrous cross
> On which the Prince of glory died,
> My richest gain I count but loss,
> And pour contempt on all my pride.[1]

Slowly they raised the cross to stand on the platform—looming, covered in nails and sins, a powerful symbol of Christ's work on our behalf.

The following Tuesday at 5:35 a.m., I arrived at Vicki's house for my small group meeting. The group is comprised of a wonderful combination of women. Some have attended church for years. For others, church is a new experience.

When I entered, the group was already talking about the weekend services. Several women spoke of the power of the cross as a worship event. But Vicki's comment, in particular, stuck with me. "Do you know," she said, "that was the first time that I got it! I mean, I have known that Jesus died on the cross. But until I nailed my sins on the cross, I really didn't get that He died for *me*."

Wow, I thought. *Praise God!*

That is truly dramatic worship at its best.

THE ORIGIN OF DRAMATIC WORSHIP

Churches that utilize drama in their worship services are often labeled in evangelical circles as "contemporary" or "seeker sensitive." These churches are considered "on the cutting edge," if one views the use of drama positively. But if one is wary of such use of the arts, these churches are accused of "selling out" or "resorting to entertainment."

The irony of either assessment lies in the fact that drama in worship is not a new phenomenon. In fact, this relationship is as old as worship itself. True dramatic worship has its origins in the very worship that God ordained for His people in both the Old and New Testaments.

Consider, for example, the feasts that God established for Israel. The Passover is perhaps the most recognized. In Exodus 12, we read of God's leading the Israelites out of Egypt. But immediately following His instruction for the first Passover comes the Lord's establishment of the Passover as a permanent ordinance. Every year God's people were to eat unleavened bread for seven days, remove leaven (a symbol of sin) from their homes, have a holy assembly on the first day and the seventh, observe the feast of Unleavened Bread, and apply blood to their doorposts.

These actions *dramatically* portrayed Israel's relationship with her God. The Passover feast illustrated in a tangible, concrete way the need of the people for God's cleansing and salvation, their willingness to depend on Him, and God's ability to deliver.

Worship as God established it in Exodus included the regular reenactment of this important event in Israel's history. Similarly, in Exodus 23 God established the Festival of Unleavened Bread, the Festival of Harvest (or Weeks), and the Festival of Ingathering (or Booths). Each of these festivals required the people to act out an aspect of their relationship with their God. Clearly, He knows the power of this exercise. He created it. Israel's experience is proof that drama (reenactment) is and has always been a fundamental format for worship.

Next, consider the Old Testament sacrificial system. In Exodus 29 God lays out clear and detailed instruction for, first of all, the cleansing and consecration of the priests. Next, the bull and the rams were to be slaughtered and offered to God on the altar. And finally, the priests were to eat the flesh of the ram. Like the feasts, this ritual of sacrifice portrayed in a dramatic fashion the people's relationship to their God.

Many other examples of drama and other art forms appear throughout the Old Testament. Genesis records the creation of the world, the greatest work of art, done by the Artist of all artists. The tabernacle (Exodus 25–27) and the temple (2 Chronicles 3–4), where God would come and people would worship, were both designed by God Himself and exemplify visual art at its very best. The book of Job is a beautiful example of dramatic literature. And, of course, poetry, music, and dance abound, the psalms and Song of Solomon containing some of the most obvious records.

Ezekiel 4 exhibits another interesting use of drama, more for educational purposes. The prophet is instructed by God to act out an unusual scene every day for over a year. To warn Israel of impending judgment, Ezekiel was to write "Jerusalem" on a brick. He was to "lay siege" against it by building a wall, a ramp, camps, and battering rams. He used an iron plate to symbolize an iron wall, set between him and the city; then he was to set his face toward it as a sign. God asked Ezekiel to lie on his left side for 390 days, bearing the iniquity of the house of Israel, and on his right side for forty days (vv. 4–6), bearing the iniquity of the house of Judah. He was bound with ropes so that he could not turn.

Ezekiel's dramatic scene, written and directed by the Lord, is a beautiful example of the power of drama. When done well, drama is an effective communication tool—drawing the attention of the viewer, articulating a vivid message, and sticking in the memory of the viewers better than words alone.

DRAMA IN THE NEW TESTAMENT

The connection between worship and drama does not end with the Old Testament. It carries into the New. Luke 22 documents the most important meal in history. Here, Jesus celebrates the Passover with His disciples, but in doing so He attaches new meaning to the bread and the wine. They now symbolize His body and His blood shed for them (see Matt. 26:26–28). And in this, His last supper, Christ commands His followers to remember Him by regularly reenacting this event (Luke 22:19), something we do every time we participate in the drama of Communion (see Paul's words in 1 Cor. 11:26).

Baptism is another example of dramatic worship found in the New Testament. Jesus sets the example in Matthew 3 when He instructs John the Baptist to baptize Him. In Romans 6 Paul clarifies the imagery: "We were therefore buried with him through baptism into death, in order that, just as Christ was raised from the dead through the glory of the Father, we too may live a new life." (v. 4). When we submit ourselves to baptism, we enact our relationship with Christ before all witnesses— dying to sin and our old self and being raised to new life.

A HOT AND COLD RELATIONSHIP

Although Christianity has its foundation in dramatic worship, the relationship between drama and the church has burned hot and cold throughout history. In the medieval era, religious drama flourished as traveling dramatists brought theater from town to town, portraying events such as Creation or the Passion (Mystery Plays), the lives of Christian saints (Miracle Plays), and the struggle of good and evil (Morality Plays). Some of the dramatic nature of worship has remained in the liturgy of many churches. The celebrations surrounding Christmas and Holy Week have often, in many congregations, relied heavily on the use of drama.

However, at various points in history the church distanced itself from the theater, even casting drama out of the church altogether. This generally occurred because the theater of the age was increasingly crude, and church leaders "threw the baby out with the bathwater," so to speak. The sad result is that, while all forms of art have their origins in God and while Christians have historically been among the world's leading artists, the artistic realm today and the theater, in particular, are sorely lacking in Christian representation. And many of our churches are devoid of artistic expression in worship.

WHY USE DRAMA IN WORSHIP?

Francis A. Schaeffer addressed the current and unfortunate gulf between the church and the arts in his pamphlet *Art and the Bible.* As he saw it, although many Christians and churches may no longer be hostile toward the arts, they have little concern for them:

> As evangelical Christians we have tended to relegate art to the very fringe of life. The rest of human life we feel is more important. Despite our constant talk about the Lordship of Christ, we have narrowed its scope to a very small area of reality. We have misunderstood the concept of the Lordship of Christ over the whole of man and the whole of the universe and have not taken to us the riches that the Bible gives us for ourselves, for our lives and for our culture.
>
> The Lordship of Christ over the whole of life means that there are no platonic areas in Christianity, no dichotomy or hierarchy between the body and the soul. . . .
>
> The Bible, however, makes four things very clear: (1) God made the whole man, (2) in Christ the whole man is redeemed, (3) Christ is Lord of the whole man now and the Lord of the whole Christian life, and (4) in the future as Christ comes back, the body will be raised from the dead and the whole man will have a whole redemption. It is within this framework that we are to understand the place of art in the Christian life.[2]

Frank E. Gaebelein was another advocate for the importance of the arts in the Christian's life and worship. As the headmaster of The Stony Brook School on Long Island, he made sure that his students received an excellent education in music, painting, and literature. After his death in 1983, his protégée D. Bruce Lockerbie collected some of his writings and published *The Christian, the Arts and Truth*. In the chapter entitled The Aesthetic Imperative," Gaebelin declares:

"The Arts are a must." Phrased in this way, it sounds drastic. "After all," someone may say, "isn't it rather radical to declare that the arts are a must? We think they are a good thing. They have a place in education and in life. When it comes to the main business of Christian life and service, they're a pleasant and helpful accessory. But to say that they are actually an imperative, and a must—well, isn't that going too far?"

No, I don't think it is—not if we stop and look at the arts in relation to the living God, who is the giver of all good gifts, and not if we face up to the responsibility of offering him the best we are capable of.[3]

And so a first reason we should include drama in our worship celebrations is that God has given us drama. He has given us art. He is *the* Creator and Artist. And He has made us in His own image. He has created us to be creative. We can do no less than offer our creativity back to Him as an act of worship. And as a church, we should provide our artists with a platform to do just that.

A second support for the use of drama in worship grows from our brief look at its origin. While it must be clear that we cannot equate a pre-sermon monologue with, say, the ordinance of baptism, we must consider the structure of worship as God ordained it for His people. We should ask: What does God know about Himself and His people that He established worship in such a dramatic fashion? And what can we learn from this? How must we plan our worship and our sermons so that God's people are not simply passive observers of good music and an interesting talk? How can we help them become dramatically active in giving honor to their God?

Third, as argued by Francis Schaeffer, the arts have an important place in worship because Christ is Lord of all, including artistic and dramatic expression. This is not to say that every attempt to create art or drama brings glory to God. We are too aware that it does not. Even art and drama done in the name of Christ can communicate false messages or can be done for impure motives. But we dare not relegate drama or the arts to the realm of "the secular." Such a distinction makes a false dichotomy. There is no such thing as "the secular." Christ is Lord of all. All truth is His. All beauty is His—including all truth and beauty communicated through music, dance, painting, literature, and drama.

Fourth, drama can play an important role in worship because of its power as a communication tool. What a sermon can tell, drama can *show*. Much of its power lies in the fact that it is both a literary and a visual art. And a message thus conveyed through multiple channels has an even better chance of being understood and remembered.

The effectiveness of drama in communicating to a congregation also comes from its fundamental use of story. As human beings, we resonate with story (as noted in chapters 16 and 19). The large percentage of Scripture itself that is in the narrative form proves the importance of this genre. A well-constructed narrative brings to life vivid characters—characters who are complex and flawed, characters with whom viewers can identify. And these characters are inevitably involved in conflict, a common denominator in all human existence. In portraying conflict, then, a play or sketch inevitably portrays the characters' struggle against the effects of sin on our world. A piece of drama may serve to convict viewers and participants of their own sin. Or it may comfort those who feel alone in a particular pain.

In addition, drama has the ability to communicate across cultural gaps. Using an appropriate musical backdrop and purposeful actions, a drama can be created that will effectively communicate without the need of language. Obviously, the message of the drama must be simplified if language is absent. But when paired with a clear sermon, this form of drama offers a wonderful opportunity for cross-cultural ministry and worship.

Finally, by opening the door for drama, a church opens the door of opportunity for many people to use their gifts in an act of worship. Drama can involve people of all age groups—from children to the elderly—and can serve to bring them together. The production of any drama—whether simple or complex—also requires a variety of skilled participants from actors and directors, to lighting and sound technicians, to set and costume designers. The opportunities are endless.

ASPECTS IN A DRAMA MINISTRY

If you're convinced of the need to incorporate dramatic elements into your congregational worship and to use drama to compliment your sermons, praise God! But before we look at specific ideas, we'll consider some important guiding principles.

Quality

A first guideline is to work for quality in your dramatic and artistic expressions of worship. God asks for our best and deserves nothing less.

Your pursuit of quality begins with your choice of scripts. More and more material is available for Christian dramatists. However, much of it—sadly—is substandard. Look for pieces that develop round characters—characters who have both virtues and vices—and that develop realistic conflict in a fresh way. Avoid pieces that portray flat or stereotypical characters or pieces that wrap up conflict in a quick and easy fashion. Drama—especially a shorter dramatic piece—usually works better when it doesn't try to give answers. Use a short dramatic sketch to raise an issue or present a problem. Leave the characters in the midst of the struggle, and let the sermon address a solution.

Your quest for quality should also carry through to every aspect of your project. Practice the piece until the actors' portrayal is natural and believable. Most directors believe this means rehearsing a piece at least thirty-five times. Also address quality in the technical aspects: lighting, sound, costumes, set, and props. Practice with your technicians so that microphones, sound effects, and lights come on and go off at the right times. Keep in mind that a well-done simple presentation is always better than a poor attempt to be elaborate. For example, a monologue done by a character who is wearing plain black clothing will be more tasteful and less distracting than an actor who is dressed in an obviously twentieth-century bathrobe and sandals and who is sporting a bushy, fake beard.

Resources

A second guideline is to make an accurate assessment of your resources. Drama can require some money, considerable time, and multiple participants. If weaving the arts into the fabric of your church is a new eavor, start small. Be realistic. And grow as God leads. If you're starting from scratch, some artistic influence is better than none, so anything you are able to do is progress.

Easy ways to begin to bring drama, in particular, into your worship are through the use of props, dramatic Scripture readings, and choral readings. See the next section ("Suggestions for the Use of Drama") for more details on these simple but effective forms of dramatic worship.

Service

Third, it is imperative for those involved in drama and the arts to maintain their focus on service. The motivation of artists must be to, first of all, glorify their Lord. Like all up-front ministers, dramatists are susceptible to the temptations of pride and self-glorification. Humbly bathing every step and every aspect in prayer is the best weapon against such an attack. During the rehearsal of any play or sketch, when the details begin to consume me and worry gains a foothold, I remind myself repeatedly that this production is all about my God and not about me. My gift is simply a tool in His hands. I will give it my all, but ultimately He is in control. And if He can receive more glory even through my failure, so be it.

Second, drama is to serve the congregation by supporting the other elements of the service. The drama should not compete with the music or the teaching. It should complement it. Dramatists must be willing, then, to hear from the pastor and the worship leader—What is the focus of the worship segment? What is the big idea of the sermon?—and to choose a piece that works in harmony with the music and the message.

Purpose

Finally, develop a clear understanding of the purpose behind each artistic presentation. Drama incorporated into a worship service should serve to enhance the congregation's experience of worship. The specific placement of the drama in the service will help determine what type of script will work best. You may use a dramatic piece to *raise a need* within the hearts of the congregation just before the sermon. This piece would likely introduce characters in crisis. No hint at resolution should be given. That would be the job of the sermon. Alternatively, you may use a sketch to *illustrate* a particular point within the sermon. This piece may depict characters attempting to work through conflict. Or here, a complete but brief dramatic monologue might work well, as would a literature reading. Lastly, drama can also serve to help a congregation *apply the principles of a passage*. Application may be aided through a sketch in which characters apply the same principles. Or, often most effectively, you may lead the congregation through a dramatic worship event during which they apply the passage themselves.

Drama used in worship may be either comic or tragic. The most effective sketches often make use of both comedy and tragedy. But be aware that the dramatic materials used in Sunday school, youth group, or mission settings will probably differ considerably from what is used in worship. In these educational situations your purpose may be other than worship, so more freedom may be taken with your artistic expression. For example, at a youth group meeting, I would feel free to use a piece that is goofy, exaggerated, over-the-top. In this situation, my purpose is likely to get the attention of a teen audience, and larger-than-life characters often fit the bill. I would not, however, use this same piece in an adult worship service. In a worship setting, our desire is to focus on God—who He is, what He has done. The drama we use here should lead the congregation to do this.

Lastly, related to purpose and our choice of material, be open to uncovering powerful pieces in unlikely places. We should not limit ourselves to scripts that portray a positive outcome or a point of view with which we agree. Drama can be very effective when it is used to stir up a congregation rather than appease them. So don't be afraid to use art to reveal human weakness and vulnerability. For example, during a seminar on communication in marriage, I might use an excerpt (or "cutting") from the classic play *Pygmalion* (from which the movie *My Fair Lady* was taken). A scene in which Eliza and Higgins engage in a verbal sparring match would gain the audience's attention, get them thinking about communication failure, and prepare them to hear what God's Word has to say about the subject.

Scripture itself is full of stories of humans who fell prey to temptation. This is not to say, however, that "anything goes" on stage. Use good judgment and decorum, always keeping in mind your purpose or goal.

SUGGESTIONS FOR THE USE OF DRAMA

The following are some ideas for incorporating drama into your worship and using drama to enhance your sermons. Some of them are quite simple and will require little effort on your part, but the benefits will be great. Other ideas will require more time and coordination. If you would like to attempt some of these more complicated suggestions, you would do well to recruit a small team of artists who will passionately offer their gifts in this area. The descriptions here are brief.[4]

Props

Probably the easiest way to bring a dramatic element into your preaching is to introduce props. Using props is as simple as finding a tangible object that relates to each of the main points of your sermon and presenting each object as you articulate the corresponding point. The props may visualize the actual points of your sermon or they may visualize your illustration or application. For example, if you are preaching from John 14 that Jesus is the way, the truth, and the life, you might use a prop to visualize each point. For "Jesus is the way," you might have a road sign. For the second point, "Jesus is the truth," you might reveal a carpenter's level. And when you articulate your third point, "Jesus is the life," you could uncover a thriving plant. These simple props would assist your congregation in focusing their attention, in understanding your message, and in remembering your outline for future growth and application.

Dramatic Scripture Reading

Another easy way to incorporate dramatic worship is through dramatic Scripture reading. The simplest form of dramatic Scripture reading involves one reader who is able to breathe life into the passage through vocal and physical expression. More complicated Scripture readings utilize multiple readers, dividing the passage up or even combining passages in artistic and significant ways (such as choral reading).

Choral Reading

A choral reading incorporates multiple readers—anywhere from two to twelve or even more. The content of a choral reading may be Scripture or any other appropriate literature. Little or no movement is involved, and readers typically read from their scripts. Choral readings are best when the composition of the material is creative and interesting. Consider compiling several Scripture passages on one topic. Divide the reading among the readers in a creative way—not simply verse by verse. For example, give certain appropriate lines to the female or male voice(s). Assign lines to a single voice or to many voices depending on the emphasis you want to achieve. The bottom line is to understand the material and assign it to readers in a manner that best communicates and enhances the meaning.

Readers Theater

Readers theater is similar to choral reading in that little movement is necessary, and the actors may use their scripts. In readers theater, however, actors generally portray specific characters and often each actor will take on multiple characters over the course of the piece. A reader "enters" and "exits" the scene by raising and bowing his head.

Readers theater often makes use of "off-stage focus," in which the actors do not look at each other. Rather, characters in dialogue look at a common point on the back wall. They interact with that point on the wall as if it were the other character, thus bringing the audience into the center of the conversation.

Readers theater is also well-suited for the church because good readers theater scripts can come from a variety of sources—Scripture, play scripts, short stories or novels, poetry, or nonfiction.

Monologue

For a monologue, one actor takes on a single character and tells that character's story directly to the congregation from the first-person point of view. Monologues should generally be kept short and should follow a good story line with a compelling rising conflict. Monologues of historical or contemporary characters can make powerful illustrations for your sermon points. If you're preaching on a Bible character, consider having an actor bring that character to life by telling the character's story for you. Or, if you're feeling really daring, consider delivering the sermon yourself as if you were that character.

Representational Theater

This is what most of us think of when we think of theater. Actors communicate with each other on stage as if the audience were not even present. There is an invisible "fourth wall" separating the audience from the life on the stage. Representational theater can be used very effectively in many places in a worship service—at the very beginning, just before the sermon, within the sermon, or even at the end. Representational theater is, however, the most difficult form. It requires skilled actors who can make the characters and story believable to the congregation. It typically requires more time to prepare than readers theater since movement (blocking) is involved.

Don't be put off, though. Well-done representational theater is powerful. And since it is the most typical form, an abundance of material is available. There are many representational theater resources that have been created specifically for the church.[5] There are many cuttings or excerpts or scenes from mainstream plays that can also be used very effectively in a worship service.[6]

CONGREGATIONAL INVOLVEMENT

Perhaps the most effective use of dramatic worship is when the congregation members, themselves, act out their relationship with God. Typically, this involves helping people respond to biblical teaching and apply it to their lives. It may be as simple as inviting people to bow in prayer, or it may be as elaborate as having five thousand people nail their sins to a cross. But whenever we lead people into dramatic and transforming worship, we are following the example of Scripture—and when it is done with clean hearts, God is pleased.

KELLI WORRALL is assistant professor of communications at the Moody Bible Institute. She is completing studies for the MFA degree at Roosevelt University, Chicago. She holds the MRE degree from Trinity Evangelical Divinity School, Deerfield, Illinois, and a degree from Cedarville University in Cedarville, Ohio.

Notes

1. "When I Survey the Wondrous Cross," Isaac Watts. In public domain.

2. Francis A. Schaeffer, *Art & the Bible* (Downers Grove, Ill.: InterVarsity, 1973), 7–8.

3. Frank E. Gaebelein, *The Christian, The Arts, and Truth*, ed. D. Bruce Lockerbie (Portland, Ore.: Multnomah, 1985), 61.

4. The following works will be helpful for refining directing and acting skills: Alex Golson, *Acting Essentials* (Boston: McGraw Hill, 2002); Robert M. Rucker, *Producing and Directing Drama for the Church*. Kansas City: Lillenas, 1993; and Robert Smyth, ed. *Developing a Drama Group: A Practical Approach for Director, Actor and Designer* (Minneapolis, World Wide Publications, 1989).

5. Three fine resources are the Drama Ministry Script Service, Lillenas Publishing, and Willowcreek Association Drama. They can be obtained through the Internet at http://www.dramaministry.com, http://www.lillenas.com, and http://www.willowcreek.com/willowdrama, respectively.

6. Consider Baker's Plays, available through the Internet at http://www.Bakers Plays.com. A good source of monologues is Marisa Smith and Kristin Graham, *Monologues from Literature: A Sourcebook for Actors* (New York: Fawcett Columbine, 1990).

Twenty-One

USING TECHNOLOGY

TO ENHANCE

THE SERMON

by
Paul Butler

Flash websites, video projectors, wireless microphones, computer presentation consoles, DVD recorders, IMAG, lighting boards, Power-Point and earbuds—many churches are awash in technology. Some even have digital surround sound, flying screens, HD cameras, podcasting, and fog machines. Those who have such technological wonders view them as necessary tools in reaching today's plugged-in world. Those who avoid them claim they are merely gadgets and gimmicks that take away from the ministry of the Word. That's the main debate—then add to this debate the tension of inadequate funds, limited personnel resources, and poorly designed spaces. No wonder some question the value of technology for a church's ministry.

The fact that you are holding this book suggests that you care about what's best for your church and not just about what everyone else is doing. This chapter will help you to develop a framework for a comprehensive media philosophy as well as to acquire some useful tips and practices. These will guide you in your personal quest for the most effective use of technology in your ministry.

ASKING THE RIGHT QUESTIONS
ABOUT MOTIVATION AND AUDIENCE

The best place to begin is by examining your motivation for using media. First, are you trying to use technology to mask a mediocre sermon, desperately hoping that no one will notice? Second, are the "bells and whistles" more of a distraction than a help, preventing you from the thoughtful construction of the message the media is supposed to be supporting? Or is the goal to use appropriate technology to reinforce the truth of God's Word? What often begins as "relevance and outreach" can easily become merely "flair and sparkle." Personally, many times I have spent more energy on the slides than the content of a presentation. When that happens, it almost always leads to style over substance.

The most important principle in determining to what extent media technologies ought to be involved in our ministries can be summed up in this axiom: *For media to be effective in the church, it must support the content of the message, not distract from it.*

Instead of simply trying to mimic what the closest megachurch does in its service each Sunday, you should begin by asking how the resources, talents, and personnel of your congregation can be effectively managed, so that the message is received.

In order to answer this question, you need to know something about those to whom you are ministering. What are their needs and desires regarding media technologies within the ministries of the church? The church's youth may feel very differently about the use of media than the senior population of the congregation. Be careful, however, not to base your conclusions on stereotypes. Too often our assumptions are oversimplified, concluding that youth need more technology and seniors less— when the opposite may actually be true.

For example, many aging members have a difficult time hearing or seeing the pastor, yet won't sit in the front of the sanctuary due to the volume of the worship music. In addition to turning down the volume, there are a number of technological approaches to this problem that can be explored, including hearing assistance technologies (broadcasting the service within the building to small FM receivers), image magnification screens (IMAG for short), or a more sophisticated mixing matrix that allows one area of the church to have reduced sound levels compared to another.

In other words, there is no single formula when it comes to media technology and ministry. Every church, and possibly every ministry within the church, will have different needs and will have to formulate ministry strategy that integrates the use of technology with its ministry goals.

While no media or technology can save you from a mediocre message or ministry, you can avoid many of the common pitfalls associated with the use of media by being intentional and proactive.

Avoiding Ten Common Mistakes

There are ten common mistakes that churches and ministry leaders make when trying to integrate media and ministry.

Mistake #1: Not Asking "Why?"

Those who are excited about technology are tempted to incorporate it into the church's ministry, even when it isn't entirely suited to the occasion or purpose of the event. Before introducing media or technology, we must always ask the "why" question. When you consider purchasing some new piece of technology, take a moment to figure out why this device is necessary. What does it do that you cannot currently do? How will it affect the current technologies you have already invested in? What might be the unintended consequences of its installation? Replace the "We have the newest and coolest" mentality with thinking that says, "We have the best solutions for the needs of our ministry." Ignore the "What can we do?" question until you have asked, "Why do we need it?" This type of decision-making requires maturity and discernment.

Mistake #2: Stagnant Media Use

Some churches introduce presentation software and projection technologies into their services because they are convinced it will make them more relevant. While this kind of technology can help, it also has the potential to be a "stagnant medium." In many cases, such technology is little more than an electronic version of the outline that used to be printed in the church bulletin.

When using presentation software during the sermon or service, it is usually more effective to include more information than just a simplified outline. Use slides to assist the congregants in understanding abstract or difficult concepts by illustrating the point visually. Sometimes, during a difficult or complex quote, projecting the words on the screen can help listeners more easily follow along and grasp the content or context.

While it is impossible to generalize the best number of slides to include with your sermon, it is clear that if the slide never changes during the message, you are not using the technology to its fullest potential. Periodic changes of visual information help keep the congregation engaged and interested.

Mistake #3: Expecting Technology to Be Perfect

Most of us have been in a situation where the speaker got up to lead a seminar, preach a media-savvy sermon, or teach a Sunday school class, only to be delayed by a technical glitch. Perhaps the equipment had the wrong cables, the operating system was frozen, or there were damaged files on the computer. Whatever the reason for the delay, it was extremely awkward for the speaker and for the audience as well.

In the best-case scenario, they lose a few minutes of time trying to fix the problem and spend the rest of the time apologizing for the delay. In the worst-case scenario, they spend the next hour talking about what you would have seen if the computer had been working properly.

Don't expect your equipment and technology to perform right every time. Whenever you introduce technology into the service, it is important to have a contingency in case it fails. A failure to have a backup system or an inability to teach without the visuals will lead to ineffective communication. Of course, pretest the system whenever possible. Even then, a breakdown may occur. When you incorporate technology into the message, expect the best but plan for the worst.

Mistake #4: Inadequate Technical Support

One of the biggest problems leaders discover when introducing media technologies into their ministry is the lack of adequate support. When considering purchasing a particular technology, there must be someone to assist in maintaining the equipment and training the leaders and lay leaders in the ministry how to properly use it. Someone needs to know how to repair the equipment if something happens to it. Finding the money to purchase equipment is not enough; we must also find people who can operate and maintain it.

Few churches are able to employ a large technical staff. You also may not find people in your church who know how to use new technologies. Be sure when raising money for new equipment that you also include funds for sending the staff (or at least one member of your staff) to one of the many excellent seminars on worship technology that are hosted all around the country each year. A number of organizations host or sponsor annual seminars, and religious media conventions include seminars and hands-on training sessions that deal with media support technologies.[1] Many companies also sell media support technology and offer informal training when requested.

Mistake #5: Copyright Infractions

The way churches use technology has legal implications. Many congregations use technology to project images, videos, or song lyrics. In many cases this material is protected by copyright. There are many misconceptions about copyright laws. Many of these false ideas are the result of misunderstanding what a copyright actually is. Simply put, copyright is legal protection for anyone who creates a work, to maintain the rights to copy, perform, and control its distribution in public or private presentations. It ensures quality control of the product and appropriate credit (and often payment) to the creator of the work.

Churches and parachurch ministries are notorious for sloppy standards or improper thinking when it comes to the area of copyright responsibilities. I have heard dozens of copyright "urban legends" that range from the merely uninformed to the bizarre. Here are a few of the untruths and excuses that lead to copyright abuse.

"If the work I want to use doesn't have a copyright symbol, it's free to use."

While looking for the copyright symbol may be a good starting place in identifying the rights to a work, it is not the determining factor in its protection. Copyrights are granted to the creator of any work. Whether or not the symbol is displayed on the work, the creator still has the right to determine if the work can be used, copied, or distributed. Look for items that are identified as "in the public domain" or "royalty free." If it doesn't say this, you should assume that it is copyrighted. There are many new sources for images and music online that are inexpensive for ministry use.

"If I only use a small portion of the work, I don't need to worry about copyright."

There is no simple equation or set time limit for determining how much of a work is legal to use. The factors that the courts have identified in copyright lawsuits include the nature of the work, the purpose of the use, the extent of the segment excerpted, and the impact of usage on the possible market of the original work. The best advice in this area is to plan ahead so that you have enough time to seek the permission of the copyright owner for the excerpt you want to use. In the case of movie clips, you must procure a motion picture license, which allows you to show excerpts from many film company releases. Even if your ministry shows a very limited portion of a work, but it is determined that it is the most crucial portion of the work, the law may support the creator in demanding restitution.

"We're such a small church/ministry that no one will come after us anyway."

Whether we get caught or not should not be the motivating factor in whether we follow the laws of the land. Sin is not a matter of degree. Besides, this is a false assumption. In recent years, a growing number of "small offenders" have been prosecuted for copyright infringements. They tend to feel the losses more acutely, since they usually do not have large enough budgets to absorb such fines.

"As long as I give credit to the author/creator, I've upheld copyright law."

This is a start in the right direction. However, all you've really accomplished by crediting the creator is to publicly identify the one from whom you've stolen the material. Crediting the source is not the same as seeking and obtaining permission to use the material. While it may be very difficult to obtain permission on short notice, most media corporations have contact information posted online. You should be able to call and ask to speak to someone in the licensing or public relations department. Do not rely on e-mail correspondence or Internet submissions that are not confirmed before your time of use. If permission is granted, it is good to get it in writing. If it is denied, don't be afraid to ask if there is some way permission can be obtained. And, of course, if it's denied, you must honor that decision.

"As long as I'm not selling it or making money off it, I'm free from copyright restrictions."

Noncommercial use does not guarantee freedom from the copyrights of the creator. Sometimes you hear the term "fair use," or someone will claim that since the material is being used for educational or ministry purposes it's fair game. The intention of the fair use doctrine is to allow for commentary or thoughtful criticism surrounding the work. But, if by copying the work you end up limiting the potential sale of the work (e.g., copying song sheets to insert into the bulletin rather than buying the hymnbooks), you've gone beyond the intentions of fair use and have infringed on the copyright of the creator.

"Getting permission is more trouble than it is worth."

Our ministries must be characterized by integrity. True, it is more work to do things legally, and it usually takes more resources to do it. But our testimony will be strong and the effort may lead to unexpected gospel opportunities as you work with the creators of media materials. There are many other issues facing the church on this topic, and there are many great materials available online with helpful suggestions and further instruction. To simplify the issue, if you are uncertain about the copyright status on a work, don't use it.

Mistake #6: Thinking "Flashy" Equals Quality

There is a misperception that the "cooler" the technology, the better it must be. While we should be committed to a high level of excellence in all we do, this does not mean our services need to look like the latest production from MTV or network television. The problem with "flashy" is that it often draws attention to the production and the process, even at the expense of the message. Major televised sporting event commercials illustrate this point perfectly. Each year, companies spend millions of dollars on the "wow factor" to sell their products. While many of the productions are talked about afterward in great detail, often the companies, products, or services are forgotten or overlooked.

I attended a service once where the IMAG projection was very professional. The church had sophisticated video camera equipment and an extremely talented crew who made the service look like a Hollywood awards show. Technically, the service was amazing. However, I began to notice that I was slipping into a passive mode, as if I was watching TV, rather than really participating in the worship or contemplating the message. I was impressed with the glitz but missed the point.

Don't forget the value of simplicity. Determine your purpose. Prepare your message. Identify your audience. Be aware of the limitations of your technologies and context. Then, determine which techniques and technology you need to meet your goals.

Mistake #7: Oversaturation

Technology is not the solution to every ministry problem in the church. If your youth group attendance is declining, it doesn't automatically mean you ought to purchase a plasma TV for the youth room to keep them coming back. Maybe there is a problem with the overall model of ministry. Too often, well-meaning technicians come up with surface answers to problems that have deeper roots. Bigger screens do not make better sermons. Brighter lights do not ensure brilliant learners. Sweeter sound systems do not guarantee keener listeners.

Before you add one more media component to the mix, recognize that your first solution to ministry ineffectiveness should not be new equipment or software. The church should not become just another media venue. Connection and community should be valued over connectivity and virtual community.

Mistake #8: Wrong Equipment

Churches face two common problems when they begin to incorporate technology into their services. The first occurs when a church ministry purchases equipment that is too sophisticated for the technical staff to install or operate. Typically a church leader visits some large church to see what equipment is being used and then purchases the identical model, without understanding the level of technical proficiency required. Before you purchase any equipment, ask the technicians at your church (and the salesperson from the company) about the level of knowledge required to operate, install, and maintain that piece of technology.

A second problem involves budgets and resources. Most ministries I have encountered are strapped for cash and have a hard time finding money in the budget, so they cut corners and purchase inexpensive equipment from a consumer electronics store. While it may seem to save money initially, it may also wear out more quickly or break under the stress of regular church use. There is no sense in going out and buying economical equipment if the ministry will need to replace it three or four times in the next dozen years. Do not do things as cheaply as possible. Rather, do them at the highest level of quality your church can afford. Wise purchases will save money in the long run.

Once you have agreed on the budget for purchasing equipment, you should also budget a certain amount of money each month or year for repairs, rentals, and replacements. If the equipment functions properly, without the need for repair, then in a few years, your maintenance monies will accrue to the point of being able to replace old equipment or to acquire new. Your budget goal should be to avoid crisis repairs or decisions.

Mistake #9: Poor Design and Execution

Some ministries buy all the right equipment, find the right people to operate it, and even plan for future growth and maintenance, but fail to understand the strengths and weaknesses of the technological medium itself. The materials they produce are poorly constructed and inadequately designed. Simplicity should be the fundamental principle when designing materials to aid your worship service.

First, don't put too much information on the screen. Limit yourself to only one idea or point from your sermon per slide. Second, consistency is important. Be sure to make each page of your presentation look as though the same person made it at the same time on the same computer. Third, use just one or two fonts (or type styles) and choose color schemes and photographs or graphics that unify the presentation (e.g., don't include a black-and-white concept photograph with cartoon clip art).

Mistake #10: Ignoring the Importance of Style

Style is a factor in good preaching. It also plays a role in the visuals that accompany the sermon. Style is a design concept that describes the look and feel of the presentation. It not only reflects the message and the messenger, but also keeps the audience in mind. Choose fonts and images that match the theme of the message and the mood of the service. I'm not advocating a certain style over another. You ought to determine the style that best reflects the message and most effectively reaches your intended audience. Keep in mind that the style should not unnecessarily draw attention to itself or distract the audience from the content.

Balance is a design concept that encourages you to use the whole screen. Balance refers to the symmetry of the design and the visual weight of the information presented. Introduce a photograph or graphic that illustrates the text and uses the visual element to provide a sense of balance on the screen that is appealing to the eye. Remember that the audience has certain expectations as they interact with your design. For example, they want to know where the primary information will be presented on the screen, so they can interpret what is important and what is not. The location may differ depending upon the nature of the presentation, but be consistent throughout each production, so your audience doesn't become distracted or confused.

Finally, don't neglect the power of the unexpected or surprise in design. If all our presentations feel like they have been mass-produced, the audience may become distracted. An unexpected picture or graphic can effectively pull listeners back into the moment, so they are more receptive to the message you are presenting.

UNDERSTANDING THE ROLE OF
THE MESSENGER AND OF TECHNOLOGY

With so many things to consider and potential pitfalls to avoid, you may wonder if it is even worth looking for ways to integrate technology into the church service or sermon. I've been in churches that have had no technical elements in their worship and other churches that have a staff of dozens to pull off the technical aspects of the service. Both can be effective and influence their congregation. I have also seen both fall short of the mark and miss an opportunity to connect with the congregation.

The key lies in a fundamental understanding of the roles of the messenger and the technician, and knowing the place of technology in the worship event. When a well-constructed message is united with appropriately chosen and well-designed technology, without drawing needless attention to the medium or the messenger, it can help the congregation hear and understand what has been preached.

Remember, though, that technology is no panacea. Effective communication will only take place as the Holy Spirit works in the hearts and minds of those who hear.

PAUL BUTLER is assistant professor of communications at Moody Bible Institute. He holds the MA in communications from Northern Illinois University and is involved in the weekly technical support at Holy Trinity Church in Hyde Park, Illinois.

NOTE

1. *Technology For Worship* magazine hosts an annual conference and has information on many other conferences; their Web site is http://www.tfwm.com. MinistryCOM also sponsors an annual conference; their Web site is http://ministrycom.org/cgi-bin/index.cgi. REACH is a conference sponsored by the National Religious Broadcasters each year. For information go to http://www.reachconference.org.

Part Four

DEVELOPING

METHODOLOGY

Twenty-Two

SERMONS

THAT

MOVE

by
Winfred Omar Neely

One way to picture a sermon is as a sequential and linear movement of language progressing toward a conclusion that can issue a life change in the listeners. The main units of the sermon's sequence of thought are sometimes called "moves." In earlier homiletical literature, these components were called "divisions" or "points." David Buttrick, professor of homiletics and worship emeritus at Vanderbilt Divinity School, refers to them as "moves," a deliberate shift in terminology that reflects his assumption that language is "inescapably linear." According to Buttrick, every sermon has a linear dimension to it and is composed of a series of rhetorical units.[1]

Thus, effective preaching formulates sermons that "move."

The literary genre of the biblical text should play a major role in determining how a move is developed. Move development in expository sermons based on the didactic portions of the New Testament will differ from those based on the narrative portions of the Old Testament. In this chapter we will consider move development in expository messages based on the didactic portions of the letters of the New Testament. The question is this: How may expositors develop moves in expository messages based on the didactic portions of the letters of the New Testament?

PRESENT THE MOVE

State the Main Point

When preaching from an epistle, the preacher should open the move with the statement of the main point. A main point is a complete sentence (with a subject and a predicate) that makes an assertion about that portion of Scripture and relates it to the life and experience of the preacher and the listener. If the expositor uses one word for a point, the statement is too broad. In the same manner, a phrase does not convey a complete thought. Further, the main point should be an assertion, not a question. If the expositor raises a question for a main point, the thought is not complete enough. A complete sentence sets the tone and mood of the move.

State the main point with language that is memorable and concise. It is a homiletical axiom that the big idea of the message should be stated in the most memorable and concise sentence possible. Nearly a century ago, J. H. Jowett said:

> I have a conviction that no sermon is ready for preaching, not ready for writing out, until we can express its theme in a short, pregnant sentence as clear as crystal. I find the getting of the sentence is the hardest, the most exacting, and the most fruitful labour in my study. To compel oneself to fashion that sentence, to dismiss every word that is vague, ragged, ambiguous, to think oneself through to a form of words, which defines the theme with scrupulous exactness. . . . this is surely one of the most vital and essential factors in the making of a sermon; and I do not think any sermon ought to be preached . . . until that sentence has emerged, clear and lucid as a cloudless moon.[2]

But why stop with the memorable statement of the big idea? Would it not improve our preaching to apply the same mental vigor to the statement of main points? Not only do we need to state the sermonic idea in the most memorable and concise sentence manner possible, the sermon ought not to be preached until the main points have emerged in sentences "clear and lucid as a cloudless moon." Of course, working with words and sentences like this is exacting labor, but expositors must compel themselves to eliminate every word that is ragged and vague and instead form sentences with words that state the main point in a memorable way, that capture with scrupulous exactness the point being made by the text. This is what John A. Broadus meant when he wrote almost 140 years ago, "The statement of the divisions . . . like that of the proposition, ought to be exact, concise, and as far as possible, suggestive and attractive. Without straining after effect, one may often state a division in terms so brief and striking that the hearer's attention will be at once awakened."[3]

Bind the following observation by Timothy Turner around your expository neck and write it on the tablet of your preaching heart: "Brevity is kinsman of clarity and the mother of all impact; don't drag out your points."[4] What William Strunk said about writing is certainly true of expository preaching, "Vigorous writing is concise. A sentence should contain no unnecessary words, a paragraph no unnecessary sentences, for the same reason that a drawing should have no unnecessary lines and a machine no unnecessary parts. This requires not that the writer make all his sentences short, or that he avoid all detail and treat his subjects only in outline, but that every word tell."[5] Vigorous Bible exposition is concise. Every word should "tell." However, the main points should be especially memorable and concise.

In addition to being memorable and concise, each main point should be stated in language that is fresh, up-to-date, and contemporary. The living God is not merely the God of yesterday; He is the God of today. Christ is our contemporary, and this great reality must come across in the way we state our main points. For starters, state the main points in the present tense. Great preaching is always in the present tense, always speaks to the concerns of the day, and speaks in the thought-forms and language of the day. It is never antiquarian, never merely nostalgic after the past, never neutral or detached in its attitude.[6]

Avoid stating the main points in an old-fashioned or distant manner. When we open a move by saying something like, "The apostle John says we are to love one another because it is our moral responsibility," we cut off the directness of the biblical exhortation, and inadvertently throw ancient water on the contemporary fire of preaching. If, however, we say, "We are to love one another because loving is our moral responsibility," we provide the audience with the opportunity to experience the directness of the exhortation and the contemporary power of God's Word. The main point is in the present tense and relates to the speaker and the listener. It is contemporary.

The words you use in the opening statement of the first move of the message are very important because they set the pattern for what follows. Use parallel construction and wording in every main point in the body of the message. Broadus suggests, "It is well that the several divisions should be stated in similar forms of expression where this can be done without artificiality. Such similarity of statement brings out the symmetry of the divisions, making them clearer and more pleasing."[7] Here is an example of main points with parallel wording:

I. *We overcome worry by* ceasing to give in to worry.

II. *We overcome worry by* taking everything to the Lord in prayer.

III. *We overcome worry by* expecting God's peace.

The parallel wording is in italics. Parallel wording gives the main points symmetry and increases clarity.

Restate the Main Point

Immediately after the memorable, concise, and contemporary statement of the main point, you should restate it. Restatement is not repetition. Restatement is saying the same thing immediately after you say it, but in different words. Restatement is one of the great tools of the expositor.

Expository preaching is an aural/oral event that requires immediacy of understanding. The listener must get the point on the spot. Restatement helps the communicator get the point across by anchoring the point in the mind of the listener and highlight various facets of the same notion. Restatement is not simply a recent homiletical innovation. There are examples of restatement in the Scriptures. The biblical writers, especially the biblical poets, were masters of restatement. Consider the use of restatement in the following passages (all NASB):

Give ear to my words, O Lord,
Consider my groaning.
Heed the sound of my cry for help, my King and my God (Ps. 5:1–3).

Help, Lord, for the godly man ceases to be,
For the faithful disappear from among the sons of men (Ps. 12:1).

The heavens are telling of the glory of God;
And their expanse is declaring the work of His hands (Ps. 19:1).

Notice how Paul underscores the nature of our real enemies by restating who our spiritual enemies are: "For our struggle is not against flesh and blood, but against the *rulers*, against the *powers*, against the *world forces of this darkness*, against the *spiritual forces of wickedness* in the heavenly places" (Eph. 6:12, emphasis added).

In the sample outline given above, the main points dealing with worry might be restated this way:

We overcome worry by ceasing to give in to worry (statement).
We conquer anxiety by turning the faucet of anxiety off (restatement).

We overcome worry by taking everything to the Lord in prayer (statement).
We conquer anxiety by talking to God about everything (restatement).

We overcome worry by expecting God's peace (statement).
We conquer anxiety by anticipating the peace of God (restatement).

The restatement of the main points is similar enough to the original wording that the audience can easily recognize the point. Yet, it is more than mere repetition.

DEVELOP THE MOVE

Expound the Supporting Scripture

Once the main point has been stated and restated, the portion of Scripture that supports it needs to be explained. The statement and restatement of the main point is not exposition. They are merely the opening statement of the move. The point must now be developed, supported from Scripture, and applied to the listener. Sometimes we struggle not only with text selection, but also with determining what needs to be explained in a passage. We have spent considerable time and effort working with the text and have met God in the course of our study. Our personal encounter with the text has brought us to a place of worship, praise, and tears. We might even dream about the passage. It is no wonder we want to share every jot and tittle of our findings in thirty to forty minutes! Young preachers who attempt to do this find themselves sinking into the exegetical quicksand of exposition and dragging their listeners down with them. There must be a better way.

Ask yourself what aspects of the main point need to be explained. What elements of the text that support the main points require exposition? Are there statements that require explanation or proof given the life situation of your listeners? It is not necessary to walk your listeners through all the exegetical processes we went through in the study to reach our conclusion. Exegetical work belongs in the study. We do the work of exposition in the pulpit.

It is critical that we be selective in what we choose to explain. As much as we would like to, we cannot share all the insights the Spirit of God has granted us during our study. Explain just enough of the portion of Scripture under consideration so the listener is able to intelligently respond to the practical implications of the passage.

This is not the time to demonstrate to our listeners how much we know about the passage. Study should not make us recondite and erudite scholars; study should make us clear. Explain the text in simple language using fresh and creative ways. Express your thoughts in language that appeals to the senses. Use contemporary language. The great theological terms of Scripture should not be jettisoned but explained in ways that are contemporary and up to date.

Use the vernacular to explain the glorious truths of Scripture. This is the heart language of your audience—the language they use at work, at home, in the gym, and on the playground. Help your audience understand that God speaks their language. This is where reading current novels, watching films, and even commercials can help. They use contemporary language and current English idioms to convey their points.

Illustrate to Support the Main Point

Some aspects of the Scripture passage will need to be illustrated. Illustration should come after exposition. The traditional method of explaining the text first, then illustrating, still works well. While the preacher should work hard at making exposition vivid with concrete and sensory language, exposition inevitably leans toward the abstract and conceptual. It is necessary to root these abstract and conceptual ideas more deeply in the fertile soil of specific illustration.

An illustration is a snapshot of life that illuminates a biblical truth in the text. An illustration is often a story, one that sheds light on some biblical concept, image, or action described in the text. Sometimes the expositor may want to highlight the image in the passage. For example, the imagery of Heb. 12:1–3 is drawn from the world of sports, in particular the long-distance run. When preaching a passage like this, the expositor might use a contemporary illustration drawn from the marathon.

Story illustrations bring abstract concepts to life. For example, Philippians 4:7 says, "And the peace of God, which surpasses all comprehension, will guard your hearts and your minds in Christ Jesus." The verb "guard" is a military term and was used for a garrison of soldiers that guarded a city from attack. Since Philippi was a Roman colony with a garrison of soldiers, the Philippians would have understood immediately the imagery associated with this verbal action. Our twenty-first- century listeners may not make such associations. In addition to explaining the imagery behind the verb "guard," the expositor may want to use a contemporary illustration to help our listeners more fully understand the action being implied. The reader will find an example of an illustration of the verbal action of "guard" in the sample move provided near the end of this chapter (see "An Example"). A word of caution is in order: Do not overload the move with illustrations. There should be only one illustration per move.[8]

Read the Scripture Passage

After stating and restating, explaining and illustrating, the expositor should now read the portion of Scripture that supports the main point. At this point, the audience is best prepared to interact with the passage. Since they have heard the main point stated and restated, explained and illustrated, the listener will be able to interact in a fuller and more meaningful way with the text. We hope that they will meet God in the text, their minds having been prepared and the Holy Spirit Himself having worked in the minds and hearts of the listeners. Sometimes preachers will state, restate, explain, illustrate, and apply their main point without ever directing the congregation to examine the biblical text. We must strategically direct the listener to the text! The truth of God is communicated through the audience's interaction with His Word. They must see that the assertions of the message do not reside in the mind or authority of the preacher but in the authority of God's Word. Reading the text at this juncture helps the expositor walk the audience through the text.

APPLY THE MAIN POINT

Every move in the body of the message should be applied to contemporary life. What difference does this truth make in the life of the listener? Of course, this question needs to be worked out in the study. (Application is discussed at greater length in chapter 4.)

BRING IT TOGETHER: REVIEW AND PREVIEW

The move closes with a review of the main point. Review the main point by stating it once more.

After bringing the move to a close, the expositor previews the next point with a transition. Transitions are brief statements that link the previous move with the one that follows. Transitions give the message a sense of flow, unify ideas, and help the audience follow the speaker's train of thought as he moves from one part of the message to another.

There are several ways to transition. Many choose to transition with numbers: first, second, third. While using numbers to transition may be a method as old as Augustine, enumeration is not creative and should be avoided. Also, using enumeration as a means of transitioning makes the audience conscious of chronological time. David Buttrick warns, "Enumeration introduces time-consciousness to sermons, and thus, enlarges congregational restlessness. After ten minutes of 'First,' when a preacher announces 'Second,' you can almost hear the congregation groaning."[9] Instead of enlarging congregational restlessness, we should move the experience of the audience from a sense of chronological time to the experience of the message as an event.[10]

Why is it that moviegoers can sit down and be totally engrossed in a film like *The Return of the King*, the climactic film of *The Lord of the Rings* trilogy, and not be conscious that three hours of time has elapsed? It is because the filmmakers have succeeded in moving the audience from chronological time to the experience of time as an event. The moment we start enumerating points in the message, we make our audience conscious of chronological time. Therefore, eliminate enumeration in the statement of main points and stop using them as transitional devices in the body of the message.

It is helpful to signal a transition of ideas with words such as "furthermore," "moreover," or "in addition to." Rhetorical questions are also an effective means of transitioning. You can use rhetorical questions like, "Why else should we love one another?" Or, "How else do we overcome worry?" These questions enable the audience to move with the speaker from one part of the message to another and help the audience *think* along with the preacher.

good

In transitioning from the previous move to the next move, the expositor repeats the process, i.e., he states and restates the main point, explains and illustrates the portion of Scripture that supports the main point, reads the portion of Scripture that supports the main point, applies the portion of Scripture that supports the main point, reviews the main point, and transitions to the next move.

AN EXAMPLE

Here is an example of a move based on Phil. 4:6–7 (as prepared by the author):

"We overcome worry by not worrying about anything. We overcome worry by taking everything to God in prayer [*review of previous main points*]. We also overcome worry by anticipating God's peace [*statement of the main point with the transitional word 'also'*]. We obtain victory in anxiety by expecting God's peace in the midst of the storm [*restatement of the main point*]. Peace in our inner world is the result of believing and prayer. Note the little word 'and.' This shows us that peace is the direct result of prayer and thankfulness. It is important for us to understand the difference between peace with God and the peace of God. While all Christians have peace with God, not all believers in Christ know and enjoy the peace of God. The peace of God is the peace, inner tranquility, serenity, and wholeness that characterize the inner life of God Himself. The Lord does not get worried; the Almighty does not have anxiety attacks. Peace marks the inner life of God and the Lord gives this peace to us in response to our prayers. The peace of God passes all comprehension.

"It seems to me that the thought here is that when God's peace inundates our hearts and minds, the experience is so wonderful that our very thoughts are limited in understanding it. Frankly, we will not be able to understand how we can have peace in the midst of difficulties. The peace of God is not the peace of circumstances. The text goes on to say that God's peace will guard our hearts and minds in Christ Jesus.

"The verb 'guard' is a military term. The word was used for a detachment of soldiers that guarded a city and protected the city from attack. This verb 'guard' pictures God's peace as a detachment of soldiers that protects our hearts and minds from the vicious assaults of anxiety and worry. In worrisome situations, when our thoughts and emotions begin to spiral out of control, God's peace will rein in our emotions and our minds from the attacks of worry. This protection is only possible in Christ Jesus. Those who know Christ and trust Him experience the protection of God's peace in the midst of worry [*exposition of the portion of Scripture that supports the main point. Note also how exposition in contemporary language carries with it contemporary relevance*].

"When George W. Bush was reelected as president, his ride along Pennsylvania Avenue to the White House was a part of the inaugural festivities. He was riding in an armored, protected limousine that was surrounded by an impressive motorcade. There were cars in front of him, cars in back of him, and cars along his side, and Secret Service agents were running along both sides of the presidential limousine in order to protect him from danger. Now, you may not be the president of the United States, but you are a child of God. And, as you move up the Pennsylvania Avenue of life, the Pennsylvania Avenue of struggle, toward your heavenly Father's house, the peace of God will come alongside of you, in front of you, in back of you, and will run with you to protect you from the vicious assaults and attacks of worry [*illustration of the main point*]. Notice what the text says: "And the peace of God, which surpasses all comprehension, will guard your hearts and your minds in Christ Jesus" [*reading of the portion of Scripture that supports the main point*].

"Some of you today might have a child who is ill. You have not rested well in months. Worry has taken your sleep away. Talk to God about this problem, bring your sick child before the Lord in prayer and commit him to God, and then ask God to give you peace. You will find yourself able to go to sleep at night [*the application of the main point— contemporary relevance*]."[11]

MOVING ALONG IN THE JOURNEY

Note that every sermon does not need to have three points. The number of moves in a message is determined by the text. For example, 1 Cor. 6:12–20 gives eight reasons why to flee immorality and glorify God in our bodies. A message structured according to the main assertions of the text will naturally have eight moves. Of course, time constraints also come into play. The expositor may not have time to develop all eight moves in thirty minutes. Therefore, the preacher may deal with three moves in two messages, and two moves in a third message. Arranging the messages in such a way generates a miniseries on the theological and biblical basics for sexual purity.

The main assertions of the text and time considerations are primary in determining how many moves an expository message should have.

Every sermon is a journey. We lead the audience into the text convinced that it will ultimately bring them to a place where they can have an encounter with God. Yet, if our listeners are to be moved by the text, they must be able to follow the reasoning of the sermon. This is why the outline, illustrations, explanations, and transitions are so important to the structure of the message. These mile markers ensure that listeners will travel with us. They enable us to create sermons that move our audience.

NOTES

1. David Buttrick, *Homiletic: Moves and Structures* (Philadelphia: Fortress, 1987), 22–23.

2. J. H. Jowett, *The Preacher, His Life And Work* (New York: Harper & Brothers, 1912), 133.

3. John A. Broadus, *On the Preparation and Delivery of Sermons,* 4th ed. (San Francisco: Harper, 1979), 95.

4. Timothy A. Turner, *Preaching to Programmed People* (Grand Rapids: Kregel, 1995), 100.

5. William Strunk, *The Elements of Style* (New York: Macmillan, 1959), 23.

6. H. G. Davis, *Design For Preaching* (Philadelphia: Fortress, 1958), 203.

7. Broadus, *On the Preparation and Delivery of Sermons,* 95.

8. Buttrick, *Homiletic,* 135.

9. Ibid., 69.

10. Eugene L. Lowry, *Doing Time in the Pulpit* (Nashville: Abingdon, 1985), 32–35.

11. Unpublished sermon by Dr. Winfred Neely, *How To Overcome Worry.*

Twenty-Three

THE LOGIC

OF THE

SERMON

by
Bryan O'Neal

Growing up in Texas in the seventies, when a waiter asked, "What would you like to drink?" I always said, "Coke." The waiter would then ask, "What kind of Coke?" which meant, "Would you prefer Coca-Cola, Pepsi, Dr. Pepper, lemonade, etc."

Coca-Cola enjoyed such a dominant portion of the beverage market that "Coke" had become a virtual synonym for "soft drink." All that changed through a serendipitous series of events, including the retirement of Coca-Cola's longtime president, Pepsi's new marketing strategy built around a blind head-to-head taste test called the "Pepsi Challenge," and the endorsement of a moonwalking singer named Michael Jackson. Faced with a challenge like none encountered previously, Coca-Cola panicked and changed the secret original formula for Coca-Cola in 1985, creating the "New Coke." In perhaps one of the greatest corporate strategic disasters in American business history, the Coca-Cola company succeeded in alienating many of its loyal fans, while failing to distinguish itself from its growing competitors.

Eventually, red-faced Coke executives withdrew "New Coke" and announced the renewed production of "Classic Coke," but the damage had already been done. The soft-drink landscape has never been the same.[1]

In recent years the Christian church and preachers of the gospel have confronted a similar challenge. From the times of the apostles to the Reformation, the intentional, faithful proclamation of the Word of God had been the cornerstone of the church's strategy for evangelism and discipleship. Now we find ourselves in a time and culture when the visual and emotional are enjoying ascendancy over the logical and rational, and many churches and preachers are rethinking their strategies. My fear is that many pastors will capitulate to the times—alienating the faithful and becoming indistinguishable from the world around them—by moving away from the careful study and exposition of the inerrant Word of God, which is itself "living and active," "useful for teaching, rebuking, correcting, and training in righteousness" (Heb. 4:12, 2 Tim. 3:16). For centuries, logic has been the servant of the exegete and the expositor; I write this chapter for those who may renew its study as they take their places in their pulpits and in the church's story.

REASONING WELL:
LOGIC AND ITS PLACE IN SCRIPTURE

No treatment as short as this one can hope to exhaustively cover a subject as broad and rich as logic or critical thinking. My more modest goals are first to convince the reader of the appropriateness of applying logic to the tasks of exegesis and exposition, and secondly to illustrate several legitimate and illegitimate logical "inferences" in these twin endeavors. If I am successful in these regards, the reader should be motivated to pursue further the study of logic in greater depth.

Some Definitions

Technical terms will be kept to a minimum, but we must begin with a few distinctions. A "proposition" is a sentence in the indicative or declarative mood; that is, it makes a claim that must be either true or false. An "argument" is a set of propositions, one of which, the "conclusion," is said to follow from the others, the "premises."

Logicians generally recognize two types of reasoning: *deductive*, in which the conclusion is supposed to follow necessarily from the premises, due to the structure or form of the argument; and *inductive*, in which the premises are supposed to provide probabilistic support (to varying degrees) for the conclusion. Both are very common: deductive reasoning often in law, computer science, and mathematics, and inductive reasoning in many sciences, medicine, and various daily tasks.[2]

Our use of reason, like the rest of the features that make us human, has been affected by the fall, so sometimes we reason well, and sometimes we reason poorly. Examples of poor reasoning are called "fallacies," many of which will be explained and illustrated below.

Deductive Reasoning

The biblical writers made extensive use of deductive reasoning patterns, as do theologians and preachers as they set about the task of interpretation and exposition. One of the most commonly used patterns goes by the Latin name *modus ponens*.[3] Most famously, "All men are mortal. Socrates is a man. Therefore, Socrates is mortal."

This pattern of reasoning is so natural to us that it is almost trivial to discuss it, and we may be surprised that it even merits a name. It is the same sort of thinking which allows us to read rightly God's instructions to Adam and Eve and to understand the events that follow.

> All who eat of the tree will surely die. (Gen. 2:17)
>
> Adam and Eve ate of the tree. (Gen. 3:6)
>
> Therefore, Adam and Eve die. (Gen. 5:5)

We employ *modus ponens* as well when we engage in application, evangelism, and exhortation. For example, we may quote Acts 2:21, "Everyone who calls on the name of the Lord will be saved," and enjoy seeing some response, as Alice, for example, calls on Christ for salvation. It is by simple "logic" then that we conclude that Alice will be saved.

As an aside, some might resist a discussion of logic, particularly being applied to exegesis and theology, on the grounds that to do so "limits God" who is after all, "above logic." The previous example

THE MOODY HANDBOOK OF PREACHING

should illustrate the error in such an objection. Presumably, Alice will someday die and stand before the Lord, and if He asks (as we learned in Evangelism Explosion that He might), "Why should I let you into heaven?" we think Alice should rightly point to texts like Acts 2:21 as well as her own conversion experience. If God scoffs at an answer like that, informing her that He is "above logic" and so not bound by *modus ponens*, then none of us have any assurance or hope of salvation.[4]

A related pattern of reasoning is called *modus tollens*. This is the pattern Jesus employs when he counters the Pharisees' claims to being true children of God:

"If God were your Father, you would love me" (John 8:42).

Clearly, the Pharisees do not love Jesus (the threat to stone Him should prove this).

Therefore, Jesus concludes, "You do not belong to God" (John 8:47).

These two patterns of reasoning share a structure in the first premise, being of the form "All As are Bs," or, equivalently, "If something is an A, then it is a B." In *modus ponens*, the initial condition (here "A," the "antecedent") is affirmed in the next premise, so the second condition (here "B," the "consequent") is inferred in the conclusion; with *modus tollens*, the denial of the consequent implies the denial of the antecedent.

Making Deductive Arguments Valid

It is critical that expositors attend carefully to these patterns, because the slightest of variations can invalidate the argument. Arguments in which the truth of the premises fails to provide for the truth of the conclusion are called "fallacies." For example, we might recall Acts 2:21, "Everyone who calls on the name of the Lord will be saved." We might next consider the prospects of an individual, call him Alec, whom we know to have never called upon the name of the Lord. Our syllogism might look like this:

Everyone who calls on the name of the Lord will be saved.

Alec does not call upon the name of the Lord.

Therefore, Alec will not be saved.

In this, however, we might be in error on both logical and biblical grounds. Second Samuel 12 records the death of David's infant son, conceived through his adultery with Bathsheba. Suppose his name was "Alec" (the text does not name him, but David seems to have a predilection for names beginning with "A"). In this instance, the two premises are undoubtedly true (as attested by those who hold to biblical inerrancy), but David seems confident that the conclusion is false. He says, "I will go to him, but he will not return to me" (2 Samuel 12:23).[5] This logical error is called "denying the antecedent," and is repeated here:

All Muslims believe Jerusalem is a holy city.

Jacob (a Jew) is not a Muslim.

Therefore, Jacob does not believe Jerusalem is a holy city.

A related fallacy is that of "affirming the consequent;" that is, concluding that because the latter clause of a conditional sentence is true, the former must be as well. A twist on the previous argument should illustrate this error:

All Muslims believe Jerusalem is a holy city.

Jacob the Jew believes Jerusalem is a holy city.

Therefore, Jacob is a Muslim.

As absurd as this particular conclusion appears, the pattern that got us here is not altogether uncommon in our churches and pulpits. Have you heard arguments like the following?

All naturalists deny that the earth was created in seven twenty-four hour days.

"Michael" does not hold to "Seven Day creationism."

Therefore, Michael is a naturalist.[6]

or,

Feminists believe women should receive the same pay as men for the same work.

Andrew believes women should receive the same pay as men for the same work.

Therefore, Andrew is a feminist.[6]

This kind of mistaken reasoning and arguing (indeed, any kind of mistaken reasoning) is doubly harmful to the church. First, Christians are led into errors—some benign and some critical. Second, this type of reasoning reinforces stereotypes of Christians as illogical and unthinking. In many respects the second offense is greater, because it is a blasphemy against the name and image of God we are privileged to bear.

There are a literally infinite number of valid deductive reasoning patterns, not all of which (obviously) are used in Scripture.[8] Happily, I'll conclude this section by illustrating only three more.

The "hypothetical syllogism" is a series of conditional statements, arranged so that the consequent of one is the antecedent of the next. The logical effect is like pushing the first of a sequence of dominoes, each causing the next to fall. For example, Paul writes, "Those God foreknew he also predestined to be conformed to the likeness of his Son, that he might be the firstborn among many brothers. And those he predestined, he also called; those he called, he also justified; those he justified, he also glorified" (Romans 8: 29–30).

We can rephrase the verses to reveal the logical structure:

All those God foreknew He predestined to conformity to Christ's likeness.

All those God predestined He also calls.

All those God calls He justifies.

All those God justifies He glorifies.

The implied conclusion: All those God foreknew will be glorified.

The preacher's task is to communicate, in the words of the sermon, the Word of God as revealed in the Scripture. The more closely the structure of the sermon conforms to the structure of the text, the more confident the preacher can be that he is faithfully discharging his duty in proclaiming the Word of God. Here is where careful attention to the logic of the text leads directly to the logical structure of the sermon. Here's an example:

Text: Romans 8:28–30

Thesis: God's eternal love for His people directs our every circumstance to our ultimate good, which is our glorification in conformity to Christ.

I. God's "foreloving" leads Him to destine us for eternal glory.

II. God's predestining of us leads Him to call us to Himself through the gospel.

III. God's gospel call is effective, as God grants us the faith by which we are justified.

IV. Having been justified by God through faith, we can be assured that we will enjoy the ultimate blessing of glorification by being conformed to Christ's likeness.

V. Therefore, God's love that He had for us before the foundation of the world is the ground of our hope of salvation.

I leave it to the individual preacher to sort out the various theological ramifications, and to illustrate appropriately.

The word *or* is also a surprisingly powerful logical engine, serving as the basis of many biblical inferences. I will conclude this section with two brief examples of common patterns. The first is the "disjunctive syllogism," in which we list our alternatives, reject the false ones, and therefore accept as true whatever remains. Paul leads the Galatians through this exercise in the third chapter of his letter to them:

You foolish Galatians! Who has bewitched you? Before your very eyes Jesus Christ was clearly portrayed as crucified. I would like to learn just one thing from you: Did you receive the Spirit by observing the law, or by believing what you heard? Are you so foolish? After beginning with the Spirit, are you now trying to attain your goal by human effort? Have you suffered so much for nothing—if it really was for nothing? Does God give you his Spirit and work miracles among you because you observe the law, or because you believe what you heard? (Gal. 3:1–5)

The text reflects the following logical structure:

The Spirit is received through observing the Law or by belief (faith).

The Spirit is not received through works of the Law.

Therefore, we receive the Spirit by faith.

This familiar pattern of reasoning is common in a variety of contexts, from the board game Clue! to the mysteries of Sherlock Holmes ("When you have eliminated the impossible, whatever remains, however improbable, must be the truth"[9]). The two critical concerns that validate this pattern are first being sure that we have initially listed all possible alternatives, and second being sure that the rejected hypotheses are in fact false.

A more indirect application of the use of "or" is to evaluate the logical and practical consequences of each of the alternatives.

John's baptism was from heaven, or from men.

If the priests and teachers believe John's baptism was from heaven, then they should have believed him.

If the priests and teachers believe John's baptism was from men, then the crowds will stone them.

Therefore, the priests and teachers are in danger of God for disbelief, or of the crowds for denying John's legitimacy (from Luke 20:4–6).

The Jewish leaders find themselves between a rock (several, actually) and a hard place, because of their correct application of the "constructive dilemma." In this sort of reasoning, we list the relevant alternatives, consider the implications of each, and then (perhaps) choose between alternatives by rejecting those that lead to unacceptable conclusions. In this text, the leaders refuse to comment on John's baptism because all outcomes are unacceptable to them.

A common cliché in Christian circles is, "Give a man a fish, you feed him for a day; teach a man to fish, you feed him for a lifetime." The size of the canon of Scripture prohibits me from producing an exhaustive and cross-referenced list of every logical inference in the Bible—I cannot give the reader that particular kettle of fish. The size of this chapter precludes me from producing a comprehensive treatment of all things logical, so I cannot even completely teach the reader how to fish. I do hope, however, that this brief overview illustrates the pervasiveness of logic in the Scriptures and the usefulness of logic's study.

If the reader thereby develops an "interest in fishing," many useful guidebooks are available to direct him further to that end.[10] The remainder of this chapter will catalogue and illustrate errors—particularly of an exegetical or theological nature—resulting from something other than the poor structure of the argument.

REASONING POORLY:
LOGICAL MISTAKES IN THE PULPIT

Informal Fallacies during Exposition

"Informal fallacies" are mistakes in reasoning arising not from poor structure (as is the case with the previously considered "affirming the consequent" and "denying the antecedent") but instead from a variety of other grounds. A quick perusal of logic textbooks will reveal that while logicians have failed to compile a "standard list" of such fallacies with consistent terminology, there are several common errors that are repeatedly identified.[11] What all such fallacies have in common is that they fail to adequately justify the conclusions that are said to follow. These errors can arise from either ignorance on the part of the arguer, in failing to see that the conclusion is not well-supported, or from intent, in that the arguer attempts to compensate for some deficiency (in either his own ability or his position's integrity) by "cheating" through the use of rhetorical devices.

Christian preachers should commit themselves to avoiding errors of both varieties. Whereas considerations of deductive reasoning and formal fallacies will have their most immediate application in the work of exegesis, the study of informal fallacies bears most closely on the work of exposition. In the sermon, the preacher hopes, among other things, to get his hearers to accept or believe a particular proposition—that they ought to turn to Christ for salvation or that husbands should love their wives self-sacrificially, for example. Given the high stakes at hand for the first proposition—the outcome for people's eternal souls—preachers might be tempted to employ any number of these fallacies. Another consideration is at hand, however: the approval of the omniscient God of truth.

Fallacies Based on Illegitimate Appeal

Recall that an argument is an attempt to persuade the hearer to accept a conclusion on the basis of the truth of the premises set forth. A fallacy is committed when the grounds offered for accepting the conclusion do not properly justify doing so. We will begin with a collection of persuasive fallacies involving some sort of illegitimate appeal. This appeal could be to an illegitimate authority, to threat or force, to the hearer's pity, or to some kind of "popular approval." Just as there are recognized "experts" and reliable sources on most subjects, there are a variety of inappropriate authorities to which we may appeal in error. In academic circles, online sources are not generally regarded as authoritative, as almost anyone with a computer can build a Web site and post their "findings." Secondhand accounts (also know as gossip), whether whispered in an ear or appearing as forwarded emails, also have no proper place in a sermon.

Of particular temptation to preachers is the opportunity to exercise personal authority in areas of doctrine and practice. Honesty compels us to admit that on a variety of issues, ranging from the timing of the return of Christ to the consumption of alcohol, reasonable Christians have through the years disagreed and debated the meaning of various biblical texts. Responsible preachers will recognize this diversity and will fairly handle these issues as they arise, rather than offering something like, "I'm the pastor, I've studied these things, so you should just accept my word on this issue."

The abuse can be more extreme: American Christians do not need to be too old to recall a series of financial and sexual scandals involving certain televangelists. As disturbing as any other part of that fiasco was the defense by some of the accused that we should "touch not the Lord's anointed." The difference is one merely of degree for the pastor who demands that his congregation just "take his word for it." The authority of the church is in the Word of God, not the human presenter of it.

Other illegitimate appeals bypass the mind to access the emotions of the hearers. One might do this through fear, by way of threat should a person resist a pastor's conclusions. "Do what I say or you'll not teach your Sunday school class any longer." "Accept my interpretation here or your little indiscretions may become public knowledge."

Equally misplaced are appeals to pity. How might a pastor persuade a parishioner to support some missionary project? Perhaps through a series of expository sermons, instructing the congregation as to, among other things, the nature of evangelism, the multinational composition of the church, and a biblical theology of financial stewardship. This would be commendable. Or he may tell stories about orphans and puppies, show a few gripping PowerPoint slides, and pass around tissues with the offering plate. These commitments, born from the latter strategy, last only until the emotion passes. Similarly, I have heard "gospel" messages, in which Jesus is displayed as breathlessly and desperately awaiting the sinner's decision. Are we not moved by compassion in response to how much He has done for us? I have no need of a god who needs my pity— such a god cannot save and is no god at all.

Children regularly justify their actions by whining, "But everyone else is doing it," and parents almost universally reply, "If everyone else jumped off a bridge, would you follow?" The "everybody is doing it, so you'd better get on board" fallacy is called the "appeal to the people." We find it employed in discussions of music ("all the other churches are dropping hymns") or theology and ethics ("it's hard to be respectable when we're the only ones opposing gay marriage"). The most egregious example of this fallacy that I have observed came during my pastoral tenure.

A particular large-scale evangelistic ministry operates in coordination with local churches, requiring an interdenominational invitation to visit a city to conduct a series of services. The churches are required as well to commit workers to attend a series of gospel-presentation training sessions, and then to serve as counselors at the big meetings. I was stunned by the closing instructions at the final training session: "Now on the night of the service, we want you to sit all over the arena, with your family, friends, and guests. The sermon will conclude with an invitation, instructing those who are interested in Christianity to come forward and to meet with trained counselors. When that invitation is given, you get up, and come forward, waiting to attach your 'Counselor' badge until you reach the front."

It was even explained to us that seeing hundreds of people spontaneously "going forward" adds a persuasive nudge to the wavering sinner under conviction. I'm not sure what sort of pneumatology motivates such an evangelistic strategy, but it is not one that really believes that it is the work of the Holy Spirit that convicts of sin and accomplishes regeneration. And, lest we believe that it is only the "big boys" who can employ such tactics, the same fallacy is committed when a pastor, while "every head is bowed and every eye is closed," primes the pump by saying "I see that hand" when no hand has been raised. Such tactics, on the large or small scale, are dishonest, disrespectful, and sub-Christian.

Fallacies Based on Attacking a Person

Another broad set of fallacies center on a strategy of ignoring an individual's position or argument, and attacking the person instead (Latin *ad hominem*—"against the person"). This attack might be of a straightforwardly abusive nature, where name-calling ("liberal," "fundamentalist," "baby-killer") replaces rational argumentation. More subtly, the "attack" may be on a person's circumstances: "You are a man, and since men cannot bear children, you should not speak to the issue of abortion." "Only those who have experienced discrimination are qualified to address the issue." "Of course the pastor favors a New Testament continuation of the tithe; he stands to benefit from so doing."

These kinds of arguments confuse ideas such as: the morality of abortion, the injustice of discrimination, and the theology of the tithe, with the people who hold or present the arguments. And, as an argument is about persuading people to accept an idea (the conclusion), the individuals who advance them are, strictly speaking, irrelevant. God has on more than one occasion allowed truth to be found in the mouth of an ass (cf. Num. 22:22–31).

A final species of attacking a person is to accuse him of hypocrisy. "The pastor has been preaching about denying self, but then he goes and buys a new car." Christians above all should resist this tactic, for two reasons. First, there is the previous distinction between a person and an idea, which applies just as appropriately here. More fundamentally for us, however, we are often on the receiving end of just this sort of accusation. "You Christians are a bunch of hypocrites, so I reject your message. You talk about loving other people, but you can be as mean-spirited and petty as the next guy." And we must admit that the charge is true—but that does not make our message false. As a matter of fact, that is our hope: that the message will bear fruit, despite the failures of the messengers.

A Mini-Catalog of Fallacies

Other fallacies are committed when an argument is ignored or misrepresented. The "straw man" fallacy is so named because it brings to mind a scarecrow—a set of clothes stuffed with straw. Someone tired of being picked on by the neighborhood bully may console himself by knocking the stuffing (literally) out of a scarecrow, but that does not actually do anything toward addressing his bully problem. Similarly, if we are confronted with a powerful argument, we might rephrase it, modifying it in ways that make it easier for us to criticize. I have heard dispensationalism attacked by covenant theologians for "disregarding the significance of the Old Testament," even though I can think of no colleague of mine who would do so. Alternatively, my Baptist friends are worried about those Reformed types who "believe that infant baptism saves them," even though I've never met a Presbyterian minister who thinks it does.

The fundamental virtues here are once more honesty and integrity. The first step in legitimately critiquing an opposing position is to characterize it legitimately. Failing to do so leaves the original position unscathed by our criticism, and undermines our credibility when our mischaracterizations are revealed.

Other fallacies abound. For example, the fallacy of the "privilege or deficiency of age," where an idea is accepted or rejected because it is of ancient or modern origin. A friend recently debated a female minister on some questions in eschatology, and her major critique of dispensationalism was that it was a late (nineteenth century) development in the church. My friend graciously refrained from pointing out that her church had begun to allow for the ordination of women only fifty years ago (he thus avoided the "hypocritical ad hominem" fallacy). Both sides in the "worship wars" appeal to age as if it were relevant. People who want to sing only the "old hymns" seem to forget that every one of them was once "brand-new," and people who insist upon using only "the new" often find themselves mindlessly mouthing some shallow drivel whose primary virtue is that it was composed this week.

What shall we say to these things? For space will fail us if we consider the "slippery slope," the "red herring," the "bad analogy," the "complex question," and the "faulty dilemma." Neither can we explicate the fallacies of "division" and "composition," nor "hasty generalizations," "circular reasoning," or "special pleading." What should be apparent from this study is that the potential for logical error is legion, and Christians are as susceptible to these fallacies as any other. Indeed, as preachers in the pulpit, we serve as particular confirmations of the maxim "when words are many, sin [or in this case, fallacy] is not absent" (Prov. 10:19).

This catalogue of fallacies should not discourage us; to the contrary, it provides for us a road map as we apply anew Paul's admonition in 1 Tim. 4:16, "Pay close attention to yourself and to your teaching (NASB)." The continued study and application of logic is yet another means by which we can "do our best to present ourselves to God as ones approved, workmen who do not need to be ashamed and who correctly handle the word of truth" (see 2 Tim. 2:15).

BRYAN O'NEAL is assistant professor of theology at the Moody Bible Institute. He is completing requirements for the Ph.D. degree at Purdue University, West Lafayette, Indiana. He holds degrees from Purdue University and Moody Bible Institute.

NOTES

1. This story is told at length in somewhat one-sided detail in Roger Enrico's semi-autobiographical *The Other Guy Blinked: How Pepsi Won the Cola Wars* (New York: Bantam, 1986).

2. The present study will consider almost exclusively deductive reasoning. General points usually apply to both sorts of reasoning, and in any event the reader will be encouraged repeatedly to make a more extensive study of the topic.

3. Almost every logical form and fallacy discussed in this chapter has a Latin designation. With very few exceptions, I will avoid the often-pretentious exercise of employing the Latin names. Ultimately, what is most important is that the readers recognize and construct good arguments, and recognize and avoid bad ones. Knowing the Latin names of the arguments contributes very little to that end. Furthermore, given the relatively nontechnical nature of this chapter, I ignore the distinction between categorical, Aristotelian logic, and the more modern modifications associated with propositional logic.

4. This account is an abbreviation of a similar discussion in my "Proclaiming Jesus Through the life of the Mind: Thinking as an Act of Worship," in *Proclaiming Jesus*, Thomas H. L. Cornman, ed. (Moody: Chicago, 2006). This is not the place for a lengthy discussion of God's relationship to logic, with the attendant concerns about sovereignty, omnipotence, divine freedom, etc. Perhaps it will suffice for now to assert that "logic" is best understood as a description of how God's mind works, and we employ logic because we are created in His image.

5. By this illustration I do not endorse any idea of universalism or pluralism in salvation. I heartily agree that it is only through Jesus that we might come to the Father. This illustration merely points out that Jesus' righteousness may be applied to some—in this case children who die in infancy—who have not "called upon the Lord" in the traditional sense of praying a particular prayer or affirming (believing) certain truths.

6. Michael might in fact be a naturalist. This argument does not prove it.

7. Again, though the conclusion *may* be true, this argument does not demonstrate it to be true.

8. Fortunately, about six or eight account for the vast majority of common inferences, and the remainders are generally variations or extensions of these simpler and more common patterns.

9. From, among other places, Sir Arthur Conan Doyle's "The Sign of the Four" in his Sherlock Holmes mysteries.

10. I recommend in particular for this readership three books initially: D. A. Carson's *Exegetical Fallacies* (Grand Rapids: Baker, 1984); Norman Geisler and Ronald Brooks, *Come Let Us Reason* (Grand Rapids: Baker, 1990); and, as an example of a comprehensive college-level logic textbook, Patrick Hurley's *A Concise*

Introduction to Logic (Belmont, Calif.: Wadsworth, 2006), available in a varied and growing number of editions.

11. Compare, for example, the lists included in the aforementioned texts by Geisler/Brooks and Hurley.

Twenty-Four

EXEGETING

YOUR

CONGREGATION

by
Michael Milco

Analyse your Audience

In my seminary days I learned the importance of exegesis in sermon preparation. Instructed in the languages of Greek and Hebrew by highly respected professors, I spent hours learning grammatical nuances, sentence structure, accents, participles, irregular constructions, and vocabulary. I learned the craft of sermon preparation and how the delivery of a good message can be compared to the parts of a healthy human body. In a well-crafted message, the points are tightly interwoven, the transitions fit like connecting ligaments, and the theme flows through the message like blood through the body.

Yet in the years of ministry following seminary, I discovered it was equally important to accurately exegete my congregation. I remember standing in the pulpit for the first time, anxiously wondering how the message would be received. Would it come from my head or my heart? Was my preparation guided by good skills or by the illumination of the Holy Spirit? For years I had rated myself on sermon application, textual depth, powerful illustrations, and intellectual stimulation. But when I turned the spotlight on my own local congregation, I failed to understand the bleating of my sheep.

"Preaching has had to change," observes Scott Gibson, director of the Center for Preaching at Gordon-Conwell Theological Seminary and one of the founders of the Evangelical Homiletics Society. "For evangelicals, hopefully, the content of the sermon has not changed. However, preachers are confronted with how they engage the challenges of a culture's shift. People who preach, moreover, people who live in the culture, cannot help but be influenced by their culture. The question is, how will preachers respond to the challenges?"[1]

KNOWING THE PEOPLE IN THE PEWS

After many years in ministry, I now understand the importance of exegeting the people in the pews. Each week they work for hours in environments filled with stress. They are weighed down by baggage from their past. They strive to live meaningful lives according to biblical principles. What class could I have taken in seminary that would help me to understand the tenses, grammar, or sentence structure of their lives?

Imagine how different our messages would be if we worked to understand our people in the same way we work to understand the biblical text? In his epistle, James says that we who are teachers of the Word will be held more accountable than others (3:1). I believe James is referring not just to what we teach, but to how passionately and accurately we encourage, heal, and strengthen our flocks.

The lives of our listeners, like many of the people in the world, are in a constant state of flux. Their marriages have seasons and pressures. Immorality, despair, and hopelessness creep in as hearts turn cold. The Holy Spirit is grieved when individuals and families become fragmented. Children turn into teenagers with unexpected twists and turns. Parents face sleepless nights and ceaseless praying. Loss creeps in; dreams are stolen; life quickly slips away. The people in our congregation feel squeezed by events and come to church longing for God's Word to give them hope and provide a secure foundation.

For all of these reasons, preaching should not just be about the Word of God, but also about the people of God. In so doing, we will handle our people with the same understanding that we handle the text—diligently, patiently, and accurately. Growing up in Chicago, my mother constantly reminded me that only two things last for eternity: God's Word and people. Like good shepherds, our role is to know our sheep so they confidently and authentically impact the sphere of influence God has given them.

How often have you seen parishioners walk out of the Sunday service shaking their heads, perhaps wondering if the pastor understands anything about their lives. From my experience as a pastor, college professor, and counselor, I have developed a "congregational hermeneutic" to serve as a tool in order that pastors can skillfully exegete the people God has placed in their lives.

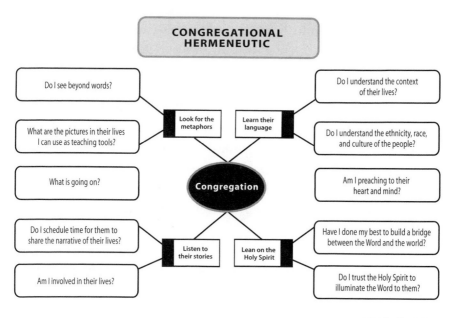

© Michael R. Milco

LISTENING TO THEIR STORIES

Recently I watched the movie *Big Fish*. The movie portrays a father who lived his life by telling stories. His adult son wants to separate the truth from fiction because his dad is dying of cancer. Throughout the movie, the son can only understand the truth as a result of his father retelling his stories. In the same way, human lives are also made up of stories. Some of these stories are documented in books, blogs, or other forms of media. But many go unnoticed waiting to be read, understood, and listened to by someone.

In his book *A Psychology for Preaching*, Edgar Jackson suggests, "The capacity for sensitivity, the ability to feel with and for his people, is the pastor's supreme art. It means he sees not himself but beyond himself. It means he sees the multitude but not as a multitude. Rather, he is sensitive to the multitude as the group of individual souls, each valuable in himself, for the soul must always of its nature be individual."[2]

I began ministry in 1983 in a rural community in Wisconsin. I had lived my whole life in Chicago. I moved from urban Chicago to rural America, from cement and skyscrapers to the rolling countryside punctuated with barns and silos. I went from the smell of diesel exhaust to the smell of cow manure, from the hectic pace of stop-and-go traffic to a town with only three stoplights. This new congregation had different priorities. They were concerned with how much milk their cows produced and whether the rains would come at the right time for their crops to grow. During those years, I learned to milk cows, haul manure, watch as sheep were birthed, and bale hay. I listened to the stories of their lives in living color. Their lives were so different from the world I had known for most of my life. This realization impacted my preaching.

Pastor Arturo Azurdia warns of the danger of preaching that focuses only on the intellect and does not connect with listeners' lives:

> Such pastors are men of books and not men of people; they know the doctrines, but they know nothing of the emotional side of religion. They set little store upon the experience or upon constant fellowship and interaction with almighty God. It is one thing to explain the truth of Christianity to men and women; it is another thing to feel the overwhelming power of the sheer loveliness and enthrallment of Jesus Christ and to communicate that dynamically to the whole person who listens so that there is a change of such dimension that he loves Him with all his heart and soul and mind and strength.[3]

Every day we add pages to the story of our lives. We share these stories with our wives, children, small groups, colleagues, and many others.

Stories bring us into the chapters and pages of people's lives. Listening to their stories brings us into relationship. When we listen, God fills our pulpits with a passion that will penetrate hearts and encourage community and connectedness.

Graham Johnston, senior pastor of Subiaco Church of Christ in western Australia and an adjunct lecturer in homiletics at the Australian College of Ministries, highlights the benefit of exegeting the congregation. He notes, "Life experiences provide a means to establishing both interest and relevance."4 Listening is a gift that must be cultivated if we are to influence a world that desperately needs to know the Word of God has relevance in the stories of their lives.

LEARNING THEIR LANGUAGE

In the spring of 2006, I accepted an invitation to preach and teach in Angola, Africa. I was asked to be the morning Bible teacher for a conference of a large Angolan evangelical denomination. This conference occurred once every four years, and this happened to be the first one since peace had come to the country in 2002. I had previously made two trips to Angola, meeting with the leaders of the denomination and teaching in their Bible Institute. These attendees would be delegates from every province of Angola. I wondered, before I came, if communicating the Word effectively would be as difficult as driving on their roads where it took eight hours to travel 120 miles!

"No speaker is more effective than the one who knows and relates to an audience, yet few things are more difficult."5 Connecting with your audience can be challenging even when we know the culture: Significantly, in Angola, I felt like I *did* know the culture. This was my tenth trip to Africa in six years. I was accustomed to working with translators and had learned some Portuguese and Umbundu, their tribal language.

My wife and I arrived several days ahead of time. We began making the adjustments to the new culture: bathing out of a bucket, eating the traditional meal of rice and soup. In Angola, I was thankful not to have my cell phone or e-mail. With my translator at my side, I walked around the mission station meeting and greeting pastors. They talked as I listened to stories of loss, pain, tragedy, and hope. Many of the pastors had fled cities, towns, and villages as bombs were dropped and tanks destroyed every building in sight. Their stories gave me insight as I prepared my text.

The stories of the people in our congregations may not be those of literal bombs and tanks, but they *are* filled with the emotional bombs such as family issues, personal struggles, and overwhelming stress. Only after we listen to their stories can we begin to learn the language of their lives. Johnston says, "People get bored when not involved, and won't listen when they fail to see the importance of the message. In fact, they'll go a step further and tune out when the message fails to connect with their interest."[6]

Learning their language means we speak in a way that connects, with words that capture their hearts and minds. We must ask, Have I listened to their stories to understand the context of their lives? Do I recognize the impact race, ethnicity, and culture have as I teach? Are my illustrations insulting or encouraging? Does my preaching include seeing, hearing, and doing? In today's postmodern mind-set, people want to know what it looks like in the context of their lives. Gone are the days of the lecture. Our sermons must avoid a critical or demeaning tone that speaks a language different from the listener.

In Angola, Monday morning came and my responsibility was to teach from 8:00 to 9:30 a.m. for six days with the help of two translators. I was asked to teach on leadership. I chose to teach from the book of Nehemiah to more than nine hundred pastors, leaders, and delegates from all over Angola. My personal goal, before I stepped into the pulpit, was to keep it simple and home in on one major point each morning. This was especially important, since I was teaching through translators. I prayed for the Spirit of God to give me words that would be in a language that would introduce them to the principles from God's Word with accuracy, precision, and understanding.

Along with precise exegetical teaching, I desired to give the delegates as much application as possible. I already had a cultural language barrier preventing me from delivering choice illustrations that would be grand slams in any pulpit in the States. My desire was to give them applicable truths to take back to their congregations, truths that they would feel confident sharing in every corner of Angola.

As I reflected on their culture, I wondered how my message would be understood. What concepts would transfer to these people in Angola? After all, we read from the same Scripture, but language can be a double-edged sword. It can help or hinder our preaching effectiveness. The language of culture can enhance or destroy our message.

Each day, as I taught in Kalukembe, Angola, I thought about what makes believers in Christ the same and different. Their differences are not as simple as where they live or what language they speak. Here in the United States some members of our congregations are Gen Xers; others are baby boomers. Each person, regardless of the language they speak or the color of their skin, faces different issues concerning relationships, finances, health, conflicts, expectations, and opposition. These issues cross lines of language and culture. If this is true, then learning the language of the people we shepherd is an essential component to how we preach.

Congregational exegesis enables me to correctly read the context of my listener's lives. It enables me to understand what they struggle with, whether they live in Angola, Chicago, Boston, or Seattle, and helps me to make the text come alive through the power of the Holy Spirit. Culture factors into my audience's understanding of the text. It can handicap them from growing and applying the Word. My understanding of their lives must be translated into language that they can feel, see, and touch!

LOOKING FOR METAPHORS

The first day I taught my Angolan audience, I felt awkward and wondered if I was connecting. I had listened to their stories and was familiar with the decades of war in Angola and the devastation it has had on the people. I wanted to teach in a language they would understand. God knew exactly how I was feeling, and in a strange way He blew a fresh breeze through the crowd.

About twenty minutes into my teaching there was a restlessness and commotion among the delegates. I looked up to see four bare-breasted Himba women, delegates from one of the churches in southwestern rural Angola, walking to a vacant bench near the front. Their bodies were adorned with necklaces, bracelets, and unique headpieces that stood tall in the air. They were painted with a deep brown lotion from head to toe. *These are the people who are photographed in* National Geographic *magazine,* I thought. As they entered, everyone began looking and whispering. I took a deep breath and said to myself, *This is Africa!*

These women were not only a sight to me, but to almost every other delegate as well. I stopped preaching as they made their way to the only empty bench, three rows from the front. I realized the dress of these Himba women provided the metaphor these pastors needed to hear. So as I began to focus on the themes of servant leadership from Nehemiah, the context of my messages were woven with themes of vulnerability, openness, and honesty.

In a simple way, the culture of the Himbas hid nothing. They were not ashamed to have their breasts exposed and to adorn themselves with meaningful symbols. Their lives gave me insight into how I should preach on leadership. Servant leadership means we "strip" ourselves of pride, the need for power, and control in order to trust God to work when we are most vulnerable. As I spoke, the people listening shook their heads affirming what I was saying with a visual of the Himbas among them.

When Jesus spoke to the woman at the well in John 4, He spoke of the living water He would give so she would never be thirsty again. As His words touched her heart, she realized He was not talking about physical but spiritual water. If you continue to read in John 6, Christ refers to Himself as the bread of life. This follows His feeding of the five thousand. Over and over, we see how Scripture uses metaphor to build a bridge between the physical and the spiritual.

As pastors and leaders, we are programmed to think in terms of vision, goals, strategy, and budgets. Yet, the majority of people who sit in our churches every week are caught up in the daily grind of life. They want the Word to be a healing balm or the scalpel in a surgeon's hand cutting out the results of sin. Instead they sometimes find a pastor who looks at every problem as a nail and uses the hammer of the Word to solve the problem. The only difference is how hard the hammer hits the nail . . . ouch! Faith, hope, and love seem to evaporate so quickly from the context of the Christian life. This misunderstanding of preaching uses the pulpit to promote a sense of power and authority from a human perspective instead of divine intervention.

Throughout the week I listened to these Angolan pastors, with the help of my translator, and learned of the stresses they wrestle with on a daily basis. They have little money, lack adequate health facilities, and their children lack education. They die from common illnesses and their crops fail. As we exegete the people we shepherd on a daily basis, we should be filled with compassion and understanding for the lives they lead. We need to listen instead of talk. We must work hard to find the balance between hiding in our offices and being among our people. Regardless of the cultural, theological, or worship trends in the church, understanding our congregation will open the arteries of hearts that desperately need to be made fully alive.

LEANING ON THE HOLY SPIRIT

"The fact that a minister has a certain status and prestige does not free him from the responsibility to present his message both winsomely and well," Edgar Jackson warns. "Too often a man who has won the hearts of his people as pastor seems to feel that he has earned the right to be a careless craftsman in the pulpit."[7] Some preachers develop a mind-set that the Word is all the audience needs to grow and teach without regard for how that Word is delivered. We become so familiar with the routine that we sometimes forget or neglect to let the Holy Spirit invade our lives and messages.

In a day when people assume that bigger is better and corporate strategy invades the church, we desperately need to remember that the real work is done through the power of the Holy Spirit in the hearts of our people. Many times I remember preaching on Sunday morning thinking I had the homiletical structure down perfectly. Included in my message were the right balance of really good illustrations, biblical exposition, and application. On the way out, as I shook people's hands, they just said "thanks" and walked away. Then there were those Sundays when I felt like my tongue was tied to the roof of my mouth. I stumbled over my words, used the wrong verb tenses; you name it. On the way out I would hear the people tell me how God spoke to them through my message. As I returned to my study, I would thank God for the work of the Holy Spirit in spite of me.

The preparation of sermons is not only to be studied and interpreted in a sterile environment called the office, but is to be lived out in community where the preaching of the Word has influence and relevance. We live in a generation that wants to give back; yet, at the same time, we have congregations that just sit back.

Shepherding God's flock is a great privilege and responsibility. The pressures can be enormous, but our success does not come by power or by might but by the Spirit of God (Zech. 4:6). As we understand how we are wired, we will be less fearful of how God has wired others. We will be listened to as we listen to others. The more we rely on the Spirit of God to take what we have prepared and use it to massage and grow the hearts of our people, the more God will be glorified. Isaiah said it best: The grass withers and the flowers fall, but the Word of our God stands forever (Isa. 40:8). Let us herald the holy Word with great insight and passion and nurture those who listen with great determination and understanding.

MICHAEL MILCO is assistant professor in the educational ministries department at the Moody Bible Institute. He holds graduate degrees from Trinity Evangelical Divinity School, Deerfield, Illinois, Wheaton College Graduate School, Wheaton, Illinois, and Loyola University, Chicago.

NOTES

1. Scott Gibson, ed., *Preaching to a Shifting Culture* (Grand Rapids: Baker, 2004), 11–12.

2. Edgar N. Jackson, *A Psychology for Preaching* (Great Neck, New York: Channel, 1961), 64.

3. Arturo G. Azurdia III, *Spirit Empowered Preaching* (Fearn, Great Britain: Christian Focus Publications, 1998), 11.

4. Graham Johnston, *Preaching to a Postmodern World* (Grand Rapids: Baker, 2001), 73.

5. James Berkley, ed., *Preaching to Convince* (Waco: Word, 1986), 18.

6. Johnston, *Preaching to a Postmodern World*, 75.

7. Jackson, *A Psychology for Preaching*, 20.

Twenty-Five

NOW,

DELIVER

THE GOODS!

by
David W. Fetzer

"If you can't help him preach any better, we're going to replace him." Harsh words, said sadly but emphatically to me by the chairman of the church's ruling committee. He went on to describe their efforts to help their pastor improve but admitted that not much had helped. It wasn't that the preacher did not have solid biblical content, but that his messages were simply poorly packaged. People got lost in his technical explanations, parts of the sermon didn't connect, the audience felt as if they had to decode and somehow reassemble his words to get any meaning. That is, if they could stay awake long enough while he labored his way through his text.

As I began to listen to tapes of his sermons, I was reminded quickly that *how* something is said is as important as *what* is said. In the world of acting, the director may demand dozens of "takes," replays of a scene, until the precisely desired meaning comes out. But preachers get one "take." We need to pay attention to the delivery of our message, not just its content. Is your delivery of the message helping accomplish your sermonic purpose? Or is your audience bored, disconnected, confused, and ultimately unplugged, even though your content is good?

SUGGESTIONS TO KEEP FROM
LOSING AN AUDIENCE

Analyze your audience to formulate a sermonic purpose that fits your congregation's circumstances (see the previous chapter) and then carefully select words that accomplish your purpose. Use words that are clear and understandable, words that stir and challenge, and words that are vivid and contemporary. Messages that go over an audience's head typically contain technicalities and details that are beyond the interest or understanding of the listener. You lose the audience when the language of the sermon is overly abstract or obsolete—or the changes you ask for are vague or unrealistic.

Decades ago communication was regarded as a simple give-and-take process: A speaker selected symbols and sent a message via verbal and nonverbal channels to listeners who decoded the symbols and then sent feedback to the speaker. Today communication is seen as a transactive event. It is more than simply sending and receiving symbols. It is an active, two-way process aimed at arriving at mutual meanings. You know you are working at transacting meaning in a conversation when the listener says, "What do you mean?" or "What are you trying to say?" or "I don't get it!"

But in preaching, with its limited, mostly nonverbal feedback, the speaker must know his listeners well and select plain, appropriate, relevant symbols. Plus he must always check and analyze the feedback. Years ago, before the days of air-conditioned auditoriums, my wise pastor would occasionally observe, "Well, it's getting pretty warm in here; give me two more minutes to wrap this up and we'll stop for today."

Listen to an audio tape or CD of several of your sermons occasionally. If you are feeling really bold, do it with your wife or kids or a couple of honest friends who will tell you the truth. Church consultant and researcher George Barna reports that "Every successful church has some formal type of review session on Monday (or Tuesday), to assess every aspect of the Sunday experience."[1] Identify the times when you move into a distinct "preacher lingo" that differs distinctly from normal language, when you use too much technical talk or clichés known only to the in-group, or when your words get so heavenly and abstract that they are not much earthly good and you miss your audience. Granted, many of the essentials of the Christian faith are abstract. But *joy, compassion, Spirit-filled power, blessings* and dozens of other frequently used words may be abstract enough to be comfortable but not too significant to many in your audience. Abstract words tend to be ambiguous and the more ambiguous we are, the greater tendency to lose our audience.

As you speak of or challenge your listeners about some spiritual truth, remember that clear, familiar, concrete, and concise language will help your audience see it, feel it, and sense it in order to personally apply it.

If you are aware of recent television programming, you know a big emphasis is on reality programming. Real people doing real activities—those becoming survivors, apprentices, or the biggest losers (of extra weight)—attract our attention. Likewise today's audiences are looking for "real" men in the pulpit using conversational language and style with a blend of formality and dignity appropriate to the church.

The pulpit is not a stage for the preacher to perform on. It is the place in our culture where one man can talk with others about worshiping God and knowing Him through His own words. This is where your choice of words, images, metaphors, nonverbal symbols, and illustrations demonstrate how connected you are to your audience and how well they will connect with you and see you as authentic. Lee Strobel observes, especially when unchurched people are present, "they don't like to be talked down to. Sooner or later, they see through leaders who are trying to project a phony image. They respond best when speakers talk to them as friends and peers, sharing with sincerity and honesty."[2]

In David Murrow's thought-provoking book *Why Men Hate Going to Church,* he carefully documents his contention that American churches of all denominations are populated primarily by women and older adults and are often feminine in atmosphere, themes, image, and vocabulary.

Weakness, humility, relationships, communication, support, and feelings are constantly held up as the ideal values of a Christian. Again, men get the message that Christlikeness is synonymous with Mom-likeness. . . . Gordon MacDonald finds it strange that Christian men use words like precious, tender, and gentle. MacDonald admits these are nice words, but not typical masculine conversation.[3]

Other words Murrow suggests that need a more masculine rendering include *sharing, passionate relationship,* and *intimacy,* words not commonly used by men. If it is true that many churches do not attract men, particularly young men, it is worth checking our preaching vocabulary to analyze the kind of atmosphere our words create, lest we lose that segment of our audience.

SUGGESTIONS TO KEEP FROM CONFUSING AN AUDIENCE

Recently I asked a group of students what bothers them most about preachers' deliveries of their sermons. A common thread was "I get lost too easily," "I can't follow him," "his message is confusing." These may represent a structural, content problem, but from the delivery side it helps to use clearer, more precise, and frequent transitions. Some transitions should stand out, like signposts on the roadside, such as "first," "on the other hand," "we also need to consider," or "finally . . . ." In a narrative style of sermon the transitions will be more time oriented, but still clear enough to keep your audience with you. Sometimes questions work well as transitions because they bring up an issue, set the audience up for the point you will then make. As you progress in the message don't neglect a brief review as a transition. The old advice still has some merit: Tell them what you are going to tell them; tell them; and then tell them what you just told them.

This is where your delivery skills can make a difference. Use your voice to make a transition. Slow down as you close out a section of your message. A deliberate brief pause followed by a change in the pitch and rate of your speaking will serve to refocus attention. This is the primary device used by most newscasters as they move from one report to another. Watch them to see how effective vocal transitions can be.

One might assume that confusion would be diminished if some type of audio-visual aid were used, especially computer, generated graphics for all to see and follow.

But, of course, that assumes that the audio-visual (an object, film clip, photos, PowerPoint, etc.) is, in fact, an *aid* to your verbal presentation. It will be of no help if it distracts or confuses with too many details. Visuals must be concise and enhance your content. They should be appropriate for the subject and the style of service.

As visual support in churches has increased, two suggestions are in order. First, emphasize quality over quantity. An outline on the screen week after week gets old. Find some fresh ways to use the tool, but do it right with high-quality graphics. Second, make certain everything is pre-set, pretested, and ready to go. When the sound won't come on or the menu is still on the screen or the image is out of focus—or a dozen other things that can go wrong—you lose. Credibility, time, the flow of your message as well as its impact can all be sacrificed with electronic media that distract rather than aid.

SUGGESTIONS TO KEEP FROM BORING AN AUDIENCE

A study of churchgoers reported by church consultants Thom and Joani Schultz revealed:

- Just 12 percent say they remember the message.
- Almost nine out of ten (87 percent) say their minds wander during sermons.
- One of three churchgoers (35 percent) say the sermons are too long.
- Eleven percent of women and 5 percent of men credit sermons as their primary source of knowledge about God.[4]

In view of these statistics, you might think that preaching is passé. But Bill Hybels, effective preacher and public speaker, asserts, "It would be difficult for you to overestimate the importance of great preaching. It's not much of an exaggeration to say it's about 85 percent of the game."[5] According to Hybels, "effective preaching creates the environment, the openness, the atmosphere, where people begin to do spiritual business."[6]

How can we deliver the sermon in a way that keeps the audience alert and engaged rather than bored and distracted? A well-designed and organized message with stimulating and clear content is a good starting point. But the method of delivery can be just as important. There are four generally recognized methods of sermon delivery, which most preachers use in combination or vary for different settings.

Impromptu speaking is "off the cuff," with little or no preparation. There may be times when a preacher is called on for an impromptu talk, but, hopefully, not in a sermonic setting.

Some preachers *memorize* their text, or at least parts of it, such as the introduction and conclusion or perhaps an illustration. However, most preachers simply don't have time to memorize or don't want to be that closely tied to a prepared text.

A third method, used by many preachers is a *manuscripted* presentation. By definition, a manuscript is a word-for-word prepared text. Some preachers who prepare a manuscript do so because they are not strong at recall and need the security of a script or at least a very full outline. Others prepare a manuscript in order to edit and polish their message. A manuscripted sermon can help the preacher stay on schedule and avoid tangents, repetition, or rambling. If you use a manuscript, it is wise to learn the art of writing for the ear rather than the eye. This means scripting in a spoken rather than a written style (in the entertainment industry, scriptwriters get paid well for that skill). The major problem with manuscripted sermons is the impersonal atmosphere that tends to be created when the message is read to an audience. To avoid this, know the message well enough to talk comfortably to the audience, referring to the script as necessary, while maintaining sufficient eye contact and supportive nonverbals.

Extemporaneous delivery is the final and most popular method. In this method of delivery the message is planned, prepared, outlined, practiced, and presented in a conversational style. The outline can be very brief or quite extensive, depending on the subject and the speaker's need for notes. However, when notes are too brief they may create a tendency to get off the subject, drift into repeated themes week after week, and not fit together all the pieces of a well-structured message.

Today's audiences prefer a natural, spontaneous, conversational delivery, no matter what type of notes one is using. This open style of speaking communicates honesty, sincerity, trust, and a transparency that comes with willingness to self-disclose when appropriate. Make your speaking come alive with a personal touch. Talk to and with people, not just at them. Create a warm intensity that makes people want to stay tuned in because they sense you care, are real, and have something of importance from God's Word for them.

SUGGESTIONS FOR USING YOUR VOICE

Pay closer attention to the *vocal* aspects of your preaching. The recognition of this part of delivery elements is as ancient as Aristotle:

> Our next subject will be the style of expression. For it is not enough to know what we ought to say; we must also say it as we ought; much help is thus afforded toward producing the right impression of a speech. . . . It is essentially the right management of the voice to express the various emotions—of speaking loudly, softly, or between the two; of high, low, or intermediate pitch; of the various rhythms that suit various subjects. These are the three things—volume of sound, modulation of pitch, and rhythm—that a speaker has in mind.[7]

Many preachers, having had some training in speech or homiletics, are familiar with these vocal elements. But your "natural" style may not fit your audience. It is necessary, from time to time, to be intentional in reviewing and evaluating aspects of your delivery, seeking feedback from respected listeners, and making change where necessary to help you keep an audience focused and interested.

The major components of the vocal side of delivery include *volume, pitch, rate,* and *force.* A good way to bore an audience is to speak with little or no variety in these elements. But the results of a flat vocal pattern actually have more serious results: "As a number of studies demonstrate, a monotonous delivery interferes with audience comprehension and later recall of the information."[8]

Variety in *volume* can provide emphasis (as long as your volume is not limited to loud and louder); it can communicate emotion, bring color, and stimulate interest. Moving to a soft, lower volume can actually be more effective in driving a point home than getting louder.

The same is true with *pitch*, the highs and lows of your voice range. Pitch inflections lend vitality and flavor to a voice and can potentially change meaning as well as emphasis. Use the three simple words *I hate you* to experiment with vocal pitch by stepping or sliding to different pitches that imply a range of meanings from hostility to playful teasing. A delivery that is monotone, with little pitch variety, is a surefire way to induce boredom.

The *rate* of most Americans' speech is about 125 words per minute. To speak slower than that, continually, invites listeners to drift into their own thoughts. One study indicates that faster rates of speech tend to increase listener comprehension and recall of the content.[9] Some start slower as their audience tunes in and increase their rate as they move toward a conclusion. For example, Martin Luther King opened his "I Have a Dream" speech at a pace of 92 words per minute and finished it at 145.[10] The use of a pause, as long as it is not filled with "ah" or "um," can break the pace, signal a change, or mark a point of emphasis. "The right word may be effective," said Mark Twain, "but no word was ever as effective as a rightly timed pause."[11] The best approach is to vary your rate, slowing down for emphasis or at transitional points, speeding up for background material, and using pauses effectively when it enhances your delivery.

Force, or the energy behind your words, is an aspect of delivery not always discussed in communication or homiletics texts. Some preachers have a high-energy, intense, in-your-face, demanding style that, if used continually, can be quite annoying. When that happens, all force equals no force. It amounts to an emotional "monotone." Force needs to be used sparingly and, in combination with the other elements, can be quite effective.

There were days when my mother would stick her head in my bedroom door and say, in a pleasant and conversational way, "Son, you need to clean your room." I would grunt "uh-huh" and keep at whatever I was doing. Later she would return and say, a little more forcefully, "It's time to clean your room." Same result. Then, a half hour later, she was standing in the doorway and as I looked up she said, *"Clean your room."* This time it was said softly, slowly, with a bit lower and descending pitch, and with quite a bit of force behind the words. She didn't yell, but I knew it was time to clean my room—*now*.

Variety isn't just the spice of life; it will also spice up your speaking. Check your verbals. Stretch yourself, experiment, practice, and don't allow your vocal delivery to be a reason for people to get bored. You *will* use your voice; so learn to use it well. Make it work for you, not against you.

A key element of delivery involves *nonverbal communication*. This aspect of preaching starts before you ever say a word. *Appearance,* a strong first-impression factor, involves dress, sitting posture, movement into the pulpit or preaching area, even the shuffling of notes or fussing with audio-visuals. For example, Kearney and Plax remind us that power and status are commonly associated with clothing. Historically, clothing has often distinguished individuals of higher social status from those of lower status.[12] Dress appropriately for the culture and the context.

Body language and movement are also aspects of nonverbal communication. Moving closer to an audience, increasing eye contact, having a pleasant facial expression, and using broad, open gestures create a sense of friendliness and closeness with the audience. This phenomenon, called nonverbal immediacy, tends to be mirrored by the audience. Because immediacy connotes liking, both you and your audience members will believe the feeling is mutual and care about each other.[13]

But trying to nail down rules and principles for body language is difficult. About *gestures*, one author wrote, "Over the years, more nonsense has been written about gesturing than any other aspect of speech delivery."[14] The way you move and gesture should fit you; in time they will become as natural as they are in conversation. But in the meanwhile, be aware of unnatural, unusual body language you might use, such as an awkward posture, jingling coins in your pocket, or gesturing excessively as if you were leading a choir. Anything that draws attention to itself will draw attention away from your content rather than complement it. For example, for a time I attended a church where the preacher often draped himself over the pulpit, elbows out, shoulders almost as high as his head, which was even with the front of the pulpit. All I could think of was my brother's bulldog. My attention suffered, to say the least.

Body language, especially *facial expression*, should mirror your content. Dismay, frustration, excitement, concern must be seen as well as heard. A rigid posture or a blank expression will not communicate the relief that comes with the forgiveness that you are telling your audience is available. If you want to keep your audience from being bored and distracted, let them see and feel as well as hear about that sense of forgiveness.

Also, remember to look at your audience. The greatest way to make contact with and establish a bond with your listeners is through your eyes. As you look at people, not past them, or above them, but at them, you show your interest in them. You are saying, nonverbally, "I care about you and what I am telling you from Scripture will benefit you." Your eye contact should not be so intense with individuals that it makes them uncomfortable. Rather, it should involve a moving, brief connection all around the audience. They will not be bothered when you refer to your notes if the majority of the time your focus is on them.

A FINAL SUGGESTION

Whether you are just starting your preaching ministry, have been preaching for a brief time or for many years, a *visual analysis* of your delivery style on a television can be very enlightening. If your church does not have video recording equipment in place, it should not be too difficult to locate someone with a home video camera, which can be placed inconspicuously to record several services.

Many speakers, when they see themselves on screen for the first time, tend to focus on one or two usually negative details such as the shape of their glasses or their big ears or that awful tie. It usually takes multiple viewings of different sermons before a speaker can start to identify and focus on specific delivery behaviors. The way you use your hands, your facial expressions, your eye contact or lack of it, and other previously mentioned behaviors all can contribute to whether you are a vibrant, interesting, attention-holding speaker, or one who has the potential to bore yourself, let alone others.

As you begin to focus on one aspect of your delivery, ask whether it is effective in communicating your point. Does it enhance the content or detract from it? Do you need to make some changes? If so, what kind? The goal is not to make immediate, radical changes in your preaching style, but to become aware of different elements in delivery that are changeable, if necessary, to make you a more effective speaker. Over the years some bad habits might have become a part of your presentation, such as jingling the loose change in your pocket or an eccentric posture or a repeated unusual gesture. Video analysis may be just the right tool that helps you identify, evaluate, and improve your sermonic delivery.

Effective preaching does not always come naturally. All good preachers work at their content, making it accurate, well organized, and clear. Some seem to be gifted and fluent, with an attractive and appealing delivery. Yet even the best sometimes need to step back and evaluate their delivery of the message God has entrusted to them. Those who preach are told to "Preach the Word . . . with . . . careful instruction" (2 Tim. 4:2). To be careful instructors, we must pay careful attention to the delivery as well as the content of the message. You've done the hard work of study. Now, deliver the goods!

DAVID W. FETZER is professor of communications at the Moody Bible Institute. He holds a D.Min. degree from Trinity International University in Deerfield, Illinois as well as degrees from Bowling Green State University in Bowling Green, Ohio; Dallas Theological Seminary; and Cedarville University, Cedarville, Ohio.

NOTES

1. George Barna, *User Friendly Churches* (Ventura, Calif.: Regal, 1991), 66.

2. G. A. Pritchard, *Willow Creek Seeker Services* (Grand Rapids: Baker, 1996), 127.

3. David Murrow, *Why Men Hate Going to Church* (Nashville: Nelson, 2005), 135.

4. Thom and Joani Shultz, *When Nobody Learns Much at Church*, 2nd ed. (Loveland, Colo.: Group, 2004), 189.

5. As quoted in Pritchard, *Willow Creek Seeker Services*, 116.

6. Ibid.

7. Aristotle, *Rhetoric*, W. R. Roberts, trans. (New York: Random House, 1984). Book III, ll.15–35; as quoted in Clella Iles Jaffe, *Public Speaking* (Belmont, Calif.: Wadsworth, 1995), 280.

8. Patricia Kearney and Timothy G. Plax, *Public Speaking in a Diverse Society* (Mountain View, Calif.: Mayfield, 1996), 378.

9. Ibid.

10. Stephen E. Lucas, *The Art of Public Speaking,* 3rd ed. (New York: Random House, 1989), 237.

11. Ibid., 238.

12. Kearney and Plax, *Public Speaking* , 371.

13. Ibid., 380.

14. Lucas, 39.

Twenty-Six

ABUSE IT

AND

LOSE IT

by
Terry Strandt and Jori Jennings

Do you picture yourself in the pulpit of a vibrant, growing congregation that hangs on your every exegetical exposition? Pretty soon you are preaching multiple services on Sunday morning and two in the middle of the week. With hundreds (or even a thousand) people now depending on your preaching for spiritual guidance, you begin to notice that your voice isn't as clear and strong as it used to be. By the end of your third Sunday sermon, you really have to push hard to get adequate volume and there are sometimes sharp pains when you do. What has happened to your voice?

This chapter considers the gift that most preachers often forget—and sometimes neglect. Your speaking voice—the way it is used and the way it is cared for—must be given serious consideration or the gospel message you are called to present may be muffled or, worst-case scenario, silenced completely.

Back in 1992, as a candidate for president, Bill Clinton struggled while on the campaign trail with chronic, recurring laryngitis. Four years later, running for reelection, President Clinton again found his voice failing. In both instances the official diagnosis from his doctors was a combination of overuse of his voice and allergies. It got so bad at one point that a speech therapist started traveling with him as he campaigned. While it is true that public speakers are especially prone to suffer from such maladies, the resultant problems are not just from overuse but medical conditions. There are several facets of Bill Clinton's speaking voice that, with careful analysis, will yield a treasure trove of "what-not-to-dos" for the preacher who uses his voice extensively.

In Clinton's case, his allergy complications were no doubt real, but of much greater concern was the way phonation (use of the laryngeal system to generate an audible source of sound which is modified and enhanced to become recognized speech) occurred. Two factors, specifically, combined to exacerbate the swelling and dryness already present from allergies and the prescription medications he was undoubtedly taking for that condition. Bill Clinton spoke with both a husky tone quality and a very low, mean pitch level. The husky, or raspy tone quality is caused by inadequate closure of the vocal cords. In laymen's terms, we might describe the sound as "gravelly" or "breathy." This is often a by-product of speaking at the bottom of one's pitch range. Speech scientists tell us that the average person has, at their disposal, about a two-octave range. Naturally, we tend to use only a small portion of that range when we speak. People who speak so low in their range that their vowels have no discernable pitch or tone quality are producing a scratchy tone known as a "glottal fry." This kind of tonal production in American speech is widespread, especially among teenage and young adult females.

PROTRACTED VERSUS PROJECTED SPEAKING

Though a large percentage of the American public speaks in this way, they encounter none of the potential speaking woes experienced by professionals such as Bill Clinton, Billy Joel, Billy Graham, or Bill Murray, not because they possess the same first names but because they all use their voices in a protracted and projected manner. Because the average person rarely has to use his voice regularly for extended periods of time, or at a louder decibel level than conversational speech, they are unlikely to damage their voices during their career despite unhealthy speech habits. Researchers A. Mathis Holbrook and C. W. Bailey compared talking time versus loud talking time in relationship to subjects' reports of vocal fatigue. Their study found that loud talking time was more relevant to vocal fatigue than amount of talking.[1] They concluded that projected speaking is more damaging than protracted speaking.

In conversational speech, the lung pressure is minimal at a normal speaking range in the male voice. But, when hertz (speaking pitch level) is increased, the lung pressure is also increased, putting more stress on the vocal cords. As well, greater decibels (volume level) mean that the impact of the vocal cords, as they collide together, is also intensified. Simply put, raised pitch and volume levels mean more friction—that's the "rub!"

It's also the bad news. The good news is that Sander and Ripich did a similar study but did not find that vocal fatigue increased with loud talking, although one-third of their subjects reported that the clarity of their voices diminished with loud talking. Sander and Ripich concluded that vocal fatigue might depend on the vocal behaviors subjects used to create more intensity: In other words, if you use your voice in a clear and supported fashion, the likelihood of fatigue and deleterious effects on your voice should be minimized.[2] That is good news because it would seem to indicate that the voice could be used with volume and inflection for prolonged periods without significant compromise of quality.

The $10,000 question (the approximate cost of vocal surgery and rehabilitation for the severely damaged voice) is, What are the methods to achieve these healthy vocal mechanics?

Most homeowners have discovered one unsettling phenomenon of lawn maintenance: The first time they rake their lawns in the fall or turn over the garden in the spring they realize how frail the skin is on the palms of their hands. The palms turn red and tender; even blisters may form. If they continued to rake and dig for several weeks, however, they would develop a nice, thick set of calluses that would then shield their skin from further harm. Now imagine that your livelihood required that you be able to press your palms flat together with no gap between them. Such is the requirement of properly functioning vocal cords. The calluses would, in that case, then become a liability.

When We Abuse Our Vocal Folds

Treating Laryngitis

That's what happens with your vocal folds when you abuse them for too long. During speaking, healthy vocal folds close together smoothly to form a straight line. With abuse of the voice, however, vocal folds deteriorate. Consider laryngitis, the most common infirmity of the vocal abuser. Laryngitis is an inflammation of the mucous membrane lining the larynx (voice box), which is located in the upper part of the respiratory tract. It causes hoarseness, and a possible temporary loss of voice. Acute laryngitis may result from excessive strain on the vocal cords, as occurs with activities such as yelling, cheering, singing, or public speaking.[3] The hoarseness, or complete loss of voice, that often accompanies laryngitis can also be brought on by a virus, tumor, or other medical condition unrelated to unhealthy phonation. Should such a condition manifest itself, vocal rest is the best course of action.

Whether it's laryngitis caused by one of these conditions or simply excess strain on the vocal cords, under chronic abuse the cords can be damaged, leading to swelling of the vocal folds, vocal nodules, and even a vocal fold hemorrhage (bleeding).

If the vocal folds become swollen, the cause can range from simple overuse to abuse. Teachers, public speakers—including preachers—stage actors, telemarketers, sports coaches, referees or cheerleaders, and youth leaders/camp directors, among others, are most susceptible. The first four occupations would most likely fall into the category of overuse. They do not tend to abuse their voices by yelling to be heard under adverse conditions; they just talk a lot. The second group of professions, beginning with sports coaches, is the abusers who are at highest risk for lengthy, debilitating pathologies. In addition, people with long-term, chronic coughs from lingering colds or allergies can also develop a sore throat and lose their voices.

Treating Vocal Nodules

The ramifications of such a condition are many. Short term, a pastor may need to cancel speaking engagements or cut back on the number of sermons he will preach on any one day. Long term, one can develop more debilitating vocal nodules, which can effectively hinder all speaking activity for several months or longer if not properly treated.

Before the advent of electronic amplification systems, orators and preachers were much more cognizant of their vocal limitations and took great pains to learn how to properly project their voices in large halls. Charles Spurgeon wrote in the July, 1875 edition of *The Sword and Trowel* that "One of the surest ways to kill yourself is to speak from the throat instead of the mouth. This misuse of nature will be terribly avenged by her; escape the penalty by avoiding the offense."[4]

Vocal nodules are the second most common disorder found in those who have crossed the threshold to unhealthy phonation. The previously discussed "calluses on the hands scenario" is an adequate vernacular metaphor. Here is how the medical lexicon describes it: Nodules are symmetric, broad-based masses ("mass" simply means "lump," and does not imply cancer) that occur at the midpoint of both vocal folds. This location suggests that nodules are the result of phonotrauma, the physical stresses on the vocal fold which occur with heavy voice use or voice use under adverse circumstances.[5]

The enumerated professions above and their accompanying abuses, when left undiagnosed or disregarded, will result in, at the least, reduced vocal stamina and quality and, at the worst, longer and longer periods of laryngeal distress following the overuse and misuse of the voice. The swelling of the mucosal lining (the outer layer of skin that covers the vocal fold) will eventually manifest symptoms at the two most irritated points. The swellings will continue to protrude farther from the edge of the vocal folds, effectively keeping the vocal cords from completely closing. When this happens, a constant hoarseness or laryngitis will accompany all talking or singing.

Vocal nodules are much more difficult to treat than straightforward laryngitis. Some studies have shown that concentrated steam inhalation and hydration might be beneficial. In one study reported in the *Journal of Speech, Language and Hearing Research*, six adult female patients with vocal nodules received five consecutive days of hydration treatment: Subjects drank eight or more glasses of water per day and took one teaspoon of the Robitussin expectorant three times a day and were exposed to high humidity environments (90 to 100 percent) in half-hour intervals for two hours each day.

The authors concluded that the study as a whole indicates that *hydration treatments are beneficial for nodules*, but that hydration treatment *should not be used as a primary or independent treatment.* [6] Water is the oil of the voice box!

The obvious application for preachers is lots of water: They should drink at least 100 ounces of water a day and operate a humidifier in their homes during winter months when humidity is low. (Homes with forced air/gas heat often have less than 10 percent humidity, about the level of the Sahara Desert!) Our bodies secrete mucous along the edge of the cords, which provides greater lubrication. Well-hydrated bodies produce a healthy, thinner mucosal film, which allows the vocal cords to function more easily. Often, relative vocal rest is recommended along with a regimen of speech therapy. Speech therapy involves teaching good vocal hygiene, eliminating vocal abuses, and direct voice treatment to alter pitch, loudness, or breath support for good voicing. Stress reduction techniques and relaxation exercises are often taught, as well.[7] If this proves ineffective, microsurgery to remove the swellings might be deemed necessary.

DIAGNOSIS OF YOUR VOCAL HEALTH

Consider the Length of the Vocal Problem

How will you know when you have a significant problem? No one is better equipped than ourselves to know when our voice isn't as clear or strong as it normally is. Consider the length of the vocal malady. A degeneration of tone quality usually happens over a fairly long period of time. Your voice may have a husky sound to it or you may have to push in order to get out very much volume: There may also be an accompanying tightness or pain when you do. In contrast, acute overuse, such as might happen at a sporting event, may quickly yield a vocal loss, but you also will recover relatively quickly, usually within forty-eight to seventy-two hours.

If vocal problems have existed for a long period, and you experience such symptoms as a husky voice, pushing to create volume, or tightness or pain when you speak, there are a couple of things to do. First, analyze any recent changes in your life that would require you to use your voice significantly more, or in an unusual way.

Test for Swelling of the Vocal Cords

Second, consider taking a test to determine whether vocal fold swelling exists. Dr. Robert Bastian has developed one such exam, and he describes the procedure:

> These tasks incorporate high pitch, very soft volume level, and sometimes-rapid onset/offset of the voice. The two swelling tests used at the Bastian Voice Institute almost exclusively are the first phrase of "Happy Birthday," and a five-note (5–4–3–2–1) descending staccato on hee, hee, hee, hee, hee. In both cases the individual should produce the voice in a tiny "boy soprano pianissimo" kind of production; this tiny dynamic is insisted on because getting even a little louder tends to conceal the problem.[8]

In the Bastian test, if your voice cuts out when you sing the words "to you," or on any of the "hee, hee's," your vocal cords are swollen, and you should use your voice as little as possible for the next day or two.

When these symptoms last more than three weeks, it is time to visit an otolaryngologist, commonly known as an ear, nose, and throat (ENT) doctor. An ENT specialist should be easy to locate by a simple search of the Yellow Pages phone directory. However, if there is a college or university in your area with a voice or speech department, you are likely to get a good recommendation. These doctors can perform a noninvasive endoscopy that will produce an actual picture of your vocal folds. The doctor can then definitively diagnose your illness and prescribe the proper regimen of treatment to return your voice to excellent health.

HARMFUL HABITS THAT CONTRIBUTE
TO POOR VOCAL HEALTH

Poor Speech Habits

Two categories of vocal misuse typically need to be confronted: poor speech habits and poor vocal health. Why a person develops peculiar and debilitating vocal production is a fascinating sociological and psychological study in itself. Some reasons are addressed below but sometimes it is as simple as familial modeling. We are all privy to numerous anecdotes or personal experiences where awkward telephone conversations were initiated because the caller mistook the speaker for a different family member. Most embarrassing is when the speaker was a pubescent male who is mistaken for his mother!

Foremost among our concerns is vocal misuse through poor speech habits. First, consider how we use our voice in daily communication. As mentioned earlier, *many people tend to speak near the very bottom of their pitch range.* The result is a "glottal fry" where the pitch is so low it is actually below the range to make an audible pitch. Such a speaker is not speaking in a monotone, but with *no tone.* It sounds more like a croaking frog than a human voice. The vocal folds then, rather than form a tight line as we speak, flutter loosely producing a raspy tone quality. Speaking in this way is in vogue in American society. A low speaking timbre is a sign of authority in the male voice. For the woman, it is a harbinger of sensuality. "If you long for that deep, authoritative voice that proclaims your masculinity and alpha-male status, there is hope," says Helen Cutting, a Chicago voice and speech coach and consultant who assists people remedying their vocal flaws, helping them speak in a powerful, persuasive, resonant voice.[9] But such "hope" is often a false hope. You see, God has granted to each person a voice that is his or her very own, distinctive in quality as well as timbre. That's why choirs are made up of sopranos, altos, tenors, and basses! When one goes to a speech coach to lower their speaking voice, they might end up harming their voice by doing something God never intended.

Ryan C. Branski, PhD, a speech scientist at the Sloan-Kettering Cancer Center, states that voice therapy must address the pitch of the voice. Often patients must become reacquainted with their natural pitch. A patient speaking at an unhealthy pitch is placing unnecessary strain on the vocal musculature; this can either cause or worsen the problem.[10] It doesn't take too much imagination to visualize the dichotomy that might occur in someone, say a Bill Clinton, when confronted with a voice coach who is trying to get him to lower his normal tenor range when speaking and a vocal therapist who is suggesting that he raise his speaking pitch.

Then there are those *who have a very loud, sometimes nasal-sounding voice*. These people suffer from the opposite complication of the "glottal fryer;" they are squeezing their voice boxes and producing speech with too much tightness and volume. (Think Fran Drescher, the actress from the television sitcom "The Nanny.") This person must learn to relax her voice more, speak softer and less often.

A third type of malfunctioning vocal production is known as *hypofunctional. People who speak softly, with too little tension in their vocal cords*, produce a breathy tone quality. This can be the result of tightening muscles that are naturally weak; or, in the case of women, they might think that a lighter, breathier sound enhances their femininity. Often, when people get more emotional, they will push extra air through their vocal cords to create more urgency in their voice. Unfortunately, these behaviors create the deleterious, increased friction spoken of earlier and long term, can produce pathological symptoms such as laryngitis or even vocal nodules.

Finally, *some people just speak much too fast.* One drawback to this kind of speech production is that a person speaking too fast cannot perceive damaging vocal habits and change them, even when they are identified. For instance, a typical injurious habit is initiating every word that begins with a vowel by closing the throat first and then pushing the air through, blowing the vocal cords apart (called a "glottal attack"). This occurs because the coordination is malfunctioning between the brain, the squeezing muscles of the larynx, and the airflow from the lungs. When the brain issues the signals to produce speech, the throat closes to initiate the vowel before the airflow gets there. The air must then "blow apart" the vocal folds in order to vibrate.

In the following phrase, for example, each of the underlined vowels would be produced with a slight, grabbing and holding on to the vowel: "In earlier times it was easier for man to travel by water rather than on land." This habit happens so quickly that it is hard enough to quantify the sound for a person speaking with slow speech; with those who communicate in "hyper-drive," it becomes nearly impossible. Also, when someone tends toward accelerated discourse, they are also prone to not taking a deep enough breath to support articulation with a good airflow. When this transpires, the support is then derived from the muscles in the throat instead of abdomen and promotes fatigue in the throat, which then leads to further deterioration of tone quality. It is a constant downward spiral, especially when the symptoms are treated rather than the causes.

Poor Vocal Health

The second category of vocal misuse has to do with poor vocal health. Several components here warrant consideration. The first factor to consider is adequate hydration. It is somewhat paradoxical that, in the last fifteen years, there has been an explosion of retail, bottled water companies: Appalachian Springs, Avita, Colorado Crystal, Dannon, Evian, Ice Mountain, San Pellegrino, just to name a few of the better-known brands. Yet water consumption remains relatively low. According to Michael Lam, M.D. and antiaging specialist, more than 50 percent of Americans are chronically dehydrated and admit not drinking the minimum recommended amounts of water. In fact, studies have shown that 35 percent of Americans drink three or fewer servings, and 9 percent drink no water at all. The average American consumes only four to six servings of water a day.[11]

How can this be in such a water-saturated society? Perhaps it's the little "sippy" tops on most retail bottles. How long do you suppose it takes someone to drink a bottle of water through one of those tops? Or maybe it's just one more example of another trendy, American pasttime, similar to the explosion of health clubs in a society that is increasingly morbidly obese: i.e., people buy a lot of water in bottles but really only consume a small fraction of it. But for someone who uses his voice prolifically, the danger of falling into the under-hydrated 50 percent of Americans is not merely a statistical reality: it is a dangerous detriment (more about hydration later).

Another mitigating consideration regarding vocal stress involves a careful evaluation of behavioral risk factors. As noted earlier, certain professions are prone to inflict abuse on the muscles and tissues of the larynx.

To make this personal, ask these questions: Do you communicate for several hours during the course of a weekend as part of your professional obligations? If so, do you coach your son's soccer team on Saturday mornings? Do you tend to raise your decibel levels to a deleterious point during that ninety-minute match, or are you in such tight control of your emotions that you never yell at the overzealous defenders who are all the way down the field in the forward's position? If you are experiencing voice fatigue and hoarseness after preaching for two services on Sundays, you may have to make a difficult decision that might even disappoint your son but save your career.

Similarly, do you converse for several hours in a crowded restaurant or attending a sporting event? Any activity that will put undue strain on your vocal mechanism should be filtered through a grid of common sense. As a general rule, one should refrain from any oral activity, louder than a normal conversational level, for at least forty-eight hours prior to delivering a speech or sermon, singing a concert, or any other vocal production requiring a refined and controlled use of the voice.

STRATEGIES FOR DEVELOPING LIFELONG VOCAL HEALTH

Vocal Production

Speak with a clear, focused tone. People with a naturally breathy or husky tone quality (think Marilyn Monroe) will want to work for a clearer, more resonant core sound. The goal is to achieve greater tensing power in the muscles that bring the vocal cords together. Techniques that can effect positive changes are: working for a more nasal quality, using brighter vowels (ee and ay), combining those with *m*, *n*, or *ñ*. Try beginning all the words in a sentence with *ñ* and then, gradually replace that consonant with the correct ones without losing the engendered focused sound. Comprehensive explanations and exercises are beyond the parameters of this brief chapter. One may find it necessary to procure the services of a speech therapist or voice teacher to effect significant changes in tonal quality.

Also crucial in healthy speaking habits is maintaining a clear tone quality even when embracing subject matter that evokes visceral emotions within. When a speaker becomes more emotionally engaged in her delivery, one of two vocalizing phenomena occurs: the timbre of the sound either becomes more breathy or more of a scream. Those are the primary methods we use to express vociferous passion about a certain subject. In both cases, the manner in which the vocal cords are brought together is causing excess abrasion of the vocal process (where the vocal folds come together).

When utilizing a whisper to grab your audience's attention, an excellent expressive tool, use an actual whisper, not a stage (breathy) whisper. In the latter (which is the typical whisper used to communicate deep sentiment), the vocal folds partially close, creating more tension and friction and a harmful effect. In a true whisper, only the anterior portion of the vocal cords closes and the bulk of the cords do not even come together, thus creating a softer but less harmful delivery.

Raising the volume level is the other favored manner by which one conveys great conviction. Unfortunately, this can lead to more propulsion of air than the muscles of the larynx can handle and result in that harsh sound we refer to as yelling. Our abdominal muscles provide the upward thrust of pressure to the lungs, forcing the air back out through the vocal cords. They are obviously much larger and stronger than the muscles operating the larynx and will, when called upon by your emotions, produce much more air than the throat can handle. Keep your tone quality clear as your decibels increase. If the rasping quality of a "sports event yell" creeps in, one has crossed the line from healthy phonation.

Use the entire pitch range of the speaking voice, trying to keep the average about three or four steps above the normal conversational level. If one forces her voice to phonate below the natural range, she can expect to incur similar debilitating results, as did Bill Clinton. Conversely (although this rarely occurs), one should not speak habitually higher than is typical for their voice type. Generally speaking, though, pitch modulation is a very important ingredient in avoiding vocal fatigue

Another key ingredient for clear, supported speech is regular, low breathing. One of my (Terry's) sons was briefly part of a running team dynasty. Our local high school cross-country team finished first in the state competition for a record twenty-seven years in a row. One of the things their coach taught them to do was keep their breathing low (in the abdominal area) and relaxed, especially when their bodies became more and more stressed. Breathing through your nose, imagine that there is an inner tube tightly around your waist. Push out all around your middle against this imaginary inner tube as you take in air.

The same wisdom should be applied to the "marathon" speaker. As the engaging communicator varies his delivery, he may be prone to speaking louder and faster. Within that stressful oration paradigm, one crucial facet tends to get subjugated to the will of the emotions: breathing. The communicator will unintentionally take progressively shorter breaths and they will invariably be high in the chest. When this happens, a constant stream of air flowing from down low in your abdomen is not possible. One telltale sign is a squeezing of the larynx at the end of long sentences that produces a pinched or hoarse tone quality. The voice struggling under such a shortage of air works less efficiently and tires more quickly.

Finally, do not allow the pitch level of your voice to drop and your tone to become raspy during extended conversation. The man who wears a counseling hat as part of his daily routine may find himself using his voice for several hours a day. Consistently, humans tend to interact with a more "laid back" persona when such social discourse is required. This unsupported, grating tone seems to be emanating straight out of the larynx instead of the mouth, or better yet, the top of the head. When this occurs the vocal cords are, once more, inadequately closed. There is too much air scraping along the edges of the vocal folds creating excess friction and potential damage. Attempts must be made to sit up straight, speak at a higher pitch level than might seem "normal," and imagine the voice floating buoyantly, on top of the airstream rather than sinking underneath.

Lifestyle Changes

Stay hydrated! Drink at least 100 ounces of water per day, especially the couple of days leading up to heavy speaking engagements. The voice-care professionals have a highly technical medical barometer that insures complete body hydration. One knows they are well hydrated if they "pee pale!"

Use the voice as little as possible the day or two before speaking. As a preacher, avoid shouting at your child's baseball games on Saturday morning. No Saturday night social engagements whenever possible, and so forth.

Minute for minute, there is probably more essential relationship building that takes place over the dining table than anyplace else. If you are one who has multiple mealtime meetings in a typical week, consider making them earlier or later to avoid having to speak over a crowded dining room ambience. A crowded restaurant's ambient noise level actually approaches the decibel production of a rock concert.

When greeting people after a worship service, stand as comfortably close as possible. Keep your voice well modulated and focused. If you speak at multiple services on Sunday mornings, it may become necessary to excuse yourself from greeting the congregants between each of them. Maybe there is a less noisy area than the immediate vestibule of your church where people could interact with you.

Learn to speak less, listen more, and breathe deeply. This is a biblical injunction as well (James 1:19, Ecclesiastes 5:2–3, Isaiah 42:5), one that reaps beneficial vocal rewards.

If you are a classic sanguine personality, strive to allow others to assume your role as "life of the party." Laryngologists Bastian and Brent Richardson, who oversee the Bastian Voice Institute, first instruct patients to rate their personality on a scale of one to seven. A "one" is reclusive and speaks very little during the course of their day. A "seven" is highly gregarious and loves to be the center of attention. The number "seven" is much more likely to encounter a chronic vocal condition than anyone else. Where do you fall on this continuum?

Perhaps the testimony of Kathleen Perez, a certified fitness instructor, will serve as motivation for readers to give serious consideration to practicing good vocal health habits.

> I never thought that could happen to me. After all, I always used a microphone and avoided screaming during class. Like many of my colleagues, I believed the ever-present gravelly quality of my voice was simply an unavoidable occupational hazard. Then I developed a chronic sore throat and severe vocal loss that lasted more than eighteen months and did not improve despite frequent voice rest. I even stopped making phone calls and going out socially, because talking became too painful.

When I did speak, my voice was raspy, deep, and choppy. A trip to the otolaryngologist . . . confirmed my fears: The diagnosis was vocal cord nodules, which are essentially small fibrous bumps. What followed were three months of medical leave, the loss of my job, months of voice therapy and hours of wondering if my teaching and lecturing career was over. I also learned I was not alone in my predicament. You, too, are at risk!"[12]

TERRY STRANDT is professor of sacred music at the Moody Bible Institute. He holds the D.M.A. degree in vocal performance and literature from the Eastman School of Music and has bachelor's and master's degrees in music from the University of Arizona, Tucson.

JORI JENNINGS is assistant professor of sacred music at the Moody Bible Institute. She holds the D.M.A. degree in vocal performance and literature from the University of Illinois at Champaign-Urbana, as well as academic degrees from New Mexico State University and Butler University.

NOTES

1. A. Mathis Holbrook and C.W. Bailey, "Talking Time and Loud Talking Time as Factors in Vocal Fatigue," presented at the annual convention of the Florida Speech and Hearing Association, 1974.

2. E. K. Sander and D. E. Ripich, "Vocal Fatigue," *Annals of Otology, Rhinology and Laryngology,* 92 (1983);141–45.

3. http://www.healthcentral.com/encyclopedia/408/444/Laryngitis.html

4. http://www.spurgeon.org/sw&tr.htm

5. http://www.voicemedicine.com/nodules.htm

6. K. Verdolini, Y. Min, I. Titze, J. Lemke, K. Brown, M. Van Mersbergen, J. Jiang, K. Fisher, "Biological Mechanisms Underlying Voice Changes Due to Dehydration," *Journal of Speech, Language, and Hearing Research* 45 (2002): 268–81.

7. http://www.asha.org/public/speech/disorders/nodules_polyps.htm

8. "Glossary," s.v. *swelling tests*, Bastian Voice Institute; http://www.bastianvoice.com/s.htm

9. "How to Be Heard—Speak Up, Brother," April 11, 2004, as cited on the Internet at http://www.voicepowr.com/ourclients/articles.html

10. Ryan C. Branski, "Voice Therapy"; http://www.emedicine.com/ent/topic683 .htm

11. Michael Lam, "Dehydration" at the Web site DrLam.com, http://www.drlam.com/A3R_brief_in_doc_format/2002-No6-Dehydration.cfm

12. Kathleen Perez, "Project, but Protect," *Idea Fitness Edge,* November-December, 1999; http://www.ideafit.com/pdf/Prevent_Vocal_Damage.pdf

Twenty-Seven

USING BIBLE

SOFTWARE TO

EXEGETE THE TEXT

by
James Coakley and David Woodall

The digital revolution now underway has the potential to transform our culture in the same way that the printing press transformed society in Gutenberg's day. The printing press provided the printed text of the Bible to everyone who was able to read; today the digital revolution is opening up the biblical languages to every pastor who has a basic understanding of the grammar and syntax of the ancient texts of Scripture. For the first time the serious Bible student has the tools in digital format to analyze and exegete the biblical text.

There are important reasons why every pastor should invest the time and energy that it takes to use Bible software for the study of biblical languages in sermon preparation. As ministers of the gospel in a changing culture, we can utilize this technology for the benefit of the body of Christ as we preach the unchanging Word of God.

As ministers committed to inspiration and inerrancy, we embrace the importance of the biblical languages for an accurate understanding of the biblical text and a powerful presentation of its message. A recent

survey of pastors attending the Pastor's Conference at Moody Bible Institute revealed that although the pastors had a high regard for the use of
Hebrew and Greek in the exegetical process, they had not internalized
the languages, almost never used them for personal devotions, and were
highly unsatisfied with their level of biblical language use. Their use of
the language was often reduced to an occasional reference to a lexicon
for a quick word study.[1] Something needs to be done in order to reverse
the current situation.

REMOVING ROADBLOCKS TO
HEBREW AND GREEK LANGUAGE STUDY

Several barriers discourage pastors from using their knowledge of
Hebrew or Greek: (1) The languages are hard to grasp, and it is difficult
for many pastors to motivate themselves to constantly drill the endless
list of paradigms that are necessary to become fluent in the original language text. (2) The languages are fleeting, and seminary knowledge is
easily lost once the syllabus requirements of the language classes are
completed. (3) The languages are time-consuming, and the duties of the
pastorate quickly devour the time needed for a consistent study of the
languages. (4) The languages are technical, and there is often a feeling
that even after receiving an M.Div., only those with Ph.D.s can really
speak with authority and avoid the exegetical fallacies that D. A. Carson
so aptly warned against.[2]

The use of digital technology, however, allows pastors to overcome
these barriers and offers ways to redeem the use of biblical languages in effective sermon preparation. Pastors are now able to gain insight into
Hebrew and Greek in a way that is ministry-friendly and produces results.
Extensive memorization is minimized, and analysis can be executed with
speed and precision. As pastors engage the original-language text on a
regular basis, proficiency will increase beyond the knowledge gained in
the classroom. Pastors can pick up the Hebrew and Greek text once
again, not with their hands but with their fingertips as they explore the
bold new world of digital technology.[3]

Bible software packages abound on the market today, and all of
them have certain advantages and disadvantages.[4] Most of this chapter

will illustrate the use of the Libronix Digital Library System contained in Logos Bible Software with only occasional reference to other software programs. The Libronix program was chosen because of the commitment of Logos to cutting-edge technology, the development of databases for original language study, and the inclusion of a massive digital library system.

BENEFITING FROM BIBLE SOFTWARE PROGRAMS

There are four reasons why those who proclaim the Word of God should use Bible software for sermon preparation. Each reason will be explained and illustrated in order to give a basic introduction to the world of digital study.

1. Space: The Final Frontier

When was the last time you could actually see your office desktop in the middle of an intense Bible study? Haphazard piles of commentaries, lexicons, dictionaries, and translations of the Bible open to various places typically lie scattered around the desk often mingling with unorganized scraps of notes. In contrast, with the use of Bible software, the study resources are neatly organized in the condensed space of the computer screen. Space on the office desktop is limited, often unorganized, and in need of constant rearrangement and re-shelving; space on the digital desktop, however, is unlimited, organized, and rearranged with the click of a mouse. The office desk now is clean (an important upgrade for the perfectionists among us), and all the work is completed in a digital workspace. In fact, the extensive amount of shelf space needed to shelve books is eliminated when these resources are saved on the hard drive.

What does the digital desktop look like for the exegete? Figure 1 illustrates a workspace for the study of the Greek New Testament.[5] It contains (1) the Nestle-Aland text of the Greek New Testament that has been marked to show various parts of speech, (2) an English Bible window that contains access to different versions of the Bible and various Greek grammars, and (3) an information window that contains morphological and lexical data. This information window identifies the gender, number, and case of the noun πειρασμός as well the semantic range of the word from Louw and Nida's *Greek-English Lexicon of the New Testament*. The English Bible window also contains tabs at the bottom of the window for quick reference to various Greek grammars, syntax databases, and additional Greek lexicons.

Figure 1

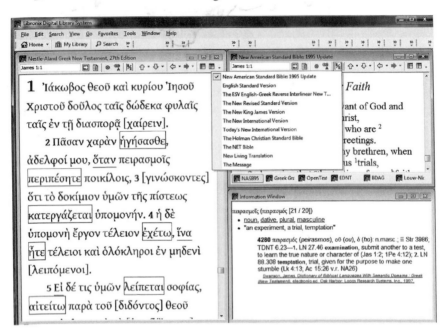

Each window of text or resource allows for quick movement between user-defined parallel resources that are similar in nature. The English Bible window, for example, contains a collection of English versions that may be organized from formal to functional equivalent translations. Clicking the arrow keys (or using the popup window illustrated in Figure 1) changes the window from the New American Standard Bible to the New International Version or any number of translations loaded on the hard drive. The same feature works with Greek texts and lexical resources. A click of the mouse or the use of an arrow key transforms the information window into lexicons like Bauer's *Greek-English Lexicon of the New Testament and Other Christian Literature* (BDAG), which are already open to the biblical language word being referenced.

All of this information is contained in the space of a computer screen! The appearance of the actual desktop is up to the expositor. The digital space can be devoted to multiple saved workspaces, and each workspace can include multiple windows that are opened to the exact page of interest every time the study begins. Create it, save it, and use it according to your own study style. Through the use of a laptop, the workspace can actually travel with the pastor. Bring your library with you to study at home or on the mission field. Pack thousands of volumes on the hard drive. Space is no longer an issue in the new digital world. The first reason for using the Bible software, therefore, concerns the space advantage of a digital workspace.

2. Functionality: How to Explore Vast New Worlds

What can the exegete do with the software during sermon preparation? Here we can only scratch the surface of the many functions of the software.

First, consider the *help available for studying the Greek text* of the New Testament. In Figure 1 the user has marked the Greek text, a feature that helps the student identify various parts of speech (called "visual filters" in Logos). In this particular workspace, finite verbs (e.g., verbs in the indicative, subjunctive, imperative, and optative moods) appear in a box; participles and infinitives appear in brackets; and adverbial conjunctions are underlined. Because the Greek text is tagged according to parts of speech and basic syntactical relationships, any combination of colors or symbols may be given to a grammatical aspect of the text.

A key exegetical task in epistolary literature involves (1) an identification of the extent and nature of various clauses in a passage and (2) an analysis of how these clauses function in the discourse. Because the words in boxes tend to function as finite verbs in independent clauses[6] and the words in brackets tend to function as nonfinite verbals in dependent clauses, the exegete can visually identify the extent and nature of the clauses in the text. The underlined adverbial conjunctions introduce dependent clauses. In James 1:2–3, for example, the boxed verb ἡγήσασθε (*consider*) stands alone as the main verb in an independent clause. The second clause begins with the underlined adverbial conjunction ὅταν (*when*), which marks the beginning of a subordinate clause that modifies the main verb. The bracketed participle γινώσκοντες (knowing) also shows that the next clause is a subordinate clause (the conjunction ὅτι introduces an embedded clause that gives the content of the knowledge). With a little practice and a basic understanding of Greek grammar, the exegete can visually identify the one independent clause and the two subordinate clauses.

Once the clauses have been identified, the next exegetical question concerns how each clause functions in the sentence. The independent clause includes a verb in the imperative mood (ἡγήσασθε, *consider*) and gives a command; the following dependent clause gives the timeframe for the implementation of the command based on the lexical meaning of the subordinating conjunction ὅταν (*when*). The function of the participle in the next dependent clause, however, demands an exegetical decision. How does the adverbial participle γινώσκοντες (*knowing*) modify the command to consider? A quick survey of English translations in the software reveals that most translators take it as causal. The brothers should consider trials pure joy *because* they know that the testing of their faith produces endurance. We are left with the following clause analysis of James 1:2 (NASB):

> Πᾶσαν χαρὰν ἡγήσασθε, ἀδελφοί μου, (command)
> ὅταν πειρασμοῖς περιπέσητε ποικίλοις, (time)
> γινώσκοντες ὅτι τὸ δοκίμιον. . . κατεργάζεται ὑπομονήν. (cause)

> Consider it all joy, my brethren, (command)
> when you encounter various trials, (time)
> knowing that the testing . . . produces endurance. (cause)

In epistolary literature, this type of analysis will often lead to an outline of the text that identifies the main and subordinate points of the sermon. The big idea of the sentence grammatically is a command to think a certain way, and this thinking occurs (a) *when* various trials are encountered and (b) *because* of the knowledge of what testing produces.

Previous Bible software was limited to the factual data of morphology. Verbs were parsed and nouns were declined, but key syntactical analysis on the phrase and clause level was mostly ignored. All of this is changing with the recent release of version 3 of the Logos software. Three new databases—the *OpenText.org Syntactically Analyzed Greek New Testament*, the *Lexham Syntactic Greek New Testament*, and the *Lexham Clausal Outlines of the Greek New Testament*—all focus on syntax at the clause level and confirm the above exegesis. The *Lexham Clausal Outlines of the Greek New Testament*, for example, separates James 1:2–3 into clauses and identifies the function of each clause as imperatival, temporal, and causal respectively. This confirms our exegesis and illustrates the increased functionality that Bible software gives to the pastor.7

Second, consider the *help available for studying the OT Hebrew*. Figure 2 illustrates a Hebrew workspace that contains the *Lexham Hebrew-English Interlinear Bible* and the NASB text opened to Exodus 9:14 as well as an information window that is open to the *Enhanced Brown-Driver-Briggs Hebrew and English Lexicon* (BDB).

Figure 2

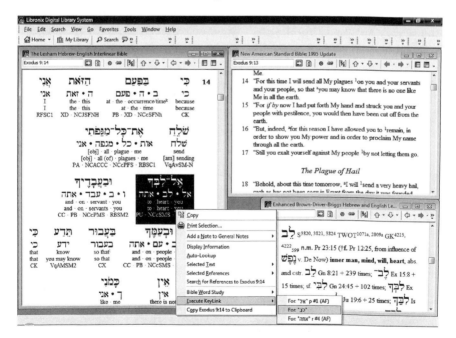

The Hebrew desktop reproduced in Figure 2 illustrates another feature that enhances functionality.8 *Keylinking* allows the user to navigate to various resources with the click of a mouse. Exodus 9:18, for example, introduces the seventh plague—the plague of hail upon Egypt. The NASB reads, "I will send all My plagues *on you*" (emphasis ours). God is telling Moses what He will do to Pharaoh. The Hebrew text reads: אֲנִי שֹׁלֵחַ אֶת־כָּל־מַגֵּפֹתַי אֶל־לִבְּךָ This literally means "I am sending all my plagues *upon your heart*" (emphasis ours). Most English translations leave out the word *heart* and simply translate the last word with the second-person singular pronoun *you*. This is a specific use of the word *heart*. The phrase *on you* in Hebrew is normally constructed with the Hebrew preposition אֶל (on) with an attached pronominal suffix (you). Here the noun לֵב (heart) is included in the phrase. A survey of English Bibles reveals the tendency to avoid using the word *heart* and the choice to translate it simply as the independent pronoun *you*. By avoiding the use of the word *heart*, translators do not allow readers to see the greater impact of this verse in the broader context. However, if the user highlights with his computer mouse the word לֵב (heart) in the *Lexham Hebrew Interlinear* (see Figure 3) and then clicks the right mouse button, a dialogue box will appear that brings up a menu list with the option *Execute Keylink*. Once this option is highlighted, the end user can click on the specific word and navigate directly to the exact entry in BDB that gives a meaning of *heart* (as well as *inner man, mind,* and *will)* for this word.

With an understanding of this information, the expositor is able to grasp the purpose of the plagues, God's specific intentions with Pharaoh and the Egyptian people, and the focus that Pharaoh's *heart* has in this passage. The rest of Exodus 9:14 states that this particular plague (the plague of hail) will teach all of Egypt (especially Pharaoh) a major theological lesson: *"that there is no one like Me in all the earth."* Verse 16 goes on to stress that God has allowed Pharaoh *"to remain, in order to show you My power and in order to proclaim My name through all the earth."* By focusing on the original language word לֵב *"heart"* instead of the traditional rendering of *"you,"* the pastor is able to share more forcefully the connection that this particular word has in the passage. It also brings the relationship of this verse to the whole discussion of the hardening of Pharaoh's heart into clearer focus.

Most expositors of this section of Exodus tend to focus on the question "who hardened Pharaoh's heart?" which is a very legitimate question. But communicators of God's Word should also stress that

Pharaoh's *heart* is the staging ground for God to make a major theological statement: with this particular plague God wishes to proclaim his "name through all the earth" (Exod. 9:16). This particular plague of hail (the seventh plague) is a pivotal one in the entire plague narrative, and the use of Bible software makes the process of utilizing the Hebrew text more functional.

It should be obvious from these examples that a book in digital format has a greater functionality than its hard-copy counterpart. For example, having the Bible in digital format allows the student to quickly search for words, phrases, and grammatical constructions: an advanced search engine executes a query for every occurrence of the word or phrase, and advanced searches explore the occurrence of simple to complex grammatical constructions. The computer functions as a highly technical mega-concordance. This function of Bible software is so powerful in its resources and speed that the bulky hard-copy concordance will soon become a dust collector. Bible software effectively eliminates the need to have a concordance, a parsing guide, or a vocabulary guide.

Figure 3 displays the results of a graphical query in a Bible Works program[9] that searched for several combinations of phrases containing the word *fear* (e.g., *fear of the Lord* and *fear of God*) by linking the word "fear" יִרְא (both in its noun and verb form) with either the word *Lord*, יהוה or *God*, אֱלֹהִים. Several phrase searches from the Hebrew text were combined together to get the results listed in the left panel.

A study of the results shows that there are different nuances of this phrase depending on the genre of the text. Richard Shultz has noticed that in narrative contexts the use of these phrases "describe exclusive, even radical trust in or worship of God and basic morality (Gen. 20:11; Exod. 14:31); in legal contexts it usually is expressed in obedience to the law (Deut. 6:2); in wisdom books, especially Proverbs, it expresses a fundamental attitude toward God that leads to wise behavior and the avoidance of every form of evil."[10] Bible software makes it easier to verify such claims and find the occurrences of specific phrases in the Hebrew text that would be beyond the scope of print concordances.

Figure 3

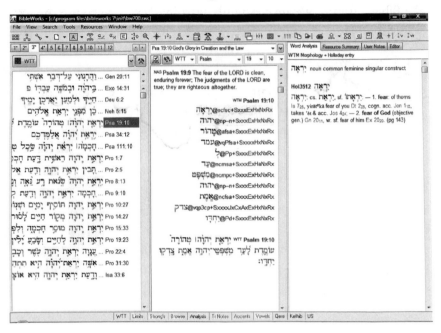

Visual filters can also be used for the analysis of Hebrew verbs. Because verbs are the "weight bearing" beams of the structure of any text,
it's helpful to identify their function on both the word and passage level.
For example, all of the *wayyiqtol* (also known as *waw consecutive imper-
fect* or *waw conversive*) verbs in a text can be highlighted with the same
color for visual analysis. Chisholm notes that "the main story of narrative, built on a succession of *wayyiqtol* verbal forms, usually proceeds
from "A-to-Z" in sequential fashion."[11] Once the *wayyiqtol* verbs are
identified, they can be isolated to provide the backbone of the main
story line. For example, by means of visual filters, all of the *wayyiqtol*
verbs in the story of the Tower of Babel in Genesis 11:1–9 are identified,
and the "backbone" of the story (with all the supporting elements
stripped away) is laid bare: they found, they settled, they said, they used,
they said, he came down, he said, he scattered, and they stopped. These
verbal actions form the backbone of the story, and with the help of Bible
software the main story line of a narrative text can be identified and
tracked. The pastor, therefore, is able to get to the heart of the message
of the narrative through the use of this technique.

This section provides only a taste of the functional benefits found in the Bible software. We are constantly learning new ways to use the software for exegesis.

3. Time: Where Does It All Go?

The use of Bible software will greatly reduce the amount of time needed to get to the heart of the message from the text. A recent time management survey concluded that 70 percent of the time a pastor spends in Bible study is actually spent in searching for resources, paper flipping, page turning, looking for information in hard-copy resources, or arranging the resources on the desk.[12] Wasted search time is virtually eliminated in the digital world, as a click of the mouse brings the resource to the exact page on the screen. More time is devoted to the actual study of the Bible.

The possibilities for the lightning-fast retrieval of information are limitless. One area of fruitful study is to compare different English Bible versions. But the process of opening several different Bibles to a specific passage and then comparing each of the versions to note the specific differences can be very time-consuming. With the Compare Parallel Bible Version tool in Logos, however, several Bible versions are compared with the differences already highlighted. This allows the pastor to read the different versions that are used in the congregation and to identify various hotspots that require more intensive study in the biblical languages.

A second time-saving benefit of the Bible software is available through the process of keylinking, which was described in the previous section. How often do pastors stop to actually look up a certain word in a hard-copy reference work? It has been our experience that the time involved in opening the book and flipping the pages discouraged the use of this resource in casual study. The information is more readily available if it is accessed quickly with the software. By establishing a keylink with various lexicons, a double click on any word can instantly link that word to a window that includes any number of preset reference works. A clicking frenzy can take one quickly from a Greek word to the Greek lexicon BDAG to the unabridged works of Josephus to the Pseudepigrapha book of Enoch and then on to the Internet for an advanced search.

Time is precious in the pastorate, and using Bible software will help the pastor redeem the time while also advancing his understanding of the biblical languages.

4. Availability: All of This at Your Fingertips

Serious sermon preparation demands access to quality reference works. The fourth reason for using technology is very simple: Bible software provides access to the major reference works, databases, and resources that are essential for Bible study. We have already seen that Bible software can quickly display the morphological information about any word in the biblical text. But a host of other resources and databases are available within Bible software to assist the pastor in the study of the original languages. Bible dictionaries, Bible background commentaries, encyclopedias, commentaries, and other topical resources are plentiful.

In addition to the Logos resources, the *New International Dictionary of Old Testament Theology and Exegesis* (NIDOTTE) is available in electronic format in Zondervan's Pradis Bible software program. The NIV text has every English word automatically tagged to keylink to the exact location in the lexical portion of NIDOTTE. By right clicking on the English word *language* in Genesis 11:1, for example, a Related Topics menu box appears, which brings up a number of resources where the word *language* is discussed in any of the Pradis resources. By selecting the transliterated Hebrew word in the menu box, the software takes the user to the specific location in NIDOTTE where the corresponding Hebrew word is discussed. Other valuable resources such as the *Expositor's Bible Commentary* are also available for consultation within Pradis.

Several exciting resource tools are also available in Logos Bible software to do a word study. In the use of any tool, there is a potential danger in simply looking up the meaning of a word. Words only have meaning in context. Words are not "orphans," and it is best to narrow down the precise meaning of a word under study by the company it keeps. Sadly, many potential expositors take a smorgasbord approach to the meaning of biblical words. They pick and choose whatever meaning they like or feel is pertinent, and then they share that meaning in a sermon. Instead, a pastor should go beyond the word level to the level of clause and discourse in order to grasp the meaning of the text. Bible software makes it much easier to study words in collocation. In fact, the software allows the student to study beyond the word level in a way that is not possible with hard-copy tools.

The study of a Hebrew or Greek word involves two basic steps: (1) the discovery of the semantic range of the word (what the word *could* mean) and (2) a decision concerning the meaning of the word in the passage being studied (what the word *does* mean in the context of the passage).[13] Logos has tools that greatly enhance the pastor's ability to understand the semantic range of the word. In order to do a personal word study (without simply reading the results of word-study dictionaries), the pastor needs to first find every reference to the biblical-language word he is studying. It is only through a study of every reference to the biblical-language word that the pastor can get a feel for its semantic range. The use of a Hebrew or Greek concordance may be difficult apart from an excellent working knowledge of Greek, and the use of an English concordance that references the biblical languages through an elaborate numbering system (Strong's numbers or Goodrick/Kohlenberger's numbers) is clumsy; several pages must be turned in order to identify all the references. With Bible software, however, the need to use a concordance and reference number is eliminated. The computer can accurately generate a list of every time a Hebrew or Greek word is used while at the same time displaying the results of the list in English.

This procedure is available in the Logos Bible software through the use of an English Standard Version Reverse Interlinear and the new database tools available in the Bible Word Study feature. In contrast to a regular Interlinear text which prints the biblical language text on the top line with a corresponding Hebrew or Greek word on the line below it, the Reverse Interlinear prints the English text of the ESV on the top line with the corresponding Hebrew or Greek word below the English word. It not only includes the biblical language word, its lexical form, and a parsing guide, but also an elaborate system of codes to show word order, ellipses, idioms, etc. This text is also available in hard copy.

The recent release of version 3 of Logos refines this resource. A right click on the word in the Reverse Interlinear leads to a keylink to the Bible Word Study feature. This is a powerful research tool that goes beyond the word studies of the past and takes advantage of the new syntax databases available in Logos.

When this feature is selected, Logos generates and collates information on several levels of study. (1) The tool provides a list of lexicons that are already opened up to the exact location of where that word is discussed. (2) It also provides a "spark line" graph that visually displays the distribution of that word throughout the Hebrew or Greek text. When the user moves the mouse over the different colored columns, a pop-up window displays the frequency of the word in the particular Bible book. (3) It generates a list of syntactic features about the word being studied. These features include a list of how the word under study is used within its clauses. For example, it will list the frequency and reference to where the word is used as the subject of a clause or the object of a clause. If it is a noun, it will automatically generate a list of verbs that are associated with that noun. If it is a verb, it will generate a list of the subjects that are associated with that verb. With this information the exegete is able to gather data that will help him determine the meaning of the word in different contexts. (4) The Bible Word Study report also generates a cluster diagram of all the English glosses for this particular original language word. It is easy to visually see the full range of translation options that a specific word has in the text.

THE FUTURE OF BIBLE REFERENCE STUDY TOOLS

Availability of resources involves more than just making hard copy texts available. Dale Pritchett, president of Logos and someone who has been on the cutting edge of new technology for years, predicts that "a large percentage of all future Bible reference work will be authored, edited, packaged, distributed, sold and read without ever making an appearance on the printed page.[14] The new world will go well beyond the resources available in hard copy.

As mathematics advanced from the abacus to the slide rule, the calculator, and finally to the computer, the accuracy of the results reached a higher level. Engineers no longer use slide rules to do their calculations. They use elaborate computer workstations that analyze complex equations and produce accurate results. In the same way, the software tools provide the exegete with the ability to accurately analyze complex constructions. The significance of research, after all, is not found in crunching numbers or parsing verbs. Multiplying six times eight to get forty-eight or parsing εὐχαριστοῦμεν as present active indicative, first-person plural does not communicate a message that changes the lives of people. The use of this information, however, to get the big idea of the message will impact people where they live. The information used by the exegete needs to be accurate, and the software provides this precision.

Occasionally a student will ask if a certain construction occurred in the biblical-language text. Before the advent of Bible software, we could only offer a feeling based on our familiarity with the text. Now the question can be answered accurately using the computer. Each exploration increases the student's understanding of the Hebrew or Greek text. Students who were not able to retain the paradigms necessary to sight-read the Bible in the biblical languages are still able to work with the text in a meaningful way.

Pastors must learn to fall in love with the biblical languages in order to resurrect the power of expository preaching that comes from work with the original text. People have often told us—and we have experienced it time and time again—that the sermons which speak with power and authority are the ones that have been built on the insights gained from the use of biblical languages. It is our prayer that the Bible software will empower pastors and students of the Word to redeem the biblical languages as the foundation for sermon preparation.

JAMES F. COAKLEY is associate professor of Bible at the Moody Graduate School. He holds the D.Min degree from Covenant Theological Seminary, St. Louis, as well as degrees from Grace Theological Seminary and Calvary Bible College.

DAVID L. WOODALL is associate professor of Greek and New Testament at Moody Graduate School. He has earned the Ph.D. degree from Trinity Evangelical Divinity School, Deerfield, Illinois, as well as degrees from Grand Rapids Theological Seminary and Cedarville University, Cedarville, Ohio.

NOTES

1. Philip N. Freeberg, "The Effect of *CAPABLE* on Biblical Language Use in Ministry" (M.Div. research project, Moody Bible Institute, July 2003). *CAPABLE* refers to the biblical language program at Moody Graduate School and stands for a *Computer Assisted Practical Approach to Biblical Languages and Exegesis.*

2. D. A. Carson, *Exegetical Fallacies*, 2nd ed. (Grand Rapids: Baker, 1996).

3. The challenge of this chapter does not stop with pastors. The seminary must likewise take the lead by preparing ministry practitioners to use the digital tools in a practical way. With this in mind, the biblical language department of Moody Graduate School has launched a program called *CAPABLE* (see footnote 1). All of the biblical language classes meet in the computer lab, and students are required to purchase the Logos Bible software. The objective is to teach the basics of Hebrew and Greek grammar and syntax and to teach ministry practitioners how to use the software tools in order to do accurate and responsible exegesis.

4. The major packages are (1) Logos (*www.logos.com*), (2) BibleWorks (*www.bibleworks.com*), (3) WordSearch (*www.wordsearchbible.com*), (4) Pradis (*http://www.zondervan.com/Cultures/en-US/Product/Software*), (5) QuickVerse (*www.quickverse.com*), and (6) E-sword (*www.e-sword.net*). The focus of this chapter will be on Windows-based systems. Macintosh users will find that the Accordance program is very useful (*www.accordancebible.com*).

5. From the Libronix Digital Library System (Logos Bible Software 3), developed by Logos Research Systems, Inc. ©2007. Those interested in purchasing this program may do so by visiting the following Web site: *http://www.logos.com* or by calling 800-875-6467. The user may purchase several different software packages. For access to the features described in this article, the user will need any of the Scholar's Libraries.

6. Notice the words *tend* to function as finite verbs; there are, of course, exceptions to this statement. The Greek word περιπέσητε, for example, is boxed, but it functions as a verb in a subordinate clause. But pastors need only to look at the introductory adverbial conjunction ὅταν (underlined in the text) to realize that this is a subordinate clause. The same is true for κατεργάζεται, which is also introduced by ὅτι.

7. The problem with this, of course, is that as we move from the hard data of morphology, there are more exegetical decisions that need to be made. But the pastor is directed toward the syntax relationships in a graphical way that gets him started beyond the word level. The same type of syntactical analysis can be done on the Hebrew text. Currently there are two syntax databases for the Hebrew Text: (1) *The Hebrew Bible: Andersen-Forbes Phrase Marker Analysis* developed by Francis I. Andersen and A. Dean Forbes, (2) The *Stuttgart Electronic Study Edition* of the BHS text based upon the morpho-syntactic database of Eep Talstra, and a third one by Wolfgang Richter in development.

8. From Libronix Digital Library System (Logos Bible Software 3), developed by Logos Research Systems, Inc. ©2007.

9. Figure 3 is a desktop image from BibleWorks 7, developed by BibleWorks, LLC ©2006-2007. Those interested in purchasing this program may do so by visiting the following Web site: *http://www.bibleworks.com* or by calling 888-747-8200.

10. Richard Schultz, *A Guide to Old Testament Theology and Exegesis*, ed. Willem VanGemeren (Grand Rapids: Zondervan, 1997), 189. It could be added that the use of the phrase *fear of the Lord* in Psalms 19:9 (English) is more likely a synonym for the *word of the Lord* or *law* since it is listed among six other phrases that clearly refer to the law rather than an attitudinal expression of reverence or awe.

11. Robert Chisholm, "History or Story? The Literary Dimension in Narrative Texts," in *Giving the Sense*, ed. David M. Howard and Michael A. Grisanti (Grand Rapids: Kregel, 2003), 65.

12. Scott Lindsey, interview by Dennis Rainey, *Family Life Today*, June 19, 2006. The entire interview is available at *http://www.oneplace.com/ministries/FamilyLife_Today/archives.asp?bcd=2006-6-19*

13. For an excellent discussion of word studies (but without reference to using Bible software), see J. Scott Duvall and J. Daniel Hays, *Grasping God's Word*, 2d ed. (Grand Rapids: Zondervan, 2005), 132–56.

14. Dale Pritchett, "Logos in the Academic Environment"; at *http://www.logos.com/academic/whitepaper*

INDEX

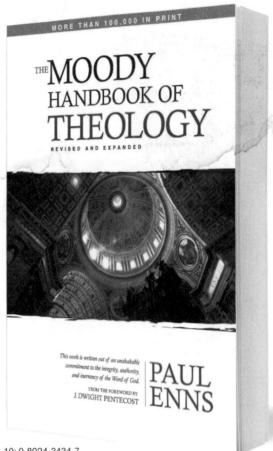

ISBN-10: 0-8024-3434-7
ISBN-13: 978-0-8024-3434-0

The Moody Handbook of Theology leads the reader into the appreciation and understanding of the essentials of Christian theology. It introduces the reader to the five dimensions that provide a comprehensive view of theology: Biblical Theology, Systematic Theology, Historical Theology, Dogmatic Theology, and Contemporary Theology. Paul Enns provides a concise doctrinal reference tool for both the newcomer and scholar. This volume includes new material on openness theology, health and wealth theology, the emergent church, various rapture interpretations, feminism, and more.

by Paul Enns
Find it now at your favorite local or online bookstore.
www.MoodyPublishers.com

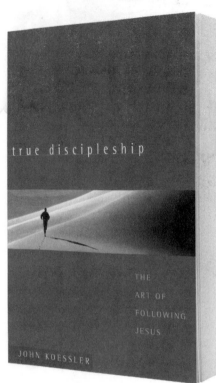

ISBN-10: 0-8024-1642-X
ISBN-13: 978-0-8024-1642-1

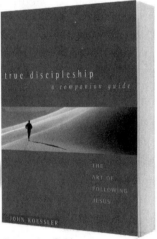

Companion Guide
ISBN-10: 0-8024-1643-8
ISBN-13: 978-0-8024-1643-8

Most of us would answer no when asked if we were like Jesus. How do we become more like Jesus? John Koessler believes the answer is by understanding and developing the marks of a true disciple in our lives. In *True Discipleship: The Art of Following Jesus* and the companion guide, he provides a straightforward presentation of the characteristics Jesus laid out for His disciples. As he offers teaching on the practice of discipleship and the responsibility of being a disciple, readers will be stretched in their thinking and encouraged in their journey.

by John Koessler
Find it now at your favorite local or online bookstore.

www.MoodyPublishers.com